PRAISE FOR *EQUALITY*

"Ideas of equality have a long and chaotic history—long before modern political battles and institutions made the rise of equality possible. At a time when the march toward equality seems so fragile and uncertain, this fascinating and refreshing book is more necessary than ever. A must-read for all citizens interested in the past and future of equality"

  – Thomas Piketty, author of *Capital in the Twenty-First Century*

"Fascinating . . . McMahon's book is less a call to action than a goad to thinking"

  – *New York Times*

"An important examination of the past, present, and future of a key concept of political thinking"

  – *Kirkus*

"A meticulous and thoughtful account"

  – *Publishers Weekly*

"McMahon's book is a rare general study of the topic . . . Sweeping and discerning"

  – *Library Journal*

"Darrin McMahon once again delivers a brilliant intellectual history of one of humanity's most important and least understood ideas. Sweeping, incisive, and provocative, *Equality* is nothing short of a masterpiece"

  – Daniel Gilbert, author of *Stumbling on Happiness*

"This is an essential book for thinking about the most pressing issues of our time. We instinctively react against inequality yet have confused and conflicting ideas about how to make equality a reality. McMahon explains why equality remains so elusive"
— Lynn Hunt, author of *Inventing Human Rights*

"McMahon places equality at the center of human history, showing us how elastic and unruly the concept is and illustrating struggles over its meaning continue to be central touchstones for our contemporary moment. This intellectual and political history is a critical resource in our age of inequality"
— Adom Getachew, author of *Worldmaking after Empire*

"McMahon uncovers the many different ways in which human beings . . . have imagined equality from prehistory to the present day. What emerges is not only an elusive idea, but a strikingly ambivalent one. Equality may be more at home with hierarchy and exclusion than modern egalitarians care to admit. Yet McMahon argues that to maintain its power—and promise—in an unequal world, one must first confront equality in all of its complexity. I count myself convinced. There is no better place to start than with his wonderful book"
— Teresa M. Bejan, University of Oxford

"A magisterial and path-breaking history of the dialectic of equality and inequality . . . The author's fine-tuned analysis demonstrates that equality-thoughts are always ambiguous and polysemic"
— Siep Stuurman, author of *The Invention of Humanity*

EQUALITY

First published in the UK by Ithaka Press
An imprint of Black & White Publishing Group
A Bonnier Books UK company

4th Floor, Victoria House,
Bloomsbury Square,
London, WC1B 4DA

Owned by Bonnier Books
Sveavägen 56, Stockholm, Sweden

Hardback – 978-1-80418-683-1
Ebook – 978-1-80418-684-8

A CIP catalogue of this book is available from the British Library.

Typeset by IDSUK (Data Connection) Ltd
Printed and bound by Clays Ltd, Elcograf S.p.A.

1 3 5 7 9 10 8 6 4 2

Ithaka Press is an imprint of Bonnier Books UK
www.bonnierbooks.co.uk

EQUALITY

The history of an elusive idea

DARRIN M. McMAHON

ITHAKA

For David Avrom Bell
Amicus et primus inter pares

CONTENTS

Imaginary equality: the first way to show inequality in action.

—GOETHE, *MAXIMS AND REFLECTIONS*, MAXIM 954

INTRODUCTION

Imaginary Equality

Very often in the course of writing this book, I met people who conflated my subject, equality, with its opposite, inequality. It didn't just happen once or twice, but over and over. "I'm looking forward to your book on inequality," they'd say, or "Here's something for your inequality project," sharing a reference or a link. In Sweden, organizers even changed the title of a lecture I was giving from "Reflections on the History of Equality" to "Reflections on the History of Inequality." The slip, as they say, is revealing.

We live at a time when it is difficult even for Swedes to imagine equality, let alone to live it. Inequality, by contrast, is the common default, part of a "new paradigm" that dominates our cultural horizon with the steep and formidably upward slope of an n-gram charting the rise in incidence of the term. A massive literature on the subject has emerged in recent years, with revealing titles and subtitles: "Ten Thousand Years of Inequality" or "Violence and the History of Inequality from the Stone Age to the Twenty-First Century." Commentators now speak of the rise of an "inequality industry" housed in well-funded think tanks and NGOs, where policy analysts focus on the problem with the best of intentions, issuing yearly "inequality reports." They are driven to do so by facts on the ground. Scarcely a week goes by without some new and startling revelation: that income and wealth inequality in the United States have approached the highest levels in its history; that almost half the world's wealth is owned by just 1 percent of the world's population; that the three richest men in America possess more wealth than the poorest 50 percent.[1]

Such headline-making revelations are embedded in powerful long-term trends. As the pioneering research of scholars such as the French economist Thomas Piketty has helped to show, virtually every country in the global north has experienced a growth in inequality of wealth and income since the late 1970s, after a previous (and perhaps anomalous) run of compression in the decades prior. Globalization, too, has had a powerful effect on inequalities of various kinds—both within countries and between them—not always for the worse.[2]

Given the salience of these trends, and their prominence in our headlines, it is little wonder that a book on equality has been difficult for many to comprehend. I confess that I have struggled to comprehend it myself. For as one observer laments, "We have lost the sense of value, and perhaps even the meaning, of [equality's] presence." Another insists, even more emphatically, that we face "a crisis of equality." We may still bandy the word about as a slogan in speeches, and philosophers may never tire of pondering its significance. But as equality has become detached, in practice, from our social and political experience, it has become increasingly difficult to conceive.[3]

That difficulty is compounded by the fact that scholars have paid surprisingly little attention to the ways in which ideas of equality have been understood in the past. One eminent historian of political thought even described equality as an idea so varied and amorphous that its history could never properly be written. Partly as a consequence, not many have tried. While a generation and more of intellectual historians have devoted themselves to exploring the history of ideas of liberty, they have tended to treat equality as its homely and neglected twin. The result, as one authority notes, is that "the conceptual history of equality remains almost entirely unwritten," with another adding that "the whole issue has been, to a quite remarkable extent, shrouded in neglect."[4]

There are, to be sure, exceptions, as well as some exciting work-in-progress that this book will call attention to throughout. I will also make use of robust literatures in the kindred fields of philosophy, politics, anthropology, and economics. But while those studies can certainly be helpful, all too often one encounters in them ideas of equality that are ill informed about their uses and meanings in the past.

It is the case that social and cultural historians have taken pains to chronicle the experience of the excluded and the formation of categories such as gender, class, sexuality, and race. But more often than not when equality itself is treated in these works, it functions as a placeholder on the horizon, hazy and indistinct. The titles are revealing: *The Struggle for Equality*, *The Pursuit of Equality*, *The Fight for Equality*. In movement histories of the kind, the focus is on the journey, not the arrival, the inequalities to be overcome and the struggles to be won. Ideas of equality themselves tend to get left out.[5]

I say "ideas" in the plural, because of course there are many, and one could easily pluralize "equality" as well. For when people speak of equality, they invariably speak of the equality *of* something, and that something can be almost anything at all. There are equalities of income and of wealth, of outcome and opportunity, of ends and means. There is civic equality, social equality, legal equality, and the equality of rights, along with the equality of education and access, welfare and well-being, dignity and respect. And that is to say nothing of the equality between men and women or people of different ethnic groups, or of those who choose to love partners of the same sex, or to transition to another. Equality can refer to all those things, and many others besides. Which begs a question: Just what kind of equality am I really talking about? As the Nobel laureate in economics Amartya Sen once insisted, echoing an insight from Aristotle, when we talk of equality, we need to ask, "Equality of what?" And, indeed, equality for whom?[6]

Those are important questions, and they must be kept in mind as we grapple with the great variety of ways in which human beings have put equality to use throughout the ages and continually fought about its meaning. But I purposefully resist parsing the word too finely at the start, for the simple reason that people in the past regularly refused to do so, in ways that can be both baffling and beguiling. Time and again, as we shall see, people employ equality with a seductive vagueness, one that gestures to its multiple meanings and significations while obscuring or covering over its contradictions. That is one of the reasons why equality is so elusive. It also helps to account for its persistence and power. As each age reimagines equality in its own image, it makes and remakes it anew.

This book presents a history of some of those imaginings, ranging over a considerable expanse of time and space in the intellectual *longue durée*. It begins at the very dawn of humanity, asking what evidence about our earliest ancestors may tell us about ideas of equality to come, and it ends in the present, when the prospects for equality's future are very much in doubt. In the interim, I explore a wide range of characters—from hunter-gatherers and foragers to patriarchs and kings to the prophets and sages, philosophers and revolutionaries, feminists and activists who called them to account. Some of those characters will be familiar, others less so, and that is by design. For a primary aim of this book is to render what can seem a familiar idea strange, forcing us to confront the fact that equality is older, more malleable, and more elusive than it commonly appears, and that our feelings about it are more conflicted than we generally acknowledge.

Consider first the widespread assumption that equality is a modern idea that was only "invented" relatively recently, in the seventeenth and eighteenth centuries. The anthropologist and archeologist team of David Graeber and David Wengrow, for example, in their recent best-selling *The Dawn of Everything: A New History of Humanity*, assert confidently that prior to the seventeenth century the notion of social equality "simply did not exist as a concept," and that it was only then that the terms "equality" and "inequality" "began to enter common currency," largely as the result of European encounters with the indigenous cultures of the New World. Others assume, more conventionally, that equality was the invention of the Enlightenment, or of the American and French Revolutions. Americans, especially, are fond of citing Thomas Jefferson's words from the Declaration of Independence, the "self-evident" truth that "all men are created equal." Here, surely, they assume, was a radical new notion, one that gradually spread to the world, even if Jefferson and the other Founding Fathers failed to apply it universally at the time.[7]

Yet what can seem a startlingly new proposition was in truth a hackneyed cliché, a commonplace of Stoic philosophy and Roman law that was given memorable formulation at the end of the sixth century by Pope Gregory the Great. "Omnes homines natura aequales genuit," Gregory affirmed: "All men are born equal by nature." Lines to that effect were repeated down through the Middle Ages, and then regularly affirmed by early modern theorists of natural law. If Jefferson regarded the equality of creation as a self-evident truth, that is largely because the "evidence" had been provided over and over. Ideas of equality had a long and rich history prior to the seventeenth and eighteenth centuries, and that deep history inevitably bore on its modern emergence, shaping and inflecting it in important ways.[8]

That is one major theme of the book, which will endeavor to make clear the deep continuities that have shaped ideas of equality over time, and that have weighed on their ruptures and breaks. Such continuity points to another of the book's principal themes—the enduring tension between difference and sameness in the long history of equality. And here it helps to bear in mind that human equality is always and invariably "imaginary." To say as much is not to suggest that equality is an illusion, or somehow less than real, although we will encounter claims to that effect throughout the book. Rather, it is to insist that equality is first and foremost a relationship that we conjure in our minds in order to draw comparisons between dissimilar things. From our fingerprints to our facial features, human beings are as different as their DNA, as different as their hopes and dreams. No two people are alike. And so equality claims necessarily involve the abstracting out of a shared characteristic (or characteristics). Philosophers call that characteristic a "host property," or the *tertium comparationis*, the third point of comparison to which any two may be likened to reveal what they share. From a common soul to a common humanity to a common place of birth, the rationales are extensive, and over time they have changed, privileging at various stages religion, reason, virtue, sex, race, age, and dignity, to name only a few. But in order for those points of comparison to have purchase, they must be taken up by members of a group. Only then does imaginary equality become the common feature of many minds, part of the social imaginary, and so a norm that is shared. That, in effect, is how imaginary equality becomes real.[9]

It follows, logically at least, that equality is perfectly compatible with difference, and even presupposes it. For beyond the stated points of comparison themselves—and the equal rights or privileges they confer—diversity will be the norm. W. E. B. Du Bois was characteristically astute when he observed, in 1915, that "the equality in political, industrial and social life which modern men must have in order to live, is not to be confounded with sameness. On the contrary . . . it is rather insistence upon the right of diversity." Equality, to put it another way, is always equality from a certain perspective and point of view. Which means, as one scholar insists, that "full or absolute equality are contradictory terms." If two individuals were equal in every respect, they would not be equals, they would be the same.[10]

Proponents of what is styled "identity politics" have reaffirmed that line of reasoning in recent years, insisting on equality's difference. They surely have a point. But to insist on it too strongly is to risk ignoring equality's deep historical connections to uniformity, similarity, and sameness. That connection is suggested by the word itself, which in English derives from the Latin *aequalitas*, which in turn is formed from the verb *aequo/aequare*, "to make equal to something else." The Latin gives off various connotations, but the root-sense of the word evokes an activity, the practice of making level, as one does in balancing two items on a scale, or of making something even, as a carpenter does when smoothing down a surface with a plane. To equalize in the latter sense is to grind down the protruding bits and straighten out the whole so that all is uniform, plumb, and straight.[11]

Such "leveling" is a recurrent tendency in the history of equality, as well as a recurrent concern. As one historian who has worked on the genesis of democracy in the early modern period points out, equality exists in tension between two poles. On the one hand, it can signify the "equality of individuals *as* individuals, empowered by rights" and attended by difference. But on the other hand it can refer to "equality in the sense of *sameness*," emphasizing homogeneity over heterogeneity and erasing individual diversity.[12]

It is revealing that early modern dictionaries regularly defined equality as "conformity" or "uniformity," or having "the same degree of dignity." An equal was "one of the same rank and age," Noah Webster's dictionary declared typically in 1806, glossing equality as "sameness." A later edition, of 1828, specified that an equal was "one not inferior or superior to another, having the same or similar age, rank, station, office, talents, strengths, etc."[13]

Such definitions reflect the older assumptions of societies arranged vertically, in which "equals" were those who occupied the same horizontal rungs of dignity on the great ladder of life, giving us, as *Webster's* noted in 1861, "the equality of nobles of a same rank," or the "equality of men on the scale of being." But the concern with sameness was only heightened by the advent of democracy and popular rule, and the accompanying challenge to societies based explicitly on noble hierarchies of birth. Especially at the time of the French Revolution, contemporaries worried intensely about social leveling as some revolutionaries tried to impose it by force. And in the revolution's aftermath, critics as diverse as Alexis de Tocqueville, Friedrich Nietzsche, and Karl Marx complained about the leveling and homogenizing tendencies of modern democracy and (vulgar) socialism alike.[14]

Marx's name may be surprising in this context, as many people today assume that equality was Marxism's overarching goal. But in fact both Marx and Friedrich Engels were far more critical of equality and egalitarian policies than is generally appreciated. Together they lampooned the belief that "equality is the *primordial intention*, the *mystical tendency*, the *providential aim*" of society. Their criticism helped shape the policies of their two most influential readers, V. I. Lenin and Joseph Stalin, who went out of their way to denounce the "concept of equality" as "a most absurd and stupid prejudice." Seeking, on the one hand, to rein in their people from "excessive leveling" and "equality mongering," they acted forcefully, on the other, to eradicate difference and dissent. Even Chairman Mao Zedong was relatively silent on the subject of equality. In short, Marxism's relationship to the idea is more complicated than commonly assumed.[15]

If Marxism's relationship to equality will be surprising to most readers, the fact that fascists in Italy and Germany developed languages of equality of their own will likely be more surprising still. Playing shrewdly on fears of diversity, and weaponizing status anxieties with psychological force, they elaborated theories of equality as homogeneous national and racial "substance." "Equality is only interesting and valuable politically so long as it has substance," the Nazi crown jurist Carl Schmitt declared, "and for that reason at least the possibility and the risk of inequality." He thought about the matter at length, developing a trenchant critique of what he regarded as the liberal and social-democratic refusal to see equality for what it actually is: a language of power and exclusion. It was largely on the force of his thought that Nazi jurists developed the consequential legal theory of the "equality of type," while exploiting to the full Schmitt's suggestion that the "elimination or eradication of heterogeneity" was real equality's necessary task. Although rarely studied or even acknowledged by scholars, such right-wing discourses of equality are very much alive, and they continue to exert a strong popular appeal, making them all the more worthy of our attention today.[16]

Animated between the competing poles of difference and sameness, historical understandings of equality help to elicit a tension that endures. They also reveal the extent to which equality as an idea is filtered through the passions, exciting powerful and conflicting emotions. Appeals to equality over the centuries have inspired yearning for recognition and distinction, emancipation and empowerment, acceptance and belonging in communities and the community of humankind. But they have also taken a darker turn, channeling animosity and resentment, while rousing the will to dominate, repress, and exclude.

That constellation of complex emotions points to this book's third running theme: human beings' fundamental ambivalence toward equality itself. To put the matter simply, we want it and we don't. We want to be treated with fairness and on equal terms, accorded recognition and respect. But at the same time we seek distinction, aiming to set ourselves apart. And we are strongly inclined to pay allegiance to those who distinguish themselves most successfully, especially when it redounds (or seems to redound) to our benefit.

Such ambivalence almost certainly has evolutionary origins, as I argue in the opening chapter, and it has been singled out repeatedly by insightful thinkers across the ages. But psychologists and sociologists who study status have done the most of late to point out what that ambivalence looks like in practice, and my work is informed by their insights. Status hierarchies take shape spontaneously in every place where human beings come together in groups.

Hungry for recognition, we crave acknowledgment and approval, and we are resentful when it is denied. But we also grant it freely to others in the form of distinction, conferring honor, esteem, and respect in order to facilitate our social interactions. All cultures have particular grammars for status—rules that shape and guide its complex norms—but none do without it. And its unequal accrual very often reflects and reinforces inequalities of more concrete kinds, whether of power, wealth, or access to other people's bodies. The most woke academic departments, just like the military, the corporation, or your social media feed, are intense arenas for status competition that necessarily impinge on (and frequently under-mine) prospects for equality in others. Human beings are status creatures par excellence, and that basic fact has shaped the way they have imagined equality over the ages, and developed conflicted feelings about it.[17]

That insight helps account for a fourth major theme of the book: the great variety of uses to which ideas of equality have been put, many of which are scarcely egalitarian at all. We tend to think of equality today largely as a "protest ideal," the prerogative of the political Left and of those groups at the forefront of the fight to expand its frontiers in the name of justice. Equality has certainly functioned in that capacity often enough, as this book will discuss at length. But history's canvas is wider.[18]

Pope Gregory's words above provide a case in point. For like the Roman jurists on whom he drew, Gregory invoked equality in the context of a discussion of slavery, an institution he had no intention of challenging or changing. Gregory, in fact, in his capacity as pope, owned enslaved persons himself, just like Thomas Jefferson. The point for now is that what can easily seem from a modern perspective a blatant contradiction—that all men are created equal, but some are slaves—was for Pope Gregory a perfectly consistent proposition and point of departure, which he used to help justify the hierarchies and domination so prevalent on earth.

That is just one example of many that will help drive a final argument of the book: that not only are understandings of equality consistent with hierarchy and exclusion, but they regularly serve as their very basis, acting to buttress and reinforce them. That may sound paradoxical, but only because of confusion about what hierarchy actually is. Modern scholars tend to be of little help on the matter. With their egalitarian sympathies, they are often uncomfortable discussing the subject at all, speaking of hierarchy only "reluctantly and with averted eyes," as if it were "taboo." And when they do invoke the term, they generally employ it as a pejorative, to mean the very opposite of equality, as if it were a simple synonym for domination or oppression.[19]

Hierarchy can certainly be those things. But at its most basic, it is a system for allocating status and access to resources, whether of food, sex, money, or power, and of establishing the criteria upon which that is to be done. Hierarchy is a way of facilitating social order, and as such, it most often enjoys social sanction, conferring legitimate authority. Indeed, human beings cannot live without hierarchies. They form spontaneously even in very small groups, and they inevitably grow more elaborate as those groups expand, helping us to work together and get along. Hierarchy, in other words, is not the same thing as domination (illegitimate authority), which is based more explicitly on force and threat, even if the line between them is often thin.[20]

Now equality claims are regularly invoked to contest or contain established hierarchies. But they invariably carry hierarchical assumptions of their own—ideas about who is equal and who is not, and what a just arrangement of the two would be. Where they are successfully implemented, those ideas sanction new ways of conceiving and arranging social order, which is to say, new ways of establishing hierarchy. From Athenian democracy to the meritocracies of the eighteenth century to the global politics of the twentieth, we will have occasion to watch that happen time and again.

We will also see that hierarchies based on equality claims can shade quickly, like hierarchy itself, into domination. For to assert a community of equals is to do so by way of reference to those who are not part of the community, meaning that equality, inequality, and exclusion are always entwined. The excluded, of course, have not always been the same, even if some groups, such as women or the poor, have been excluded with a disturbing frequency throughout human history. But the general act of exclusion itself has been surprisingly consistent. Human beings are good at banishing "unequals" from their midst. Over the long run, ideas of equality have been used just as often to consolidate the position of elites in power as to contest or overthrow them. And they have presided faithfully over regimes of domination.

I thread each of these five principal themes throughout the book as a whole. But they are woven in particular chapters around a series of what I call "figures" of the way equality has been imagined and represented in the past. I use that word loosely, in both the rhetorical sense, of a "figure of speech"—what ancients and early Christians called *figurae*—and also in the artistic and literary sense, of a "figurative" rendering that can be true to life and at the same time metaphorical or stylized in some way. The "figures" of equality that figure in this book are a selection of some of the principal representations that have shaped and given contours to abstract ideas of equality as they have been conceived and experienced over time.[21]

Each chapter introduces a figure of its own—I discuss eleven in all—and the book unfolds chronologically, beginning in prehistory and moving forward to the present day. The figures themselves, however, are not meant to be perfectly sequential, even though I introduce them in periods when they took on particular resonance and force. The book presents the figure of "leveling," for instance, only explicitly at the time of the French Revolution, when the "razor of equality" (the guillotine) was busy doing its best to cut down those who dared to rise above the rest. But leveling stretches back all the way to ancient Israel and the classical world. It was associated with equality from very early on.

Similarly, although I introduce equality in the figure of justice as it emerged as a focal point of reflection in ancient Greece, justice's connection to equality was there already, and it has remained to the present day. The figures endure; each is written over the others like a palimpsest, so that they remain legible across time if one strives to see beneath the surface. And the figures of equality prefigure, as well, suggesting shapes and forms to be assumed later. Any idea as old, complex, and essentially contested as equality can only have come down to us in this layered and multifaceted way. To read it deeply requires that we hold as many of the different facets and figures in our minds as we can at once, even if it will never be possible to see them all.

I begin in Part I with the figure of "Reversal," the challenge to the dominance hierarchies that likely characterized life among our oldest hominid ancestors and the more equal social relations that may have reigned among their hunter-gatherer successors for tens of thousands of years. Asking what evidence about our earliest ancestors can tell us about ideas of equality to come, I contrast the figure of reversal, in the following chapter, with that of "Loss," which narrates the emergence of the immense inequalities of wealth and power that were slowly put in place with the development of civilization. The last several thousand years before the Common Era were among the most unequal periods in the whole of human history on many parts of earth, giving rise to god-kings, slavery, patriarchy, and an original "one percent." Understandably, men and women mourned what they had left behind, imagining a mythic past in which human beings were more equal than they had since become. But at the same time, they opened themselves up to the appeal of the masters, prophets, ascetics, and sages who emerged in what is known as the "Axial Age" of the first millennium BCE. The period saw the birth of the world's first major religious traditions, and strikingly, they all articulated versions of the figure I call

"Fellowship," preaching the unity of humanity and denouncing many of the inequalities of the world. Giving birth to some of the world's first explicit representations of human equality, they laid the basis at the same time for new forms of exclusion and division.

Part I of this book is thus global in its scope, reflecting the fact that ideas of equality have roots in virtually every culture. But although equality is by no means a uniquely Western value, it was politicized and instrumentalized in the West in ways that ultimately exerted an undue influence across the globe, sometimes for the better, often for the worse.

In Part II, accordingly, I trace four figures—"Justice," "Recovery," "Fraternity," and "Leveling"—that helped give contours to influential ideas of equality that emerged in classical antiquity, Western Christendom, the European and American Enlightenments, and the American, French, and Haitian Revolutions. It is toward the end of that period, in the long eighteenth century, that one witnesses the "reinvention" of equality culled from classical, Christian, and Enlightenment sources, as well as the first articulations of what was destined to be a powerful faith that equality is humanity's final frontier. To some extent, this reinvention involved a creative engagement with the Christian figure of "Recovery," which had long imagined equality as human beings' natural and intended state. Christians had speculated for centuries about the possibility of equality's retrieval, but in the eighteenth century, altogether new energies were also unleashed, moving men and women to question their place in the reigning hierarchies of humanity, challenging them outright in bloody revolutions. At the very same time, however, actors in Europe and the United States put the reinventions of the age to familiar and tested uses, employing new assertions of equality to construct new forms of hierarchy and new justifications for exclusion. They did so, moreover, on the very eve of Europe's divergence from, and conquest of, much of the world, with the consequence that the better part of the globe was relegated to unequal status. In the West's emerging epistemological map, equality would be cordoned off and bounded, in space as well as time.

Whereas Part II cautions against treating the history of equality as the triumphant march of progress, opening up new sight lines to equality's complicated past, Part III opens up new sight lines to the present. I introduce four figures that emerged initially in the global north, but that over time significantly impacted many places in the world. The first, "Illusion," reveals the surprising story of how Marx and Engels presented equality as just that, an illusion, combating the utopian and ultimately mystifying embrace of egalitarian notions in the aftermath of the French Revolution by fellow socialists, democrats, and liberals. The second figure, "Domination," frames the no less surprising story of how right-wing forces responded to new doctrines of equality with their own. Theorists in fascist Italy and Germany exposed the ugly mechanisms of power that those employing languages of equality often hide from themselves. Openly embracing those mechanisms, fascists generated combustible theories that weaponized status anxieties, making populist appeals to the equality of the people that demanded not only the exclusion and suppression of others, but their total eradication.

The language of equality as domination has resurfaced in recent times, but the language of equality in the figure of "Balance" has never gone away. In the penultimate chapter I examine understandings of sovereign equality and world order as they took shape in the twentieth century in the global north and were in turn challenged by anticolonial activists in the global south. Synthesizing egalitarian currents in their own traditions with ideas appropriated from their colonizers, activists facilitated the "globalization of equality" as a stated aim of politics, economics, and society. But although the countries of the global north achieved significant social and economic compression over much of the twentieth century, their policies opened up a gap with the rest of the world that their egalitarian languages could not hide. What many economists today describe as the "Great Compression"—the run of contraction of inequalities of wealth and income from roughly 1914 to 1970—was experienced in much of the world as the continuation of a "Great Squeeze."

I close with the figure of the "Dream," the idea that equality and the arc of history coincide, by tracing the uses of equality by Martin Luther King Jr. in the civil rights movement, and its subsequent refashioning in second-wave feminism, Black Power, and the politics of identity. Here the long-standing tension between difference and sameness bursts into the open once again, exposing fault lines in the United States and the world that have only been exacerbated by the stunning reemergence of inequalities of income and wealth of the past several decades. I conclude by trying to take stock of our current moment in light of the past, speculating about the prospects of equality's future.

In presenting these eleven figures, I make no claims to completeness. There are more figures of equality in heaven and earth than any single history can conceive. Rather than engaging in a quixotic attempt to write equality's complete and integrated history (as if any such thing were possible in the first place), I offer instead a series of revealing instances and iterations over the intellectual *longue durée*. There is a governing logic to my choices, as I have tried to make clear, but I have inevitably selected subjects in keeping with my own predilections and areas of expertise, as well as in line with my stated aim of presenting equality in a new and unaccustomed light, making strange what is seemingly familiar.

As a consequence, I pay less attention to topics that have already received considerable treatment elsewhere, such as the emancipation of the enslaved at the time of the Civil War, the genesis and triumphs of first-wave feminism, the egalitarian politics of the welfare state, the history of utopian thinking, or the history of human rights. And there is much that I touch on only sporadically or leave out altogether, such as the global reception of socialism, leveling in Mao's China or Pol Pot's Cambodia, and ideas of equality elaborated outside the West following the Axial Age and prior to the twentieth century. Despite its acknowledged lacunae, however, this book offers a history of ideas of equality that I hope will spur thinking beyond them, generating more reflection and new imaginings to come.

For clearly we have lost, of late, our ability to imagine equality together. The renewed salience of inequality in our time is so powerful that it can blind us to the fact that until only recently many assumed that the world was struggling steadily forward in the direction of an ever greater equality for all. Some optimists continue to cherish that hope, and they look to the past to sustain it. Thomas Piketty, for example, in his most recent book, *A Brief History of Equality*, discerns "a long-term movement over the course of history toward more social, economic, and political equality." My book adopts a less sanguine perspective, opting instead to embrace the ways in which our current historical moment disrupts teleological assumptions put in place since the eighteenth century. If what once seemed safely on the horizon can no longer be safely assumed, it should be easier to see equality not as a natural destination, but as the contingent historical creation that it is.[22]

In short, the crisis of the moment is also an opportunity, a chance to reexamine old assumptions, excavate lost resources, and cast a glance in the eerie light of the times on an idea we thought we knew. At a moment in history when equality is difficult for many to conceive, we can at least conceive it more clearly in the past. By studying a history of imaginary equalities, we can begin to imagine it anew.

PART I

PART 1

1

REVERSAL

The Deep History of Equality

Down dusty roads in the Spanish Levant, about an hour and a half northwest of Valencia by car, lies the Stone Age site of Remigia. A series of caves and rock shelters whose walls contain some 750 megalithic figures and drawings, the site was only discovered in 1934. It is now well known to specialists, though less so by tourists, who tend to favor the older and more celebrated sites of Altamira (35,000 BCE) or Lascaux (15,000 BCE). Still, the figures at Remigia—executed over different periods, but perhaps as recently as 6500 BCE—may tell us something interesting about a much earlier period in human history. Their faint lines in ocher and black offer a rare glimpse into the deep history of equality.[1]

Most intriguing in this connection are a number of drawings in Cave 5, and in particular, three powerful scenes of what appear to be acts of banishment and execution. In one drawing, fourteen gathered individuals stand and watch as a lone figure departs from the group, apparently in the process of being cast out and excluded. In another, a bloodied and splayed figure, with body and head pierced by arrows, lies broken in the foreground before an exultant group of five others, who raise their arms in triumph. And in the third drawing, a larger band, of ten men, brandish their bows above their heads in seeming celebration before a recumbent figure,

"Execution Scenes" at Cave 5, Cova Remigia, Spain, in the tracing of Joan Baptiste Porcare. Courtesy of the Societat Castellonenca de Cultura, Castelló, Spain.

unarmed but pierced by six arrows. As in the other image, only the head of the victim is upright, as if looking plaintively to the group.[2]

Faint and difficult to see in the uneven light and surface of the cave, these figures recover their full graphic power when transposed to the page in black and white. Violence and strong emotion emanate from their minimalist lines, which seem to defy their time and place of origin. We could almost be looking at the primitivist drawings of a Picasso or a Miró, executed at the very moment of Remigia's (re-)discovery. But such apparent timelessness only begs the historical question: What can these haunting figures mean?

We will never know for sure, and any answer can only be speculative. But paleoanthropologists and archeologists point out that such scenes of execution and exclusion likely played an important role in the group dynamics of the small bands of hunter-gatherers who roamed the earth in the wake of the emergence of modern *Homo sapiens* some 300,000 years ago. Such scenes are well documented among more recent hunter-gatherers, the itinerant bands who move regularly between foraging and hunting grounds, living without fixed habitation or cultivation of the soil. And while anthropologists are quick to caution against the dangers of treating modern hunter-gatherers as "living fossils"—as if the activities recorded by ethnographers since the nineteenth century provide a perfect picture, frozen in time, of the earliest human past—they do point out certain patterns of convergence. The exclusion—or in extreme cases, the execution—of outcasts and upstarts seems to be one such pattern. In the power dynamics of hunter-gatherer societies, individuals are "removed" when they attempt to place themselves above the group or act consistently to dominate or bully their fellows. Upstarts, in other words, put themselves at risk when they threaten the group cohesion and solidarity.[3]

Over the past several decades, anthropologists have done a great deal of work to understand this phenomenon, what they describe as the "fierce egalitarianism" of hunter-gatherer societies. In a celebrated analysis of the !Kung, the San people of the Kalahari Desert in south-western Africa, the anthropologist Richard B. Lee detailed the practice of what he called "insulting the meat." Every time a hunter of the band made a kill, the other members would belittle the achievement with razzing and slights, mocking the hunter and his paltry prey, even (and especially) if it was prodigious. An informant explained the rationale: "When a young man kills much meat, he comes to think of himself as a chief or big man and he thinks of the rest of us as his servants or inferiors. We can't accept this. So we always speak of his meat as worthless. This way we cool his heart and make him gentle." Such ribbing—formulaic and often good natured—is accompanied by strong social pressure to limit boasting or arrogance of any kind. The mechanism is further reinforced by a social ethos that emphasizes altruism, sharing, and group solidarity. In itinerant societies where people can only accumulate what they can carry on their backs, private possessions are few. Food, like almost everything else, is divided and shared. The meat of one becomes the meat of all.[4]

The San people are thought to have lived as hunter-gatherers for at least 20,000 years, and their ancestry has been traced back some 200,000 years, making them the oldest surviving people on earth. But their "fierce egalitarianism" and "aggressive rejection of hierarchy" are by no means an isolated phenomenon. On the contrary, they are the norm among hunter-gatherer peoples.[5]

Anthropologists describe variations on the same pattern on every inhabited continent, drawing attention to recurrent features: broad material equality among members of the group; "acephalous" social arrangements (without formalized leadership structures); and a variety of policing mechanisms to reinforce the dominant "egalitarian ethos." The latter can include formal prescriptions for food-sharing, particularly of large game, such as the elaborate rules governing the distribution of seal meat observed among the Inuit people of the Canadian Arctic. Invariably, though, these mechanisms feature strong social sanctioning to reinforce altruism, reciprocity, self-sacrifice, and humility, along with a variety of leveling mechanisms designed to forestall the emergence of domi-nant individuals. The kind of ridicule observed among the San people of the Kalahari is widespread in this regard, as are various forms of gossiping, shaming, and censoring, all of which serve to police the behavior of potential upstarts and exact social confor-mity while keeping those with authority in check.[6]

Hunter-gatherer peoples are by no means leaderless, even if they tend to make their crucial decisions collectively. Admired individuals—respected for their physical prowess, intelligence, experience, or skill—inevitably play an outsized role in delibera-tions, and they assume special prominence in times of emergency or war. But if they are in some sense firsts, they are firsts among relative equals. Their authority is never institutionalized, and it is predicated on the understanding that it is to be carried out with due deference to the group. Behavior is continually scrutinized for incipient signs of arrogance or presumption, and if individuals over-step their bounds, social sanctioning and other leveling mechanisms are brought to bear. When these fail, more extreme measures are pursued, including ostracism, banishment, and, in the last resort, murder. Anthropologists have provided accounts of the executions of upstarts and aggressors among a wide variety of hunter-gatherer peoples, including Inuit, Indigenous North Americans and Australians, and Africans. In the judgment of one authority, the suite of measures and sanctions that serve to enforce the fierce egalitarianism of hunter-gatherers is "universal."[7]

Are the apparent depictions of banishment and execution on the stones of Remigia early illustrations of such sanctioning—dramatic accounts of social leveling and the terrible justice imposed on upstarts by a band of equals? Again, it is impossible to say with any certainty. Given that other drawings at the site clearly depict episodes of war, it is possible that these figures merely represent the release or execution of captives. The dating of the drawings, moreover, while uncertain, appears to fall somewhat after the period of exclusive hunter-gatherer dominance that began to end with the transition from the Paleolithic to the Neolithic—that is, the "Old Stone Age" to the "New Stone Age"—roughly 12,000 years ago. By the time these drawings were likely produced, a variety of other social forms had made their appearance on earth, rendering the illustrations that much more difficult to interpret. The truth is that we will never know for sure what they were meant to depict.

But if they *were* intended to illustrate the policing of pretenders to power—the banishment or elimination of potential upstarts—that would hardly be surprising. For such images are consistent with a good deal of forceful speculation about early human development, and it is not hard to imagine that they played out with some frequency across the landscape of our early human past. Such speculation yields, in turn, a powerful image of early equality in the making. In order to more fully understand that image—the figure of equality as reversal—we need to spend a little more time thinking about the kinds of animals that human beings once were, and the kind that we have since become.

There may be a little monkey in all of us, but there is a lot of great ape. Modern human beings share a common ancestry with all four of the living great apes: orangutans, gorillas, bonobos, and chimps. Which is to say that we evolved along the same branch of the great tree of life that connects every living thing on the planet. We know, based largely on genetic evidence, that orangutans departed from our common branch of descent some 14 million years ago. Gorillas did the same roughly 7.5 million years ago, and the genus *Homo* (which includes not only our own species, *sapiens*, but a host of others, now extinct, including *Homo erectus*, *Homo habilis*, *Homo heidelbergensis*, and *Homo neanderthalensis*) branched off about 5.5 million years ago from the common ancestor that yielded both bonobos and chimps. Orangutans today, confined to Indonesia and Malaysia, live as solitary creatures, and so are something of an outlier. But the other great apes of Africa are intensely social, like human beings, and it is clear that we share a good deal in common.

To be sure, we're talking about many more degrees of separation than six. Millions of years and countless adaptations lie between us. But in evolutionary terms, we in the hominid family, which embraces both *Homo sapiens* and the great apes, are closely related. Modern human beings share about 98.8 percent of their DNA with bonobos and chimps, and some 98.4 percent with gorillas. It is true that those numbers can be a little deceptive—for context, bear in mind that we share DNA with *all* living things, and show surprising genetic similarities to mice, dogs, and even the banana! Still, the numbers are close enough for some scientists to argue that bonobos and chimps ought really to be included with humans in a common genus *Homo*. To study them, as primatologists have long recognized, is to gain insight into our own "inner ape." They can help us understand our nature, to see a little better who we are.[8]

Historians, for some time, have been resistant to this kind of inquiry, and arguably with good reason. Trained to study the particular, they are instinctively allergic to the general, and acutely sensitive to human beings' plasticity in different cultural contexts. They rightly point out how often claims about an essential or universal human nature have been used to constrain and confine. Reasoning by analogy to our ancestry to the apes has been employed to justify all kinds of unsavory things—from violence and war to male domination to the survival of the "racially fit"—as if all that were somehow justified by our genes. Clearly, researchers today must be mindful of this unsavory past, treading warily where socio-biologists and social Darwinists before them have fallen.[9]

And yet to dismiss the inquiry into our ancestral human natures altogether—as if we humans were entirely free to fashion ourselves as we would, unconstrained by our biological inheritance—would be naïve at the extreme. And where questions of equality are concerned it would be to miss out on a crucial insight into what makes us not only typically hominid, but uniquely *Homo sapiens*. As one of the early pioneers of the speculative history of equality, Jean-Jacques Rousseau, once rightly asked, "For how can the source of the inequality among men be known unless one begins by knowing men themselves?" Our nearest relations may well have something important to tell us in this regard, if only we take the time to listen.[10]

What is most striking, at first glance, is how little equality one finds. The social organization of all the great African apes is intensely hierarchical, ranging in the classificatory schemes of animal behaviorists from "despotic" (gorillas and chimpanzees) to "semi-despotic" (bonobos). Gorillas and chimpanzees organize themselves in dominance hierarchies around an alpha male. Among gorillas, in whom sexual dimorphism is pronounced (males are about twice the size of females), a single dominant male will control a harem of females (on average about six), using bluffing, aggressive display, and ultimately violence to drive off competitors, who must live as rogue individuals or gain control of their own harems by overthrowing a dominant male somewhere else.[11]

Chimpanzee societies, which typically number between fifty and one hundred members, are more complex. Here the alpha male enforces a strict linear hierarchy of dominance and submission that dictates the place of every animal in the group. From highest to lowest, each member knows its place. But unlike some species— monkeys, for instance, among whom hierarchies are frozen and fixed—chimps continually jockey for position. Given that dominant individuals enjoy greater access to food and mates, they must constantly defend their positions through aggressive displays, intimidation, bullying, and force, as well as by effecting alliances to challenge superiors or put down threats from below. Chimpanzee society is thus the scene of constant struggle for status and rank, with rivals competing for their places in the hierarchy, and the power and benefits precedence confers. When an erstwhile alpha is defeated by challengers—demoted, driven off, or killed—the hierarchy rearranges itself in a new order of dominance and submission. The rule of each alpha is comparatively short—rarely lasting more than four or five years. But the hierarchy itself endures.[12]

Bonobo society is less severe. For one thing, the sexes are codominant. Unlike in chimpanzee society, in which every female is subordinate to every male in the hierarchy, bonobos are governed by both an alpha female and an alpha male. In many ways, it is the females who run the show, forming alliances and coalitions to mediate power and access to food. Male bonobos do not form alliances with other males, but wisely work through their mothers instead. Often, females use sex to establish and solidify their alliances, engaging freely with female and male partners alike. The result is a far lower level of fighting and aggressive dominance displays among males engaged in status rivalries for females. Highly sexual, bonobos, not surprisingly, are peaceful and relaxed. As the primatologist Frans de Waal has observed, they are the "hippies" of the ape world, making love not war.[13]

That said, bonobos are hardly egalitarians. Though their social interaction is less fraught than that of chimpanzees, they are hierarchical creatures all the same. In fact, the relative absence of conflict is itself a sign of the strength of their hierarchical order, which is more stable than that of chimps, who are constantly challenging one another for pride of place. And as with chimps, one's position in the hierarchy among bonobos largely determines the "pecking order" of access to food and sex. The first and best portions of each go to the dominants, and violence, though less common, is employed when needed to ensure that "inferiors" know their place. It is little wonder that bonobo mothers expend so much energy trying to ensure that their offspring get into the upper echelons of the elite. Even among laid-back bonobo hippies, it is better to be on top of the establishment than at the bottom.

Just how much of this primate predilection for hierarchy still lurks in the minds of human beings is difficult to say. The question is inevitably controversial, and not only because of the crude uses to which the study of apes has been put in the past. It is made more so by an unwillingness to talk about hierarchy frankly. With their ostensible commitments to equality, observers in modern democratic societies often skirt the subject, treating it, as one group of eminent scholars recently complained, as "taboo." Alternatively, they speak of it exclusively in pejorative terms, as if hierarchy were only synonymous with oppression, rather than what it most often is: a socially sanctioned system that formalizes access to resources, be these food or power, salary or status.[14]

Still, although the subject of hierarchy has received less attention than it deserves, a wealth of evidence points to the fact that human beings, just like monkeys and apes, are hierarchical creatures, exquisitely sensitive to cues of status, rank, dominance, and submission. Patterns of gaze, vocal and speech characteristics, posture, body size, age, and height are just a few of the traits to which all social primates are carefully attuned, and we are wired with specific neural networks to detect them. Within forty milliseconds, human beings can tell the difference between a dominant face staring them in the eyes and a subordinate one, with averted glance. Human beings draw on a range of other indicators—including intelligence, reputation, attractiveness, income, profession, and the ever-nebulous prestige—that our primate relations don't in order to make judgments about status and rank. And, unlike animals, we regularly inhabit multiple hierarchies at once, with the result that a low-status individual in one environment, say a janitor at a corporation, may be a high-status individual, the captain of the company softball team, in another. That said, there can be no doubt that among our many complicated criteria for assessing other human beings lie some fairly primitive measures. There is a reason (if not justice) behind the fact that tall men are statistically more likely than their shorter counterparts to succeed in business or get elected to high office, just as there is a reason why interviewers process body language and gaze as signs of inner confidence and worth. We may not be fully comfortable with these judgments—and often they are made unconsciously. But anyone who has ever attended an American high school will know how crude our species can be at assessing and assigning status. The "popular" are not always well liked. But like it or not, they draw disproportionately from the alluring, the athletic, the strong. And the tendency of others to gossip about them, just like the tendency of human beings to gossip in general, is driven by an intense interest in rank differences. As the biologist Robert Sapolsky has remarked, "Gossip is mostly about the status of status." And status is part of the air we breathe.[15]

Yet however much we are prone to assess status according to criteria we share, uncomfortably, with the apes, we are undoubtedly moved by far more than simply the residual crudeness of dominance and submission. Human beings, after all, are social creatures—more so than any other creature on earth. We are the "cooperative species" par excellence. Our sprawling networks, institutions, and metropoles testify to our capacity to work together. And while hierarchy and status are certainly important means by which we arrange ourselves to cooperate and coexist, we draw on other capacities besides the restless pursuit of power and prestige to do so.[16]

Here again the great African apes can be our guide, for they, too, are social creatures, and even, as primatologists in the wake of the pioneering Jane Goodall insist, "political animals," consciously developing strategies and alliances to protect and further their interests. Chimps form coalitions to protect their places in the hierarchy of the group, to put down pretenders, or to oust erstwhile alphas. They also work together to gather food, police their frontiers, and even to hunt collectively, sharing meat after a kill. Bonobos, too, are political animals, if less intensely so, given the stability of their groups. Female bonobos act in solidarity to protect their interests and collectively dominate males, and also to further the fortunes of their younger protégés of both sexes, who in turn cultivate alliances with those who can help them. The point being that the great apes pursue conscious strategies to attain their ends, forming alliances and working in concert to manage power within their ranks.[17]

Not only that, but they quite clearly display sentiments and emotions that in human beings we would call "moral sentiments"— prosocial feelings and the associated actions that serve, beyond naked power and force, to maintain group solidarity and cohesion. As millions of YouTube viewers know, capuchin monkeys, for example, seem to possess a sense of fairness. In a famous experiment first performed by the lab of Frans de Waal and readily viewable online, two monkeys are given cucumbers to perform the same simple task. But after a while, one is given a tastier grape in the plain sight of the other. The shorted monkey rebels, clearly displaying resentment at the "unfair" treatment, refusing to accept the cucumber while the other gets the grape. Such experiments have been repeated widely with many different animals, including chimpanzees. They testify to something like a basic sense of fairness, as well as to the resentment that can arise when an animal feels that it has been wronged.[18]

The sentiment is closely related to reciprocity, which bonobos and chimps exhibit all the time. The phrase "If I scratch your back, you scratch mine" may be a human adage, but for apes, it is a way of life. Grooming, like food and sexual pleasure, is one of the key favors they share. And, like human beings, apes keep tabs on who owes what. When they feel short-changed, they let the others know.

Sharing and performing favors, little acts of kindness, including sexual favors, are two of the ways that apes bind their groups together. But they also exhibit empathy, compassion, consolation, and other forms of prosocial behavior. After they engage in conflict, bonobos and chimps make efforts to reconcile through grooming, placation, and sex, and when a member of the group acts in such a way as to incur resentment, the transgressor can be punished or run out of the group in a form of collective "justice."

The point of these observations is not to insist that animals are moral agents, but to emphasize that where their behavior is concerned, power and interest are not the only games in town. The same chimps and bonobos who jockey for position in environments shaped profoundly by hierarchical arrangements based on status and power also act in ways that redound to the benefit of others, cooperating for the benefit of all.

Human beings, clearly, harbor similar tendencies. We compete *and* we cooperate. We are self-seeking *and* we are prosocial. We pursue power and domination, but we are also concerned with fairness and reciprocity. And although we possess the capacity for great altruism and generosity, we are quick to take umbrage when we feel slighted and to take measures to exact our revenge.

Many towering thinkers throughout the ages have recognized one or the other of these basic tendencies. But more often than not they have chosen sides. The likes of Machiavelli, Thomas Hobbes, or Friedrich Nietzsche, for example, have insisted on human beings' will to power, their relentless self-interest, and their ceaseless striving for domination. Others, from Jesus of Nazareth to Karl Marx to Gandhi, have emphasized that we are, at our core and at our best, social creatures, moved by concerns for others as much as by the desire for our own preservation and preferment. Many of the anthropologists and biologists who have speculated about the behavior of our early hominid ancestors over the years have been similarly inclined to choose between extremes, presenting human beings in their infancy either as noble savages or as ruthless aggressors. They have grappled less frequently with the possibility that we might be both of these things, and so neither, harboring competing tendencies at once.[19]

That is the great insight of recent primatology and evolutionary biology, which insist on the "relentless ambivalence and ambiguity" of the human mind bequeathed to us as part of our primate inheritance. As de Waal puts it succinctly, our inner ape is "bipolar." We are at once selfish and selfless, despotic and democratic, moved by interests of power *and* by the common good. On the one hand, the urge to dominate, or at least to get a leg up, is clearly part of our nature. We seek status and we measure it all the time, in others and in ourselves. But if a tendency to hierarchy lurks in our DNA, so, too, on the other hand, does an inclination to resist it. "To be human," the biologist E. O. Wilson insists, "is also to level others, especially those who appear to receive more than they have earned." What in Australia is called the "tall-poppy syndrome," the urge to lop off the head of anyone who dares to rise above the rest, or, in Chile, *chaqueteo* (jacketing), the teasing sport of grabbing another by the lapels and pulling them down to size, has analogues in almost every culture, from the razzing of the !Kung to the grumblings at the water cooler about the boss.[20]

In short, human beings are a conflicted bunch. We naturally seek our own status and preferment, striving to get ahead, while at the same time grumbling about, and often trying to impede, the same pretensions in others. That contradiction undoubtedly explains a good deal of human hypocrisy and a lot about our individual psychologies. But it can do even more than that, giving us insight into the deep history of equality. For there is every reason to conclude that our contradictory impulses helped to shape, just as they were shaped by, our early social evolution. And although it is no more possible to say precisely how this process unfolded than it is to establish with certainty the meaning of the cave paintings of

Remigia, we can entertain a plausible conjecture. That imagining—the image of an early, and lasting, form of imaginary equality—looks something like this.

The farther back in time we go, the more apelike we were. Which is to say that our early hominid ancestors were a lot hairier. Hair now clings mainly to our heads, and in patches under our arms and between our legs. But at one point our ancestors would have been covered almost entirely. If there is a general consensus among specialists that human beings had largely shed their thick covering by the time they achieved their modern body form, there is similar agreement that for long periods of our development, we were shaggy beasts.[21]

We were also longer in the tooth. At least that is the hypothesis. Darwin famously speculated in *The Descent of Man* (1871) that our early male forefathers were "probably furnished with great canine teeth." Ever since, researchers have entertained the notion. The theory runs that over time the length of those powerful canines was reduced, along with an earlier, and more pronounced, disparity in size between the teeth of men and women. Canine sexual dimorphism, in other words, gradually diminished as we evolved, so that men's and women's teeth became more and more alike.[22]

Given the imperfect state of the fossil record, all of that remains somewhat conjectural, and may even be misleading. The same is true for the related theory of the reduction in body size dimorphism between men and women. Fossils from *Australopithecus afarensis* and *Australopithecus anamensis*, the apelike ancestors from whom the genus *Homo* began to depart some 2 or 3 million years ago, suggest considerable disparities in size, with males perhaps as much as 50 percent larger than females. That contrasts sharply with the 15 percent difference evident in modern human beings. Until recently, that was the standard account, and in some respects still is. But researchers of late have begun to question the evidence, suggesting that the body size of male and female australopiths may have been closer than we thought.[23]

Still, if one admits some gradual reduction—in either teeth or body size dimorphism—here is why the change would matter to the subject of human equality. Armed with powerful jaws, menacing canines, and erectile hair that could stand up in hackles in bristling displays, our distant male ancestors would likely have engaged in similar kinds of fighting, bluffing, and intimidation for dominance and control that we still observe among the apes. Domination, to put it simply—between and among males and females—based on agonistic competition was probably much greater and more rigidly enforced the farther back in time we go.

We know, too, that conspicuous sexual dimorphism in primates is associated either with polygamous harem arrangements, like those of gorillas, or with fierce competition among males, such as that witnessed among chimpanzees. The social organization of our more apelike ancestors would likely have been similarly "despotic," characterized by struggles for dominance among males in which size and strength were all-important.[24]

Yet as they gradually lost their body hair and aggressive canines, and as the size difference between males and females decreased, the evolutionary forces abetting domination and competition based exclusively on displays of prowess and the strength of one's jaws and fists would have weakened. As we evolved, the theory runs, we grew gradually more equal—both in our physical constitutions and in our social arrangements.

A number of factors would have aided that development, but the introduction of weaponry was undoubtedly a critical equalizer. Although we have firm evidence of general tool use dating back at least 2.6 million years—and quite possibly well before that—the earliest confirmed fossil evidence of "bespoke" weaponry is much more recent: a lone, and rather unimposing, wooden spear from the Schöningen Valley in Germany from approximately 400,000 years ago. Fire-hardening technology—employed to shape strong and sturdy tips—is even more recent, and stone arrowheads and darts are not attested until about 70,000 years ago. But our ancestors were employing cruder instruments far earlier: the controlled use of fire can be confirmed some 800,000 years ago, and the introduction of hand-axes dates from roughly 1.5 million years ago. Surely, we were picking up rocks and throwing them from at least that time. And that seems to be the key. For the most effective weapon in the early fight for equality was likely the shoulder.

Human beings are unmatched among primates in their capacity to throw at a high velocity and with precision aim, and paleobiologists tell us that perhaps as early as the time of *Homo erectus*, roughly 2 million years ago, the shoulder was well adapted to throwing. Brain evolution in the succeeding million years would have refined the capacity to target, giving our ancestors an edge not only against predators and prey, but against each other. A well-aimed stone can fell a much larger opponent, as the mythic tale of David and Goliath makes clear. And so projectiles—whether flung by the hand, or, in due course, by sling, spear-launcher, or bow—meant that rivals were placed on a more equal footing. Projectile weapons facilitated flight if an attack went awry. And crucially, they obviated the need for fighting in close quarters, where larger and stronger opponents inevitably had the advantage. Competence in delivery helped to balance sheer size and strength, reducing evolutionary pressures that selected for brawn over brain. A skilled opponent could more easily resist an aggressor who tried to bully or dominate. And weapons of all kinds—hand-axes, spears, blunt instruments, and rudimentary knives—made it easier to kill by stealth or surprise. Stronger rivals or aggressors could be dispatched quickly while they slept. As Thomas Hobbes famously pointed out in his *Leviathan*, one of the earliest bases of human equality was our equal capacity to kill.[25]

Weapons, in all these ways, made it easier to constrain or take out would-be alphas and dominant males. They also made it easier to scavenge and kill game, providing precious protein that served to feed the growing hominid brain. And that tool—the brain—in the end, proved to be the most important egalitarian force of them all, for it allowed our ancestors to cooperate to an unprecedented degree. If tools helped us to contest the dictates of biology and nature, the brain permitted us to imagine—and to shape—a world that was very different from what we first encountered.

Our remarkable human intelligence is to a large degree a *social* intelligence, permitting us to communicate and to act to secure common ends. Bonobos and chimps possess aspects of that intelligence, forming coalitions and engaging in sophisticated assessments of power and "politics." But as our hominid ancestors broke away from the branch of common descent and their brains steadily increased in size, their political or "actuarial" acumen grew. That gave them an enhanced capacity not only to work together, but to see the benefits of cooperation and sharing. Keeping track of favors, obligations, and slights, they were able to evaluate complex systems and negotiate power. The upshot is that subordinates were presented with a new tool that could help them limit the power of aggressors. By working together, the many could contain and even dominate the few.

And so the foundations of what the anthropologist Christopher Boehm describes as a "reverse dominance hierarchy," or an "egalitarian hierarchy," in which the many combine to dominate the few, were put in place. In reverse dominance hierarchies, the normal top-down or pyramid-shaped order of primates is inverted. Rather than pointing upward, with one or a few individuals at the top exerting authority over a submissive rank and file, the pyramid of power is turned upside down. Subordinates band together to suppress or remove potential bullies while enforcing cooperation and sharing on equal terms. It is, in effect, the basis of the order that prevails in a large number of the hunter-gatherer societies that have been studied ethnographically, which employ a variety of tactics and leveling mechanisms—from social sanctioning, gossip, and ridicule to coercion, ostracism, and murder—to prevent the emergence of upstarts, enforcing a broadly egalitarian ethos among the group. The belief is that our Paleolithic ancestors employed similar mechanisms, forming coalitions among subordinates to challenge bullies and alphas while simultaneously policing and putting into place collective and prosocial norms.[26]

The theory of reverse dominance hierarchy thus assumes an innate human propensity to hierarchy, inherited from our hominid ancestors and shared with nonhuman primates, while also fully recognizing our social and prosocial capacities, which would have been further reinforced by cognitive development and evolutionary pressures. Taking into account both the dynamics of more recent hunter-gatherer societies and our knowledge of our closest primate relations, the theory balances nicely the bipolarities of our nature. For at work in the construction of reverse dominance hierarchies is both something like a will to power and a will to parity, a drive for dominance and a drive for fairness, a desire to rise up the ranks and a resentment of those who do so by bullying others. The reverse dominance hierarchy accommodates both hierarchical and anti-hierarchical feelings at once. As one anthropologist's East African informant summed up the logic, "All men seek to rule, but if they cannot rule they prefer to remain equal."[27]

Just when such reverse dominance hierarchies might first have formed is far from clear. Boehm speculates that the process could have gotten underway as early as *Homo erectus*, some 2 million years ago. But at the very latest, he believes, egalitarian groups emerged with the advent of anatomically modern humans—human beings, that is, who looked like us—whose remains can now be traced back some 300,000 years. What is clearer, though, is that the prodigious development of the brain of *Homo sapiens* aided this process considerably. And while that, too, was necessarily a protracted affair, many specialists now believe that the critical innovations leading to the emergence of language and full symbolic consciousness, which allowed us to understand and manipulate our experience of the world through signs, occurred rapidly, by dint of a genetic mutation occurring sometime *after* the appearance of modern *Homo sapiens*.

The timing of that development is far from certain—estimates for the emergence of language range from 100,000 to 300,000 years ago, and the achievement of full symbolic cognition may well have been more recent. But by approximately 70,000 years ago, we have unambiguous evidence of the advent of a full-scale "Cognitive Revolution" that empowered *Homo sapiens* to do what they have been doing ever since: transform the world, for better and for worse, through cognition and cooperation. This is the point at which human beings began to create culture—processing their environments through symbols and signs, which they continuously recombined and rearranged in language. It is the point, we can be certain, at which human beings began to stop treating the world, as other creatures do, essentially as a given, and their relationship to it as fixed. It is the point, as one observer aptly puts it, "when history declared its independence from biology."[28]

That applies most directly to our social arrangements. In nonhuman animals, hierarchies are fundamentally mechanical. They form naturally, like the pecking order of chickens, and are accepted without question. But the hierarchies of modern human beings are to a large extent conscious creations—and the reverse dominance hierarchy is no exception. It, too, is an invention, a cultural creation that brought into being moral and political communities that needed to be consciously enforced.

But because they are cultural creations, reverse dominance hierarchies admit of endless varieties and permutations—no two hunter-gatherer bands are exactly alike. And because they are creatures of culture, modern human beings are not bound by them. We should not assume, in other words, that the social arrangements of our Paleolithic ancestors were unchanging, or as extensively or exclusively egalitarian as the experience of more recent hunter-gatherers would seem to suggest. More likely, they were fluid, with many different power arrangements emerging in the small groups that roamed Africa and then gradually began to make their way out into Europe and Asia roughly 75,000 years ago.[29]

There is, in fact, direct evidence of that variety, most famously at the Pleistocene site of Sunghir, about 120 miles north of Moscow. The site contains the remains of hunter-gatherers who lived between 30,000 and 34,000 years ago and were evidently skilled at slaying large game (bison, mammoth, bears). The graves of three individuals, one adult and two children, stand out for the conspicuous presence of various luxury items: art objects, fine weapons, jewelry, fox teeth, and thousands of ivory beads carved from the tusks of mammoths. Scholars estimate that it would have taken a single worker somewhere between fifteen and forty-five minutes to carve a single bead. The children's graves alone had close to 10,000 of the beads, which means that years of human labor were expended in their preparation. Given that the children were too young to have earned their reward through personal merit or achievement, we can only assume that they were the benefactors of special consideration. Here is a sign of incipient social and economic inequality.[30]

There are other such examples—scattered gravesites that hint at economic disparities and inherited power as well as sites of early monumental building, such as the sprawling stone temples at Göbekli Tepe on the Turkish-Syrian border, now thought to have been built by hunter-gatherers at the very end of the most recent ice age, some 11,500 years ago. Even though, like most evidence that ancient, such examples are few and far between, they are nonetheless an important reminder that human beings from early on were likely experimenting with a variety of different social arrangements, not all of which were as egalitarian or small in scale as the bands of reverse dominance hierarchies discussed here.[31]

Still, the preponderance of evidence suggests that significant inequalities between people were more likely the exception than the norm. As one leading scholar concludes, "For all we can tell, social or economic inequality in the Paleolithic remained sporadic and transient." The very fact that hunter-gatherers were constantly on the move, and so had to carry everything they owned on their backs, precluded significant accumulation. When economists try to estimate distribution levels among hunter-gatherers using the standard modern metric known as the Gini coefficient (with 1 representing perfect inequality and 0 perfect equality), they conclude that hunter-gatherer numbers were low. Those are very rough estimates, of course, and we shouldn't put too much stock in them. But if we can be sure that our ancient ancestors were poor by modern standards, we can also say with some conviction that by those same standards they lived far more equally than we do.[32]

And what of women in these early groups? Did they participate fully in the egalitarian possibilities of reverse dominance hierarchies? The subject, understandably, is fraught, for in the history of the world, women have suffered more than any other subset of our species from systematic oppression. To offer judgments on how they were in the beginning suggests to some how they ever shall be, as if the "is" or the "was" necessarily implied the "ought." To make matters even more complicated, the history of science is replete with examples of (male) researchers dressing up their prejudices as universal truths. There is, then, every reason to exercise caution.

What can be said is that the experience of contemporary hunter-gatherers is varied. In the majority of cases described in the ethnographic record, it is true, conditions of equality apply first and foremost to relations among men, who are inclined to treat each other as equals in the "public realm," while exerting varying degrees of dominance over women and children in the privacy of the domestic setting. It is also the case that the vast majority of recorded upstarts—those whom the reverse dominance hierarchies aim to contain—are men, and one of the typical ways they lord it over others is by attempting to possess females. Given the continued sexual dimorphism of the species, which gives males an advantage in average size and strength, and so allowed them in the past to play a more central role in the crucial activities of big-game hunting and combat, it is hard to avoid the conclusion that many probably dominated Paleolithic women when they could.[33]

That points to a general pattern that we will see play out repeatedly: efforts to constrain hierarchy in one realm can easily displace domination onto another. In the case of hunter-gatherers, the more equal relations enforced among men in "public" by reverse dominance hierarchies were likely predicated in many cases on domination over women and children in "private."

Yet that is by no means the end of the story. Just as there is plasticity and play among males and females in the animal kingdom, there was undoubtedly plasticity and play in the gender relations of the early human past. Examples from modern hunter-gatherer societies are intriguing in this regard. Among the Agta people of the Philippines, for example, women take part in the hunting of wild boar and other animals, enjoying high status within society. At the level of both the family and the group, they appear to participate equally in decision-making.[34]

Nor should we assume that the "nuclear family" is everywhere the norm. Sexual mores regarding infidelity tend to be somewhat relaxed among hunter-gatherers, and anthropologists have chronicled numerous examples of "polyandry," in which women take on more than one lover and more than one husband in what appears to be a deliberate attempt to confuse parenthood within the group. If men can't be sure who their children are, the thinking runs—or better, if they suspect that many children might be theirs—they are more inclined to care equally for others.[35]

Evidence of polyandry certainly goes against the grain of the more standard account proposed by Darwin and developed since by sociobiologists and evolutionary psychologists. Pair bonding, they assert, is a consequence of the vulnerability of both women and children in the long gestational and developmental periods of human child-rearing. In need of protection, women granted sex and fidelity to men, who in return gained reasonable certainty about the provenance of their offspring (as well as built-in day care), which was to their evolutionary advantage. Free to go out and hunt big game (or chase down other women), our male ancestors brought home the wooly-mammoth bacon while their wives stayed home with the kids. Patriarchy was born in the home.

In its cruder forms, this conventional view can read a little bit like a tale of prehistoric prostitution, with women selling their bodies in return for security and food. Complicating the picture even further is the fact that there is significant genetic evidence for the prevalence of polygamy in our past, and specifically polygyny (one man, many women), with males fathering multiple children by multiple wives. One shocking study from more recent times estimates that as many as sixteen million people alive today are descended from just one man, the Mongolian emperor and warlord Genghis Khan. The great Khan was no hunter-gatherer, of course. Far from it. But the case highlights the potential for polygyny that surely lurked among our hominid ancestors, and that has been permitted in close to 85 percent of all human societies. Men, on this view, really are gorillas when they can get away with it—or, at best, chimpanzees. And although such apelike behavior is precisely one of the things that the reverse dominance hierarchy aimed to prevent, we can hardly be sure it always did.[36]

But what if, some critics counter, women in the past were more like bonobos—at once free-loving and in control? To many that thought has an undeniable appeal, and the evidence for poly-andry would seem to give it an element of credence. At the very least it has prompted an orgy of speculation about the sex lives of our prehistoric ancestors, with some popular writers going so far as to fantasize about the swinging Stone Age—a time, they suggest, of multiple partners and multiple orgasms before monogamy, jeal-ousy, and the repressive patriarchal pair-bond set in. There is a venerable tradition of thinking about life in paradise before the Fall as unconstrained by later taboos. And modern anthropolo-gists—from Enlightenment accounts of sensual Pacific Islanders to the twentieth-century fieldwork of Bronisław Malinowski and Margaret Mead—have sometimes echoed it in their reports of the "sexuality of savages." The more recent fantasies of sex in the Stone

Age fall into that tradition. It is surely fun to think of the egalitarian communes of the Paleolithic as places not just of freedom
and equality, but of free love. And by putting bonobo-like women
more on top, we would be giving a whole new meaning to the
reverse dominance hierarchy.[37]

But the truth is that when it comes to family arrangements,
human beings are neither bonobos nor chimpanzees (still less
gorillas). Pair bonding is one of the things that make us distinctive—
there is no parallel for it among the apes. And although polyandry
(just like polygyny) can certainly arise under certain environmental
conditions—most notably in societies with low birth rates or a
shortage of women—even there, the unions tend to be tight. A
woman with two mates is in effect living in two pair-bonds, a pair of
a pair. In the majority of cases, though, one was probably enough.
And among our hunter-gatherer ancestors, that way of pairing off
was probably the norm.[38]

That doesn't mean that women in those groups were the play-
things of powerful men. For one thing, there is good reason to
believe that women also exerted considerable agency in their choice
of partners. Males had to appeal to females just as much as the other
way around, and those who offered charm in place of coercion were
likely more favored. The readiness to play a significant role in child
care, as is the case among men in many hunter-gatherer societies
today, would not have hurt men's fortunes or those of the group.
And in fact there is evidence, based in part on computer modeling,
that a greater degree of sex egalitarianism would have been instrumental to hunter-gatherers' social evolution.[39]

What is more, women certainly played a critical role in the
most basic activity of these groups: gathering food. From modern
hunter-gatherer societies we know that women's foraging activities account for a significant share of the food supply—as high as
between 60 and 90 percent in the tropics—giving them a share of
the power and autonomy that economic importance confers. Among
our ancestors, we can reason, even if men more often brought home

the main course in the form of big game, women were providing the starters, staples, and side plates, along with a wealth of other valuable materials and tools. Finally, it bears repeating that while reverse dominance hierarchies constrain the predations of dominant males, women participate centrally in the moral communities that lie at their heart. It is they, as much as men, who enforce the strictures of reverse dominance—shaming, censoring, gossiping, calling to account. Women in hunter-gatherer societies of more recent times have often played vital roles as well in making key collective decisions, such as when and where to move. They likely did so in the past.[40]

Thus, although we shouldn't overstate the case, there is cause to think that some of the fruits of forager egalitarianism extended to women. In comparison to the kinds of social arrangements that likely preceded them among their hominid forebears and those that came after, the conditions of women in the hunter-gatherer societies of the Paleolithic look, if less than perfect, then still comparatively good. As one observer summarized the situation, "What matters is that our female ancestors almost certainly enjoyed more bargaining power in relation to men than they were ever to do once agriculture arrived." Much the same can be said about the comparative conditions of equality among men. So much so that when they were later challenged and taken away, many would mourn them, as some have ever since, looking on our early human past as an innocent idyll of freedom, happiness, and equality before a fatal Fall took place.[41]

We must be wary of that tendency. For whether construed as a paradise lost; extolled in a "hymn of praise" to a time before our corruption, as Rousseau would later do; or framed as a "primitive communism," as Marx and Engels did, such imaginings tend to tell us more about the worlds that produced them than about those that came before. Whatever else it may have been, the life of our ancestors, we can be certain, was no idyll.

The "fierce egalitarianism" of foragers in that respect is well named, for it is precisely that—fierce—with the violence and aggression that its mechanisms aim to contain threatening always to burst out. The high rates of violence documented among contemporary hunter-gatherers, it is true, may be somewhat distorting, belying the stressors of societies that in the modern world have been pushed to the margins. But there is ample evidence nonetheless among the impaled bones and shattered skulls of the Paleolithic to make clear that our ancestors were ready to resort to violence when the opportunity presented itself or the situation demanded—not just against upstarts in their midst, but against rivals from outside.[42]

We will have occasion to discuss war and its consequences at greater length in the next chapter. But it should be emphasized here that *Homo sapiens*, just like the other social primates, are an in-group/out-group species, capable of showing intense loyalty and devotion within their respective "tribes," but prone to "tribalism" when confronting others. Just like chimpanzees who police the borders of their communities relentlessly and harass, and even kill, chimps from outside, human beings are quick to constitute themselves through opposition, often of a frankly invidious kind.[43]

Indeed, in a phenomenon that psychologists describe as "social dominance," human beings (and men in particular) pursue status precisely through such in-group/out-group orientations. Modern sports affiliation is a good example. Studies show that male fans receive a spike in testosterone when their team wins—as if they had dominated the losing side themselves. But not all instances are so harmless. The same propensity is at play in nearly all cases of human "othering"—from racism to virulent nationalism to religious sectarianism to political combat—in which one group bands together and in the process deems another inferior, unequal, unfit. In-groups need little prompting to see themselves as superior. And the criteria used to establish who is in, and who is out, and which group is "better" and which is "worse," can be almost anything. The distinctions are arbitrary, but the effects are real.[44]

Evolutionary biologists have spent a great deal of time and energy thinking about the intricate dynamics of such group behavior and its effects on competition and fitness. But what matters here is the general point that such in-group/out-group dispositions undoubtedly played a role in the cohesion and competition of our hunter-gatherer ancestors, at once binding their groups together and placing them at odds.

Appreciating that fact helps us to understand an aspect of equality that, although readily on display, can be easily overlooked: that equality is a relation not only of fairness, but also of power, and as such very often involves domination. That is clear enough in the context of reverse dominance hierarchies, in which the many band together to dominate the few (and frequently women as well). But the dynamic can be coercive and exclusionary in other ways, too, with the equality of the group predicated, either explicitly or implicitly, on its relations of dominance to others in its midst or to those who lie outside. To be equal, in other words, is always a relational proposition, and the relation is generally drawn not only between those who share some quality (or qualities) in common, but in comparison to those who do not. In the closed context of the reverse dominance hierarchies of hunter-gatherers, the unequal someone is the potential aggressor (or aggressors) who must be leveled and brought low. But taking a wider view, the role can additionally be played by the members of the (out-)group on the other side of the forest or beyond the hill, whose alleged difference or inferiority serves to help bind together the band of equals.

Just how early *Homo sapiens* might have viewed those groups beyond the hill—or how, for that matter, they might have viewed the other species and creatures with whom they shared the world—is anyone's guess. But we can offer a number of grounded speculations that help to establish parameters. On the one hand, there is plenty of evidence to suggest that even if fantasies of perpetual peace among our early ancestors are precisely that—fantasies—they nonetheless found ways to get along. From genetic evidence and rudimentary patterns of trade we know that relations among groups in the late Paleolithic could be friendly across significant distances, with different bands exchanging partners and goods, or coming together in what were probably large seasonal gatherings around the migration of game, which likely involved shared religious celebrations. There are also indications, again from genetics, that small bands avoided inbreeding when they could, meaning that our ancestors looked beyond the next hill for mates who were not directly related to them. That says nothing, of course, about whether they regarded each other as similar or the same. History is sadly replete with examples of close associates who have viewed each other as fundamentally distinct. Still, it is hard not to suspect that the glimpse of another *Homo sapiens* face across the savanna or through the trees brought a quick thrill of recognition: *Here is someone like me!* [45]

And what of the other species of the genus *Homo* with whom *Homo sapiens* shared the earth? If the survival of the fittest is to be our measure, then *Homo sapiens* was clearly the master race. In evolutionary terms, they were extraordinarily successful. Flexible and adaptive in the critical tasks of ensuring group safety, raising children, and gathering and preparing food, they began to push out of Africa from the time of the Cognitive Revolution, entering the Arabian Peninsula about 70,000 years ago and occupying, shortly thereafter, the entire Eurasian landmass. By 55,000 to 60,000 years ago they were present in Western Europe and Australia. And by 16,000 years ago they had made their way across the Bering Strait and were rapidly populating North and South America. In a remarkably short span of time—between 50,000 and 100,000 years—*Homo sapiens* quite literally conquered the world.

Conquer, they did. One historian has likened the expansion of *Homo sapiens* to a kind of *Blitzkrieg*, which left a trail of destruction everywhere in its wake. Flora and fauna were trampled down, animals hunted to extinction, fields and forests scorched in massive fires set to drive out game. The spread of *Homo sapiens* constituted nothing less than an ecological disaster, and it spelled the end of the other species within the genus *Homo*, most notably the large-brained *Homo neanderthalensis* and *Homo denisova*. Both species were close enough to our own kind to allow for successful inter-breeding, which, we now know, certainly took place. With the exception of indigenous Africans, modern human beings possess between 1 and 4 percent of Neanderthal DNA, while Melanesians and Indigenous Australians have close to 6 percent of the DNA of Denisovans. All the same, by about 30,000 years ago, or 15,000 years after *Homo sapiens'* first arrival in Europe, the Neanderthals were extinct. The Denisovans seemed to have died out even before that, along with *Homo floresiensis*, a race of hobbit-like people with a maximum height of 3.5 feet, who inhabited the Indonesian island of Flores. Of the six types of the genus *Homo* cohabiting the earth as recently as 100,000 years ago—*Homo erectus, Homo soloensis, Homo floresiensis, Homo denisova, Homo neanderthalensis,* and *Homo sapiens*—only the last in this list prevailed.[46]

Whether our close relatives were ethnically cleansed in delib-erate campaigns of genocide, or simply killed off by competition, changing environmental conditions, or infectious disease is far from clear. We would probably be wise, though, not to put too much stock in our own species' tolerance. For we know too much about human beings' propensity to stigmatize others on the basis of ascribed differences to imagine that our ancestors always greeted their rivals—of their own species, or any other—with a smile.

And just as *Homo sapiens* dominated other representatives of the genus *Homo*, they dominated the other animals of the animal kingdom, gradually subjugating them to their will. In the long-term story of the hierarchies of the earth, that development is dramatic. For hundreds of thousands of years, after all, the vaunted "man the hunter" was, in truth, "man the hunted." The fossil record is clear. Prey to hyenas and wild dogs, to saber-toothed cats and lions, and to carnivorous tigers, leopards, and bears, we were also squeezed or struck by serpents, crushed by wooly rhinoceroses and mammoths, and trampled by giant elk. Our ancestors even fell to feasting fowl. The famous "Taung child," we now know, the 2-million-year-old *Australopithecus afarensis* fossil found in 1924 by Raymond Dart, was probably killed and carried off into the sky by a giant raptor, as the talon holes in the child's skull suggest. To this day, a shadow overhead can induce an instinctive shudder, and with good reason. For millions of years our ancestors were nowhere near the top of the food chain.[47]

Given that fact, it is hard to conceive that our distant ancestors thought of themselves as anything other than one of the beasts, and a rather lowly one at that. It was only in the past several hundred thousand years—and only through our intelligence, cooperation, and use of fire and tools—that we grew more accustomed to eating other species than to being eaten ourselves. Even with that development, human pride of place may have been slow to take hold. What little we can glean from speculation about our ancestors' earliest religions and myths would suggest that they continued to think of themselves for some time as akin to the other living things of the earth they collectively shared. Even as *Homo sapiens* hunted some creatures to extinction and killed off others in droves, animals served as totems, sacred founders of peoples and clans, to whom we were related and whom we therefore honored. Animals provided sustenance, the stuff of life, and they were justly chosen as among the first subjects of human art. The very same caves at Remigia that seem to tell the tale of reverse dominance hierarchies pay homage as well to the many wild oxen, deer, and ibex that were victims of another reversal, the triumph of man over beast.[48]

It is difficult, of course, to say much beyond such vague pronouncements. Which is a reminder of the obvious, but essential, point that whatever our earliest ancestors may have thought of themselves in relation to one another and the many different species of the earth, they did not leave conscious mental representations of those thoughts behind. And to the extent that equality is largely a human contrivance and representation—less an empirical fact than an idea that must first be conceived so that it can be claimed—we can conclude that our hunter-gatherer ancestors probably had no concept of equality at all. The image and imaginary are ours. Their equality, such as it was, was one of shared emotion and experience, not of abstract ideas.

Still, in the long history of humanity that experience was significant. If we began to emerge as hunter-gatherers some 300,000 years ago, that way of life was only fundamentally challenged within the past 12,000 years, leading some to conclude that the members of *Homo sapiens* have lived the vast majority of their total time on earth in roughly equal conditions—something on the order of 97 percent. Their experience was likely much more varied than that, and we should beware the tendency of anthropologists and others to hypostatize our primitive past as if it were all one thing or another. But where reverse dominance hierarchies were put in place, that meant the active inversion of pyramids of power that were likely typical among our hominid ancestors and remain so among our primate kin. It would also have meant the cultivation of leveling mechanisms and norms of reciprocity, altruism, sharing, and sympathy in order to reinforce the equal standing of those in the group.

That experience contrasts starkly, as we shall see, with the extreme forms of domination and inequality that would succeed it. Yet the succession itself is a reminder that for all our capacity for cooperation, we *Homo sapiens* have ever been creatures of power. On the continuum of animal behavior, we are "semi-despotic," a little less prone to domination and the seductions of status than the great apes, but not that much in the end. Which means that where and when equality of conditions can be made to flourish, they must be actively put in place, guarded vigilantly against upstarts and aggressors both within and without. When human vigilance fails, reversion threatens, and those pyramids of power balanced ever so delicately on their points can be toppled, or turned upright. Equality may then appear predominately in the figure that is the subject of the next chapter: as loss.

2

LOSS

The Human Surrender to Slavery and Exploitation

The idea of a paradise lost, a vanished golden age, is nearly universal in human culture, and myths recounting the happiness and abundance of a time long ago can be traced back to a surprising number of the world's earliest civilizations. The ancient Sumerians cultivated such beliefs, as did the Persians, Mayans, Egyptians, Indians, and Chinese, whose myths teem with images of flowing waters, ripe fruit, and bounteous gardens and glens. The ancient Greeks and Romans indulged their own visions of "Arcadia" and a "golden age," but perhaps the best-known account of a paradise lost is that of the Book of Genesis in the Jewish (and Christian) Bible. For believers, the tale recounts the grandeur and generosity of God, and the contrasting weakness and concupiscence of human beings. But for those of a more anthropological bent, the tale offers something else: clues about the fateful human passage from life as hunter-gatherers to life as tillers of the soil.[1]

In truth, as biblical scholars have long made clear, the Book of Genesis contains two accounts of creation. In the first, which ends at Genesis 2:4, God forms Adam and Eve in his own image and likeness. In the second, he blows Adam into being from the dust, later pulling a rib from the poor man's side to fashion his female companion. Both accounts concur, however, in presenting the world that awaits them as a veritable cornucopia, bursting with every plant and every tree, and teeming with animals, birds, and game that are there for the taking. True, God fashions a garden for his children, and bids Adam to "till it and keep it." He also takes care to note that in addition to "every green plant for food," he has provided "every plant yielding seed" and "every tree with seed in its fruit." Seeds, presumably, shall one day be planted. And yet despite a bit of mild cultivation, Adam and Eve would seem to have lived more or less as foragers, gathering and collecting their fill.

The contrast with their condition after the Fall could not be more clear. Having eaten of the tree of the knowledge of good and evil, they are banished from the garden and forced to work the land. As God makes plain to Adam, their lives henceforth will be hard:

> Cursed is the ground because of you;
> in toil you shall eat of it all the days of your life;
> thorns and thistles it shall bring forth to you;
> and you shall eat the plants of the field.
> By the sweat of your face
> you shall eat bread
> until you return to the ground,
> for out of it you were taken;
> you are dust,
> and to dust you shall return.
>   (Genesis 3:17–19)

The leisure and abundance of the Garden of Eden have been exchanged for the hardship of an agricultural existence. Life will now be struggle and pain. And not only that, but human beings have relinquished the freedom and equality they once knew. To the dominion over the beasts that had reigned in the Garden of Eden, God adds man's dominion over woman in punishment for

Eve's alleged sin, telling her, "He shall rule over you" (Genesis 3:16). And men themselves will know enmity and division. Adam and Eve's first son, Cain, slays his brother, Abel, leading to human beings' further alienation and estrangement from the earth. "When you till the ground," God tells Cain, "it shall no longer yield to you its strength" (Genesis 4:12). It is upon this primal act of violence, in which one brother slays another, that the first city is founded to the east of Eden by Enoch, Cain's son.[2]

Read in this way, the early chapters of Genesis become a parable of human beings' exit from their hunter-gatherer past and their entry into an altogether different world, one shaped by agriculture, inequality, conflict, and toil. Respected biblical scholars argue for the merits of such a reading. And although few, if any, would want to reduce early scripture *simply* to anthropology, it is nonetheless intriguing to consider Genesis, along with other early accounts of a vanished golden age, as a kind of elegy or mourning for a way of life that had been lost. Happier, more abundant, more equal, more free, that remote time could now only be imagined. To do so was to cast in stark relief a present that was invariably very far from Eden, east of the garden.[3]

Indeed, for the majority of those who experienced the full force of transition to agricultural society and the emergence of the world's first civilizations and states, life was anything but a paradise. The process, we now know, was ultimately painful, accompanied by the creation of steep hierarchies and inequalities that present a striking contrast with the conditions of our hunter-gatherer past. Within a space of several thousand years, human life was radically transformed in what one historian has called, fittingly, "the great disequalization." Inequality in its many forms—between conqueror and conquered, ruler and ruled, rich and poor, men and women, freeborn and slave—became the new normal. Should we be surprised if many looked to the past with longing as they learned to bear the shackles that bound them? Human existence would never be the same, and human equality, most conspicuous now in its absence, took shape in the abiding figure of loss.[4]

Whether or not we *should* be surprised by the plaintiveness of these early laments, the fact remains that it is easy enough to be so. For a powerful narrative has long dismissed them as mere myths while presenting our true primordial past as wretched—so wretched, in fact, that it would seem to make little sense to mourn its loss. That narrative is the history of civilization, the "ascent of man," and even for those who know better, it can be seductive.[5]

For we tend to think of civilization as a force for the better. Even Gandhi, speaking ironically of the Western kind, thought it would be a good idea. And for a long while that was how scholars treated the development of the complex cultures and states that grew up in the great river valleys that many of us read about in school: the Tigris and Euphrates (Mesopotamia), the Nile (Egypt), the Indus (India), the Yellow and Yangtze Rivers (China). Here, beginning in the third millennium BCE, is where civilization got underway, and the settings are important. For if "civilization" means the stage of social development that is most advanced, the word derives from the Latin *civitas*, or city. Those who were civilized had settled down. And they did so, it was believed, because they had figured out how to farm.

Agriculture and animal husbandry, the story goes, freed human beings from the wretchedness of their foraging past, which men and women were quick to leave for the safety and superior comforts of the sedentary life. Agriculture yielded surplus, permitting better living standards and the wherewithal to innovate. Government followed, replacing anarchy with order and license with law. When writing was invented, the rest was (recorded) history. The march of civilization was underway.

History, as Voltaire is said to have remarked, is "but a pack of tricks we play on the dead," and the history of civilization may be one of the biggest tricks of all. The line, it is true, is probably apocryphal. Still, Voltaire was in a position to know, for he was a trickster himself. When his eighteenth-century contemporary Jean-Jacques Rousseau published his celebrated *Discourse on the Origin and Foundation of Inequality Among Men* (1755), which romanticized the early human past and described civilization as something to regret, Voltaire scoffed. Not for him such encomia to a time, he chided, when our ancestors had walked on all fours. Like the biblical Eden and other tales of a vanished golden age, Rousseau's paradise lost was for Voltaire a story of misplaced regret.

Yet over the past several decades, archeologists, anthropologists, and historians of early human history have been playing tricks of their own. And the collective story that emerges from their work is one that presents the emergence of civilization in a light slightly more in keeping with the judgment of Rousseau. We now know, for example, that group settlement—along coasts and in fertile wetlands, especially—often preceded agriculture, rather than the other way around. And even when people did begin to farm—gradually, experimentally, in fits and starts over the course of several thousand years—they did not always stay put, but continued to forage and hunt, moving seasonally as the game and pickings allowed. There was nothing ineluctable, in other words, about the transition from foraging to farming and an exclusively agricultural way of life, and still less to the intensive cultivation of the major domesticated grains and cereal crops that in time would come to feed the world's first civilizations, like the bread that fed Adam and Eve after the Fall.

Nor was the transition to the states that ruled such civilizations foreordained. Many thousands of years separate the fledgling appearance of "sedentism"—cultural anthropologists' term for the practice of settling down in one place that began in the wake of the Neolithic Revolution approximately twelve thousand years ago—from the appearance of the world's first "states" in Mesopotamia and the Fertile Crescent in roughly the middle of the fourth millennium BCE. Similar time lags—between four

and six thousand years, or, on average, some two hundred generations—divide the appearance of agriculture and the emergence
of archaic states in other parts of the world, whether in India,
the Nile Delta, China, West Africa, or the pre-Columbian civilizations of Mesoamerica and the Andes. Humanity, clearly,
was in no rush to become civilized. Not only did it experiment
with numerous social forms along the way, but more democratic
pockets of resistance to civilized autocracy held out in places
around the globe long after the emergence of the archaic states.[6]

Given what we know about life in these earliest civilizations,
and the contrasting circumstances of ancient hunter-gatherers, the
reluctance to join them is understandable. For one thing, hunter-gatherers often ate better. It is true that the development of
agriculture ultimately fed more mouths, with greater productivity
leading to the expanding populations needed to work the land. But
the food turned out to be less varied and less nutritious than the
food of hunter-gatherers. The carbohydrate-rich starches and grains
that served as the staples of agricultural societies—and still account
for a large percentage of the human diet today—are high in calo-
ries, but low in nutrients. The "Paleo" diet, by contrast, is healthier
and ever-changing, with the result, as the fossil evidence makes
clear, that ancient hunter-gatherers were less likely to suffer from
malnutrition than their agricultural successors. Strikingly, average
human stature actually *declined* with the development of agricultural civilization, and it did not begin to return to hunter-gatherer
levels until the nineteenth century in the industrialized West (and
in many parts of the world much later than that, if at all).[7]

Life expectancy, similarly, showed little improvement, and in
many cases it got worse. After adjusting for death in childbirth,
which among hunter-gatherers was always a dicey affair, our Paleolithic ancestors stood a good chance of living into their sixties or
longer, which compares well with most people on earth into the
twentieth century. They were also less likely to suffer from famine
or disease. People who subsist largely on crops are susceptible to

crop failure, and hence to periodic starvation. And plagues and parasites thrive in proximity to livestock and among densely packed human beings. The horrors of mass famine and raging pandemics— from smallpox and measles to cholera and bubonic plague—are as much a part of civilization as refined manners and monumental buildings.[8]

Then there is the issue of leisure and toil. For the average peasant forced to work the land, an agricultural existence was, quite literally, backbreaking. Fossil evidence—of bones gnarled with arthritis, stooped spines, deformed knees, and herniated disks—is as eloquent on the subject as the Book of Genesis. From ashes to ashes and dust to dust, agricultural existence was hard. And though being a hunter-gatherer was never a cakewalk, studies of the amount of labor necessary to procure the necessities of life suggest that ancient foragers had it comparatively good. The average Paleolithic workweek was probably close to about thirty-five hours, even less than that of the most generously funded welfare state today. But in any case, hunter-gatherer life likely afforded greater leisure and abundance than that known by the domesticated laborers who later worked the land. As the anthropologist Marshall Sahlins once provocatively claimed, far from being wretched, early hunter-gatherers lived in the "original affluent society."[9]

And that is to say nothing of the subject of this book, equality, and its early concomitant, freedom, which were arguably among the greatest blessings our foraging ancestors knew, even if they didn't know it. The two went together. Equality among members of the group prevented the domination of all save the would-be upstarts, forestalling severe constraints on the liberty of others. Equality served as liberty's foundation and guarantee.

The twists and turns of the paths leading to the surrender of liberty and equality is a complex affair, with countless variations along the way. Scholars debate how small bands might have given way to larger tribes and tribal confederations, and how so-called big-man societies, based on personal achievement and tacit consent, could have ceded their place to hereditary chiefdoms and the trappings of formalized rule. Bound up with these discussions is the perennially vexing question of the origins of the "state," a subject of endless scholarly conjecture. But here it is enough to point out that although the steps along the way are hotly contested, what is not in doubt is the place of arrival. For the simple fact is that human beings living in complex societies invariably live in complex hierarchies. There are no exceptions to that rule, only greater and lesser degrees, and the hierarchies that emerged with the archaic states and the world's first civilizations would prove extreme, the most extreme the world has ever known. Reverse dominance hierarchies, in effect, were reversed yet again, yielding domination on a hitherto unprecedented scale. Pyramids of power were turned upright, and the few gazed down as gods at the many.[10]

Gods are exactly what rulers in many of the archaic states claimed to be, deified kings who invoked the power of the heavens in support of their earthly might. The consummate example is that of the Egyptian pharaohs, able to command their followers in the tens of thousands to lug stones across the sands from the middle of the third millennium BCE to build the tombs that proclaimed their exalted status to the heavens and earth. The pyramids of Egypt stand to this day as wonders of civilization. They are at the same time vivid testaments to human beings' capacity to dominate their fellow human beings for their own exaltation.[11]

There were many other such wonders of civilization—from the ancient towers of Babylon to the foundation stones of the Great Wall of China. In those places, too, rulers proclaimed themselves, like Hammurabi, gods among men, or maintained, like the emperors of China, that they ruled by the "mandate of heaven." Not all, it is true, sought apotheosis, and the extent of deification could vary. It is likely the case that the very first states that emerged in southern Mesopotamia during the Uruk period, in the fourth millennium BCE, were more prosaic affairs, essentially walled cities, whose rulers operated something like protection rackets, extorting resources from their stratified populations in return for defense and the imposition of order. The metaphor here is less god-king than mafioso boss, less theocracy than kleptocracy. Yet however configured, consolidation of power was the eventual norm, not only in the archaic states of Mesopotamia and the neighboring regions of Syria, southeastern Anatolia, and southern Iran, but wherever civilization emerged. As one authority summarizes these changes, on the basis of extensive global comsparison, "The development of early civilizations appears inevitably to have produced monarchs," along with extensive "social and economic inequality which informed the understanding of society as a whole."[12]

Inequalities of power and resources were guaranteed by a tiny emergent caste of government officials, nobles, and priests and backed up by powerful armies, who stood ready at a moment's notice to inflict punishing violence. Together they ensured that their god-kings were able to demand extraordinary sacrifices from their subjects, which ranged from crippling levels of taxation and tribute to forced labor and work quotas to military service and outright slavery and bondage. The archaic states exacted their pound of flesh—often quite literally, in the form of human sacrifice, a common feature of nearly all the principal early civilizations. It was practiced in ancient Egypt and Mesopotamia, in northern China and Nigeria, in the Indus Valley, and in the pre-Columbian civilizations of Latin America, among others. In some civilizations, such as that of Egypt, human sacrifice seems to have died out over time. But in others it long endured.[13]

Slavery in its many forms was also institutionalized and widespread. Hunter-gatherers may have occasionally enslaved captives, but never on the scale of civilization, where children were bought and sold outright, and individuals could sell themselves as a means to satisfy debt. Others, such as criminals and the destitute, were regularly forced into service for extended periods, while war captives and prisoners were very often permanently enslaved. And although early slavery was not based primarily on racial or ethnic distinctions, it proved incredibly persistent as an institution and practice. As recently as 1800, over three-quarters of the world's population was living in bondage of one kind or another, from outright chattel slavery to serfdom, indentured servitude, and regimes of forced labor and confinement to the land. And despite concerted efforts since, tens of millions of people continue to languish in slavery around the world still today.[14]

The persistence of slavery is a sobering thought, and it needs to be considered alongside the no less sobering persistence of patriarchy. The two, in fact, often went together. It is hardly a coincidence that in a number of languages, the word for "slave" is closely related to the word for "woman" or "concubine" (*nu*, for example, in Chinese). Women were generally the first to be taken captive by raiders in war, and they were regularly sold and exchanged. And even when they were not formally enslaved, their independence was severely constrained. Indeed, although early civilizations may not have invented violence against women or initiated attempts at male domination, they gave them moral sanction and legal authority. Patriarchy as a system was created in the archaic states, where in places such as Mesopotamia, in the second millennium BCE, male authority within the family was first set into law.[15]

It is telling that the three major law codes of ancient Mesopotamia—the Code of Hammurabi, the Middle Assyrian Laws, and the Hittite Laws—all devote considerable attention to the regulation of women's sexual behavior and their commodification and exchange in marriage. At the same time, the laws established patrilineal descent and the inheritance rights of sons, while working to ensure male priority in property and professional relations. Proscribing women from many occupations, these laws and the norms that grew up around them also denied women education, above all in the new technology of writing, which was used to inscribe patriarchal authority at the very heart of repressive legal regimes.[16]

The ancient law codes testify to the creation of patriarchy as a legal and social system. They exercised a major influence on the covenant laws governing relations between the sexes in the Hebrew Bible, and their influence radiated outward from there. But patriarchal authority was hardly confined to the civilizations of the Near East. Male rule necessarily varied considerably according to context, and there may have been more space for women in the play of social forms at civilization's infancy. But as civilization "advanced," the "radical subordination of women," as David Graeber and David Wengrow put it in *The Dawn of Everything*, was reproduced nearly everywhere.[17]

Patriarchy's grip proved powerful and lasting. More than two thousand years later, that pillar of enlightened jurisprudence, the Napoleonic Code of 1804, continued to lay out the legal duties of women and wives in depressingly familiar terms. As Napoleon himself is said to have observed, in explaining the underlying rationale of the code's provisions regarding the female sex, "Women ought to obey us, [because] nature has made women our slaves."[18]

In pointing out these broad continuities in attitudes toward women, scholars note that they are of a piece with the more general social and economic stratification common to agricultural societies virtually everywhere in the world. "Great inequality and sharp stratification" constitute their "most general feature," the sociologist Ernest Gellner remarks.

Which is not to say that agriculture alone was responsible for their emergence. One can detect the gradual accrual of economic disparities even before the development of farming, and long after, human beings seem to have cultivated the land in ways that didn't lead ineluctably to patriarchy, inequality, and subjugation. The full "Neolithic package" resulting from sedentism, the cultivation of major cereal crops, accumulation, and the rise of repressive states took time to put in place.[19]

Archeologists trace incipient stratification in the possessions left behind at gravesites, as well as in the walls and remains of buildings, which, then as now, reflect differences in status and wealth. Such evidence makes clear that the "basic ingredients" of structural inequality were put in place between 6000 and 4000 BCE. But it was ultimately the process of state formation that increased inequality dramatically, inventing new possibilities for accumulation, enrichment, and deprivation.[20]

Organized violence was central to that process, permitting states and their rulers to impose tributary obligations on existing landholders, and conquer new territories outright, while providing ample opportunity for the accumulation of property. A whole suite of civilizational innovations facilitated those general developments. They include the elaboration of formal ownership rights in land and live stock, along with inheritance laws and other legal mechanisms that helped to guarantee the transfer of wealth from one generation to the next. That greatest of civilizational achievements—writing itself—and the advanced record-keeping that went with it, in the form of land surveys, censuses, and tax rolls, also proved crucial to the ability of landowners and state officials to track the flow of tribute.

The earliest cuneiform tablets of the Sumerians are eloquent on the subject. They also make clear to what extent the chief cereal crops of the Agricultural Revolution served as the perfect currency of exchange. Visible, divisible, and difficult to hide, grains and cereals could be taken in kind at the source, as they were with great rapacity. The first business of civilization, we might say, was extraction, and the first civilizations were good at extracting, fielding their legions of soldiers, tax collectors, and officials to orchestrate and oversee the plunder.[21]

The collective result of this process was the creation of an "original one percent," composed of vastly wealthy cohorts of landowners, government officials, priests, and commercial elites who benefited disproportionately from the tributary and trade networks they helped to put in place. One might play with the percentage points here and there: they varied, of course, from region to region, and they were always subject to setbacks, shocks, and reversals. But the basic fact remains that a general pattern of inequality—with a tiny cohort of elites dominating all but a fraction of the total income and wealth generated from the primary producers of the land—was the norm, and would remain so in most parts of the world for millennia. Well into the late modern period, over 90 percent of the world's inhabitants were peasants, and the great majority of them were desperately poor. The spoils of civilization went overwhelmingly to the few.[22]

The Neolithic Revolution, then, and the rise of civilizations that followed in its wake, entailed far more than simply the passage from foraging to farming. A "great disequalization" transformed human society in nearly every way, spelling the reversal of reverse dominance hierarchies and the erosion of hunter-gatherer egalitarianism while opening up huge chasms between rich and poor. Stratification accompanied this process nearly everywhere it took hold, portioning out power on highly unequal terms. And whether these hierarchies were constructed on the basis of wealth, power, status, or sex, they could easily congeal and be passed on to one's offspring. Archeological evidence suggests that hereditary aristocracies began to form in the Near East as early as roughly 7,300 years ago, and in the New World civilizations of Peru and Mexico between about 3,200 and 3,000 years ago, respectively. In any case, within a few thousand years of the development of agriculture, and in places as far afield as Mesopotamia and Egypt, China and the Andes, huge disparities divided the people of the earth, and centralized, authoritarian states were out-competing their rivals in contests for land, people, and power.[23]

For the winners in this process—the small percentage who were able to leverage the increased productivity of the land in their favor—the benefits were enormous. They used them to build the wonders of civilization that in many parts of the world still stand.

But for the overwhelming majority, the benefits were fewer and farther between. It is not surprising that those whose not-so-distant ancestors had experienced the upheaval might regard the departure from paradise as a tragic lapse of judgment. And we can similarly understand why historians and social scientists analyzing them now might do the same. As the scholar Jared Diamond concluded on the basis of the kind of evidence summarized here, human beings' departure from their early foraging and communal life might be reckoned "the worst mistake in the history of the human race."[24]

One needn't agree with that judgment to see the point. And to do so is immediately to beg a question. If the foraging life was so good, and the agricultural life in cities and states so bad, why would our ancestors ever have left it? Why would human beings, who apparently lived so long in conditions of relative freedom and equality, surrender to the forces of civilization and the many constraints that entailed?

The biblical response is that the first humans turned away from God, sinning in the act of seeking more than they were meant to possess. Other religions offer variations on that theme, presenting the expulsion from paradise as either divine punishment or the way of the world. But historians and scientists necessarily seek different kinds of answers, and the first answer they are likely to offer is that hindsight is twenty-twenty. When our early ancestors settled down to tend the fields, they could no more have foreseen the consequences of their actions than Adam and Eve would have foreseen the repercussions of sampling a tasty piece of fruit. The development of inequalities took time, as did the transition to civilization and states. And although in deep historical terms that transition was fairly rapid, in human terms the change was painstakingly slow. Could it be that our ancestors were like frogs simmering in hot water, lulled to sleep before they awoke to find themselves being boiled alive? On this view, no one set out to throw themselves into bondage. It just happened.

That explanation has much to recommend it. But it also poses an explanatory problem of its own. For given that human beings in hunting and foraging societies had developed, to the best of our knowledge, sophisticated means to guard against the emergence of upstarts, how is it that they let their guard down, and slowly surrendered their power?

One answer is that they were tricked. That was effectively Rousseau's response—that "easily seduced" men ran "headlong into chains" without full knowledge of what they were doing. A similar perspective has been taken up more recently by some who point to religion as the culprit. Tracing in careful detail the succession of societal forms that stand between hunter-gatherers and the god-kings of the archaic states, they follow the "incremental changes in social logic" that might have chipped away at the egalitarian ethos of hunter-gatherers. In so-called big-man societies, they note, individuals rise to special prominence within the group on the basis of a particular trait or traits, such as age, wisdom, virtue, strength, or generosity in gift-giving. But although examples of those types of societies are legion in the anthropological record, their leadership hierarchies tend to be achievement based, not hereditary. Figuring out how the transition to hereditary inequality may have happened is the puzzle. And religion can be made to provide the missing piece.[25]

The logic goes like this. Contemporary hunter-gatherers often believe that the world is animated by hidden spirits or gods, and that their ancestors can intervene with those spirits on behalf of the living. In such orders, the gods serve as the alphas and the ancestors as the betas, with equality reigning among the omegas of the living. But by introducing this wrinkle into the reverse dominance hierarchy, religion opens the door for its demise. For what happens when a shaman, priest, or medicine man begins to claim proximity to the gods in the cosmic hierarchy of the universe? Archeologists and anthropologists have argued that it was on the basis of such original deceit that the theocracies of the archaic states came about, and they trace the emergence in the archeological record of ritual houses and temples to attest to the gradual emergence of a dominant priestly caste. Reversing the reverse dominance hierarchies of our foraging ancestors, they not only overthrew the reign of equals on earth but took the place of the spirits themselves. It was in this way that god-kings were eventually able to command their fellows to fall on their knees before them.

Few would deny that religion played an important role in social evolution, and the recent speculation that the world's oldest known religious structure—the massive pillars of Göbekli Tepe in southeastern Turkey—may actually have been built by hunter-gatherers is intriguing in that connection. Dating from some 11,500 years ago, the Neolithic complex seems to have preceded the development of agriculture in the region, suggesting that religion was the impetus to settle and begin farming there, rather than the other way around. But regardless of precisely when or how it arose, religion is clearly bound up with the early origins of settled societies, and there is a strong case to be made that gods, and particularly "big gods," were instrumental in facilitating the networks of cooperation necessary for the emergence of larger-scale civilizations.[26]

And yet, if religion's later role in legitimating various forms of hierarchy is clear, the theory that it stood at their origin is less so. That is not only because any such theory must be speculative to a considerable degree, but also because it rests on the proposition that our hunter-gatherer ancestors were dupes. Adept at detecting the first stirrings of the upstart, they were most likely people on the lookout for bullies and aggressors. It is not immediately clear why they would have allowed themselves to be permanently tricked into surrendering their power to pretenders claiming connections to the gods. Surely, it is just as likely that these pretenders would have been banished, put down, or killed?

A more compelling suggestion is that our ancestors were not so much tricked into surrendering their power as constrained. And here the likely culprit was war. The scholar Peter Turchin and others have pointed out that with the end of the most recent ice age, about 12,000 years ago, the human population began to expand, and then did so rapidly with the advent of agriculture. Whereas in 10,000 BCE there were roughly 5 million to 8 million inhabitants on earth, by the first century CE there were some 250 million—evidence, some might suggest, that civilization is good, at least, at generating bodies. But it is also good at dispatching them. There is considerable empirical evidence that with expanding populations and greater competition for resources, warfare escalated significantly. In that context, there would have been strong pressure to band together in large, well-organized groups. In war, size matters—it is a force multiplier, as is hierarchical discipline and chain of command. Competitive pressures, then, favored both size and stratification. Larger and better-regimented fighting forces could simply outperform smaller, less disciplined rivals, giving the communities that could sustain them a competitive edge. In that scenario, it is not difficult to imagine how the authority of a skilled or charismatic leader might gradually have hardened and become permanent, with religion invoked in due course to help solidify the arrangement. The demise of hunter-gatherer bands and the eventual rise of the imposing theocracies of god-kings, in this view, were the perverse outcome of cultural competition that favored larger and more unequal states.[27]

Although they differ about essentials, what both these theories share is the conviction that domination was essentially imposed, foisted upon the unsuspecting or unwilling. There are, it is true, other accounts that seek to explain stratification and the genesis of authoritarian states in more spontaneous ways, such as the notion that these were the largely unanticipated outcomes of the need to build dams and canals to provide for the irrigation necessary for farming, or to solve other large-scale problems of information processing or economic complexity. Others see the Agricultural Revolution and all that followed from it as more or less inevitable.[28]

And yet there is good evidence to suggest that, when they had the opportunity, hunter-gatherers resisted permanent settlement in states with determination, much as Native Americans later resisted confinement to reservations. Seen from the outside, civilization, with its diseases and coercion, could easily seem a bad proposition, to be fled or resisted. Many did so, living on the periphery of empires as "barbarians" or stateless peoples, raiding, trading, or slaving as best they could. Viewed in this way, the early walled states—which the anthropologist and political scientist James Scott describes harrowingly as "late Neolithic resettlement camps"— were constructed as much to keep their subjects confined as to keep the barbarians at bay. Like the later Great Wall of China, or the Berlin Wall, their ramparts secured against escape as much as they protected against invasion. Outside, genuine hunter-gatherers were pushed ever farther to the margins, their numbers dwindling, so that by the first century CE, only 1 million or 2 million remained, largely in remote regions of Africa, Australia, and the Americas. Where civilization on earth reigned, inequality was triumphant.[29]

And that is the essential point. For although accounts of the causes of inequality may differ, the consequences are clear. As one pair of scholars has explained, by about 2500 BCE, "virtually every form of inequality known to mankind had been created somewhere in the world, and truly egalitarian societies were being relegated to places no one else wanted." The archaic states produced some of the greatest inequalities the world has ever known, making it possible to conceive of rulers as beings who literally devoured and consumed their people, and of the people themselves as the rubbish or excrement they produced. It is perhaps not surprising that it was among them, at the very heart of civilization, that voices arose to challenge the legitimacy of the archaic states, proclaiming, for the first time in human history, the fellowship of all.[30]

3

FELLOWSHIP

The Invention of Equality in the Axial Age

The very same text that recounts humanity's fall in the garden and the passing of primitive equality plants the seed of another powerful thought: that human beings are made in the image of God. "Let us make mankind in our image, in our likeness," God declares in the Hebrew (and Christian) Bible. And so he does:

> In the image of God he created them;
> male and female he created them.
> (Genesis 1:26–27)

The second creation account in Genesis 2 is less exalted, with God forming man of dust and then woman of man: "bone of my bones and flesh of my flesh," as Adam exclaims (Genesis 2:23). But whether conceived as God's direct progeny or the muddy offspring of the soil beneath our feet, we are siblings either way. All are God's children. All are brothers and sisters.

Here in embryo was a compelling vision of human likeness: the common standing of the children of the earth before their patriarch and lord. "Have we not all one father?" asks the author of the prophetic Book of Malachi. "Has not one God created us?" (Malachi 2:10). Job, in his afflictions, poses a similar question. "Did not he who made me in the womb make them?" he asks, speaking of servants, slaves, and the poor, male and female alike (Job 31:15). Such sentiments are scattered throughout the Hebrew scriptures. The God of Abraham is the God of all: his "house shall be called a place of prayer for all people," and his law is universal (Isaiah 56:7). The other Abrahamic faiths—Christianity and Islam—would later concur. "There is neither Jew nor Greek, slave nor free, male nor female," St. Paul famously explains to the Christian community of Galatia in what is modern-day Turkey. "For you are all one in Christ Jesus" (Galatians 3:28). The Koran emphasizes a similar commonality among the peoples of the world, stressing repeatedly that God created man from a single cell, a single soul, a single embryo, and that the whole of humanity descends from the coupling of Adam and Eve. If, later, God formed his offspring into "nations and tribes," that was only so they might "recognize each other" (Koran 49:13). They are enjoined to do so. As a canonical hadith, a saying attributed to the prophet Muhammad, insists, "Oh humankind, truly your Lord is one, and surely your father is one, and thus an Arab has no superiority over a non-Arab, nor a non-Arab over an Arab; nor a white man over a black man, nor a black man over a white man, *except* as a consequence of [their] virtue."[1]

That is hardly the end of the story, of course. Not all would be equal in the eyes of Muslims, Christians, and Jews, and the final qualifying phrase of the hadith just cited indicates one way that distinctions could be drawn. To separate the members of God's family by orders of sanctity and virtue was a potent means to divide them. The religious would devise other such means. And that is to say nothing of the fact that Abrahamic assertions of the common standing of humanity were founded upon claims to the domination of all other living things, which, if you happen to be a cow or a snake or even a lion, the king of the beasts, may not seem fair.

But the point for now is that classical Judaism, like its later monotheistic descendants, helped give expression to an understanding and ideal of the relations between human beings that was emerging in a number of the religious and philosophical traditions of the first millennium BCE. Calling to account the dominant social relations that had developed among the archaic states, those traditions asserted that behind or beyond the great cleavages of wealth, power, and position that divided men and women in the world lay a common humanity to which even the most wretched might appeal. Conceiving of disparate persons as fundamentally alike, the Axial traditions imagined equality in the figure of fellowship, the ideal association that united human beings in their common participation in the divine. To invoke the fellowship of humanity was to imagine new ties of solidarity that could be put to egalitarian ends, used to challenge the brutal domination and inequities that wracked the archaic states. But the figure also provided a powerful warrant to justify the subjugation and exclusion of the unregenerate. All those who stubbornly refused the common submission to the divine and the prompting of its most virtuous adherents could be outcast, banished from the fellowship of humanity.

The german philosopher Karl Jaspers was the first to call this period *die Achsenzeit*, the "Axial Age." For it was then, he argued, between 800 and 300 BCE, to be precise, that the world's principal religious and philosophical traditions were brought into being, and it was around their central "axes" that our contemporary moral notions still turn. Jaspers was writing just after World War II, and scholars of religion have since complicated his notion of a foundational moment in which the moral concerns of humanity were formed for all time. They tend now to speak of "Axial breakthroughs" among different civilizations rather than a unified Axial age, and they have broadened Jasper's chronology. Still, they largely concur that the rough period in question, with the first millennium BCE at its heart, marked an extraordinarily fertile moment in human history. On multiple continents and within a strikingly concentrated period of time, the world witnessed the simultaneous emergence of powerful wisdom traditions that continue to influence us to this day: the crystallization of classical Judaism and the canonization of the Torah; the rise of the Buddhist and Jain traditions in India, along with the *Upanishads* and the *Bhagavad Gita*, the central texts of the Hindu tradition; the Confucian and Daoist traditions of China; and sweeping and influential systems of thought in Persia, Mesopotamia, and Greece. It was a period of moral creativity and spiritual innovation when great sages walked the earth in the company of the Hebrew prophets: Confucius, Mencius, and Zhuangzi in China; Siddhartha Gautama (the Buddha) and Mahavira in India; Zarathustra in Persia; Socrates, Plato, and Zeno in Greece. From their collective cries and assertions would echo back those of countless later innovators, acolytes, and interpreters, including, not least, Jesus and Muhammad. To a remarkable extent, the Axial Age furnished the principal values, faiths, and philosophies around which our moral universe continues to turn.[2]

Needless to say, those various traditions differed extensively in their particular doctrines and spiritual practices. Yet they shared a readiness to reflect critically upon human existence and to imagine it otherwise. Together they brought forth new conceptions of being and the social order, "questioning," as Jaspers put it, "all human activity and conferring upon it a new meaning." From the denunciations of Elijah and Jeremiah in Palestine to the renunciations of the Buddha and Socrates in India and Greece, the prophets of the Axial traditions were generally critical of the societies in which they lived, and they staked out novel visions of the good life and human flourishing to make amends for the suffering of their time.[3]

Most often they did so by appealing to a transcendent being or reality, invoking the righteous judgments of Yahweh, the consoling peace of Nirvana, the animating spirit of *Logos*, the World Soul, or the Dao, that simultaneously grounded existence and offered refuge from its pains. Most often they did so, too, by condemning injustice and criticizing those who sought fulfillment by more conventional means. "Let not the wise boast of their wisdom, or the strong boast of their strength or the rich boast of their riches,"

Jeremiah enjoined (Jeremiah 9:23). Power and wealth, like the conventional wisdom of the wise, were paths that often deceived, leading not to justice and righteousness, but to self-importance and false pride. The Daoist sage Zhuangzi offered a similar thought, warning that those who sought fulfillment solely in power, pleasure, status, or wealth were "upside down men," human beings whose priorities were inverted.

To declare that people should live right-side-up was not necessarily to demand that the world be set on its head. The Axial traditions were seldom explicitly revolutionary. Yet nearly all were critical of the abuse of worldly power and the seductions and disparities of wealth. Calling their times to account, they demanded that rulers serve with righteousness and that the rich tend to the poor. Denouncing the worship of idols, they warned that those who did not repent and reform would be consumed by their own iniquity. The prophet Jeremiah was a model of the type—the Jeremiah, as it were, of Jeremiahs. But many a hermit and wandering sage invoked the calamities on hand for those who oppressed their fellows:

> Woe to you who devour the finest of the wheat,
> And drink wine in large bowls,
> And tread underfoot the lowly with your might.
> (Enoch 96:4–5)

These lines, from the Book of Enoch, were found with the Dead Sea Scrolls. And though they are not considered part of the Jewish biblical canon, there are plenty of canonical scriptures to trouble the sleep of the powerful. The prophet Amos, for example, repeatedly castigates the rich and those who

> trample on the heads of the poor
> as on the dust of the ground
> and deny justice to the oppressed.
> (Amos 2:7)

Other of the Axial sages leveled similar condemnations, extending their messages broadly to all who would hear.

Siddhartha Gautama, for his part, was born into privilege and power sometime, it seems, in the fifth century BCE in what is now northern India or Nepal. Yet he famously turned his back on the riches of his youth, concluding that true fulfillment lay elsewhere. In the pursuit of enlightenment could be found the only true wealth, and every man and woman, he believed, had the capacity to earn it. Such was the Buddha's broad message of inclusion, which emphasized compassion for all sentient beings.

The Buddha's rough contemporary, Mahavira, one of the important early sages of the Jain tradition, made a similar claim, teaching that every living thing in the universe should be cherished, even the lowliest insect or worm. Jains, to this day, often strain their water before drinking it, or cover their mouths with gauze to avoid ingesting small insects by mistake. They walk with a mindful step, sweeping the way before them with a small brush to avoid harming even the tiniest creatures, in the conviction that all life is sacred and that we must love and protect it in all its forms.

Although the Master Kong (Kongzi), better known in the West as Confucius, had little to say about animals, one of his best-known disciples, Mencius, preached benevolence and love (*ai*) toward all things. And though neither Confucius nor his disciples ever declared the universal equality of people—and indeed made a virtue of deference toward just authorities—they did, like the Buddha, extend their message to all. "I educate everyone without [regard for] categories," Confucius declares in the *Analects* (15.39), by which he is taken to mean that his moral teachings were on offer to anyone who would hear them, regardless of wealth, social standing, or birth. Even ordinary people could be induced to follow what he called "the Way," though he stressed that they would need the guidance of good teachers. Mencius and another great acolyte of Confucius, Xun Zi, also emphasized the point, stressing that all people, regardless of their background, were endowed with an equal moral capacity and potential, and so might aspire to live as a *junzi*, a noble or exemplary person. The *junzi*, it is clear, aspired to fairness and care for the basic needs of the people. "Exemplary persons," Confucius says, "help out the needy; they do not make the rich richer." Service to the people, and especially the less fortunate, became in his hands a moral ideal.[4]

There were even stronger warrants for heeding the value of creatures great and small in China's other abiding Axial tradition, Daoism. Though often traced backed to the semi-mythical "old philosopher" Lao Tzu, the tradition really took shape in the teachings of the master Zhuan (Zhuangzi) in the late fourth century BCE. In a celebrated chapter of the foundational collection of writings that bear his name, readers are presented, as the title proclaims, with a "Discussion on Making All Things Equal." The three Chinese characters that form the title—Qi Wu Lun (齊物論)—are each pregnant with possible meanings, and their grouping is slightly ambiguous in the text, yielding a variety of different interpretations depending on how they are parsed (*qiwu lun* or *qi wulun*). Yet whether they are rendered, as various translators have done, as "Seeing Things as Equal" or "The Equality of Things and Opinions," or "Equalizing Opinions on Things," the general sense is that human beings should approach all manifestations of the universe with tremendous openness and acceptance, and be wary of those—whether high officials and rulers, or self-professed masters and sages—who declare their superiority to others.[5]

From the Daoist perspective, the world is ever changing and fluid, and so the labels we seek to impose on it are illusory. Good and bad, beautiful and ugly, better and worse have no fixed or inherent meaning, but are rather the misleading categories through which we draw false distinctions between others and ourselves. The very idea of the stable self—of the clear separation between subject and object—is one of those false distinctions. Each of us is continuous with the universe and its myriad things, and so we must view all elements alike, whether a fish, a person, or a bird. In the famous passage that concludes the chapter, Zhuangzi dreams that he is a butterfly and then awakens to question not only the distinction between human beings and insects but also that between waking and dreaming. In a universe of continual transformation, such hard and fast distinctions can only lead us astray.

And so, just as the lines between things—whether animate or inanimate, living or dead—are broken down and blurred, so are the hierarchies with which we rank and order them, with potentially far-reaching consequences. Throughout the text Zhuangzi scoffs at the pretensions of high officials and kings, whom he likens to robbers on a massive scale, and he takes pains to exalt the down-trodden and oppressed. A high official who refuses to break rank to walk with a former criminal, whose foot has been cut off, is mocked in one chapter for asserting that the mutilated man is not his equal. Elsewhere Zhuangzi takes pains to glorify the maimed and to praise the conventionally ugly. The Dao is present in all alike, present in all things—from the ant to the grass, even, he insists, "in piss and shit."[6]

Such shocking and paradoxical assertations were intended to befuddle, and they can easily do so today. Yet it should be clear nevertheless that they provide ample grounds for "making all things equal," or at least for attempting to see them as such. It is hardly surprising that in our own time, a wide range of commentators, including feminists, animal activists, and defenders of the rights of the disabled, have discovered in the *Zhuangzi* strong principles for upholding the equality of all living things. For generations of his followers, the Daoist sage has offered a model of free and easy wandering that could be drawn upon to challenge the established hierarchies of the day.[7]

But why these initial expressions of concern for ordinary humanity? Why, in other words, does one detect in the Axial Age—from Babylon to Palestine, from India to China, from Greece to Persia—repeated assertions of the moral value of life lived outside the narrow confines of the original "one percent"? Why this collective protest against the inequalities of the archaic states? Although any detailed explanation would need to attend to the particular circumstances and contexts of each individual case, a general answer lurks in the question itself. As the late sociologist of religion Robert Bellah concluded in his exhaustive comparative study of this period, the masters, prophets, and ascetics of the Axial Age were "moral upstarts." Responding to the heightened social tensions that had emerged with the tremendous inequalities of the archaic states, they challenged the hegemony and social domination that sustained them. The Axial reformers, therefore, can be seen at once as symptoms and expressions of a "legitimation crisis" of the ruling elites. Inequality, in effect, had reached a breaking point.[8]

Bellah bolstered his thesis by pointing out that the Axial reformers served both as "denouncers," who criticized the injustice and exploitation of contemporary elites, and as "renouncers," who willfully abandoned the pursuit of worldly ends. Setting powerful moral examples of different ways of living and relating to fellow human beings, they spurned wealth and power, glory and office. In the process, they revealed that those very things were mere trappings that obscured the essential similarities of all humanity. The insight allowed for a crucial innovation. "It is part of the definition of the Axial age," Bellah stressed, "that it was then that a universally egalitarian ethic first appeared." If hunter-gatherers, broadly speaking, had *lived* as equals, or so we now imagine, to the best of our knowledge they never *conceived* of themselves as such. The prophets of the Axial Age began to do so for the very first time, sketching the initial outlines of human equality as a self-conscious value and representation.[9]

Their notion took shape in the figure of human fellowship, which combined a strong assertion of the common humanity of the peoples of the world with a weaker one regarding the actual egalitarian relations that should be made to hold between them. To be sure, the upstarts of the Axial traditions dramatized their own authority as prophets, teachers, and guides. And, as we shall see, their emphatic insistence on the need for moral renewal provided the basis for new and invidious distinctions between the virtuous and the unregenerate, setting up what the historian Siep Stuurman calls "a powerful dialectic of universalism and exclusion."[10]

Still, the appeal to human fellowship was without precedent. Universal in its potential and scope, it was a call to unity and belonging to which all might aspire. Vastly different peoples could thus be conceived in likeness. Human beings harbored sameness in their difference. They were invited to recognize that sameness, acknowledging their common provenance and connection, their common struggles against suffering, their common fate as mortals in the face of death. Together, and despite the vast differences of doctrine and approach of the Axial faiths, they called attention to what human beings shared. In doing so, they imagined worlds more equal than their own.

Very often those imaginings took utopian form, with the figure of fellowship invoked on the horizon as a place of arrival to be reached in time, like the Jewish Promised Land, or to be achieved outside it, such as the Buddhist Kingdom of Temiya, the mythical place of the Buddha's early incarnation, where all citizens are true renouncers. Plato's famous account of the perfect city in the *Republic* provides another example of an imagined place, a *polis* painted in words that made provisions for the shared ownership of property—and equality between the sexes—even as it imagined steep hierarchies of citizens (and probably slaves) based on the "noble lie" of stratified souls.[11]

Zeno of Citium, similarly, who was born toward the end of the fourth century BCE in what is modern-day Cyprus, is known to have treated private property as a social convention to be overcome, a view he developed in his own now lost treatise on the ideal city, also titled *The Republic* (*Politeia*). Zeno was the principal founder of the Stoic school, and Stoics in general imagined reason (*Logos*) as the common fund of the cosmos on which all human beings could draw. It was precisely that conception that led Stoics to conceive of borders as artificial frontiers. In their cosmopolitan account, there were no foreigners, barbarians, or slaves; all were citizens of the universe, and all were subject equally to the dictates of reason and natural law. Indeed, as we will see, it was in just such Stoic assertions, and in sayings attributed to their predecessors, the Sophists, that one finds the first explicit statements that all human beings are created equal.[12]

Although utopias, as the name implies, are "good places" that do not exist, they invariably serve as criticisms of places that do. Which is to say that the utopian views of the Axial sages were denunciations and callings to account of extant social and political practices. As criticisms of real worlds, they had real-world consequences. And amid their varied speculations and musings are concrete proposals of ways in which human beings in fellowship might relate to one another on more equal terms.

It has been argued, for example, that a kind of practical egalitarianism runs throughout the Torah (or Pentateuch), the first five books of the Jewish Bible. Whereas other ancient Near Eastern religions, such as those of Mesopotamia, Ugarit, or Egypt, imagined the cosmic order as a model for hierarchical relations on earth, the covenant that Yahweh establishes with the entire people of Israel provides for a different kind of regime. Downplaying the prerogatives of class, caste, and birth, it mitigates clan and tribal hierarchies, and takes steps to circumscribe monarchy by rejecting tyranny and dividing political and judicial authority. The fifth book of the Hebrew Bible, the Book of Deuteronomy, even contains the foundations of the principle of equality before the law, which binds all of God's people, regardless of their individual status. And the many provisions throughout the Torah regarding manumission, land redemption, and debt forgiveness provide a warrant for thinking that equity and the fellowship of God's people must go hand in hand. At the very least, they are reminders of the importance of reciprocity, fairness, and the need to attenuate extremes of property and wealth in community.[13]

A case in point are the provisions in the Book of Leviticus regarding the celebration of Jubilee years in seven-year and seven-times-seven-year cycles. Calling for the forgiveness of debts, the release of prisoners, and the manumission of slaves, their purpose, though much debated, seems to have been in part to maintain balance in the community, and to ensure, as one scholar observes, that "wealth is not concentrated in the hands of a few." How regularly and to what extent those radical measures were actually enacted is far from clear. But their promise remained vibrant enough in Jesus's day to fuel hopes that monetary debts might be forgiven along with those of sin. It is significant that when, much later—in the seventeenth century—European political thinkers introduced a crucial innovation into the classical republican tradition, "placing redistribution (in the form of agrarian laws) at the very center of republican politics," as one modern historian has put it, they did so by turning to those very same passages in Leviticus and their rabbinical commentators and interpreters. The reach of their moral example was long.[14]

The Axial religions in China, above all Daoism and Buddhism, provided a similarly lasting source of moral authority. The so-called Yellow Scarf or Yellow Turban Rebellion in the second century, for example, prompted hundreds of thousands of peasants to rise up and nearly overthrow the Han emperor. Their calls for the distribution of food, land, and a more egalitarian social order drew on a combustible mix of popular religious doctrines that combined faith healing, alchemy, and demonology in apocalyptic and millenarian strains. But Daoist principles of the equal worth of human beings seem to have helped inspire the movement's leaders and broadened its reception. For many centuries thereafter, both Daoism and Buddhism would serve as fertile sources of messianic rebellion and period revolt. And when, in the nineteenth century, Christianity was added to the mix, syncretic religion helped stoke the massive

Taiping Rebellion between 1845 and 1864. Its results were cata-
strophic—upward of twenty million dead. But its radical demands
for shared property and resources, and the abolition of distinctions
of caste, drew deeply on China's Axial traditions and their Abrahamic successor.[15]

Influences such as these are a reminder that creative interpreters
seeking greater equality in the world would draw upon Axial affir-
mations about basic human worth for centuries to come. But, more
immediately, their consequence was to tame the rapacity of the
archaic states. Urged to act with greater restraint, rulers and elites
were forced to make concessions to the moral claims of religious
reformers, taking into account their obligations to the poor and
powerless, and to the transcendent forces that unite us all. Henceforth, it would prove more difficult (though hardly impossible) to
pose as god-kings, and more difficult (though hardly impossible) to
justify such practices as human sacrifice.

Consider the example of the emperor Ashoka the Great, the
Buddhist convert who ruled over the extensive Mauryan Empire
in the third century BCE. Though he inherited a throne that
encompassed much of the Indian subcontinent and possessed
the nearly unlimited powers of a god-king, Ashoka experienced
a sudden and evidently heartfelt conversion to Buddhism, which
dramatically transformed his reign. Abolishing human and animal
sacrifice, he established orphanages, hospitals, and nursing homes.
He encouraged munificence, the giving of alms, and consideration
of the public good. And he sought to rule with a greater degree of
justice. No doubt, his efforts were imperfect. But they were meaningful nonetheless, signaling a remarkable change in message and
tone. Nor was Ashoka's case an isolated example. It was repeated
throughout the heart of Eurasia, where the Axial Age found its spiritual center and home. Henceforth, rulers were obliged to pay at
least lip service to higher ideals.[16]

The Axial religions, then, took the edge off archaic despotism.
By conferring a greater degree of legitimacy on the rulers who

adopted them, they helped the rulers respond to the very legitimation crisis they had helped provoke. With a kinder, gentler face, the archaic states could be reconstituted on sounder footing, garnering wider social acceptance. At the same time, by preaching a new egalitarian ethic and urging greater respect for humanity's brothers and sisters, the Axial religions generated an important resource for social cohesion.

That, in turn, allowed rulers and their heirs to push their frontiers outward and to scale up in size. The Axial traditions, with their "big gods," their universal pretensions, and their broad appeal, acted as forces for social integration in expanding empires. Binding people together across vast distances, they encouraged prosocial values in the communities that heeded their calls, fostering assimilation, cooperation, and trust among networks promoting greater moral (self-)vigilance. In the so-called mega-empires that began to emerge at roughly the same time as the Axial faiths—in India, Persia, China, and the Near East—Axial religions provided a kind of social glue that allowed peoples of many different ethnicities, traditions, and backgrounds to see themselves as similar. Later, Christianity and Islam would do much the same.[17]

When considered from the point of view of (in)equality over the long term, the results were paradoxical. On the one hand, the Axial religions likely contributed to an overall reduction in human inequality, which arguably had reached its greatest extent in world history at the time of the archaic states. If this is true, what is sometimes described as the "U-shaped curve" of human inequality—which begins at a high point with our early hominid ancestors, falls with hunter-gatherer egalitarianism, and then rises again with the Agricultural Revolution and the archaic states—would need to be reconceived. Turchin proposes a "Z-curve," which adds another twist to the story by accounting for a reduction in inequality as a consequence of the Axial reforms. Whether that curve continues on its egalitarian course toward the future is

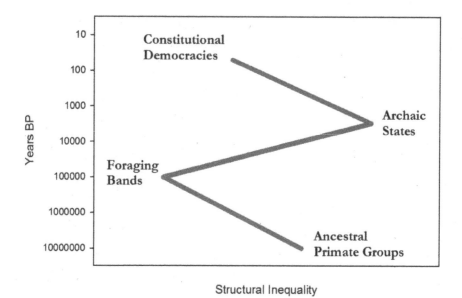

"The Z-Curve of Human Egalitarianism." Reproduced by permission of Peter Turchin.

more controversial, and what it might look like if it were plotted more finely, with data that distinguished between different types of equality, is far from clear. What, at the very least, *is* clear is that the Axial traditions offered new ways of conceiving commonalities and equal relations among persons.[18]

And yet in the long run these same Axial traditions often proved to be highly compatible with domination and power—and how this was possible is a no less salient story. The empires that rose in their wake largely succeeded in co-opting their Axial critics and taking the sting out of the more radical propositions of the Axial faiths. Examples could be culled from all the major traditions, but Stoicism provides a case in point. Like Confucianism, it effectively became a state philosophy and quasi state religion, serving both the Roman Republic and the Roman Empire to uphold, rather than challenge, the deep and profound hierarchies that divided citizen and slave, rich and poor, man and woman, noble and pleb. It was as a committed Stoic, who proclaimed that all human beings share in a "portion of the divine," that the philosopher-emperor Marcus Aurelius would later persecute the Christians of his realm. So far as Roman emperors are concerned, Marcus was of the better sort. Yet in a world in which, as the philosopher and statesman Cicero put it in Stoically inflected terms, there is "no difference in kind between man and man," some, clearly, were very different.[19]

Which highlights an essential point about the Axial faiths and equality-claims more generally. They are, to repeat, "imaginary." Which is not to say that they are a mirage, but only that equality claims are mental representations. Equality, in other words, is not a primordial fact about the universe, or a truth that can be established by observing the vastly different peoples of the earth. It is only by appealing to principles that are most often metaphysical in their foundations, rather than empirical, that we can imagine ourselves as possessing some common property or connection that all of us share. It follows, naturally enough, that equality can be imagined in very different ways. And it follows further that equality invariably presupposes difference, both within the community of equals, who are deemed alike only in certain respects, and more emphatically, vis-à-vis those who are excluded, on whatever grounds, from the community itself, whether they be nonhuman animals, noncitizens, nonbelievers, or people regarded as somehow less than men.

Those dynamics were clearly at work among the Axial faiths, which, however universal in theory, proved to be considerably more circumscribed in practice. Very often, in fact, assertions of human equality provided the basis for powerful new exclusionary claims. That was most dramatically the case with the monotheistic religions—Judaism, and later Christianity and Islam—which affirmed the unity of humanity under a common creator but simultaneously divided the world between the family of the faithful and those who rejected the father. The very same Book of Deuteronomy that curbs the power of kings, priests, and clans, laying what one scholar calls the foundation of an "egalitarian agenda" for God's chosen people, also contains exhortations to massacre any who might entice the chosen to worship other gods (13:6–15). And as for the towns in the Promised Land which God has vowed to give to his people, the directive is clear: "You must not let anything that breathes remain alive. You shall annihilate them—the Hittites, and the Amorites, the Canaanites and the Perizzites, the Hivites and the Jebusites— just as the Lord your God has commanded" (20:16–17). The fellowship of the chosen is here based on the domination, indeed the destruction, of the excluded. Nor was that move in any way restricted to Jewish monotheism. It would play out again and again with the advent of Christianity and Islam and the vastly greater empires they fashioned for themselves.[20]

The monotheistic religions were in that respect both universalistic and dualistic: they proclaimed fellowship among the children of God, but generally were quick to banish from the family those who rejected the faith. Even in the most tolerant circumstances, infidels, unbelievers, and apostates were rarely treated on equal terms. Distant human relatives at best, they were more often regarded as enemies and inferiors. To treat them that way, defenders of the faiths learned, provided a powerful means of binding the faithful together, forging the affective ties of fellowship that gave equality its lifeblood and force.[21]

And even within the ostensible communities of equals who formed the fellowship of the faith, there was ample room for separating the blessed from the damned, the faithful from the faithless, the upright from the immoral. To explain away the many differences that divided human beings on earth by reference to their ritual purity, their proximity to the sacred, or their possession of virtue or grace was a common practice, and it allowed whole classes of sages, monks, and priests to raise themselves above the rest. Stoics drew distinctions between philosophers and fools, or between those who lived by reason and those who did not. Confucians were inclined to divide the world between the superior persons who knew and delighted in the teachings of the Way, and those who did not. "One divides into two," Mao Zedong would later remark in a related connection. The common human family is split apart. Such splitting would prove a consistent feature of virtually all subsequent discourses about equality. For if what makes us equal as humans is a property that admits of degree, then some will readily be regarded as more human, more equal, than others, with the prerogatives and privileges such distinction confers.[22]

Thus, although Confucians might assert a common potential for moral excellence, it was the duty of the *junzi*, the superior person who actually possessed it, to lead, and it was the duty of others to follow. Hence the central importance in Confucian teaching of *Li*, the outward decorum intended to govern the five essential social relationships: between ruler and subject, husband and wife, parent and child, older and younger siblings, friend and friend. Only the latter was free of imbalance, with Confucius stressing, like Aristotle and other philosophers since, that genuine friendship should be a relation of equals. The other four relationships were profoundly hierarchical. True, they were intended to be reciprocal—rulers should be benevolent and their subjects loyal; parents loving, their children obedient; husbands forgiving, their wives submissive. But the chain of command is clear. Humanity might be a family, but not all blood relations are the same. Mencius put it nicely when he observed of the world, "The fact that things are not equal is the essence of things." Inequality remained the norm.[23]

Similarly, if even more starkly, in the Hindu tradition(s), the assertion of the qualitative equality of all expressions of spirit or soul (*Atman*) proved perfectly compatible with the hierarchies of caste. The universal world-soul (*Brahman*) was deemed equal and alike in all its emanations, but the vessels that housed them were weighed down by the ethical accumulations of *dharma*, meaning that some were born into bodies to labor and serve, while others were meant to cultivate the mind or lead. Again, norms of reciprocity applied. But the differences between priests, merchants, and members of the Dalit caste, then called "untouchables"—to say nothing of beasts of burden or dogs—were profound. At a cosmic level, the oneness and unity of all existence might be the universe's essential truth. But when looked at on the surface, the differences and inequalities were striking.[24]

What was true of the religions of the Indian subcontinent, moreover, was true, in effect, of all the Axial faiths. The equality of souls before God did not rule out inequality among men, and still less did it rule out inequality among men and women. However open in theory they were to the universality of creation—with some of the Axial traditions, such as Stoicism, making room for improved treatment of elite women—none of them significantly challenged the dominant forms of patriarchy that had emerged with the archaic states. Frequently they were used to reinforce them, sacralizing women's duties to men in marriage as in other forms of social relations.

And so men and women, rich and poor, noble and common, religious and profane learned to get along in the societies forged by the Axial traditions, finding their respective places in what Christians would later call the Great Chain of Being, that long ladder of life that articulated every living thing on earth from the lowest to the highest and put them in their place. Very often, the Axial traditions and their successors consolidated and buttressed such hierarchies.

It would be easy, if insufficient, to leave the story at that. For the role of religion in legitimating domination is a familiar tale, one that has been told repeatedly since the eighteenth century, when critics in the Age of Enlightenment perfected the charge that religion was the ideological tool that kept the people down. Later, Karl Marx presented religion as a drug that dulled the mind, acting like opium or OxyContin in our own time, and thus permitting the wretched to tolerate the intolerable. For the nineteenth-century Russian anarchist Mikhail Bakunin, the very idea of an almighty God towering above lowly mortals was inconsistent with human equality—unless, he added, "it were to be an equality merely in slavery and abjection." Religion, in this tenacious view, was inextricably bound up with subjugation and power.[25]

No doubt religions have often functioned that way. As psychologists tell us, they are particularly good at channeling one of the most basic forms of human social interaction—that of "Authority Ranking"—in which hierarchical relationships spell out duty, obligation, sacrifice, and deference. But religion is also particularly good at cultivating the contrasting, and no less central, mode of "Communal Sharing," in which people identify in collective terms, breaking bread together, pooling resources or possessions, exchanging empathy and compassion. Whereas the one mode's quintessential expression in religious terms is reverence and sacrifice—emphasizing obligation and debt—the other is fellowship and universal love.[26]

Which should remind us that if the story of religion as a source of domination is one we choose to tell ourselves, that story needs to be told while bearing in mind the no less central tale of religion's capacity to bring human beings together on more equal terms. The Axial religions cultivated both of those tendencies, but initially they served to mitigate the extreme inequalities that had come before. However imperfectly, they bent the U-curve back, introducing norms that censured oppression and exploitation while urging kindness, reciprocity, and the equal moral capacity of fellow human beings. In doing so, they bequeathed a legacy that has inspired moralists and reformers down to the present day, providing ample material to spark creative reflection on the meaning and practice of equality. When Mohandas Gandhi later asserted the "inherent equality of all men," and used that assertion to "fight the doctrine of superiority which many of our rulers arrogate to themselves," he was drawing deeply, as we shall see, on his Axial faith. He was not alone.[27]

PART II

PART II

4

JUSTICE

The Equality of Equals in Ancient Greece

Deep into his epic account of the great war between the Greeks and the Persians, Herodotus, the "father of history," pauses to explain the spectacular rise of Athens. The city-state, together with its surrounding settlements, had taken a leading role in the protracted struggle, which pitted an alliance of Greek-speaking peoples against the vast and powerful Persian Empire. Following the Greeks' victory in 479 BCE, Athens entered its golden age. The cause, Herodotus believed, was clear. Athens had rid itself of the rule of princes, doing away with the oligarchs, aristocrats, and kings who had long dominated the city. Athenians now ruled themselves, taking the field of battle not as subjects who slavishly received orders from superiors, but as equals who aimed to achieve the very best of their own free will. Free men fought better than servants, Herodotus maintained. Free men and equals were brothers in arms.[1]

In this way Herodotus hit upon an insight that French revolutionary soldiers, like Black regiments in the Civil War, would later impress upon their enemies: equality and its prospect can be good for combat, and other things besides. As the Athenians grew in power, they showed that equality is a good thing "not in one respect only, but in all." Equality served as the foundation of the city's greatness in every respect, supporting good soldiers, good sailors, and good men.[2]

Herodotus was well disposed in Athens's favor. Although born in the Greek settlement of Halicarnassus in what is modern-day Turkey, he identified with Athens, which he used as his base amid his many travels, and where he was celebrated as the great historian he was. Still, he could be critical of Athenian imperial ambitions; he was hardly a credulous booster. Modern historians agree that in singling out Athenian equality for special praise, he was giving voice to more than just prejudice. As one classical historian observes, "Of all the ancient cities, Athens was surely the one that most fervently preached the gospel of equality."[3]

It was a gospel of a very different sort from the good news spread by the religious traditions of the Axial Age and, later, by the Abrahamic faiths of Christianity and Islam. Which is not to say that the different gospels were incompatible. The Greeks themselves participated centrally in the Axial revolution, furnishing a number of its leading voices. Plato, for one, and the Stoics for another, put forth doctrines that would later be embraced by Christians, used to explain the ascent of the soul and the equality of God's children before their maker. In those respects, as in others, Athens undoubtedly had something to do with Jerusalem.

And yet the ideas of equality that were worked out in Greece in the late sixth and fifth centuries BCE were something different, more practical, political, and concrete. The difference comes across nicely in the words that Herodotus used to describe the "equality" he regarded as such a good thing. One central term, employed in the passages cited above, is *isegoria*, which referred generally to "political equality," but more specifically to the right of all citizens to speak freely in the *Ecclesia*, the great assembly that in Herodotus's day brought together as many as six thousand men at once to debate and legislate their public affairs. *Isegoria* thus made allusion to practice, and the same is true of the other main term that Herodotus employed in reference to equality, *isonomia*. The term is sometimes translated as "equality of rights" (or, less anachronistically, as "equality before the law"). But in its true sense it alludes, once again, to an activity—that of granting citizens the same access to legal proceedings and the courts. When invoked by the Athenians of Herodotus's time, the equality of *isegoria* and *isonomia* were inextricably bound up with their ways of doing things, of interacting together in the *polis* on equal footing and on equal terms.[4]

Not that language of this kind was confined solely to Athens, or even to Greece. Tellingly, Herodotus places the book's most eloquent praise of popular government, which "has the finest of all names to describe it, equality [*isonomia*]," in the mouth of Otanes, a Persian prince. It is a reminder that equality may be invoked by anyone, in any place. And although the examples from Greece recounted in this chapter are better attested—and largely as a consequence, more influential—than those of any other ancient culture, they have analogues elsewhere. Early democracy was not confined to Athens, but was practiced in places as far afield as ancient India, Mesopotamia, and Mesoamerica.[5]

Otanes's intervention also reminds us that equality claims are not solely the province of the people. He is, after all, a prince. Nor are they restricted to those who support *demos-kratia*, the people's power. Greeks had long contested who would be true "equals," and they continued to do so under Athenian democracy. Yet even as they disagreed, not infrequently with violence, they reaffirmed a shared sense that justice and equality were intertwined. Conceiving of the one as the expression of the other, they took steps to realize equality as harmony and balance, the just arrangement of the *polis*'s principal parts. More than any other place, Athens reaffirmed a notion that has since become a commonplace, presenting equality in the figure of justice, whose most widely recognized symbol is the scale.

Scholars trace notions of equality back to the very bedrock of the *polis*, the city-state and its surrounding territories, which served as the central organizing principle of ancient Greek life. "The *polis* aims to be composed, as much as possible, of similars and equals [*homoioi kai isoi*]," Aristotle would later point out in the *Politics*, his comparative study of the many different political regimes of the ancient world. His, to be sure, was a retrospective account, written in the fourth century BCE. But there is no doubt that long before that, general conceptions of equality had come to be widely shared among a considerable number of the nearly one thousand city-states (*poleis*) that dotted the peninsulas and islands of classical Greece. "In all Greek cities," one scholar makes clear, "some semblance of equality, at least as an ideological ideal, was a *sine qua non* of the very existence of a citizen body of the Greek type."[6]

Equality, we might say, was in the air, part of the very atmosphere that permeated the Greek world. And that is more than just a turn of phrase. For the earliest glimpses we have of Greek cosmology suggest a widespread view of the cosmos itself as a place of "justice" (*dike*), which is to say of balance, harmony, and order. "Equality," expressed as *isonomia*, and sometimes as *isomoiria* (equal portions or parts), functioned as the central guarantee of that justice. It was the principle that balanced the various forces of the universe, assuring its harmony and order.[7]

Thus, one finds in the writings of the earliest Greek natural philosophers, from Anaximander to Parmenides to Empedocles, the proposition that the whole of nature pursues "equality," and so justice. In Anaximander's reckoning, to view the universe was to see equality on display: in the intervals between the earth, the fixed stars, the moon, and the sun, or in the opposing land-masses of Asia and Europe. For Empedocles, the four elements of the universe (earth, air, water, and fire) could all be conceived as "equal," and so, too, the climate and the seasons. Temperate climates were those that balanced hot and cold, moist and dry, in equal measure, and the "equinox" was the moment when day and night, sunlight and darkness, were aligned in equality, perfectly in sync.[8]

The same principle applied to health. As the early Greek medical writer Alcmaeon of Croton observed, health was the "equality [*isonomia*] of the powers," the balance of dynamic forces in the body that produced harmony and stasis. Later that notion would be joined to the Hippocratic theory of the humors, with equality, and so health, achieved when the four constituents of the body—black and yellow bile, blood and phlegm—were in equal balance and proportion.[9]

Such views would continue to influence notions of equilibrium and balance in medicine and commercial exchange well into the Middle Ages. But they also had political implications. Famously, Plato and Aristotle treated the health (and so justice) of the *polis*, like the health and justice of the body, as the harmonious balance of forces. And that, in effect, was what equality for the Greeks was—a kind of balance of constituent parts. Its governing image was the scale, a symbol already of justice for ancient Babylonians and Egyptians, as it would be ever after, and a ubiquitous feature, as the historian of political thought Teresa Bejan reminds us, of every *agora* in ancient Greece. There in the central square, at the very nexus of political and commercial activity, goods and specie were weighed publicly on balance-beam scales, counterbalanced by the official weights and measures of the city. To calibrate items

"Man Weighing Merchandise," attributed to the Taleides Painter, c. 540–530 BCE. Metropolitan Museum of Art, New York. Purchase, Joseph Pulitzer Bequest, 1947.

The obverse side of a silver denarius from 96 CE of the Roman emperor Nerva. Aequitas, a divine personification of justice, equity, and balance, holds a cornucopia in one hand and a balance scale (*libra*) in the other. American Numismatic Society.

in this way was to ensure that they were "equal," which is to say "level." The Greek term *to ison* (the equal thing) reflects both senses together, as does the Latin *aequo/aequare* (to make equal or level). To weigh items in the balance, aligning the pans of the scale, was to make them just, make them equal.[10]

The same was true of people in the *polis*. For they, too, needed to be justly balanced and weighed. And so, together with a general science and aesthetics that favored proportion and harmony, the Greeks developed a vocabulary that invested notions of equality with social and political heft. They spoke not only of *isonomia* and

A balance-beam scale from the Egyptian *Book of the Dead*, c. 1250 BCE. The jackal-headed god Anubis weighs a deceased person's heart to pass judgment on the life. From early on, the balance scale was associated with justice.

isegoria, but of *isokratia* (equal access to power), and of *isomoiria* (equal parcels of land). They spoke of *isogonia* (equality of birth), and of those who were *isopsephos* (enjoying equal access to the vote). And finally, they spoke of equality (*isotēs*), the likeness or similarity of condition of those who were genuinely equal (*isos*).[11]

All of these words were formed from the prefix-root *isos*, which readers may recall from their time at school. To this day, students learn that an *isosceles* triangle is a triangle with two equal legs (*skelēs*). The diligent may even go on to apply that knowledge, drawing on the principles of Pythagoras, he of the famous theorem, or Euclid, the father of geometry, to alter the space about them. Abraham Lincoln, a great admirer of both men, did just that, moving from mathematical postulates about equality ("Things which are equal to the same thing are also equal to each other") to greater equality in the world. In a similar fashion, the Greeks applied their abstract understandings of equality to alter the societies in which they lived.[12]

That happened, to varying degrees, across the Greek-speaking world. But it did so most powerfully and self-consciously in Athens in the sixth century BCE, when a "strong principle of equality"

Howbeit, for easie alteratiõ of *equations*. I will pro-
pounde a fewe eráples, bicause the ertraction of their
rootes, maie the more aptly bec wroughte. And to a-
uoide the tedioufe repetition of thefe woordes: is e-
qualle to: I will fette as I doe often in woorke bfe, a
paire of paralleles, or Gemowe lines of one lengthe,
thus:======,bicaufe noe. 2. thynges, can be moare
equalle. And now marke thefe noimbers.

$$14.\text{—}.\text{——}|\text{——}.15.\text{——}======71.\text{—}.$$

Although the Greeks thought of equalities in mathematical terms, they did not employ the "equals sign." The Welsh mathematician Robert Recorde is credited with the invention. Here it appears for the first time in his book *The Whetstone of Witte* (1557).

began to crystallize out of earlier efforts to ease social tensions and constrain the power of elites. By expanding the bounded group of free men qualified to participate on equal terms in public life, Athenians sought to achieve a more harmonious balance, and so greater justice, in the *polis*.[13]

Reforms undertaken by the Athenian lawgiver Solon in 594 BCE initiated the process of bringing balance to the city. Solon, it is true, like his counterpart Lycurgus of Sparta, comes down to us largely as myth. Yet he was apparently motivated by the desire to reduce social tensions that had long divided the city. Today, we think of ancient Athens in the image of its democratic golden age, but for much of its early existence, and long thereafter, the city was ruled by a succession of tyrants, aristocrats, strongmen, and kings. Solon set out to curb their influence. "I wrote laws for the lowborn and the noble alike," he claims in a surviving fragment, "fitting out straight justice for each person." Jettisoning aristocratic birth requirements for office, he created popular law courts open to most citizens, and expanded the governing council of four hundred (the *Boule*) to five hundred, to admit representatives of the different social classes. And although he refused demands to redistribute land, he forgave existing debts and abolished the practice of debt-bondage, by which individuals pledged themselves as collateral for loans and were enslaved if they didn't pay. Finally, in what is known as a hubris law, Solon discouraged excessive displays of arrogance and aggression toward others, including toward slaves.[14]

That is not to say that Solon abolished slavery—far from it. That ubiquitous practice was assumed throughout the ancient world—in Athens, as elsewhere. Estimates of the size of the city's enslaved population vary widely, running anywhere from 15 to 40 percent of the whole at its height. There is no question that slavery was central to Athenian society and remained so throughout the period of democracy. There is also no question that it was brutal. Although ethnicity was not the foundation of ancient slavery, meaning that the enslaved were generally indistinguishable in appearance from citizens, they were treated as chattel, bought and sold in markets as adults and children, and used and abused sexually and in sundry other ways. A common Greek term for slave—*andrapodon*, or "man-footed thing"—captures perfectly the way in which the enslaved were likened to cattle and the other livestock sold alongside them, reduced to the level of beasts.[15]

The enslaved, along with other groups, such as women and resident aliens, were largely excluded from Greek public life, and all talk of Athenian equality was predicated on this foundation of domination and exclusion. Like equality throughout human history, the equality of Athens was bounded and confined. Its circle of equals was a privileged group of male citizens, distinguished from those who were not in the inner circle.

Solon's reforms set an important precedent for expanding that circle. But they didn't end aristocratic machinations or prevent the relapse of the city into rule by a succession of tyrants. It was only in the aftermath of what historians characterize as the "revolution" of 508–507 BCE, which ousted an oligarchy of noble families, that Athenians adopted a series of more robust measures, instituted by the statesman Cleisthenes, designed to secure greater balance and equality in the city.[16]

The measures took a variety of approaches. Cleisthenes began by reorganizing Athens's tribes, which, long structured according to clan, had been subject to aristocratic clientage and kinship control. Henceforth, the tribes (ten in all) were organized geographically, divided among the three major regions that constituted the Athenian *polis*: the city of Athens itself, the surrounding countryside, and the coastal region. Incorporating local villages and wards of the city, this new arrangement broke up long-standing aristocratic alliances and clientage networks while at the same time allowing for a broader and more consistent definition of "citizen." Earlier, aristocratic alliances had exercised control over who was recognized as a citizen: Cleisthenes's system shifted this power to the local village and ward assemblies, the demes, in which simple soldiers and farmers had a say. The demes decided at the grassroots level who the true citizens of Athens were, verifying descent from an Athenian father, and, after Pericles's more restrictive citizenship law of 451/450, descent from an Athenian father *and* an Athenian mother. They were thus empowered to send a wider cross-section of their fellows to the newly expanded main governing body of the *polis*, the Council of Five Hundred. Over time, property qualifications to serve on the council and in other administrative positions

"The Tyrannicides," National Archeological Museum, Naples. The statue, a Roman copy of the Greek original, commissioned soon after Cleisthenes's reforms, depicts the lovers Harmodious and Aristogeiton, slayers of the would-be tyrant Hipparchus in 514 BCE. A drinking song in their honor provides one of the first attested uses of *isonomia*: "In a myrtle bough I will carry my sword / Like Harmodius and Aristogeiton / When they slew the tyrant / And made Athens *isonomous* [equal under the law]." Photo credit: Album / Art Resource, New York.

were reduced, so that most Athenian citizens of age could serve in government, as well as attend and vote in the debates of the grand assembly and serve on juries and in courts of law.[17]

Cleisthenes encouraged other measures to broaden civic participation and to curb aristocratic dominance, and these were strengthened in the succeeding decades. Athenians, for example, instituted a lottery system to select individuals for government service, as opposed to putting their offices up for election. We tend to think today of elections as the freest and fairest means to choose our leaders. But in practice, elections grant a huge advantage to those with name recognition, or the power, influence, and money to make themselves known. That remains very much the case in democracies today, where the scion of a political family, a movie star, or a sports hero can jump to the top of the ticket by virtue of a familiar name and face.

Athenians were sensitive to such dangers, and so they randomized public service. Much like jury duty in the contemporary United States, many positions of public office in Athens were chosen by lot, a practice known as sortition: when your number came up, you served. Exceptions were made for magistracies and positions requiring specialized knowledge—in finance, say, or military affairs. But the number of terms that officials served was limited, in order to prevent corruption and domination by specific groups. Athens also paid a decent wage to those performing public service, so that positions in government or in the courts didn't fall only to those with the means and leisure to take them. And as a final safeguard against corruption and abuse, Athenians could resort to ostracism, which allowed citizens to vote to expel dangerous or troublesome members from the *polis*. Although employed infrequently, the measure served as a useful deterrent, not unlike the practices of hunter-gatherers that, when the situation demanded, enabled them to banish troublesome upstarts from their midst.

In certain distinct ways, in fact, the democratic government of Athens is reminiscent of the reverse dominance hierarchies put in place by foragers. Like them, Athenians aimed to keep down upstarts and elites, protecting the many from the predations of the few. And like them, they maintained a vigilant moral ethos that enforced group solidarity and fairness, urged self-sacrifice, and discouraged excessive pride. Of all the institutions of democracy, this "ethos" is perhaps the most intangible. But it may also be the most important. For without it, human beings in society tend to succumb to what Rousseau would later call, in *The Social Contract*, "the force of things," that inertial tendency toward pride and the accumulation of power and means that in his view "tends always to destroy equality." An egalitarian ethos is a crucial counterbalance to that force. And as with hunter-gatherers, it helps when it is fierce.[18]

Ferocity was encouraged in the Athenian case by the constant threat of war. Whether or not Herodotus was right to assert that Athenian equality was good for its soldiers' performance in battle, war was certainly good for Athenian equality. The tremendous sacrifices demanded of all Athenians in the shared emergencies of the Persian conflict—when the very existence of the state was at stake—and the constant need for manpower to staff its armies and vast navy in the decades thereafter created circumstances especially conducive to the extension of rights of citizenship. As more and more men demonstrated their devotion to the *polis* by putting their lives on the line, their claims on the public grew. And as the citizens of Athens asked more of their fellows, it was increasingly difficult to deny them. Just as American and French revolutionary soldiers, like women in World War II, later took strides toward greater equality on the strength of their wartime service, Athenians who gave freely in combat put themselves in a good position to demand rights and privileges they had earned.[19]

The martial ethos of duty and sacrifice in defense of the *polis* was reinforced by a broader ethos of public service, which conceived of civic virtue as devotion to the public good. It is revealing that the ancient Greek word *idiōtēs*, a private person unconcerned with public life, is cognate with "idiot." As the great

Athenian leader Pericles put it, "We are unique in the way we regard anyone who takes no part in public affairs" as living "a useless life." Citizens were taught from early on to be resolute in Athens's defense, training as children in the arts of war, and later performing service as watchmen and guards, literal keepers of the public trust. When they eventually came of age—twenty years to attend sessions in the *Ecclesia*, and thirty to serve in the *Boule* or the lawcourts—citizens were expected to lead when asked, and to know how to follow when they were not leading. Civic virtue in a democracy rested upon just this kind of knowledge—of how to rule and how to be ruled.[20]

For not all citizens could command or legislate at once, serving directly in the *Boule* or even exercising the right of *isegoria* in the assembly. To project one's words before thousands of spectators was a daunting prospect that most preferred to leave to highly trained rhetoricians (*rhetores*). But that citizens possessed this right was not in doubt. And though Athens had, like any other place, its leaders and eminent men who took a prominent role in public affairs, what distinguished it was the outsized attention it paid to men of the middling sort, the average Athenian Joe. These were the so-called *metrioi* or *mesoi*, words that one classicist translates, in a nod to Walt Whitman, as "middling men." Whitman, in his *Democratic Vistas* of 1871, celebrated "middling property owners" as the bedrock and future of the American republic, the kind of individuals whom the British had long referred to as the "middling sort," possessing neither too little nor too much. The *metrioi* fit that description, and in fact a striking feature of classical Athens was the presence of a substantial middle class of those living well above the subsistence level, yet considerably below the highest echelons of wealth. What we know of Athenian land distribution reinforces this picture. A "middling" group of hoplite farmers—those who manned the formidable phalanxes of the Athenian infantry, serving as brothers in arms—owned a substantial proportion of the land, somewhere between 35 and 45 percent of the total.[21]

The architectural record reveals patterns that are similarly balanced. The early urban planner Hippodamus of Miletus, who designed the Athenian port district known as Piraeus along with a number of Hellenic cities, put egalitarian principles to work in the streets, giving architectural form to the new notion of *isonomia*. His city blocks were laid out on an orthogonal grid plan, rectangular in form, symmetrical, and proportional, in accordance with Pythagorean number theory. They contained an equal number of equally sized and equally shaped homes. Democratic Athens, in fact, seems to have had almost no great palaces or mansions, meaning that most people lived in relatively modest dwellings. And the city, like many others throughout the Hellenic world, enacted sumptuary laws designed to prevent the conspicuous display of wealth, which only served to inspire jealousy and accentuate difference.[22]

That doesn't mean that Athens was poor. On the contrary, it was a prosperous trading empire, with high real wages and an average standard of living that was the envy of the classical world. It also taxed heavily, imposing significantly on its wealthier citizens, which is significant in its own right. For as extraordinary as it may seem, taxes prior to that point, and in most places in the world long thereafter, were taken from the poor and given to the rich, rather than the other way around. Tithes, levies, dues, and payments in kind were the privilege of the powerful, exacted by coercion. The weak sustained them, making taxes the great curse of the downtrodden. That general pattern held until the modern era, but Athens was an exception. Taxing its citizens progressively, it spread the wealth, financing not only war, but also public religious festivals, theater performances, and public buildings, while providing state payment for services to as many as twenty thousand people, including the poor men who rowed the navy's ships. In short, Athens achieved a level of economic equality that was significant for its time. And although we shouldn't exaggerate its extent—the city never aspired to level all distinctions of income or to eradicate all differences of wealth—in comparative terms there was relatively equitable distribution across the citizenry.[23]

The presence of a sizable "middle class" undoubtedly contributed to the ethos of the *metrioi* in important ways. Yet it is important to appreciate that the term was not, strictly speaking, a category of economic standing, but rather an identity and ideal, capable of being assumed both by comparatively wealthy men and those with just enough to get by. The term encompassed notions of "same-mindedness" (*homonoia*), friendship (*philia*), and reciprocity, along with connotations of frugality, simplicity, and modesty. A good provider and caretaker, an honest and upright citizen, resistant to the seductions of luxury and to the vulnerabilities and indignities of poverty, the "middling man" reflected the broader social imaginary of people who understood that there was such a thing as too little and too much, and who aspired to be somewhere in between.

In between was a good place to be for people who desired harmony and balance in their lives as well as in their art and architecture. Aristotle would later famously urge his students to live by the golden mean, and in politics he saw the middle class as occupying precisely that privileged space. "A city," he wrote, "ought to be composed as far as possible of equals and similars, and these are generally the middle classes." Every society would have its rich and poor at the extremes, but given that "moderation and the mean are best," it was clear to Aristotle that the best political community was formed by citizens of the middle classes. Government in the interests of the few necessarily did injustice to the many, and where the poor were motivated by rapacity and envy, they threatened anarchy and social breakdown.[24]

But if the middle was a good place to be, it was also precarious, prone to contestation from the extremes of rich and poor, who vied continually to tip the scales of justice—and so equality—in their favor. Fights over just who the equals were, and on what terms, were endemic to Greek political culture. Although all might agree, as Aristotle maintained, to think of justice as "a sort of equality," they did their calculations differently. It was in part for that reason that Aristotle, like Plato before him, distinguished between what the two men described as "arithmetic" (or "numerical") equality, on the one hand, and "geometric" (or "proportional") equality, on the other.

Arithmetic equality was a simple tally by numbers, or, as Plato put it, a counting by lots or heads. Applied to citizens, it meant treating all alike, or giving them the same honors and things. Proportional equality, by contrast, was carried out by weight, according to the principle that all were not equal by nature and so should not be treated equally. Some were nobler than others, some more intelligent, some richer, weighing more in the balance. It followed by this logic that although it was just to treat equals as equals, it was unjust to treat unequals the same. "When equality is given to unequal things," Plato observed in the *Laws*, "the resultant will be unequal." The trick was to work out who the genuine equals were, a task that varied from regime to regime. In an aristocracy, the equals were the *aristoi*, the best. In an oligarchy, those of comparable wealth and power. And in the perfect *politeia* of Plato's imagining, the equals were those of supreme virtue and wisdom, the guardians, from whose midst might emerge philosopher kings. Equality, in the justice of the city, was accorded to peers.[25]

It is partly for that reason that Aristotle stressed that the *polis* aimed to be composed not just of equals, but of those who were similar (*homoioi kai isoi*). And since not all were, it followed that "the passion for equality" was very often "at the root of faction." Those who were similar in their social standing, in other words, would seek to prevail as equals over those who were not, and the latter would clamor for the equality and status they were denied. That was the way of politics, and another reason, in Aristotle's reckoning, why it was so important to have a strong middle class to keep the balance.[26]

If the passion for equality was in Aristotle's opinion at the root of faction and social struggle, Plato made the same point the other way around. After observing in the *Laws* that masters and slaves, just like good men and scoundrels, can never be friends, he adds, "There is an old and true saying that 'equality [*isotēs*] produces amity,'" or, as another translator renders the same phrase, "'equality leads to friendship.'" Equality created affective ties that bound those of equal standing together, while keeping unequals apart. What Plato called "political justice" was knowing how to draw the proper distinctions. It consisted, he says, in "granting the 'equality' that unequals deserve to get."[27]

Plato was no friend of Athenian democracy. He lived through its unraveling, and likely wrote the words above, as Aristotle wrote his, well after its demise. But together their reflections underscore how equality talk in Athens, and throughout the Greek world, was not only compatible with inequality, but assumed and reinforced it. Their reflections also make plain the extent to which equality claims from early on were bound up in tension with discussions of similarity and difference. That was true in democratic Athens. But it can be observed with even more clarity in Athens's great contemporary and rival, Sparta.

The *polis* of Sparta offers a vivid illustration of how equality could be marshaled to bind the socially similar, fusing counterparts in a group to rule in domination over others. Although Sparta's form of government was a hybrid that changed substantially over time, the Spartan *polis* combined elements of oligarchy and kingship to create a regime that understood itself as Athens's antithesis, which in many ways it was. Allowing for hierarchical discrimination by birth, wealth, age, and attainment, it at the same time created a powerful ethos among its citizen-soldier elite of likeness, reciprocity, and equality.

Spartans called those privileged warriors the *homoioi*. The name is revealing. It means the "like" or "similar" ones, and Sparta worked hard to ensure that they were indeed as alike as possible. Following a selection at birth, in which senior soldiers examined newborns for signs of weakness or deformity—selling the "unfit" into slavery or exposing them to the elements to die—young Spartan boys of means were taken from their homes and raised together in what functioned as a military boarding school. There, they lived and bonded for years, training to be citizens and soldiers, imbibing common values and norms.

As adults, Spartan men continued their communal existence in the city's celebrated mess halls. Virtually the entire Spartan citizenry of nine thousand men dined together communally in messes made up of fifteen individuals each. Each member of the mess was required to contribute food and wine for the year, and although the meals were certainly not frugal—the portions were hearty and nutritious, and the *homoioi* were waited on by servants—neither were they overly lavish. And that seems to have been part of the point. By imposing a uniformity of lifestyle, while encouraging some sharing of property, the messes aimed to smooth over any tensions that might otherwise be created by economic disparities among the elite. Modern boarding schools often do the same, requiring their privileged students to wear a common uniform, sleep in common barracks, and eat in common dining halls, where the food is frequently not so good. In this way they strive to make "similar ones" more similar, equal in their proclivities and tastes.[28]

The boarding schools and mess halls of the *homoioi* thus took measures to fashion equals who were peers, notable and distinct in part by their very likeness. Another series of measures, attributed to the legendary Spartan lawgiver Lycurgus, discouraged conspicuous consumption, expensive clothing, and other displays of wealth. These sumptuary laws may also have been supplemented by land reforms and efforts to equalize property holdings among citizens. Later observers, such as the historians Polybius and Plutarch, writing under the Roman Empire, would claim that the reforms of Lycurgus promoted the radical redistribution of property, and that they even outlawed the use of gold and silver coins in favor of a heavy iron currency that was difficult to lug around, discouraging spending. Modern historians now regard much of that talk as exaggeration—Sparta's emphasis on discouraging wealth and power should not be overstated. And yet there does appear to be some truth behind the legend of Spartan simplicity and the lack of ostentation in the *polis*.[29]

The ethic of relative similarity among the *homoioi*—what the historian Thucydides called, in a term he coined, an "equality of lifestyle" (*isodiaitoi*) and appearance—was important, fostering a common culture for those equals who constituted the elite. All others were regarded as inferiors as a matter of course, unequal in their difference. They included not only slaves and resident aliens, but the *perioikoi*, free men who lacked citizenship status, along with the many *helots* in Sparta, the members of a kind of subjugated servant class who vastly outnumbered the *homoioi*. Finally, there were women, who, though faring better in Sparta than in many other places in Greece, were nonetheless denied the rights, privileges, and prerogatives of their husbands, brothers, and sons. The equality of the *homoioi*, like that of men throughout Greece, was a feature of public life. In private, among their families, they ruled more like kings. After crossing the threshold, men assumed the full prerogatives of power that their sex conferred, ruling over women, who were categorically excluded among the equals.[30]

Similar exclusions applied throughout the over one thousand separate *poleis* of classical Greece. Equality was always relative, always selective, and always based on difference with unequals. Athens was no exception. Women, slaves, and resident aliens (metics) there made up well over half the population, but they were kept outside the privileged circle of male citizens who constituted the true community of equals. And although women do appear to have enjoyed a parallel status in Athens as citizens of sorts, their role was decidedly secondary. Included in religious ceremonies and rituals that helped foster social cohesion, they were excluded from power in the assembly, the council, and the courts. As one scholar puts it, democratic Athens was truly a "men's club," where women's role was conceived overwhelmingly in domestic terms.[31]

And that is to say nothing of the fact that Athens at its democratic height, not unlike the United States at its own, was a vast, sea-born empire, whose vaunted equality for its citizens in the *polis* was based on the tribute, exactions, and offerings of its colonies and subject peoples. As an Athenian envoy explained to the Spartans, as recorded in Thucydides's history of the war between the two great powers, "It has always been the way of the world that the weaker is kept down by the stronger. And we think we are worthy of our power." Later, in Thucydides's account, the Athenians make that conviction brutally clear, explaining to the representatives of the rebellious island of Melos that "questions of justice only arise when there is equal power." Where there is not, "the dominant exact what they can and the weak concede what they must." The Athenians acted in keeping with that dictum, crushing the rebellion and then executing "all the grown men that came into their hands," as well as enslaving the women and children. The fate of the Melians was arguably worse than most, but it dramatizes the suggestion of one historian that at the height of its "thalassocracy" (maritime supremacy), Athenian power impacted the lives of as many as twenty million people. The golden age of Athenian equality coincided with its golden age of empire. Equality at home spelled domination abroad.[32]

In short, equality in Athens, as elsewhere, was bounded by the space that its soldiers could defend, demarcated by special privileges and laws, reserved for its citizen-elite in the metropole. "Equality consists in the same treatment of similar persons," Aristotle observed. And not all, in his view, were similar. Even at the height of the democracy, Athenians agreed.[33]

Of course, one could say much the same of the small caste of Athenian equals themselves, all of whom were differently endowed, and who enjoyed distinct pedigrees, backgrounds, educations, and possibilities, to say nothing of aptitudes, reputations, tastes, and skills. Ancient Greece was a competitive place, where individuals constantly vied to be the best in everything, from elegance in language to skill at war to the ability to hurl a discus. If anything, Athenian democracy only heightened such competition, which can be even more intense among the equally matched. In Athens, equality and rivalry, *isotēs* and *eris*, competed on equal terms. No less than its rival Sparta, it was a site of struggle (*agon*), a place of victory and excellence for the garland-crowned, who aimed to be better than all others.[34]

That highlights one other distinctive feature of ancient equality. The equality of the Greeks—their *isonomia* or *isegoria*—was an attribute of the *polis*, not of individuals, conferred by convention and law (*nomos*), not by nature (*physis*) and natural right. Whereas moderns have long held that all men, and in due course all women, are *created* equal as individuals, and only become unequal through social and political institutions, the Greeks reasoned the other way around. They took it for granted that human beings are unequal at birth—in all kinds of ways—and only become equal through an imaginative leap. That was the alchemy of the Athenian *polis*. By dint of its practices and laws, it made imaginary equality real.[35]

In doing so, moreover, the Greeks linked equality directly to freedom, which was only possible, they believed, among true equals and peers. Equality, in the Greek view—equal treatment and consideration in the public space—was freedom's prerequisite, its sine qua non. It was only as equals that men could be free, for it was only when they had overcome domination between them that they could throw off dependence and constraint. That the equal and free might impose such domination and dependence on those who were not was no matter—it was a sign and confirmation that they were genuinely so.

The codependence of liberty and equality would remain a crucial assumption in Western thought well until the eighteenth century, when equality was still regularly extolled as the "principle and foundation of liberty." They were only conceived in essential opposition, as we shall see, in the aftermath of the French Revolution, in a view that is still widely shared.[36]

The fact that Athenian equality, like Athenian freedom, was in practice highly constrained should not prevent us from appreciating the extent of Athens's achievement. For one thing, as the rest of this book will insist, equality has always been curtailed in some way, defined as much by who or what gets factored out of the privileged circle of equals as by the qualities that unite the privileged within. And although it is certainly true that when measured against an ideal standard of inclusivity, or the more universal norms of our own day, Athenian equality falls lamentably short, when considered in the context of what human beings had known until that time, the achievement was historic.

Widening its circle of citizens to include, at its height, somewhere between twenty thousand and thirty thousand active male participants, Athenians formed a community of equals that was without precedent—larger, more reflective, more deliberate, and more intense than any that had come before. "For the first time in the history of a complex society," one leading classicist emphasizes, "*all* native freeborn males, irrespective of their ability, family connections, or wealth, were [deemed] political equals, with equal rights to determine state policy." That was something. It wasn't always so.[37]

Nor would it always be. Athens's democracy, in the end, proved short-lived, a victim of internal tensions and its long and losing confrontation with Sparta. In 411 BCE, the city resorted to rule by oligarchs, and then, in 404, the year of Sparta's victory, to the rule of thirty tyrants. And though some aspects of the democracy would be restored in succeeding decades, along with the rule of *isonomia* and *isegoria*, a growing concentration of wealth and the slow evisceration of the ethos of public-spirited equality meant that the stabilizing balance of the middling men was permanently upset. The scales of justice were thrown off kilter by rich and poor alike, and then recalibrated by the power of Macedonian kings. "It has now become a habit among the citizens of states not even to care about equality," Aristotle lamented as he worked on the *Politics* sometime in the last third of the fourth century BCE. "All men seek dominion, or if conquered, are willing to submit." It would prove a fitting epitaph for the equality of the Greeks, though the memory would linger, inspiring new aspirations in the millennia to come.[38]

5

RECOVERY

Christian Equality and the Image of the Trinity

They are probably not the first figures to catch the eye, the three bearded men in togas in the upper left-hand corner of the lavishly carved, early Christian sarcophagus. More impressive at first glance is the image of the deceased themselves—a prominent couple, man and wife, in the central clypeus—or the muscular Daniel with his lions just below. To either side, scenes of Christian drama, replete with serpent and angels, Adam and Eve, meet the eye: Jesus turning water into wine at Cana or feeding the multitude with loaves and fish; Lazarus rising from the dead; Peter seized by soldiers; the Magi offering their gifts. By comparison, the three bearded men clinging to the corner look rather staid, and, on closer inspection, rather alike. Stern and solemn, they seem lost in contemplation of themselves.

Yet those same three men lend the tomb its title. The "Trinity" or "Dogmatic" sarcophagus, as it is known, was originally interred in St. Paul's Basilica in Rome sometime around 340 CE. Now housed at the Vatican Museum, it is a masterpiece of early Christian art. It is also among the very first visual representations of the dogma of the Trinity, formally proclaimed just years before at the Council of Nicaea in 325 CE. The three men—representing the Father, the Son, and the Holy Ghost—are it (the Trinity), *coeterni et coaequales* (coeternal and coequal), of one being and substance.

"The Trinity Sarcophagus," c. 340. The three persons of God may be seen in the upper far left. Photo copyright © Governorate of the Vatican City State–Directorate of the Vatican Museum.

Here was an altogether new image of equality, one that seemed to defy the evidence of the senses and perhaps even reason itself. For how could three so apparently different beings—God the Father, who appears to the apostles as a rushing wind or cloven tongues of fire; God the Son, who writhes in the pain of human flesh as Jesus on the cross; and God the Holy Spirit, who soars in the sky as a dove—be "equals," and rendered in art to look the same? It is hardly surprising that the mystery of the Trinity has long confounded confessing Christians. "Who can understand [it]?" St. Augustine asked toward the end of the fourth century. He would devote an entire work, *De Trinitate* (*On the Trinity*), to formulating an answer, probing the relations of equality at the very heart of the Christian message.[1]

"We should say three persons [*personae*], the Father, Son, and Holy Spirit," Augustine affirmed, "just as we speak of three friends, three relatives, or three neighbors." He drew here on a social analogy as well as the technical vocabulary worked out by the Cappadocian Fathers—St. Gregory of Nazianzus, St. Gregory of Nyssa, and St. Basil the Great—in the wake of the Council of Nicaea. Making use of a distinction first introduced by the North African theologian Tertullian in the early third century, they argued that the Father, the Son, and the Holy Ghost were each unique beings (*hypostases* in Greek; *personae* in Latin), who nonetheless shared a common essence (*ousia* in Greek; *substantia* in Latin). Such reflections gave rise to the formula "three *hypostases* in one *ousia*" used to describe the coequal relations of the Trinity. But the analogy could also be applied to human beings to account for the way that three particular men—say Peter, Paul, and Barnabas—were at one and the same time unique beings but shared in the common nature of humanity. "The distinction between *ousia* and *hypostases*," Basil explained, "is the same as that between the general and the particular; as, for instance, between the animal [man] and the particular man."[2]

Augustine adopted this same idea. However separate and distinct the "persons" of the Trinity, they shared a common essence, which reaffirmed their "indivisible equality" (*inseparabilis aequalitas*), their "absolute equality" (*summa aequalitas*). And although human beings, of course, are not equal to God "by parity" in majesty or standing—or "equal to the Trinity as the Son is equal to the Father"—they were nevertheless "made in God's image," and so approached him by "a sort of likeness." Indeed, the "image of the Trinity," Augustine affirmed, was reflected in the "mind itself," in the threefold relation between memory, understanding, and will.[3]

Augustine would make a great deal of this last point, so much so that the psychological analogy he used to relate the Trinity to the parts of the soul would effectively overshadow the social one. But the latter was there in his work, and it begged a question. If the Trinity could serve as a model of the mind and the harmonious relations of the parts of the soul, might it also model the

"The Holy Trinity Enthroned," Master of James IV of Scotland, c. 1510–1520. The J. Paul Getty Museum, Los Angeles.

relations that should hold between human beings? God's children, after all, likewise share a common nature. They, too, are consubstantial in their humanity, even in their difference. Each is unique, yet each is the same. The mystery of the Trinity seemed to reaffirm the essential likeness of human beings in relation to one another—seemed to reaffirm their essential equality—however different they might be.[4]

Whether the Trinity should serve as a model, aspiration, and intimation of how God's children might relate to one another on earth would prove, like so many matters of the faith, a subject of dispute. Augustine, among many others, worked to deny it. Mindful of the dangers of idolatry, he cautioned against efforts to represent the "invisible, incorporeal, immutable Trinity" in anthropomorphic terms. Making too quick a leap from the inscrutable nature of the Godhead to the fleshly nature of human beings was perilous. Partly as a consequence, figurative representations of the kind that graced the Dogmatic Sarcophagus would prove increasingly rare in Western Christendom, even as they enjoyed popularity in plaster and paint in the Orthodox East.[5]

The Holy Trinity as triangle, Saint Étienne du Mont, Paris. The common Christian image is frequently represented with an eye of Providence or a Hebrew tetragrammaton, the transliterated name of Yahweh/Jehovah, at the center. Godong / Bridgeman Images.

In the Latin West, however, the three persons of God were largely replaced by a more abstract symbol—the equilateral triangle—with its three sides representing the coequal status of the Father, Son, and Holy Ghost. It is in fact the oldest known Trinitarian symbol, and it would emerge in the centuries to come as a ubiquitous and absolutely central image of the triune God, adorning, to this day, Christian altars and churches throughout the world. To those who would see it, the image is a reminder of the relational equality that animated the Christian tradition from early on. At the same time, it poses a question that is the subject of this chapter. How should human beings, created unique in God's image, relate to one another? What, in effect, did Christian equality really mean?[6]

Although Christianity marked a turning point in the history of equality, as in the history of world religion, its trajectory was determined, like so many other large-scale historical changes, by the momentum and inertia that preceded it. The anonymous craftsman who took his chisel to the Dogmatic Sarcophagus, fashioning the figures of a coequal God, worked with Jewish and Christian, Roman and classical forms. In the same way, the men and women who labored around him to craft meanings of equality in the evolving Christian tradition worked with materials ready at hand.

That meant, first and foremost, the complicated legacy of Judaism. Jesus of Nazareth, after all—*Yeshua* of Nazareth—was a Jew, and although he preached a new law to fulfill and complement the old, much of his message was steeped in the Abrahamic tradition from which it sprang. His special ministry to the poor, his beatitudes for the marginalized and the oppressed, his scathing condemnations of mammon and greed all resonate with the denunciatory power of the Hebrew prophets, whose descendent and heir he took himself to be. Like the Axial sages before him, Jesus was a denouncer, and he called his times to account, preaching against the powerful while pleading the interests of the afflicted.

It has been argued in this connection that Jesus sought, like the prophet Isaiah, to restore or put in place the sabbatical and Jubilee laws spelled out in the Book of Leviticus. Those laws, recall, had proclaimed the manumission of slaves, the forgiveness of debts, and the redistribution of land on a seven-year and seven-times-seven-year basis. In the Gospel of Luke, Jesus appears to invoke them. Returning to Nazareth in Galilee after his time in the wilderness, he reads from a scroll in the synagogue. It is a passage from the Book of Isaiah (61:1–2), which in the Gospel of Luke is rendered as follows:

> The Spirit of the Lord is on me,
> because he has anointed me
> to proclaim good news to the poor.
> He has sent me to proclaim freedom for the prisoners
> and recovery of sight for the blind,
> to set the oppressed free,
> to proclaim the year of the Lord's favor.
> (Luke 4:18–19)

When Jesus finishes reading, he declares to those assembled, "Today this scripture is fulfilled in your hearing" (Luke 4:21).[7]

Just what the "year of the Lord's favor" might refer to is ambiguous. But some scholars have argued it is a reference to the Jubilee year, a claim that would appear to be in keeping with Jesus's calls for the forgiveness of sins and debts alike, as well as with his insistent attacks on the Pharisees, a powerful Jewish sect transformed, however unfairly by early Christians, into a symbol of hypocrisy and privileged resistance to change. Their leader, the great rabbi and scholar Hillel the Elder, had partially suspended the sabbatical laws in an effort to reform them in a legal writ known as the *prosbul*. The circumstances are complicated, but what is clear is that the *prosbul* was issued at a time of growing tensions in Jewish society between rich and poor, and it seemed to some to favor the interests of Jewish creditors, who would have had ample reason to resent the sabbatical laws. Another Jewish sect, known as the Essenes, with whom Jesus was probably familiar, dramatized the tensions of the times between rich and poor by taking vows of poverty, spurning luxury, and living communally. According to the Jewish historian Flavius Josephus, they were "despisers of riches," who pooled their resources so that "every one's possessions are intermingled with every other's possessions." The first Christians, notably, also lived in that way, as we are told in the Acts of the Apostles: "The believers were one in heart and mind. No one claimed that any of their possessions was their own, but they shared everything they had" (Acts 4:32).[8]

To what extent Jesus and the apostles were influenced by the Essenes is, like the meaning of Jesus's proclamation of the "year of the Lord's favor," open to interpretation. But there can be no doubt from the accounts provided by the authors of the gospels that Jesus was a vigorous denouncer of the unequal distribution of wealth, however often that fact has been downplayed or ignored, not least in the contemporary United States. Behold the man who chases the money changers from the temple with a whip and who declares, as reported in the synoptic gospels of Matthew, Mark, and Luke, that it would be "easier for a camel to go through the eye of a needle than for someone who is rich to enter the kingdom of God" (Matthew 19:23–24; Mark 10:23–25; Luke 18:24–25). Behold the man who warns time and again of the corrupting power of avarice, urging, in his parable of the rich fool, to "be on your guard against all kinds of greed," because "life does not consist in an abundance of possessions" (Luke 12:13–21). And behold the man who repeats throughout the gospels the message that you cannot serve two masters: God and mammon, God and wealth (Matthew 6:24; Mark 4:19; and Luke 16:13). One must choose.

That message had force among early Christians, who sold their land and homes, shared their resources in common, or gave them away in the expectation of Jesus's imminent return. Breaking bread together, they lived simply, even "communistically," as radical Protestants at the time of the European Reformation and socialists in the nineteenth century later remarked. Their example proved lasting, yet Jesus's censure of wealth was more short-lived. With the demise of the eschatological hope that the Kingdom of God was ready at hand, its force waned. Particularly in the wake of the conversion of the emperor Constantine in 312 CE and the spread of Christianity throughout the wealthy Roman Empire, the condemnation of the rich was increasingly passed over in embarrassed silence. As the great scholar of late antiquity Peter Brown memorably observed, it is tempting to call this period the "Age of the Camel."[9]

Still, the warning to the rich was there to be heard. It would be revived periodically ever after in complement to the good news to the poor. A simple carpenter and craftsman, Jesus was at home among ordinary folk (four of the twelve apostles were fishermen), and he ministered to the marginalized and least fortunate, feeding the hungry and healing the sick. "Blessed are you who are poor," he says in one of the most famous of the beatitudes. "Blessed are you who are hungry." "Blessed are you who are meek and thirst for righteousness." Jesus's preferential option for the poor and oppressed is well attested.

Yet this potentially revolutionary message—with its prospect of turning the world upside down so that "the first will be last and the last will be first" (Matthew 19:30)—came couched in a message of universal love. His affinities and aversions notwithstanding, Jesus insisted that God the Father loved all his children, and we the children were commanded to do the same, loving our neighbors as ourselves. That is the message of the Parable of the Good Samaritan in Luke 10, in which we are told that the way to eternal life is to love God with all our hearts and souls, and to love our neighbors as ourselves. The neighbor, we learn, may well be a stranger, a beggar by the roadside, or, like Judas Iscariot or the penitent on the cross, a thief. Our neighbor may be an adulterer or a prostitute, a woman whom others would stone; a Pharisee, like the apostle Paul; or a rich tax collector, like Matthew. No matter. We are called to love without condition, extending charity, mercy, and compassion to *all*.

The enjoinder to universal love is consistent with the figure of fellowship, and has close affinities in Judaism and the other Axial faiths. Yet the radical assertion of equality in love affirmed by early Christians took on an even greater resonance as the message spread beyond Jesus's initial circle of Jewish followers to appeal to the vast gentile populations of the Roman Empire. The apostle Paul, himself a Jewish convert who played a crucial role in Christianity's spread, captured the universal aspirations of the faith perfectly in his letter to the Christian community in Galatia (modern Turkey). There he notes, in the famous line cited earlier in Chapter 3, that Jesus had abolished old distinctions—of Jew and Greek, slave and free, male and female (Galatians 3:28). He repeated the message in his letter to the Colossians, stressing that for the chosen people of God, formed in the image of the Creator, "there is no Gentile or Jew, circumcised or uncircumcised, barbarian, Scythian, slave or free." All, it seemed, would be equal in love, equal in the mystical body of Christ, for "Christ is all, and is in all" (Colossians 3:11).

Written sometime in the middle of the first century CE, Paul's lines hint at the other crucial context for understanding early Christian views of equality: Rome. For Paul, like Jesus, was not only a Jew, but an inhabitant (and in Paul's case perhaps even a citizen) of the sprawling empire whose power was pressed into Jesus's very person. Rome broke Christ's body, and it left indelible marks on his message as well, shaping and facilitating the gospel in its aim to be *catholicus*, universal. Global in aspiration, yet marked by the place of its birth, Roman Catholicism, as it came to be known, is well named.

Just what was "Roman" about this religion in relation to equality can be traced via the influence of another Axial tradition, Stoicism, and its connections to Roman law. Although Stoic doctrines emerged in classical Greece, as we have seen, they flourished in unique ways in what scholars describe as the Middle Stoicism of the waning Roman Republic (c. 150–50 BCE) and the Late or Neo-Stoicism of the principate and empire during the first two centuries of the Common Era. In those periods, Stoicism func-tioned as "*the* idea system" for broad sections of the Roman elite, as well as for Jews and Christians such as Paul. It was crucial to the latter's "Christian Stoicism," and they found their way into the thought of many of the early church fathers and theologians, including Tertullian, Origen, St. Cyprian, Lactantius, St. Jerome, St. Ambrose, and St. Augustine, among various others.[10]

Like their Greek predecessors, Roman Stoics posited the essen-tial likeness of human beings, who they said shared in the divine reason (*Logos* or *ratio*) that permeated the universe as it permeated our souls. All the world's inhabitants were thus children of God, brothers and sisters in a common family, fellow citizens in the shared *polis* or *patria* that is the cosmos. Such "cosmopolitan" doctrines followed naturally from Stoic premises, and in the vast spaces opened up in the Roman Empire, where roads and rules brought together inhabitants of many different kinds, metaphors of humanity as a great collective body comprising different members and parts took on added force. As the Roman philosopher and statesman Cicero explained, "They [the Stoics] hold that the universe is governed by divine will; it is a city or state of which both men and gods are members, and each one of us is a part of this universe." Although Cicero did not identify as a direct disciple of the Stoic school, he was a lucid translator of its doctrines, and he clearly shared and admired many Stoic views. His successor under the empire, the philosopher-statesman Seneca, agreed: "All that you behold, all that comprises both God and man, is one—we are the parts of one great body" ("Membra sumus corporis magni"). It followed, in Seneca's reasoning, that since each us possessed an equal share in the divine *Logos*, every one of us was "sacred." "Homo, sacra res homini." "Man is a sacred thing to man."[11]

Men and women as members in a great divine body; the world's peoples as co-citizens in a cosmic city of God; the human being as "sacred"—these were themes that could be, and were, adapted readily to Christian conceptions. And although Stoics and Christians found different ways to parse them, on the whole they tended to reject essentialist accounts of human difference. Cicero was eloquent on the subject, maintaining, in a well-known passage in his treatise *On the Laws*, that "however we may define man, a single definition will apply to all." People varied, he acknowledged, in how they applied themselves and what they managed to learn. But the capacity of reason was widely shared. "There is no difference in kind within the species," he emphasized, and "there is no one, from any people whatsoever, who, if he finds a guide, cannot attain to virtue."[12]

In that sense, human beings were created equal. It was a common Stoic thought, and it was readily extended to the enslaved, whose status and identity in the Roman world were not tied to markers of ethnicity or color in the way asserted by the later fictions of race. Slaves could be many things in the ancient world, but often they were simply men and women taken captive in war—a fate, Romans knew, that might befall anyone. Whereas Aristotle had argued that slaves were inferior by nature—unequal by birth, and so fundamentally different in kind from free men—Stoics maintained that apparent differences between human beings, whether Roman or barbarian, freeborn or slave, were acquired, not innate. "It is a mistake to imagine that slavery pervades a man's whole being," Seneca observed. Fortune might hand the body of a man over to a master, but not the mind. Epictetus, among the greatest of the Stoic philosophers of imperial Rome, was himself a former slave. His very existence called attention to the point that there were no essential differences between the free and the bonded.[13]

Epictetus's celebrated teacher, the first-century CE Stoic Gaius Musonius Rufus, extended the claim to women. They had, he argued, the same capacity for reason and virtue as men. Rufus, the "Roman Socrates," was an early advocate of women's education. Among his few surviving works is an essay titled "That Women Too Should Study Philosophy," and another, "Should Daughters Receive the Same Educations as Sons?," to which his answer was a resounding yes.[14]

Stoic assertions of equal human capacity, then, could have liberating potential—literally so on the occasions when they were invoked to justify the manumission of the enslaved. More often, however—and this is the essential point—such assertions rested comfortably amid the hierarchical realities of Rome. For whether as republic or principate, the Roman world was a highly stratified place. And although ordinary people had made efforts, early in Rome's history, to shape the city on the Greek model of the democratic *polis*, they had largely failed. Struggles endured—between plebians and patricians, *populares* and *optimates*, subjects and citizens, the enslaved and the free. But few challenged the apparently unalterable fact that inequality of many different kinds was the basic human norm.

Nor was that acceptance simply the consequence of hypocrisy or failure of nerve—the inability, somehow, to live one's convictions or to fully reconcile principle with practice. On the contrary, Stoic assertions of natural equality were fully consonant with the acceptance of social distinctions. Stoics placed a strong emphasis on duty and the need to accept one's fate in the world. Every one of us had a role to play, and those roles were necessarily different, as the parts of the body were to the whole. And while some actions might be considered beneath the dignity of human beings—Epictetus debates, for example, whether it is right for a slave to hold his master's chamber pot—a great deal of inequality (between the rich and poor, the free and enslaved, the noble and common, citizen and subject, male and female) was simply assumed.[15]

Cicero offers an instructive example. A "new man" (*novus homo*) of provincial and not particularly illustrious origins in the minor gentry, he rose to become a landed magnate of the oligarchic Roman republic, a powerful slave-owning senator, comfortably ensconced at the center of the ruling class. His property holdings at his height were valued at thirteen million sesterces, enough to feed twenty-five thousand families for a year. Notwithstanding his eloquent assertions regarding the equal capacity of human beings, and his rhetorical flourishes in defense of the Roman people, he was quick to malign the lower orders—the *vulgus* or *multitudo*, covered as they were with dishonor (*ignominia*) and disgrace (*ignobilitas*). It is altogether revealing that the word Cicero and his contemporaries used most often to describe the lower classes—*faeces*, or "dregs"—literally means "shit" (feces).[16]

Seneca, too, as personal adviser to the Roman emperor Nero a century later, commanded and defended enormous wealth, privilege, and power. And while both Cicero and Seneca lost their lives and estates in opposition to the predations of tyrants, the point is that neither saw a conflict between their philosophical beliefs and the infinite gradations of Roman hierarchy or the harsh realities of social difference. Inequality was just the way of the Roman world.

Indeed, in Cicero's hands, assertions of equality became the basis for a novel justification of difference. If all, as Stoics maintained, had equal potential for reason and virtue, but only some were reasonable and virtuous, then the failure to be so was presumably one's own fault. Some simply cultivated their potential more aptly than others, employing their reason, tenacity, and will to better effect. That way of thinking opened the door to assertions of a "natural aristocracy," an aristocracy of cultivated accomplishment as opposed to title, birth, and blood. That allegedly meritocratic defense of social distinction would prove particularly attractive in the eighteenth century to the American Founding Fathers, among others, who turned to Cicero himself in support. As Cicero put it, "Nature has provided that . . . those men who are superior in virtue and spirit should rule the weaker." Social distinction, in that reckoning, owed less to birth than to what individuals did with their lives. Power and success were earned; poverty and abjection, it followed, were deserved.[17]

Christians would have less recourse to such arguments in the near term than their offspring in distant centuries later would. Still, the Stoic capacity to see unity in difference, reconciling equality with inequality while offering the one as the premise of the other, is a move that Christians would make their own. To do so, they drew on another influential source: the Roman law (*ius*).[18]

The Roman law served in its own right as an "equalizing device," a "veritable machine of equality," in the words of its leading historian. It performed that function through formalism and abstraction, reducing the diverse Roman citizenry, comprising from the very beginning different clans, tribes, ethnicities, and orders, to a common or equal standing, offering, as Livy put it, in a slightly different context, "equality of *ius* for all, both high and low." That was a crucial function amid the conflicts that wracked early Rome and the long "battle of the orders" that pitted citizen against citizen, plebian versus patrician. By treating all heads of households (*patresfamilias*) as patriarchs, sovereign in their dominion over family and slaves yet legally equal among themselves, the law created a neutral space, impervious in theory to special pleading and the influence of money, status, and power that prevailed outside.[19]

Facilitating social interactions and social control, the law also protected the *aequa libertas* (the equal liberty) of citizens from the domination of stronger individuals or groups, and in so doing introduced a powerful logic of abstraction. A father was a father before the law, a debtor a debtor, the owner of property an owner of property, and so on and so forth in the myriad roles that citizens might assume in their "private" interactions with others, which is to say all those interactions—social, commercial, financial, or familial—that fell outside the "public" matters of state (*res publica*). In the cold and impersonal logic of the expanding matrix of the civil law, citizens were not only equals, they were the same, interchangeable in their private abstraction, defined by the role they had played in the particular case under examination. As Cicero put it, that was the point of the civil law: "to maintain in the affairs and conflicts among citizens an impartial equality."[20]

The development of the civil law in this way was particular to Rome. Whereas law in ancient Athens, and other Greek city-states, was treated as an extension of public politics, emanating from the will of the people in the assemblies, and so closely bound up with questions of public justice, civil law in Rome developed independently, the domain of an increasingly professionalized group of jurists who treated it as an objective realm unto itself. Largely detached from politics, where public law (*lex*) was made in the assemblies, Roman jurists dealt very little with "public" matters at all, a divorce that was only heightened with the fall of the republic. Ironically, the equalizing machine of the civil law operated to its greatest extent under some of the most repressive emperors in Roman history—codifying, classifying, making equal in its justice (*iusticia*). That process, to be sure, was confined to full citizens. Slaves were not legal persons, but considered the property of others—and women, *peregrini* (free noncitizens), and the lowest social strata were excluded. But within the privileged circle of the citizen elite, legal rights were identical, their bearers the same.[21]

Thus, whereas early Christian thought assumed an irreducible human particularity before the common and equal love of God, Roman law took its departure from the opposite assumption, of undifferentiated equivalence, objectifying and formalizing all who fell under its sway. If every person was singular and unique in the eyes of the Christian God, every citizen was the same before the law, whose justice was not only impartial, but blind. And yet despite their contrasting perspectives and points of departure, both Christianity and the Roman law had the reinforcing effect of treating equality as an abstraction, independent of one's real-life situation.

In the Christian case, it was God's love that put human beings into a relation of equality, however different they might be. The slave and the free man, as Paul said, were one in Christ Jesus. But as he also stressed, on multiple occasions, slaves must obey their "earthly masters in everything"—in "fear and trembling," as the King James Bible later rendered the phrase (Colossians 3:22; Ephesians 6:5). There was no question, in other words, of denying the ever-present reality of slavery itself, or indeed of any of the worldly distinctions of wealth, status, dignity, and sex that divided human beings on earth. Master and slave might be equals before God, but they were still master and slave. The same was true for man and woman, citizen and noncitizen, rich and poor. God, as the historian of political thought Teresa Bejan has observed, was "indifferent" to the particulars of social station or status, interested only in the unique quality of our souls. The rest didn't matter. "Ça m'est égal," God might have said: It is all the same (all equal) to me.[22]

If that pithy French phrase captures nicely the sense of equality as indifference operating in early Christianity, it also applies to the perspective of Roman law, which in rendering all male citizens equal in their formal abstraction, necessarily turned a blind eye to their particular circumstances in the world. As heirs or testates, fathers or husbands, lenders or debtors, Roman citizens were all alike. But that some were very different—richer, more powerful, of greater status, dignity, or prestige—the law also refused to see. It was, in that sense, willfully blind.[23]

That, at least, was the ideal. In practice, Roman citizenship was subject to numerous gradations, divided among "orders" (*ordines*)—senators and knights, tribunes and scribes, freeborn and freedmen—and distinguished by "classes" (*classes*), each with their own legal prerogatives and privileges. And that is to say nothing of the "dignity" (*dignitas*) that accompanied each order. It, too, was hierarchical and distinct: the dignity of a senator was not that of a pleb. And just as social status differed enormously across the citizenry, so did social standing. It was for that reason that the Romans distinguished between those who were equal (*aequales*) in the eyes of the law and those who were equal (*pares*) in dignity and status as "peers." The Latin word *par*, in fact, is the root of "peer" and "peerage" in English and other languages. Those who were *pares* were not only equal, they were similar in rank and social standing, which was classified formally by order and degree of *dignitas*. At the bottom, below them all, were the vast legions of the enslaved; workers in despised trades; the *vulgus*, the dregs who had no dignity whatsoever; and women, who, properly speaking, had no dignity of their own, only that of their patriarchal families. The consequence, as one classical scholar has remarked, was that the "equality of the full *cives* [citizens], the *pares*, the *homoioi* was perfectly consistent with a state composed of a number of groups radically unequal."[24]

Thus did the Roman law and Christian theology work together, each in its own way, to situate equality amid inequality, while concealing inequality in equality itself. The one justified the other. And as both the empire of Christianity and the empire of Rome grew, so did that complementary and reinforcing function.

The machinations of the Roman law's equalizing machine only intensified as its citizenry expanded. Their numbers had grown, slowly if steadily, throughout Roman history, but never more spectacularly than in the year 212 CE, when the emperor Caracalla (Marcus Aurelius Antoninus) of the Severan dynasty extended citizenship to more than thirty million men in the provinces overnight. The reasons for that dramatic gesture are unclear: The need for greater tax revenue? More recruits for the Roman legions? An act of imperial goodwill? Historians debate them, though they generally concur in pointing out that the results were not as radical as they might seem. New distinctions—between upright citizens (*honestiores*) and the lesser sort (*humiliores*), between order (*ordo*) and grouping (*classis*)—quickly reinforced the old, and the rights of citizenship themselves were watered down.[25]

Still, the fact remains that the massive expansion of Roman citizenship was without precedent in world history. It made of the entirety of the empire's free male subjects—whether Latins or "barbarians," Gauls or *Germani*, Syrians or Jews—nominal legal equals overnight. And as a result, it required jurists to think through the now widely expanded parameters of the civil law (*ius civile*) in relation to the law of nations (*ius gentium*) that Romans had developed to govern interactions with foreigners in their midst.[26]

It was as part of that effort of integration that the jurists turned to Stoicism, and in particular to Stoic reflection on natural law as mediated and refined by Cicero. Cicero's thoughts are fascinating on the subject, flirting with the prospect that natural law, as divine reason in the universe, might ground the positive law of nations. And while that never came to pass within the *orbis Romanum*, the jurists' reengagement with natural law yielded nonetheless what to modern ears will sound like a striking proclamation.[27]

It was first set forth in the early third century by Domitius Ulpianus—Ulpian—the greatest of the Severan jurists and an adviser to the emperor Caracalla. In a vast work of commentary on the civil law and the writings of the first-century jurist Sabinus, Ulpian observed, almost in passing, "As far as the law of nature is concerned, all men are equal" ("Quod ad ius naturale attinet, omnes homines aequales sunt"). Elsewhere he added, "By the law of nature, all men were born free" ("Cum iure naturali omnes liberi nascerentur").[28]

Ulpian, it should be stressed, made both of these assertions in the context of discussions of slavery, and he was quick to note that according to positive law, slaves were not legal persons, neither equal nor free. His assertion in no way questioned slavery's legal basis in Roman statute or in the law of peoples or nations (*ius gentium*); he and his contemporaries accepted slavery as a matter of course. But in declaring the universal likeness of all men, Ulpian did provide a rationale for the incorporation of distant peoples into the empire. Barbarians and even slaves were no different from free Romans by nature, and so could receive Roman law and citizenship, as the emperor saw fit, just as they could be enslaved. Ulpian's rough contemporaries, the jurists Florentinus and Tryphoninus, recorded similar reflections regarding natural human freedom, also in the context of discussions of slavery. And while the claim that human beings were by nature equal and free had long circulated in Stoic philosophical circles, Ulpian and his colleagues were the first to bring them directly and explicitly into the law. Their opinions were later collated and included in the great compendium of Roman law and legal reflection compiled by the emperor Justinian in the early sixth century. There, Ulpian's lapidary formulation was repeated for all posterity: "Omnes homines aequales sunt": According to the natural law, all men are equal.[29]

The phrase was destined to have an important impact on the natural law tradition as it developed and was interpreted down through the eighteenth century. But however it might be interpreted later, it is crucial to see that the phrase provided no standard of critique to the Romans, no rule or precedent by which to call out inequality in practice or to challenge unequal laws on the books. Just as Stoic assertions of the natural equality of all men were nested comfortably in the realities of a highly stratified Roman society, so, too, the assertions of the jurists. They were, in this respect, politically "sterile."[30]

And that is how they were received by Christians, as they labored, in the wake of Paul and the apostles, to articulate a coherent theology that would appeal not only to Jews but to gentiles. Latin theologians, in effect, worked in complement to the Roman jurists in an effort to extend citizenship in the kingdom of God to the empire's many different peoples. Confirming Paul's assertion that all are one in Christ Jesus, they drew on the legal maxims of the jurists to emphasize the point, affirming natural human equality with great insistence.

Time and again they repeated the assertion, claiming, like Minucius Felix, a Roman solicitor and Christian convert who died in 250 CE, that no matter our parentage, "we are all born equals by lot, and are distinguished by virtue alone" ("Omnes tamen pari sorte nascimur, sola virtute distinguimir"). Felix employs the word *pari* here, the ablative form of *par*, and modifies it with *sorte*, an inflection of the Latin for "lot" (the root of our English "sortition"). The implication is that regardless of the actual position human beings are *allotted* in life by God, they are all born full citizens and peers in God's kingdom. The only meaningful distinction is virtue.[31]

Lactantius, the North African theologian who was adviser to the emperor Constantine and tutor to the emperor's son, agreed: "God, who produces and gives breath to men, willed that all should be equal [*aequos*], that is, equally matched as peers [*pares*]." He developed the point at some length in his main theological work, the *Divine Institutes*, emphasizing in one chapter that God's promise of immortality extended to all. In God's sight, "no one is a slave, no one is a master": "For if all have the same Father, by an equal right all are free." By the same reasoning, "no one is poor in the sight of God," save for those lacking in virtue, and "no one is rich," save for those who possess virtue in full. God's justice was unique in that way. Neither the Romans nor the Greeks had true justice, Lactantius claimed, for "they had men differing from one another by many degrees, from the poor to the rich, from the humble to the powerful." And where "all are not equally matched [*pares*], there is not equity [*aequitas*]; and inequality of itself excludes justice, the whole force of which consists in this, that it makes those equal who have by an equal lot [*pari sorte*] arrived at the condition of this life."[32]

Late antique Christians echoed such sentiments, emphasizing, like St. Jerome, that "equally we are born, emperors and the poor alike, and equally we die. For equal is our condition." Or, as St. Ambrose put it succinctly, nature "creates us all alike [*omnes similes creat*]." Such was early Christian unanimity on the point that all the fathers of the church maintained that men were free and equal in their original nature. And so, when Pope Gregory the Great observed, in his influential commentary on the Book of Job in the late sixth century, "All men are equal by nature" ("Omnes namque homines natura aequales sumus"), adding shortly thereafter, "All men are created equal by nature" ("Omnes homines natura aequales genuit"), he was summing up centuries of Christian reflection.[33]

They were memorable lines, and they would be invoked on the authority of the pope for centuries to come. But so, too, would Gregory's further reminder in the very same passage that by a "secret dispensation" (*dispensatio occulta*), God had chosen in his righteousness and mysterious wisdom to subject some to the authority of others, according to what Gregory describes as a "different order of merits." Gregory included servants and slaves in that subjection, an inclusion that was hardly hypothetical, for the papacy owned enslaved persons in considerable numbers, and Gregory, like many late antique Christians, made regular use of their services. He cautioned that they, too, were equal by nature, a fact that should be kept in mind by their masters. But like the Roman Stoics and jurists of the Roman law on whom Christians so often drew, Gregory saw no conflict between natural human equality and the realities of slavery and subordination. Where Gregory and his fellow Christians innovated was in their explanation of this seeming paradox.

In the doctrine of sin they found a powerful tool for explaining God's secret dispensation and the inequality that followed from it. But in developing that doctrine they also opened a pathway to the recovery of the equality we had lost.[34]

When Romans justified slavery in the context of natural human equality, they did so by reference to history, experience, and positive law. Slavery was a feature of all nations and had grown, in Rome itself, out of the realities of war and conquest. When captives were spared instead of killed, they were pressed into "legitimate" service in return for their lives. Slavery, then, was perfectly consistent with the *ius gentium* and the *ius civile*, if not the *ius naturale*. Stoics supplemented those explanations with the strong medicine of duty and references to a golden age now lost. Christians added sin. Human beings, in their innocence, were created to live as equals, as God intended. But when they sinned of their own free will, they upset the natural order of human relations, introducing bondage, domination, and oppression as the consequence of human pride.[35]

It was St. Augustine, on whom Gregory drew deeply, who gave that view its most thorough and lasting formulation. God, Augustine stressed in his early fifth-century magnum opus, *De civitate Dei*, the *City of God*, "did not wish the rational being, made in his own image, to have dominion over any but irrational creatures, not man over man, but man over the beasts." That is why, Augustine continued, the "first just men were set up as shepherds of flocks, rather than as kings of men." And that is why, he added, "we do not hear of a slave anywhere in the Scriptures until Noah." When sin took hold, however, the human soul was set in opposition to itself and to others. Men became lawless and wicked, now contemptuous and condescending, now filled with lust for domination and pride. Human beings looked down upon their fellows in their self-love, while others sought to rise against them, and in this situation of enmity and war, only subordination could bring about a temporary peace until that final peace when "all injustice disappears and all human lordship and power is annihilated, and God is all in all." Until that time, the end of time, when Christ would return in judgment to gather the full citizens of the City of God to live in perfect freedom and equality, domination would reign in the City of Man. Order required it, and order was precisely, Augustine insisted, "the arrangement and distribution of 'equal and unequal things' [*parium dispariumque rerum*]," each in its proper place. Just as sin was the "first cause of slavery," so was it the source of all subjugation, of man to man and of woman to man.[36]

In this way did Augustine offer his own variation on the theme of paradise lost. Human beings, as he put it elsewhere, were "naturally equal" (*naturaliter pares sunt*). God had intended them to live in fellowship, and to share the things of the earth. It followed that private property, too, was a consequence of sin, a view that was widely shared among the early church fathers. As Augustine's close friend and teacher St. Ambrose stressed in his book on the duties of the clergy, *De officiis ministrorum*, the earth had been given by God as a "common possession" (*communis possessio*). Private property, like domination, had come about only with Adam and Eve's Fall from innocence. In the beginning, all was equal.[37]

But that time was no longer. Our original freedom and equality were gone. And so, although Augustine might think of the Trinity as a model for aligning the various parts of the human mind in greater relational harmony, he refused to think of the relations between human beings in those terms. Whatever the equality of the three persons of the Godhead, fallen human beings could not approach it. They must live in unequal relations, not as coequals, accepting their place on earth.

Gregory reaffirmed Augustine's essential teaching in his massive treatise on the moral lessons of the Book of Job, and together the two men bequeathed to posterity an explanation of inequality that would be recycled and reworked for at least the next millennium. But whereas Augustine urged acceptance from the downtrodden, Gregory counseled restraint on the part of those in positions of authority. "To powerful men, the virtue of humility is a great one, considering the equality of their [natural] condition," he observed. Let them think of that equality, lest they be "swollen" with pride. For it was pride—the original sin—that explained why human beings found themselves in their earthly predicament in the first place, with some men set above and others beneath. The "distributive arrangements" of the world—the diversity of our earthly conditions—could be deceiving. At once punitive and providential, they issued from sin (*ex vitio*) as punishment, but they were also preparing a new order, which God in his mystery had postponed and was making ready. That final judgment and accounting would be reckoned by "another order of merit." It would put human beings in their true and rightful place.[38]

Gregory thus cautioned against presumption on the part of those in power. But he in no way questioned the earthly order. Returning to the same subject in his great book of pastoral rule, the *Liber regulae pastoralis*, he emphasized that the "very diversity which has accrued from vice is ordered by divine judgment, so that, since all men cannot stand on an equal footing, one should be ruled by another." All societies required order and distinction, even that of the angels. As Gregory pointed out elsewhere, they, too, were arranged by "order and power," according to rank, in what the influential sixth-century theologian known as Pseudo-Dionysius the Areopagite described as "hierarchy."[39]

The word is a Christian term. In Pseudo-Dionysius's influential account, which blended Neoplatonic doctrine with the teachings of Christ, hierarchy was a "sacred order," a "perfect arrangement," ordained by God, to organize the whole of creation according to relative proximity and likeness to him. There was a "Celestial Hierarchy" of higher beings—angels and archangels, cherubim and seraphim. And there was an "Ecclesiastical Hierarchy" that governed relations in the church, from the pope down to the lowliest parish priest. "An image of the beauty of God," hierarchy, it followed, should be replicated everywhere on earth.[40]

Gregory made that point explicitly in a pastoral letter to his bishops in the Frankish Kingdom of Childebert, noting that a "great order of differences" spanned the universe. "That creation cannot be governed, or live, in a state of absolute equality we are taught by the example of the heavenly hosts, since, there being angels and also archangels, it is manifest that they are not equal; but in power and rank, as you know, one differs from another." He drew the ready conclusion, asking, rhetorically, "If then among these who are without sin there is evidently this distinction, who of men can refuse to submit himself willingly to this order of things which he knows that even angels obey?" If even the sinless angels knew authority and rank, so should we.[41]

But Gregory's question contained another, which he, however, did not address. What of the condition of our ancestors in their innocence before the Fall? Like the angels, they, too, were without sin. Did they also know distinctions? It was a vexing question, and centuries later, another theological heavyweight, St. Thomas Aquinas, took it up directly in his monumental *Summa theologiae*. Deeply influenced by Aristotle, who denied natural equality outright, Aquinas wrestled with the twin authority of Augustine and Gregory, asking explicitly "whether men were equal [*aequales*] in the state of innocence."[42]

In typical scholastic style, Aquinas began by considering various responses or objections, and in the first he drew on Gregory's reflections on Job to reason as follows: "It seems that in the state of innocence men would all have been equal. For Gregory says: 'Where there is no sin, there is no inequality.' But in the state of innocence there was no sin. Therefore, all were equal [*pares*]." Aquinas then considered the objection that because "similarity and equality [*similitudo et aequalitas*] were the essence of mutual love," therefore "all were equal [*pares*] in the state of innocence." But after entertaining one more contrary opinion, he responded, on the authority of Paul and Augustine, "It is said: 'The things that are from God, are well ordered.' But order chiefly consists in inequality [*in disparitate consistere*]; for Augustine says: 'Order disposes things equal and unequal [*parium dispariumque*] in their proper place.' Therefore, in the original state, which would have been supremely well ordered, inequality would have existed." It followed, Aquinas concluded, that "there would have been some disparity [*aliquam disparitatem*]" in the original state—of sex, especially, but also mental and moral differences, and differences in knowledge, age, physical endowment, and the pursuit of justice. Even in our innocence, it seemed, inequality reigned supreme.[43]

Aquinas's speculative conclusions were by no means definitive. But they certainly carried weight, not least because they reflected the broader assumptions of his time. No less than late antiquity, medieval Europe was a profoundly hierarchical place, a society of formal orders and estates both religious and secular. In Aquinas and his contemporaries' hands, the hierarchies of Pseudo-Dionysius were combined with Aristotle's classifications of nature in what came to be known as the "Great Chain" or "Great Ladder of Being" (*scala naturae*) that linked everything in the universe in hierarchical rank from lowest to highest. Not only was hierarchy projected back onto our prelapsarian past, it was mapped onto the heavens themselves, with immortal souls in the afterlife ranked according to their respective merit.[44]

Even the Godhead was not completely spared. True, to contest the coeternal and coequal status of the three persons of the Trinity was to flirt with the old Arian heresy that made the Father superior to the Son. But that venerable symbol of equality, the equilateral triangle, could still be pressed into service as a symbol of divinely ordered authority, effectively turned on its head to depict a vast hierarchical order with the triune God at its apex. Inverted, the equilateral triangle became a pyramid of power.[45]

As formidable a theologian as he was, Aquinas hardly had the last word on the question of natural equality. The medieval revival of the study of Roman law helped ensure that its postulates were not forgotten, and careful students of the early Christian past recalled in the centuries to come that the patristic fathers had claimed time and again that human beings were equal in their innocence, and that distinctions of rank, fortune, and power had only come about as the result of our fall from grace. Aquinas himself entertained such objections. But even if one conceded his point that *some* inequality had accompanied our original state, it was surely a more equal place than the world that followed. Had not God intended it to be so—intended that we live, if not as perfect equals, then at least as more perfectly equal and more perfectly free than we did in our corruption? Surely that was an important part of the message of his beloved son, Jesus, who urged his followers to be "born again" so that they would be fit to witness the birth of the "kingdom of God"? (John 3:3). Whatever the subtleties of the scholastic philosophers, they could never banish the thought that Christians should do more than simply suffer their punishment in sin—that those who loved God most should work to recover what human beings had lost, if only to better prepare for the New Jerusalem to come.

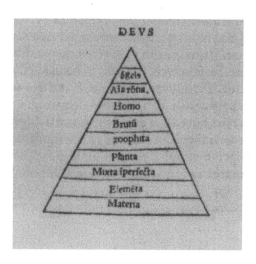

A triangle diagram of the scale of being, reproduced in a sixteenth-century edition of the late antique author Boethius's *Arithmetica* (1520). Houghton Library, Harvard University.

From the first days of the early church, Jesus's followers had wondered what that recovery and restoration would look like, and they had worked to bring it about. With the Holy Spirit upon them, the apostles shared their resources, as they shared their love, in fellowship and charity, as brothers, sisters, and peers. Countless monks and nuns pursued a similar calling, living communally in voluntary poverty. They did so, to be sure, under the authority of an abbot or abbess and according to the rule of an "order" (*ordo*). But among themselves, they attempted, however imperfectly, to cultivate charity in fraternity and sorority, living equally and without distinctions of status in anticipation of the way the world would be when Christ came again in glory to judge the living and the dead and to restore the righteous to the fullness of themselves.[46]

What would that restoration entail? A New Jerusalem, a heavenly city on earth, rightly ordered so that the last would be first? A millennium, a thousand-year reign to precede the *Parousia*, the return of Christ, as the Book of Revelation seemed to suggest? A time of prosperity and peace when all envy and iniquity would be washed away? The church gave its followers ample grounds for contemplation, sometimes of a surprising sort. Close readers of the *Decretum Gratiani* (or *Concordia discordantium canonum*), for example, the principal source of canon law, compiled in the twelfth century by the Benedictine monk Gratian, would have discovered a curious passage falsely attributed to a first-century pope, Clement I. The passage reaffirmed the widely held view that private property was the consequence of sin. More shockingly, the passage extended the same view to wives! "Everything ought to be held in common by friends. And without doubt, spouses are also included in 'everything,'" it noted on the authority of Plato, the "wisest of the Greeks." On that logic, there was both communism and free love in our innocence, and we could look forward to having them again when we were restored.[47]

The popular imagination was certainly ready to entertain such thoughts. "Medieval fantasies of the perfect life," one scholar observes, were lavishly abundant, above all among ordinary people. Combining visions culled from the Christian imaginary with legends and folklore of places of plenty and ease, such as the bountiful Land of Cockaigne, they produced vivid accounts of shared delights. These ranged from ravenous dreams of the milk and honey of abundance to fantasies of childbirth without pain, or sex without sin, or to mouth-watering visions of turkeys and geese that flew, ready-roasted, into open mouths. Invariably they represented a *mundus inversus*, an inverted world very different from the one in which the great majority lived with their hierarchies, hungers, and hardships. In the popular imagination, the New Jerusalem was "a city of peace, equality, and plenty."[48]

Most often those reveries served as mere fantasies of compensation, idylls of recompense for the repressions exacted by sin. They were a way to let off steam, like the annual festivals and charivaris, when ordinary rules were flaunted and society was turned upside down. They had their counterparts in works of fiction, including Jean de Meun's popular thirteenth-century *Romance of the Rose*, which invoked a golden age and sinless state before private property, and Christine de Pizan's *Book of the City of Ladies*, musings on a kingdom ruled by women that claimed for the ages that "human inferiority or superiority is not determined by sexual difference."[49]

But fantasies could also give rise to efforts to make them come true, and in the case of the millenarian imagination, to a more concrete "striving to restore the Garden of Eden," and to hasten the arrival of the New Jerusalem. Fueling the dream that a paradise lost could be restored, the millenarian imagination returned to the myth of original equality to challenge domination in the present as a foretaste of the world to come. "When Adam delved and Eve span / Who was then the Gentleman?" the radical preacher John Ball is said to have asked in a sermon delivered amid the great English peasant revolt of 1381. Whether he actually did so is unclear. But the man who recorded the lines, the contemporary English chronicler Thomas Walsingham, also said Ball began his sermon by invoking the theological doctrine of the natural equality of mankind: "Ab initio omnes pares creatos natura" (From the beginning, all were created equal by nature). Whether or not Ball uttered those exact words, what is clear is that the lines circulated widely, not just in England but across the Continent, and that contemporaries pulled from them the very message that the church itself had taught for centuries: that Adam and Eve had been free and equal by birth, and that the domination that ensued in the wake of the Fall was an expedient of sin. Now that those sins were to be washed away— or so millenarians believed—every effort must be made to hasten the new egalitarian community that would flourish as a result. The invocation of a more equal past thus served as the basis for criticism of the unequal present, providing an image of the restoration and recovery to follow.[50]

The Christian millenarian dream surfaced periodically in the Middle Ages and the early modern period, but never so spectacularly as it did amid the eruptions of the Protestant Reformation and the revolutions and wars that ensued in the sixteenth and seventeenth centuries. Those multifaceted events impacted Christian thinking about equality and its practice in complex ways, as historians are now coming to appreciate more fully. But at its heart the Reformation dramatized and brought to the fore a set of questions that have animated this chapter throughout: In what condition were God's children created? How, if at all, might we recover that condition? And what were the implications for how human beings should relate to one another as they attempted to bring that about?[51]

One way of coming at those questions is to ask, with Martin Luther, How are human beings saved? For that was precisely the question that exercised the Augustinian monk, who as a young man went to extraordinary lengths in an effort to save himself. He exposed his body to the bitter cold to mortify his flesh; he prayed at every hour of the day and night; he performed countless good works and acts of contrition—all in an attempt to pull himself up the Great Ladder of Being to get closer to God. Until, in his striving, he came to realize that all such efforts were in vain.

Sometime around 1517—while studying in the great "cloaca tower" at the monastery in Wittenberg, as legend has it—Luther had an epiphany. Human beings could never save themselves, he came to see. They could only be "justified" (made right) by God. Soon Luther was drawing out the implications of that thought. Salvation was a gift, a testament and offering, not a contractual negotiation, still less a contest to be won. It was an act of mercy and clemency from God. Salvation could never be earned. Salvation, rather, was by faith alone, and faith was granted by grace alone, and that saving message was revealed in scripture alone. Salvation was alone by Christ. *Sola fides, sola gratia, sola scriptura, solus Christus,* in the celebrated formulations.

Concise and powerful, Luther's formulations struck at the authority of the institutional church as the treasury of grace and indispensable mediator between God and humanity. In the place of its hierarchies, Luther posited the "priesthood of all believers," where every individual could develop a relationship with the Savior. "Whence comes this great distinction between those who are equally Christians?" he asked. It was a pointed question, and it opened the way not only for an attack on the church's elaborate hierarchies and chains of command, but for new thinking about how Christians should relate to one another in the secular realm of ordinary life where most pursued their callings. The simpler and purer arrangements of the early church, and the apparently equal relations of the apostles, many came to believe, provided a basis for conceiving ecclesiastical relations—and other types of relations in due course, such as political relations—on more equal terms.[52]

Lutherans, to be sure, no less than Catholics, restricted their circle of equals to fellow Christians. Although God, as Peter explained in the Acts of the Apostles, might show no "partiality" or favoritism among the peoples of the world, his blessings were reserved for those who accepted his love (Acts 10:34; Romans 2:11).

In that respect, Christianity closely resembled the other monotheistic faiths: it was prone to dualism in its universalism and quick to exclude from the family of God those errant children who did not embrace the Father. In the Middle Ages and early modern period, that meant heretics and heathens, Muslims and Jews. Luther was no exception, especially vis-à-vis the latter, whose homes and synagogues he urged Christians to burn in one screed, *On the Jews and Their Lies* (1543), while campaigning to have them expelled from Christian lands. Catholics were hardly better. Luther denied that the followers of the "whore of Babylon," the pope, were true Christians. The church returned the favor with its own denunciations and excommunications.[53]

But the question of who would be saved, and so raised to exalted standing, cut even deeper. Luther's two most important intellectual influences were St. Paul and St. Augustine, and both men had suggested that no one—not even Christians themselves—*deserved* salvation, because all had sinned. God's grace was a gift freely given to those without sufficient merit of their own. Why he chose to grant it to some, extending them full citizenship in his heavenly city, while banishing others to the city of man, was indeed a mystery, a "secret dispensation," as Pope Gregory had put it. Yet the church had long resisted confronting the full implications of that thought: what St. Augustine himself acknowledged as "double predestination"—two paths, one for the saved and another for the damned. Martin Luther and the Reformers confronted those implications head on. On the authority of Augustine and Paul, they stressed that human beings, vitiated by sin, could only be justified—made right and whole—by grace. And marked as we all are by the stain of concupiscence, there was nothing we could do to earn it by good works or striving. Grace was given, not taken. The community of the saints was foreordained.[54]

That (re-)emphasis on the theology of grace—stressed first by Luther in the wake of his initial challenge to the church in 1517 and then even more resolutely by the towering French Reformer Jean

("John") Calvin in the decades that followed—affected Christian thinking about equality in a number of ways. Most dramatically, it seemed, as the German theologian Ernst Troeltsch once put it, to "cut the nerve of the absolute and abstract idea of equality." If some were saved and others were damned, and God in his wisdom knew the difference, the consequences seemed clear. Calvin faced it directly. "Non enim pares creantur omnes," he asserted: "All are not created equal." Some are preordained to eternal life, others to eternal damnation. The community of true equals—the full citizens and peers of God's heavenly city—comprised only the elect.[55]

That thought could embolden, giving new impetus to the millenarian imagination. Within years of Luther's first public interventions in Wittenberg in 1517, erstwhile students and new sectarians, including the Anabaptist preacher Thomas Müntzer, were interpreting his theories as a summons to rise up against established authority. The true "freedom of the Christian," Luther argued in a famous pamphlet of 1520, meant that those redeemed by grace were "kings and priests and therefore lords of all." Luther meant that to apply to spiritual matters only, but Müntzer and hundreds of thousands of Swabian peasants in southwestern Germany understood him to be speaking of matters temporal as well. In what proved the largest rebellion in Europe prior to the French Revolution, they rose up in 1524 and 1525 against taxes and tithes and the excesses of feudal and aristocratic authority, clamoring to assert their freedom and to elect their own priests. Luther was conciliatory at first. But dependent on the power of the German princes, he ended by encouraging the slaughter that crushed the rebellion. In his pamphlet *Against the Murderous, Thieving Hordes of Peasants* (1525), he urged that they be cut down like dogs. Tens of thousands of them were.[56]

Luther was no less contemptuous when, a decade later, Dutch and German Anabaptists convened on the Westphalian city of Münster in 1534–1535. Proclaiming there the "New Jerusalem" that would serve as refuge for God's elect in the coming Apocalypse, they dissolved the distinction between mine and thine, shared out goods and commodities in common, instituted adult baptism and compulsory polygamy, and took steps to hasten the recovery of their sinless state. As one of their leaders, the former Lutheran pastor Bernhard Rothman, observed, "Among us, God . . . has restored community, as it was in the beginning and as befits the Saints of God." Another of Münster's principal leaders, John of Leiden, took sixteen wives in celebration of his restoration. Luther attacked both men as dangerous fanatics, styling John, a man of humble origins, "a tailor king." He applauded when the Anabaptists of Münster, like the peasants of Swabia, were crushed.[57]

Luther's response to both uprisings makes clear that there were real limits to how he conceived of earthly equality. As he insisted in a public reply to the demands of the Swabian peasants, their leaders "would make all men equal and turn the spiritual kingdom of Christ into a worldly, external kingdom; and that is impossible." "For a worldly kingdom cannot stand unless there is in it an inequality of persons, so that some are free, some imprisoned, some lords, some subjects." The logic was impeccably Augustinian, which is a reminder that given their emphasis on sin, Protestants could be just as insistent as Catholics on the need for powerful hierarchies to restrain the errant in the world. Calvin would show himself similarly exacting, and many of his followers in Europe and the New World would too.[58]

Yet there was potential for a twist. For by denying the logic of personal merit in the process of salvation, the Reformers made room for a different kind of equality, a "negative equality." All human beings were equally unworthy before God, they argued. None of us deserved to be saved. Feelings of superiority themselves could be dismissed as the consequence of sin, the root of which was pride. "For so blindly do we all rush in the direction of self-love," Calvin observed, "that everyone thinks he has a good reason for exalting himself and despising others in comparison." To believe yourself better than your neighbor was to be reminded that you were not.

That was a lesson in humility. But the contrasting sentiment—that no man is better than I am!—could be empowering. It had, like the priesthood of all believers, the potential to serve as a solvent of arrogant authority, and not just that of bishops, cardinals, and popes. When combined, however uneasily, with the contrasting sentiment of the special election of the saints, the results could be explosive.[59]

And from Bohemia to the Rhineland to the Netherlands they were, but arguably nowhere with as much creative force as in Great Britain amid the English Civil War and its aftermath in the 1640s and 1650s. That upheaval was, in many respects, the last of Europe's great religious wars that issued from the Reformation. It precipitated a flood of millenarian expectations embraced by a bewildering number of radical Protestant sects and movements: Baptists and Muggletonians, Levellers and True Levellers (Diggers), Fifth Monarchists, Quakers, and Ranters. There was considerable fluidity between them, but they tended to share, as one scholar notes, the sense that Christ would come "to reign through, with or even within his saints." As they readied themselves for his return, a great many of these believers spoke of the equality that had been lost and could now be restored in the interim between birth and death. They worked to hasten the arrival of a right world, a justified world, that would look more like the world God had conceived.[60]

And so Baptists took pains to organize themselves democratically, electing their own ministers and allowing even women to preach in voluntary churches composed of visible saints. Quakers walked naked to announce our equality before God and used what were then informal forms of address—"thee" and "thou"—to spurn formality, while daring to keep their hats on in the presence of social "betters." Since God was no "respecter of persons," as the King James Bible (1604) translated Acts 10:34 and Romans 2:11, then why should true Christians bow and scrape before ancestry and title, station and social rank that meant nothing in the end to God?[61]

Muggletonians and Diggers, too, refused to bestow "hat honor," the act of removing or doffing one's hat in the presence of a recognized superior. Their refusal to do so was in keeping with their broader conviction that the hierarchies of the old world would have no place in the New Jerusalem. The condemned would be punished, and the righteous redeemed. The world would be free of the distinctions, differences, and restraints long necessitated by sin. As the Digger leader Gerrard Winstanley proclaimed, woe to anyone who "lifts up themselves as Lords and Rulers over others, and that doth not look upon themselves equal to others in the Creation." The Lord would lay his hand upon them.[62]

Winstanley and his followers went so far as to declare that with Christ's return, the "common treasury" of the earth would be restored to what it was in the beginning: the common possession of all. Private property, they knew, was a remnant and perpetuator of sin. Remove the one and you would help hasten the removal of the other. Hence their name: Diggers broke up the earth with their spades, taking possession of common lands, while leveling the hedges and filling in the ditches used to enclose them for private use. The Ranter and Oxford-educated Abiezier Coppe spoke of God himself as "that mighty Leveller," recalling the God of Isaiah who leveled mountains and hills and called worldly riches and titles into contempt (Isaiah 23:9, 45:2). Now the Lord of Hosts would take an axe to all "Honour, Pompe, Greatnesse, [and] Superfluity and confound it into parity, equality, community," as he "chopt off" the "neck of horrid pride"![63]

The Levellers themselves, it is true, tended to resist the leveling label. It was cast in aspersion. But there was no denying that they aimed to raise up the lowly while pulling down the proud, putting men on an equal standing. Before God, they believed, freeborn Englishmen were peers, and they should be treated as such in his kingdom on earth, "leveled up" so that men below might enjoy the same rights as the current peers of the realm. As one of their leading spokesmen, Thomas Rainsborough, famously said, "The poorest he that is in England hath a life to live as the greatest he." Every man should be granted the right to vote and equal treatment under the law, bearing in mind always, as the Leveller John Lilburne put it in *The Freeman's Freedom Vindicated* (1646), that "every particular and individual man and woman that ever breathed in the world since [Adam and Eve] are and were by nature all equal and alike in power, dignity, authority, and majesty, none of them having (by nature) any authority, dominion, or magisterial power, one over the other." It followed, on this account, that authority could only ever be legitimate when granted by "free consent." In applying the spiritual equality of creation to the world, Lilburne and others were making of Christian equality an earthly affair.[64]

The views of these radical Protestant sects are undoubtedly striking in their audacity. For that very reason, they were always in the minority. By the time of the Restoration of the Stuart monarchy in 1660, their militant expression had been largely curtailed. Given the boldness and apparent prescience of their views on equality, it is perhaps not surprising that modern commentators have seen in them a kind of foundational moment, a time of origins from which to trace modern doctrines of civil, political, material, and even gender equality that lead ultimately to us. It is to sects like the Levellers, these commentators agree, that we should trace the emergence of modern "egalitarianism."[65]

Christian notions of equality were certainly not without their bearing on the future. Yet we would do well to view these seventeenth-century claims less as a new beginning than as a long continuation, the contractions of a tradition ever pregnant with the possibility of new birth. The most radical proponents of equality at the time of the English Civil War continued to express themselves in the language of salvation and grace, redemption and sin, that had long bounded Christian reflection. And they were shaped profoundly by millenarian expectations of the relations that would be forged with our restoration and renewal upon Christ's imminent return. The community of equals they imagined would perforce be a community of the elect. Even the Levellers, expansive and democratic in so many respects, could not conceive of women, servants, and beggars as full equals of the earth, to say nothing of royalists and foreigners. Which is a reminder that Christian equality beyond the Garden, whether in this world or the next, depended always on exclusions. The forms that would succeed it in the following centuries would do so too.

Yet the very fact that equality was on the horizon at all owed much to these varied Christian efforts. Over the course of centuries, Christians had made of equality a moral good, investing it with a sacral status, even as they sought to explain and justify its absence on earth. Equal was how God had made us; equal was how God intended his beloved to be. Singular and unique in our persons, we were somehow, all of us, the same. Surely those who worked in the service of recovering what humanity had lost were laboring on righteous ground?

Even the adamant could acknowledge the force of that thought, which surfaced in surprising places. Meditating on the Trinity toward the end of the seventeenth century, no less a figure than Jacques-Bénigne Bossuet, the Catholic bishop of Meaux—and an implacable enemy of what he considered the Protestant heresy in its many forms—moved seamlessly from the equality of the three persons of God to the equality of all people. Just as Jesus could say to the Father "that you are in me and I am in you," human beings must acknowledge that "we are all of but one nature," and we are "all formed of the same clay." We carry the image of God in our souls. "Let charity equalize everything in keeping with the message of Saint Paul that we must establish equality," Bossuet affirmed. He invoked the example of the disciples of the early church, who had "but one heart and one soul," and who claimed no private possessions. "Everything was common between them." "Consolation and affliction, good and evil, all must be equal between brothers," Bossuet affirmed. And in order to accomplish that, "the one who is rich must make up for what the poor lacks, so that, as the Apostle repeats, everyone is reduced to equality."[66]

Court preacher to Louis XIV and theoretician of absolute monarchy, Bossuet was hardly a revolutionary. His admonitions to the rich that they humble their pride and give freely to the poor were predicated on a view of Christian charity and love that accepted the inequalities of the world even as it challenged them. We needn't share the later view of Henri de Saint-Simon, the utopian visionary who in the early nineteenth century credited Bossuet with having fixed "general attention on the idea of equality," and so injected "revolution" into the national bloodstream of France. Still, we might at least grant Saint-Simon a certain exaggerated insight. For the reflections of a broad array of Christians like Bossuet, both Catholic and Protestant, in France and elsewhere, had indeed drawn attention to equality across the ages.

That attention generated conflicting and at times confounding views. For, broadly speaking, Christian perspectives on equality can be both "anticipatory" and "antipathetic." They can be used, that is, to endorse earthly efforts to recover and remake the equality we have lost in anticipation of a more equal world to come—but they can also be used to thwart those efforts, by reaffirming and accepting the inequalities of the City of Man, which are only to be transcended at some distant time in another dimension, the City of God. Christianity, just like the Axial faiths, offers resources to do both, and since its inception it has done so in a tension that continues to the present day.[67]

The contradictions were already clear in the seventeenth century. Not long after English radicals had preached the coming of equality on earth, the staunch Calvinist minister William Hubbard observed, from his Congregationalist parish in Ipswich, Massachusetts, in 1676, that "nothing therefore can be imagined more remote either from right reason or true religion, than to think that because we were all once equal at our birth, and shall be again at our death, therefore we should be so in the course of our lives." Despite his own inability to imagine, however, others were beginning to do precisely that—in Hubbard's very own backyard. Combining religion, reason, and republican reflection, they recovered equality from its classical and Christian past and reinvented it to better suit the conditions of modern life, making "all men are created equal" anew.[68]

6

FRATERNITY

*The Reinvention of Equality in the
Age of Enlightenment*

In session in Philadelphia in the late afternoon of July 4, 1776, the Continental Congress resolved "that Dr. Franklin, Mr. J. Adams and Mr. Jefferson be a committee to prepare a device for a Seal of the United States of America." The erstwhile colonies, now newly united states, were in need of a sign and symbol of their collective endeavor, and over the following weeks the committee considered its options. Among them was a proposal by the painter and polymath Pierre Eugène du Simitière. A Genevan by birth, Simitière had left Europe as a young man and spent more than a decade traveling in Jamaica and the West Indies, making sketches and gathering specimens for a collection that would eventually form the basis of the first American museum of natural history. He seems to have arrived on American shores in 1764, spending time in Boston and New York before settling in the "city of brotherly love," so named from its Greek roots, *phileo* (love) and *adelphos* (brother): Philadelphia. By 1776, he was a prominent resident of the city's large French-speaking community, a sought-after portraitist, and a member of the American Philosophical Society. A cosmopolitan figure, he proposed, fittingly, a cosmopolitan design.[1]

Pierre Eugène du Simitière's draft sketch of the proposal for the Great Seal of the United States, 1776. Courtesy of the Library of Congress.

It featured the coats of arms of the various European nations of the world from "whence America has been peopled"—including England, Scotland, Ireland, Germany, Holland, and France. Africans and the indigenous were not mentioned as people of the peopling sort, though that was hardly a stumbling block for the committee, whose members were intrigued. "His designs are very ingenious, and his drawings well executed," John Adams noted in a letter to his wife, Abigail. And although the committee eventually passed on the proposal, and Congress delayed its final decision for several more years, two key elements of Simitière's sketch found their way into the final version of the Great Seal. They can tell us something important about understandings of equality on both sides of the Atlantic as they were emerging at this revolutionary time.[2]

The first is the radiant equilateral triangle at the top, with the "eye of providence" in its center, emitting golden rays of light. The image now adorns one side of the Great Seal, and also, as many will know, the one-dollar bill. Its Latin legend reads, "Annuit Coeptis," which in a loose translation means, "[God or Providence] favors our undertaking," and "Novus Ordo Seclorum," the "New Order of the Ages," a line culled from Virgil's Fourth Eclogue signaling the advent of an era of prosperity and happiness, but long interpreted by Christians as a prophecy of the coming of Christ. The pyramid underneath is unfinished, a work in progress; the triangle serves as its capstone. And the eye in its center represents the omniscient gaze of the Supreme Being, all-seeing and all-knowing.

The equilateral triangle and eye of providence were symbols of great antiquity. The eye traces back as far as the ancient Egyptians, but, like the equilateral triangle in which it was housed, it would have been better known to contemporaries through its close association to the coequal Trinitarian God. Triangles with the eye of providence were common features of Christian churches on both sides of the Atlantic in the eighteenth century, and they also featured centrally in Masonic temples, whose members traced their (mythological) origins back to the builders of the Egyptian pyramids and the great Gothic cathedrals. In truth, the Masons were moderns, with the first lodges appearing only toward the end of the seventeenth century in Scotland and England, and slightly later in North America and on the European Continent. But like those whom they claimed as distant forebears—and like the men gathered in Philadelphia—the Masons believed they were engaged in building something wondrous and new.[3]

That new building and construction—the "New Order of the Ages"—appeared to involve nothing less than a novel way for human beings to relate to one another. The very idea that societies could be constituted, and nations willed into being as the sum of their individual parts, was a novelty of its own. And while the triangle continued to serve as inspiration in that project as a symbol of Christian equality, it could also be imagined more literally as an instrument of construction. The carpenter's square and plumb bob, with two equal sides and a piece of string to take the level, was an instrument for laying new foundations, for building and making straight. It had a venerable pedigree as a symbol of equality.

The ancient Romans used it to suggest both leveling and the leveling of death, and readers of scripture would have recalled the dramatic appearance of the Lord in the Book of Amos, with a

"Memento Mori," first century, suggesting the leveling of death. The mosaic, discovered at a villa in Pompeii, is now housed at the National Archeological Museum, Naples. Photo © Stefano Baldini / Bridgeman Images.

"plumb-line in his hand," which he vows to set amid the people of Israel to terrible effect: "And the high places of Isaac shall be desolate, and the sanctuaries of Israel shall be laid waste; and I will rise against the house of Jeroboam with the sword" (Amos 7:7–10). At the end of the eighteenth century, during the upheavals of the French Revolution, the symbol would assume once again some of that leveling menace. But for most of the century, the carpenter's level in the triangular shape—with or without its leveling line— evoked gentler connotations: of equal association, solidarity, and fraternity. Worn as a fraternal pin, close to the heart, it bound together brothers as equals and friends.[4]

The image embraced the sentiment expressed in the second of the elements in Simitière's sketch adopted by Adams, Jefferson,

Masonic badge worn by the members of the Grand Lodge of England, showing the triangular carpenter's level and plumb line, 1735. © Museum of Freemasonry. Reproduced by permission of the Grand Lodge of England / Bridgeman Images.

and Franklin: the Latin phrase "E pluribus unum," "Out of many one." It, too, had both classical and Christian associations. Words to that effect turn up in St. Augustine's *Confessions*, in the context of the joys of friendship, which can "kindle a blaze to melt our hearts and weld them into one" ("conflare animos et ex pluribus unum facere"). Cicero also employs variants of the phrase in that way, noting, in his treatise *De amicitia* (On friendship) that "the effect of friendship is to make, as it were, one soul out of many" ("cum amicitiae vis sit in eo ut unus quasi animus fiat ex pluribus"). In *De officiis* (On duties) he adds that when two people have the same ideals and the same tastes, it is natural that each should love the other as himself, with the result, as Pythagoras requires of ideal friendship, that several are united in one ("ut unus fiat ex pluribus"). Finally, in his well-known chapter on friendship in the *Nicomachean Ethics*, Aristotle insists that friendship "is equality," and that the most fitting politics is the just arrangement of friends as brothers, "since they are equal . . . and generally alike."[5]

Simitière and the Founders were well versed in all those writings, though whether they drew on them directly for the phrase in question is unclear. What is clear is that the ideal of friendship—Christian, classical, and modern—was bound up with the project of constructing a new society of equals. To make one of many, it helped to build with those who were alike, with those who considered themselves brothers and friends. And to do that involved not only binding people together, but keeping them apart. In the figure of equality as fraternity, eighteenth-century men found a means to do both.[6]

When scholars trace the origins of modern equality, they generally begin in the long eighteenth century, the Age of Enlightenment. It is the exceptional period, we are told, that witnessed the transition from *Homo hierarchicus* to *Homo aequalis*, hierarchical man to equal man. It is the age of the "invention of equality," which became the "credo" of revolutionaries on both sides of the Atlantic, and the "test of truth for eighteenth-century ideas." Some scholars, it is true, set the timeline back a bit to take in the early origins of the Enlightenment, the Glorious Revolution, or the upheavals of the English Civil War. And others spill over into the early nineteenth century to consider the full sweep of the Age of Atlantic Revolutions, with its later conflagrations in Haiti and Latin America. But, broadly conceived, the long eighteenth century is treated as ground zero for modern equality—the site of an explosion whose reverberations continue to be felt to the present day.[7]

There are good reasons for that view. The long eighteenth century *did* generate new discoveries, new processes, new ideas, and even new fashions that made talk of equality appealing. The very breadth of that appeal renders the task of explaining its origins challenging. It is hardly surprising that historians have come up with a great many explanations.

One set follows the leads of the great nineteenth-century thinkers Alexis de Tocqueville and Karl Marx to argue that either centralizing states or nascent capitalism drove the process of eroding social privileges and distinctions, bringing a new public of equals into being. But whether the driver was ultimately political, economic, or some combination of the two, novel forms of sociability certainly sprang up in the long eighteenth century. In coffeehouses, salons, learned academies, Masonic lodges, and other gathering places, people related to one another in new ways. The economic possibilities of commercial society allowed for careers open to talent and the confluence of peoples of different social standing. And thanks to developments in the fashion industry, in London and Paris especially, those people increasingly looked more alike in dress and appearance. Mingling in public promenades, they blurred social distinctions in ways that made it possible to conceive of a shared civic equality.[8]

Another set of explanations focuses on how new Enlightenment and Radical Enlightenment theories about common humanity, the moral equivalence of human beings, and natural human rights hastened the advent of equality in the long eighteenth century. It has even been argued ingeniously that the rise and popularity of the novel in that time encouraged new reading practices that fostered empathy for strangers, allowing men and women to "think of others as their equals," or similar to them in fundamental ways.[9]

Finally, some have argued recently that equality was not a Western invention at all, but rather an idea borrowed from the indigenous. As Europeans came into closer contact with the various peoples of the New World, they encountered forms of social organization that were evidently more equal than their own, and that seemed to provide a glimpse of humanity in its pristine state. What followed, then, was a calling to account of what "civilized" humanity had become.[10]

Clearly, a good deal of innovation was happening in the long eighteenth century, which suggests that no single causal explanation can fully account for the emergence of new ideas about equality at this time. Equality's modern origins, we might say, were overdetermined.

Yet all of this talk of novelty can also be obscuring, for it prevents us from appreciating the pull of the past, from seeing that equality was not so much invented in this period, ex nihilo, as reinvented from materials that were not all shiny and new. Like the venerable equilateral triangle, long admired by Christians, or assertions of fraternity and friendship, now reconceived to imagine the many as one, equality was neither as novel nor as newfangled as it might at first appear. Concepts, after all, come to us laden with their pasts. And despite all the innovative forces giving impetus and momentum to equality in the eighteenth century, history's inertia was strong.

We can better appreciate that fact by returning to Philadelphia on July 4, 1776. For the decision to form a committee to vet designs for the Great Seal was not, of course, the only resolution decreed by the Continental Congress on that day. Far better known is the other collaborative venture undertaken by Thomas Jefferson, Benjamin Franklin, and John Adams—the Declaration of Independence—with its ringing pronouncement that "all men are created equal." Americans have long regarded those words as revolutionary, a bold statement of the Founders' dedication to a radical "new proposition," as Abraham Lincoln put it some four score and seven years later in the little town of Gettysburg, just 140 miles to Philadelphia's west. Lincoln spoke in a period of fratricide, amid the Civil War, when Americans were required, as the Declaration had lamented of its own age, to serve as "executioners of their friends and Brethren." He urged them to continue the "unfinished work" that the Declaration had undertaken, echoing a theme he had spelled out two years earlier in a speech delivered at Independence Hall in Philadelphia, when he had noted that the Declaration was a promise to the future: "that in due time the weights would be lifted from the shoulders of all men, and that all should have an equal chance."[11]

The Declaration has certainly inspired over the years. Even though African Americans, like the Connecticut preacher Lemuel

Haynes, who first penned a response to the Declaration in 1776, tended to read it as a damning document of white hypocrisy and failure, they could also see it as a source of "saving principles," as Frederick Douglass would do in his celebrated "What, to a Slave, Is the Fourth of July?" of 1852. But white contemporaries in the eighteenth century tended to hear the words differently. To them, the Declaration was less a promissory note for the future, or a charter of individual rights, than an intervention in international law that justified secession from the British Empire. Read in that way, the natural equality of the created was hardly remarkable. Indeed, it was something of a cliché.[12]

The proposition, after all, had long been a truism in the Christian world. Already by the Middle Ages, as we have seen, Pope Gregory the Great's affirmation in late antiquity that nature had begotten all men equal was regarded as "axiomatic," which is to say self-evident. And time and again, early modern theorists of natural law had invoked the proposition—so often, in fact, that by 1631, the arch apologist for absolute monarchy Robert Filmer was complaining that the "supposed natural equality and freedom of mankind" had achieved the status of a "truth unquestionable." Filmer no doubt exaggerated. But it is revealing that the seventeenth century's other great pretender to the defense of English kings, Thomas Hobbes, took natural equality in the state of nature as his point of departure.[13]

So did Hobbes's and Filmer's great antagonists, Algernon Sidney and John Locke. Sidney, whose book *Discourses Concerning Government* (1698) was so influential in eighteenth-century America that he has been described as the "forgotten founding father," regarded the "natural equality in which all men are born" as "such evident truth," such "unquestionable truth," as to hardly require proof. Locke thought the same, insisting, in his *Second Treatise on Government* (1689), that the state of nature was not only a "state of perfect freedom," but a state of perfect equality, "without subordination or subjection." There was "nothing more evident," he declared. Locke cited the Anglican theologian Richard Hooker to reaffirm the point, noting that "this equality of men by nature . . . is so evident in itself, and beyond all question," that Hooker had made it the foundation of the "obligation to mutual love amongst men." We should love our equals as our friends. Hobbes, interestingly, agreed. For although he understood natural equality, in the end, to be a source of conflict, he believed that natural law imposed a duty to overcome our "pride," so, as he put it, "that every man acknowledge other as his equall by nature." That we had great trouble doing so was for him a problem to be overcome.[14]

Jefferson, to his credit, never claimed that the Declaration was entirely new, even if he saw it as charting a novel course for the future. As he pointed out toward the end of his life, the document aimed neither for "originality of principle [n]or sentiment," but sought to capture the "common sense" of the age.[15]

That all men are created equal was undoubtedly part of the eighteenth century's common sense. But what did it mean? To Lincoln, as to so many after him, it was the statement of a principle and ideal with logical force that had eventually broken free from the strictures of its time to extend to all those who were overlooked when the premise was first applied. That would include not only, as Lincoln came to insist, the nation's enslaved, but the other half of humanity, women, along with the indigenous, the propertyless, the poor, and all those originally forgotten, left out, and overlooked by blindness, prejudice, or failure of nerve.[16]

Yet here is where looking to equality's past, rather than to its future, is revealing. For assertions of equality, as we have seen, had always been compatible with inequality. Indeed, they regularly functioned as a hierarchical premise, serving as the very basis for difference and distinction. Philosophers might regret this, or regard it as going against equality's "logic," but the fact remains that conceptions of equality can comfortably exist with beliefs and practices of a highly unequal kind, and frequently lend them foundation and support. That was true of the major Axial traditions, and it was true of the theories and practices of the classical world. It was inscribed in the Roman law, and long maintained by Christians. And it was perfectly compatible with modern natural rights doctrine, which developed in the seventeenth century in part to provide new justifications for slavery. In the very same book that John Locke asserted the "equality of men by nature," and mounted arguments in support of government on the basis of our equal natural rights, he offered a rationalization of slavery in the case of captives taken in just war. Most of the other major natural rights theorists, including Hobbes, Hugo Grotius, and Samuel von Pufendorf, did the same.[17]

In light of those precedents, there are grounds for considering an even stronger view, which would hold not only that claims of equality are consistent with inequality and difference, or that they serve as their foundation, but that they *require* them. Assertions of equality, that is, require assertions of inequality to have potency and political force. That, in effect, was the position espoused by the influential German legal theorist Carl Schmitt, who argued in the 1920s that "any form of equality receives its significance and sense from the corresponding possibility of inequality," and that "this equality becomes more intense as the inequality opposing it grows." Schmitt, to be clear, was the jurist who went on to provide legal and ideological cover for the Nazis, as will be explored at length in Chapter 9. And yet his observation here—that claims to equality draw their political force by reference to the unequals they exclude—is no less trenchant for that. Scholars considerably to his left—and above all those who work on questions of gender and race—have developed similar lines of inquiry, often drawing on Schmitt himself, to probe the "constitutive exclusions" at the heart of modern politics.[18]

The thought accords well, moreover, with what historians have been telling us for some time about the history of freedom. Stretching all the way back to the ancients, freedom was conceived as slavery's opposite. Yet it was also, at the same time, predicated upon it. To be free was to be free of the authority of another, to be free of domination or dependence. That was what it meant to be *independent*. But a central measure of such independence was in turn the ability to exercise authority oneself, ruling like the Greek citizen or Roman *paterfamilias* over dependents of one's own, whether wives and children, servants or slaves. That had not changed much by the time Jefferson and his colleagues gathered in Philadelphia in 1776. The eminent scholar of colonial America Edmund Morgan famously called it the "Paradox of American Freedom." For Morgan, the fact that one-fifth of all Americans in the eighteenth century were in bondage meant that slavery couldn't just be written off as freedom's aberration. It was, rather, its "structural prerequisite," or what another leading scholar has called its "symbiotic relation." Freedom and slavery, freedom and dependence, were intertwined. And in the American context, as in the slave-trading nations of Europe, freedom overwhelmingly meant "white freedom." They were one and the same.[19]

Thinking about equality in similar terms—as a concept that depends upon and generates inequalities—helps us to explain why the eighteenth century produced not only new egalitarian assertions, but also novel ways of conceiving and justifying inequality. The period in that respect was what the historian Siep Stuurman describes as "Janus-faced," after the Roman God who looks in two directions at once. When we look at the eighteenth century, we see new theories of racial and sexual difference coming into being alongside new assertions of fraternity and equality. And together with new claims about the equality of humanity arose new theories of economic development and historical progress, which relegated the majority of the world's peoples to backwardness, equal only in name.[20]

Yet Janus was not only a god of duality and new beginnings, but of transitions and time. His double vision was temporal as well as spatial, looking simultaneously to the past and to the future.

That is true of eighteenth-century equality, as well. And it is especially true of "all men are created equal," whose Christian roots
were deep. They had been tended assiduously in the seventeenth
century in the fertile soil of natural rights theorists such as Locke
and Sidney, on whom the mark of John Calvin remained strong.
Both men were important influences on Thomas Jefferson, and
that raises an intriguing question. Was the long germination of
Christian equality finally giving flower? Perhaps the equality of the
eighteenth century was really just a Christian notion in disguise?[21]

The question of equality's Christian roots is sometimes raised only to
be quickly dismissed. It shouldn't be. No less an eighteenth-century
authority on common sense than Thomas Paine saw a relation to
equality's religious past, pointing out that "the equality of man, so
far from being a modern doctrine, is the oldest upon record." Louis
Alexandre de La Rochefoucauld d'Enville, a French duke who
strongly supported the American Revolution and later took part
in his country's own revolution, similarly regarded the Declaration's proposition that "all men are created equal" as an established
truth of Christianity, and indeed of all religions. The great Dutch
patriot Peter Paulus, who met Jefferson in Paris and was one of the
"founding fathers" of the Batavian republic, argued the connection
and compatibility between Christianity and equality at length in a
1793 treatise, *Verhandeling over de vrage: in welken zin kunnen de
menschen gezegd worden gelyk te zyn?* (Treatise on the question: In
which sense can people be said to be equal?).[22]

In the nineteenth century, such conjecture was continued even
more famously by Tocqueville, who regarded Christianity, along
with the absolutist state, as an important source of the equality
of conditions. In the United States and "wherever we look in
the Christian world," one could see its work. Equality began to
"insinuate itself into government through the church," Tocqueville
argued in the introduction to the first volume of his monumental
Democracy in America (1835). The process, he believed, stretched

back hundreds of years, and it continued still: "Christianity, which made all men equal in the sight of God, will not shrink from seeing all citizens as equal in the eyes of the law." Writing several decades later, Friedrich Nietzsche reached a similar conclusion, albeit from a hostile point of view. "Mankind was first taught to stammer the proposition of equality in a religious context," he observed with contempt. The "equality of souls before God" was just another "crazy" Christian concept that had passed "deeply into the tissue of modernity," furnishing "the prototype of all theories of equal rights."[23]

More recently, a number of contemporary scholars have made a similar point in connection to rights, albeit with little of Nietzsche's venom, and some have extended the insight to the United States. One noted historian of the American Revolution, for example, points out that Americans "secularized the Christian belief in the equality of all souls before God." Another observes of Jefferson specifically that "he shared the belief, common among American partisans of Enlightenment regardless of their denominational affiliations, that principles of political, economic, and social equality derive from God's law."[24]

Yet in order for those derivations to have broad purchase, barriers needed to be overcome. One of them was sin. It had long stood in the way of human beings' efforts to live as they were created, serving to justify slavery, patriarchy, and all manner of hierarchical rule. It was the theological linchpin of domination, and human beings would only be able to recover the freedom and equality of their prelapsarian state when it was removed. Radicals in the Reformation had dramatized that thought, as had, more recently, radicals in the English Civil War. Some even wondered aloud whether all should be equal as fellow citizens and peers, equal in rights, and they began to put that equality to work briefly in seventeenth-century England, making it an important and generative site for what the political theorist Teresa Bejan calls "equality before egalitarianism."[25]

Such uses, however, were still largely steeped in sin. They required God or grace to set us free while limiting the circle of equals to the saints. But what if sin could be removed by another means—not extricated by divine intervention, but simply thought away? Locke, for all his Calvinist upbringing and residual belief, had begun to speculate along those lines, famously conceiving of the mind as a *tabula rasa* at birth, shaped by education and experience, not hardwired by iniquity or innate ideas. Others in the eighteenth century continued to speculate along those same lines, and as they did so, they entertained a thought that followed perfectly from centuries of Christian assumption. If sin could be banished, surely equality could be cultivated in its place?

That, in effect, was the thought experiment pursued by another man with a Calvinist past, Jean-Jacques Rousseau, whose *Discourse on the Origin and Foundation of Inequality Among Men* was the most influential statement on equality of the eighteenth century. It was conceived as an answer to an essay competition sponsored by the French Academy of Dijon in 1754, regarding the origins of the inequality of conditions and whether that inequality was autho-rized by natural law. "Religion commands us to believe," Rousseau began, "that since God himself drew men out of the state of nature, they are unequal because he wanted them to be so." But religion, Rousseau continued, does not forbid us to "form conjectures" drawn solely from the nature of man regarding what the human race might have become. And although the story Rousseau tells is ultimately, like the religious account, the story of how natural goodness and equality are overcome by corruption, the crucial difference is that Rousseau depicts this process as contingent, not congenital, the consequence of human developments and choices, rather than the divine alteration of our souls.

Rousseau left open the possibility that human beings might live differently. For if our original nature was disfigured as a conse-quence of social relations, and not irrevocably altered by God, perhaps we could undo the damage by organizing ourselves in another way. "Instead of destroying natural equality," Rousseau later insisted in his best-known work, *The Social Contract*, a just society would "substitute a moral and legitimate equality" to replace the equality we had lost. What was clear to him was that "the sort of inequality that reigns among all civilized people" was "obviously contrary to the law of nature." Human beings were equal at birth and should, in a more just world, be treated so still. In this way did Rousseau break through the barrier of sin, weaponizing the potential of natural equality as a tool to criticize hierarchy in the status quo without the need for absolution or grace.[26]

To fully appreciate that departure, as well as how closely it stayed to the Christian soil from which it sprang, it helps to compare Rousseau's essay to the one that actually won the Dijon essay prize, a short treatise by the abbé François Xavier Talbert, canon of the church of Besançon in eastern France, and a member of that city's academy. Talbert, whose only other published work was a eulogy of the great Trinitarian, Bishop Bossuet, is entirely forgotten today, and understandably so, given that his views on equality were unremarkably orthodox, even if they are all the more interesting for that. For in fact Talbert agreed entirely with Rousseau that "natural law did not authorize inequality of conditions" in our natural state. "The Creator made us alike [*semblables*]," he wrote, establishing a uniformity in our species that "incontestably granted us the same rights" and excluded "all distinction of estates." "What good was subordination, power, or force" in that state? Talbert asks. "What kind of inequality could have insinuated itself [*se glisser*] in human society?" None at all. Man was not made "to suffer the yoke imposed by his equals [*semblables*]." Inequality of rank and fortune was wholly proscribed. In the beginning, we lived as we were supposed to have lived, and if the heart of man had not been corrupted, we would be living that way still—in perfect equality.[27]

Of course, according to Talbert, all that had changed with the Fall, and the accompanying original sin of pride (*amour propre*), which furnished human beings with an entirely new nature that rendered inequality not only legitimate but necessary. But the crucial point is that he wholly concurred with Rousseau regarding both the equality of our original state *and* its ultimate desirability. God had intended us to live as equals. Human beings were not made "to suffer a yoke imposed by their counterparts [*semblables*]."[28]

Nor do the similarities end there. For despite the old canard that thinkers of the Enlightenment were overly optimistic about human nature, the truth is that the vast majority of them, in removing the congenital sin of Christians, did not dispense with its cause and consequence. Self-love, the excessive pride that Augustine had identified as the root of human evil, continued to stand in the way. A strong Augustinian streak runs through much of Enlightenment thought, which wrestled with pride as a passion and a problem, sometimes to be condemned and sometimes to be condoned and explained. Pride is precisely the term that Hobbes gives to the "breach" of his ninth law of nature (that we should recognize others as equals), and Rousseau, Hobbes's close reader, if often his antagonist, fully agreed. What Rousseau famously calls *amour propre*, a term he likely borrowed from the arch-Augustinian Blaise Pascal, is both the cause and the consequence of our passage from primitive equality. *Amour propre*, to be distinguished from the healthy impetus to self-preservation that Rousseau called *l'amour de soi-même*, is not congenital to our nature, or in any case only lies dormant in our natural state. It is activated and inflamed in society, when we become conscious of our standing vis-à-vis others. *Amour propre* is relational, but it "moves each individual to value himself more than anyone else," setting off a "furor to distinguish oneself," and a "universal desire for reputation, honors, and preferences, which devours us all." Although it is related to the legitimate human need for recognition, and so is bound up with the desire for status, *amour propre* is most definitely in Rousseau's handling a "corruption." It feeds on narcissism, and it excites in us a mania of invidious comparison and competition. It is the psychological source of inequality in all its forms—whether of merit, power, rank, or wealth—and in Rousseau's opinion it determines that "inequality of prestige and authority becomes inevitable among private individuals as soon as they are united in a single society and are forced to make comparisons among themselves and to take into account the differences they discover."[29]

Rousseau's powerful psychological analysis of the sources of what contemporary social scientists call "status competition" is, in the modern philosophical tradition, rivaled only by that of Hobbes and Nietzsche. It has been described, in a nod to its Christian associations, as "a theodicy," an explanation of the evil of self-love. And yet despite Rousseau's recognition that an inflamed *amour propre*, and so inequality, become "inevitable" once human beings enter into society, he did not leave the discussion at that. There could be no going back to our lost innocence, he insisted, however much we might regret the loss. "The human race of one age is not the human race of another." And despite a certain elegy for the more equal life of peoples with whom Europeans, in their conquest and exploration, were coming into contact—the indigenous of North America, the Inuit of Greenland or Iceland, the hunter-gatherers of Tierra del Fuego or the Cape of Good Hope—he did not see the life of the "noble savage" as a viable model for Europeans. Rather, Rousseau later explored, in *The Social Contract*, how human beings might be rendered more equal and free in the civil state. That would involve nothing less than changing human nature to correct for the corruptions of pride, a project that, as we will see in the next chapter, was undertaken amid the French Revolution, in part at the prompting of Rousseau.[30]

In America, however, despite Rousseau's renown, *The Social Contract* was little read. The deep Puritan, Protestant, and Augustinian roots of the country discouraged the growth of confidence in the power to radically alter human nature by social means. The legacy of sin endured, generating suspicion toward men in power, in keeping with the older Calvinist view that human beings in their damnation were equally depraved. A stubborn recollection of the sinful capacity of human beings favored vigilance toward authority, underscoring the need to erect fences to contain it. And it limited the extent to which Americans could imagine themselves or their neighbors as free of self-interest and self-love. Negative equality, like negative liberty, was a circumspect affair. Serving as a powerful solvent of arrogant authority, it nonetheless constrained Americans' capacity to think of their fellows as equals in more expansive and more positive ways.[31]

Recollections of sin also encouraged skepticism toward the presumed innocence of humanity in its early stages of development. When Americans looked to the example of the "primitive" peoples in their midst, they were less inclined than Rousseau to think of natural goodness. And while it is true that, like Europeans, they could on occasion regard indigenous life as a "symbol of equality," they tended to interpret that symbol less as an ideal to be emulated and more as a reminder of the advantages of civilization.[32]

That tendency was motivated in part by invidious observations of Native Americans, whom John Adams described as "blood Hounds" ready to "scalp Men, and to butcher Women and Children," and whom the Declaration of Independence decried as "merciless Indian savages." Prejudice of the sort—born of conflict, tense encounter, violence, and fear—was certainly prevalent, and probably the norm. And yet it would be misleading to dismiss the attitudes of eighteenth-century Americans, and still less those of the Founding Fathers, simply as "racist," and to leave the matter at that.[33]

Many among the enlightened in fact expressed admiration for Native Americans' ingenuity, imagination, and valor, with Jefferson, for one, ready "to place them on a level with Whites in the same uncultivated state." "I believe," Jefferson continued, in a long letter to a like-minded French philosophe, François Jean de Beauvoir, Marquis de Chastellux, "the Indian then to be in body and mind equal to the white man. I have supposed the black man, in his present state, might not be so. But it would be hazardous to affirm that, equally cultivated for a few generations, he would not become so." The words are revealing—and not only of the fact that Jefferson thought Indians more nearly equal to whites than Africans, a point he developed at somewhat greater length in his *Notes on the State of Virginia* (1785). They also make clear that the crucial distinguishing feature between peoples in his mind was less natural difference than stages of civilizational advance.[34]

In the very same letter, Jefferson invoked the influential French naturalist, Georges-Louis Leclerc, Comte de Buffon, who held that all the peoples of the world were inherently alike. "Man, white in Europe, black in Africa, yellow in Asia, and red in America is always the same man," Buffon had noted in the crude taxonomy of pigmentation that was a product of the eighteenth century. Skin color, in other words, like other superficial differences, could be explained by reference to environment, and still others could be attributed to culture. "Everything thus supports the thesis that humanity is not composed of essentially different species: that on the contrary there originally only was a sole species of men, which . . . has undergone diverse modifications by the influence of the climate, different diets, ways of living," and the like.[35]

Buffon thus provided a scientific explanation to replace the older Christian monogenetic account of the unity of the human species as the sons and daughters of Adam. Yet while his universalist language may well seem preferable to theories of biological race that were just then coming into being, it was not without its own causes for concern. For one thing, Buffon assumed whiteness as the natural standard of beauty and fitness by which to judge all other hues of humanity. For another, his environmental theories provided readily for what he described as "degenerations" of the species due to climate or culture. And although it is true that neither he nor Jefferson believed that the indigenous people of the Americas had degenerated in that way, others certainly did, and they used his theories to buttress their case. The crucial point for now is that environmental explanations like Buffon's, no less than theories of biological race, could be employed to mark categorical distinctions between peoples.[36]

The same is true of eighteenth-century "stadial" accounts of human development, known in France as *histoire philosophique*, and in the Anglo-American world, and particularly Scotland, where it was especially strong, as "conjectural history." That body of work drew on the enhanced knowledge of human diversity garnered by European explorers, travelers, and soldiers to speculate on the origins of human society and the various stages of its development. Like Rousseau in the *Discourse on Inequality*, conjectural historians combined history with a nascent anthropology and ethnography to put forth a general account of human development. But unlike him, they tended to see the story of humanity as one of progress. As the Scottish historian John Millar observed, "There is thus in human society, a natural progress from ignorance to knowledge, and from rude to civilized manners, the several stages of which are usually accompanied with peculiar laws and customs."[37]

Millar, like his teacher and colleague at the University of Glasgow Adam Smith, specified that there were four of these stages: the age of hunters, the age of shepherds, the age of agriculture, and the age of commerce. In the "four-stage theory" of development, peoples generally progressed from common origins, and they tended in similar directions. But they did so at different speeds, developing different laws, values, customs, and beliefs. And so, although conjectural historians generally agreed with John Locke, who said famously, in his *Second Treatise on Government*, that "in the beginning, all the world was America," meaning that the indigenous peoples there provided a picture of human beings in their infancy, the point was not to stay a child. Conjectural historians valued "maturity," and growth toward the affluence and sophistication of commercial society, and they tended, accordingly, to relegate the less developed peoples of the world to an inferior place, even as they regarded them as equals by nature. In such descriptions, what another Scot, Adam Ferguson, described as the "history of rude nations," the romanticized "noble savage" became an "ignoble savage," a barbarian primitive and crude.[38]

Thus, just like the natural history of Buffon, conjectural history could be used to account for difference in human development in the past while also explaining different levels of civilization in the present. When plotted on the "great map of mankind," the commercial societies of the Atlantic rim stood out as the most civilized and advanced, while the hunting and pastoral peoples of the world, clustered in places such as sub-Saharan Africa, the rainforests and plains of the Americas, and the great Eurasian Steppe, were cast as occupying a stage of delayed or arrested development. Human beings might have been created equal, but they were not all so now.[39]

When viewed through this developmental lens, equality itself could look less appealing. For it was not lost on observers in Europe and North America that the indigenous peoples they encountered in the New World—the Iroquois and Algonquians, the Huron and Cherokee—lived much more equally than they did in social, material, and political terms. Yet when viewed on a continuum of the stages of historical progress, such equality seemed like a relic of the past, primitive and perhaps charming in its simplicity and undifferentiated sameness, but primitive all the same.

It was also desperately poor. As Smith described the condition of hunters and gatherers in the earliest stage of society in *The Wealth of Nations*, "Universal poverty establishes there universal equality." Unlike later observers, Smith saw no evidence of an "original affluent society" in the early human past. He and his contemporaries largely abandoned the myth of a cornucopian golden age. And while Smith continued to worry—more than is generally acknowledged—about the morally corrupting effects of extensive inequalities in modern commercial society, even sympathizing with

Rousseau's critique to some extent, he regarded prosperity as ample compensation for the crude equality of poverty we had lost.[40]

Others were less sanguine about the tradeoffs involved, but they agreed that the progress of civilization led inexorably to inequalities. As the French author Claude Adrien Helvétius insisted, in recounting his own version of the four-stage theory, "When societies have reached this point of perfection [the development of agriculture], all equality between men will be shattered." The point for those living in commercial societies in the present was to use law and reason to try to bring some degree of equality back. As Helvétius's colleague the Chevalier Louis de Jaucourt, the author of the article on "natural equality" in the great French *Encyclopédie*, emphasized, "In the state of nature men are truly born into equality but do not know how to remain there. Society forces them to lose it, and they only become equal again by laws."[41]

Jaucourt's lines were cribbed almost verbatim from Montesquieu's *Spirit of the Laws* (1748), a book read widely on both sides of the Atlantic. It likewise insisted that primitive equality was a thing of the past. In Montesquieu's view, the only kind of equality that could be recovered at all must be fashioned by law, and in thinking about that prospect, he relied heavily on examples from classical Greece and Rome. Americans did, too. Whereas Christianity provided one set of resources for equality's reinvention, the ancients provided another. Their example loomed large.[42]

Eighteenth-century observers widely believed that the ancients had achieved a recovery of sorts of what human beings had abandoned when they departed their primitive state, refashioning forms of equality that were fit for civil society. To those interested in reinventing equality in the modern world, Greece and Rome served as a rich quarry of materials with which to build.

Of course, there were different Greeces, from Athens to Sparta, just as there were different Romes, from the republic to the principate. European commentators had long culled from them freely, putting them to varied uses. Readers in the eighteenth century did the same. They were particularly drawn to "classical republicanism," that broad tradition that harkened back to antiquity, flowered in the Renaissance, and continued to nourish the seventeenth and eighteenth centuries in Europe and the New World. In truth the name is misleading, for there was no single republicanism, classical or otherwise, just as there was no single classical republic. Eighteenth-century observers found examples to admire in both Greece and Rome and in the traditions of commentary that flowed from them over the centuries, which included a "neo-Roman" as well as a "Greek" tradition of republican thought. Though conceptually distinct, they were freely combined in practice, with important implications for the recovery and reinvention of equality.[43]

From the Greeks, republicans developed a keen sense of the importance of balance and moderation, in power and property alike. The example of Sparta proved instructive in this regard, for everyone in the eighteenth century who had read their Plutarch "knew" that the great lawgiver Lycurgus had fashioned a state of striking equality. Even Talbert, Rousseau's rival for the Dijon prize, confessed that Sparta offered "an image of this equality that we so regret." He alluded to the alleged equality of wealth and land of the Spartan *homoioi*, a widely received understanding of Spartan society prevalent in the eighteenth century. The image cast Sparta as a simple but staunchly egalitarian place, one of the "happy community of goods" and the "perfect equality" of fortunes, as the influential French republican thinker Gabriel Bonnot de Mably put it, forged by the sumptuary laws, land reforms, and redistributions attributed to the great lawgiver.[44]

Other commentators drew from Plato or Aristotle, who both insisted on the importance of balancing extremes of wealth and poverty in a well-run state in keeping with their conceptions of justice. But Aristotle also emphasized, where Plato did not, the importance of the middle classes in balancing extremes. "A city ought to be composed, as far as possible," Aristotle observed in the *Politics*, "of equals and similars; and these are generally the middle classes." The "best political community," he continued, "is formed by citizens of the middle class," who possess a "moderate and sufficient property," and so are able to balance the predatory instincts of rich and poor alike.[45]

Although there were many republican interpreters and admirers of that view in the early modern period—not least the Florentine Niccolò Machiavelli—the most important for eighteenth-century Americans was the Englishman James Harrington. Harrington's 1656 *Commonwealth of Oceana* drew explicitly on Aristotle, as well as the long tradition of Jewish reflection on biblical land law, to make a concerted case for the need to balance power and property in a well-ordered republic. "Equality of estates causeth equality of power," he asserted famously, "and equality of power is the liberty not only of the commonwealth, but of every man." Equality and liberty went hand in hand, a view that the famed American patriot Samuel Adams echoed when he insisted, in the pages of his republican journal, *The Independent Advertiser*, in 1748, that "liberty can never subsist without equality."[46]

The close connection between liberty and equality was a common republican view, and it followed perfectly from Harrington's assertion that the way to balance power in a republic was to balance property. Conversely, where there was imbalance between rich and poor, there was bound to be domination as well as civil strife. "For to make a commonwealth unequal is to divide it into parties," he wrote, "which setteth them at perpetual variance, the one party endeavoring to preserve their eminence and inequality, and the other to attain unto equality." In Harrington's opinion, that is precisely what had happened to the Roman republic, where the rough equality of its founding was gradually eroded, and society descended into the long battle of the orders and the widening chasm between the nobility and the people. The failure of the late republic to enact the agrarian laws proposed by the brothers Tiberius and

Gaius Gracchus, which aimed to redistribute newly conquered lands to the people, marked the republic's downfall.[47]

Harrington's defense of the Gracchi went against the long-standing view that the brothers had furthered Rome's instability by inflaming the appetites of the people through demagoguery. His related proposal, that commonwealths should employ agrarian laws to control the acquisition and distribution of land in an effort to ensure the "balance of justice," was similarly controversial. Even the radical Jacobins Louis Antoine de St. Just and Maximilien Robespierre shuddered at the thought at the time of the French Revolution, voting the death sentence in the spring of 1793 for anyone who dared to propose a *lex agraria*, an agrarian law.[48]

Yet in colonial America, with its plentiful land, its absence of a feudal past, and a more equal distribution of property than anywhere in Europe, the Harringtonian vision of an agrarian republic of modest yeomen flourished. "Harrington has shown that power always follows property," John Adams observed in 1776. "The only possible way, then, of preserving the balance of power on the side of equal liberty and public virtue, is to make the acquisition of land easy to every member of society." Property gave owners a stake in society, and where it was not amassed in huge and disproportionate concentrations, it provided citizens the means to forestall dependence on others. Property ownership, in fact, was widely considered a prerequisite of citizenship itself, and so of the right to vote.[49]

To be sure, the white settlers of America rarely contemplated the confiscation or redistribution of property, at least not among themselves (the lands of the indigenous, of course, were another matter). For those of European origin, property rights were paramount. But unlike in Europe, where the ubiquity of large and settled estates posed a daunting challenge to Harrington's vision, in America there was seemingly enough land to go around. Americans boasted of their small but abundant farms, which seemed to accord with a vision of ancient republican yeomen, each with a plot of his own. European visitors frequently remarked on the same, noting the relative absence in the New World of sprawling aristocratic estates and the miserable hovels of the landless peasantry. Portraits of the kind were often exaggerated and romanticized, it is true. But they were not wholly inaccurate either. As Thomas Jefferson boasted late in life to John Adams, laws passed at his urging at the time of the revolution "abolishing the privilege of Primogeniture, and dividing the lands of intestates," limited the growth of large estates. It was among his proudest achievements, "a foundation laid for a government truly republican," and the "best of all agrarian laws."[50]

Indeed, even after accounting for indentured servants and the enslaved, who owned neither land nor their persons, the level of income inequality in colonial America at the time of the revolution was significantly lower than it is today, and lower, for that matter, than in any other place in the eighteenth-century world for which we have measures. The fund of land that could be appropriated from indigenous inhabitants ensured that the white European settlers had plenty to go around. The tragic irony, however, is that this early American equality was built upon a foundation of predation and theft. As one scholar rightly observes, "It was farmland taken from Native Americans that became the most significant source of American equality, both as a reality and as an ideal."[51]

The particular circumstances of the New World, then, favored the reception of Harrington and his insight that any just and stable commonwealth be balanced by a rough equality of property. Americans could find further support for that belief in the writings of Gerrard Winstanley, John Lilburne, and the Levellers, or in reflections on Jewish landholding and Jubilee laws of a kind that had influenced Harrington himself. They also found support in the writings of authors popular in America, who had read Harrington closely and incorporated his views, such as Montesquieu and Mably. Although Montesquieu himself doubted that large modern states could successfully adopt the forms of the comparatively small ancient republics, and was himself in many ways an apologist for inequality, he nonetheless famously observed that virtue in the republic was the "love of equality," and that "real equality" in democracies was the "soul of the state." Pointing out how ancient legislators, such as Lycurgus and Romulus, had "divided up the land equally" in small shares, he emphasized how important frugality and balance were in Sparta, Athens, and early Rome.[52]

Modern republicans borrowed freely from such eclectic sources to fashion what has been described as America's "lost" or "forgotten" egalitarian tradition. It was of a piece with the criticism of the vanity of royal and aristocratic privilege. "Pomp, titles, and wealth are means and devices to make the world think that they who possess them are superior in merit to those that want them," the British commonwealthmen Thomas Gordon and John Trenchard declared. Their serialized *Cato's Letters* were widely read in the colonies, and they made clear that an appeal to superiority on the basis of ancestry, wealth, or title was an appeal to prejudice, redolent of false pride. "That nature has made men equal," they insisted, "we know and feel, and when people come to think otherwise, there is no excess of folly and superstition which they may not be brought to practice."[53]

Trenchard and Gordon's republican critique, with its Protestant suspicion of pride, was well received in the colonies, where the absence of a hereditary nobility only emboldened attacks on its trappings and pretensions. In Thomas Paine's view, opposition to blood aristocracy and the hereditary privileges of kings was part of the "common sense" of the country. And as the historian Sophia Rosenfeld has shown, a belief in common sense was widely shared. Adult men possessed the modicum of good judgment necessary to make good decisions for themselves. They needn't bow and scrape before the titled. "For all men being originally equals," Paine continued, "no one by birth could have a right to set up his own family in perpetual preference to all others." John Adams agreed. The very idea of a peerage,

whether hereditary or for life, was antithetical to public sentiment. "Nothing could be more abhorrent to the general Sense
of America." Thomas Jefferson likewise pilloried until the end of
his life what he called the "tinsel-aristocracy," linking his proud
efforts to pass agrarian laws to the desire to take "the axe to the
root of the Pseudo-aristocracy."[54]

Yet fears of the aristocratic hydra persisted, with Americans
continually sounding "the alarm bell of aristocracy," as George
Washington put it, to better guard the republic. In the 1780s, an
effort to create a hereditary club for military officers who had served
in the American Revolution, the Society of the Cincinnati, named
after the famed Roman general, provoked a widespread outcry.
"An order of peerage may do very well under the petty princes of
Germany," one critic, writing under the name of Cassius, noted in
response. "Yet in America it is incompatible with our freedom."
Samuel Adams declared the effort "disgustful to common feeling."
With good reason did the United States Constitution specify in its
emoluments clause (Article I, Section 9, Clause 8) that "no Title of
Nobility shall be granted by the United States."[55]

But if Americans agreed in dismissing what Adams called the
"artificial aristocracy" and Jefferson the "pseudo-aristoi," he and
others were more confident about the genuine article. Ideas about
a "natural aristocracy," in fact, were central to republican reflection
going all the way back to the ancients, and republicans in the seventeenth and eighteenth centuries invoked the term and the concept
repeatedly. For all his talk of equal power and estate, Harrington
was adamant in his belief in the existence of a "natural aristocracy
diffused by God through the whole body of mankind," whose job it
would be to lead. Indeed, the very purpose of equalizing conditions
was not only to ensure that no one man could buy or dominate
another, on the understanding that the possession of property
was the bedrock of liberty, but even more to allow these natural
aristocrats to compete on equal terms. The point of republics, as
the Greeks and Romans alike had insisted, was to allow talent to

flourish and the best men to rule. Remove special privilege and specious title, and the true aristocracy of mankind would emerge to take its rightful place in society. Whereas Paine mocked the nobility of the Old World as a "no-ability," a genuine equality of opportunity would reveal the true aristocracy of talent, merit, and virtue always hidden in humanity's midst. Alexander Hamilton, whom Adams described as "the bastard brat of a Scotch Pedler [*sic*]," was convinced that "there are strong minds in every walk of life that will rise superior to the disadvantages of station, and will command the tribute due to their merit. The door ought to be open equally to all." And he firmly believed that "while property continues to be pretty equally divided, and a considerable share of information pervades the community, the tendency of the people's suffrage will be to elevate merit even from obscurity."[56]

Hamilton did, it is true, warn elsewhere that, as "riches increase and accumulate in a few hands . . . the tendency of things will be to depart from the republican standard." But for the time being, at least, the relative equality of the republic helped ensure that voters identified and rewarded the genuine best. David Ramsay, the South Carolina historian and member of the Continental Congress, singled out that same dynamic when he observed, of the advantages of American independence on its second anniversary in 1778, that "all offices lie open to men of merit, of whatever condition," and that the "reins of state may be held by the son of the poorest man, if possessed of abilities equal to the important position." By drawing as widely as possible from its pool of talent, and granting opportunity on equal terms, Americans would reveal the natural aristocrats hidden among them.[57]

It is true that commentators disagreed as to whether the attributes of the natural aristocracy were acquired or innate, the product of learning, tenacity, and experience, or rather of an inborn genius or gift of nature that was there from the start. The controversy ran right through the eighteenth century. One pole tended to agree with the Scots David Hume and Adam Smith, both closely read and admired in America. Hume pointed out "how nearly equal all men are in their bodily force, and even in their mental powers and faculties, 'ere cultivated by education." And Smith famously insisted, in the *Wealth of Nations*, that "the difference between the most dissimilar characters, between a philosopher and a common street porter, for example, seems to arise not so much from nature, as from habit, custom, and education." The "difference of natural talents in different men," Smith claimed, was, "in reality, much less than we are aware of."[58]

John Adams, for his part, waffled on the question. At times he could sound very much like Smith, emphasizing that "genius" was the product of circumstances and freely scattered throughout the world, evident even in those "planting corn, freighting oysters, and killing deer." At other times, however, he stressed the prerogatives of birth. In that respect, he was not unlike his intellectual hero, the Roman statesman Cicero, who was never really clear whether natural aristocrats were born or made. In either case, however, the final outcome was apparent. The cream of society would rise to the top. As Adams asked rhetorically, "Was there, or will there ever be, a nation whose individuals were all equal in natural and acquired qualities, in virtues, talents, and riches? The answer of all mankind is in the negative."[59]

Adams's assumption that inequalities of outcome, despite equality of rights, were inevitable was widely shared. The statesman, legal scholar, and eventual associate justice of the Supreme Court James Wilson put the matter succinctly: "When we say, that all men are [created] equal, we mean not to apply this equality to their virtues, their talents, their dispositions, or their acquirements. In all these respects, there is, and it is fit for the purposes of society that there should be, great inequality among men." Wilson, it should be noted, was the architect of the infamous three-fifths compromise that counted the enslaved as "three-fifths" of a person for the purposes of apportioning seats to the House of Representatives. We might say ruefully that he knew a thing or two about inequality.

But his point here was actually less controversial than his compromise. The equality of creation did not imply equality of outcome for eighteenth-century Americans any more than it did for Roman Stoics or the Christians of earlier eras. And the language of merit provided a convenient justification of the gap, just as it did for Cicero. If human beings really were equally endowed at birth, then the differences that opened up between them, whether of status, wealth, or political power, could be plausibly presented as fitting and deserved. They were to the benefit of society, Wilson averred, encouraging striving and competition with reward.[60]

By contrast, those most concerned to ensure equality of outcome in the centuries to follow could be even more insistent on the inequalities of birth. For if competition between human beings was not equal from the start, then equity demanded that they be given according to their needs, not their abilities, righting, as it were, nature's wrong. For all his talk of the equality of our distant ancestors, Rousseau effectively took that line. Although what he called "natural or physical inequality," consisting in the "difference of age, health, bodily strength, and qualities of mind or soul" between human beings, meant little in the state of nature, those natural differences exercised a kind of multiplier effect in society. "Thus it is that natural inequality imperceptibly manifests itself together with inequality occasioned by the socialization process," he wrote. "Thus it is that the differences among men, developed by those of circumstances, make themselves more noticeable, more permanent in their effect." For Rousseau, the point of the social contract would be to correct for and to restrain those differences, both natural and unnatural, bringing about a "moral or political" equality in a just society. Inequality based on merit was for him as indefensible as inequality of rank, power, or wealth.[61]

Most Americans dismissed Rousseau's position outright. In a new world and new society bursting with opportunities, they embraced the meritocratic position wholeheartedly, along with its inevitable consequences. For meritocratic equality not only tolerated and produced distinctions in status and reward, it honored them. Equality begat inequality, producing *meritocracy*, a new order in society, which is to say, a new hierarchy. The same language of merit that could be used to such devastating effect against inherited privilege or aristocratic title could thus be put to the defense of the endowments of natural aristocrats and all those who simply did better than others in the game of life. Not all equals would be equal.

It is true that a few farsighted observers, including Patrick Henry (he of "Give me liberty or give me death!" fame), might worry about the emergence of a new "aristocracy of the rich." Anti-Federalist opponents of the Constitution feared the concentration of power in the hands of a new elite, while some Federalists, such as Adams, fretted about the dangers of oligarchy. Meanwhile, "everyday Americans," who constituted a different type of "revolutionary founder," showed themselves ready to challenge the pretensions of founding elites from below. They pushed for an expanded democracy in language that could take on a hard egalitarian edge.[62]

All that notwithstanding, intense concerns about the great disparities in wealth and reward that might be generated by the unimpeded *agon* of competition were still largely on the horizon. In the precapitalist vision of eighteenth-century republicans, a language of frugality and moderation prevailed. And while that meant curbing luxurious excess, it also meant avoiding what Montesquieu called, on the example of the ancients, the "spirit of extreme equality," in which "everyone commands, or in which no one is commanded." The "spirit of true equality," by contrast, involved "obeying and commanding only our equals," along with the recognition that "men are equal only as citizens." Where the spirit of extreme equality went astray was by extending that principle to everything in the mistaken belief that men were equal as men and "magistrates, senators, judges, fathers, husbands, or as masters." As in the ancient view, true equality seen in this light was simply another way to organize hierarchy. Indeed, it served as its very platform and basis, allowing the best men to come forth and to lead.[63]

That these men should be men was widely assumed. It is true that the American Revolution "opened up a brief window of opportunity" for women, and also that, in its aftermath, an Abigail Adams or a Judith Sargent Murray might, like Mary Wollstonecraft, assert the equal capacity of women in matters of the mind, dismissing as so much prejudice the contrary claims of the majority, and doing so with brio. The publication of Wollstonecraft's *Vindication of the Rights of Women* in 1792 prompted a heated discussion in the United States, opening the door for a relatively small if vocal group of women, who sought to vindicate those rights in practice, to set about "negotiating equality" in small circles of mixed company. Wollstonecraft's own husband, William Godwin, did the same back in London in the 1790s in the mixed company of radical women. And as we will see in the next chapter, they were not alone.[64]

Yet, however actively American women might involve themselves in the vital life of their communities—in the home or on the farm, in the study or on the streets, in field hospitals, meeting houses, churches, or even, briefly, in the state of New Jersey, by voting at the ballot box—they seldom were accorded, or even accorded themselves, the full measure of their due. The Founding Fathers, as the name implies, were patriarchs, their social contract a sexual contract, their republican fraternity that of a band of brothers. All their ancient inheritance reinforced that belief, as did their Christian learning. When they said that all men were created equal, they meant only men.[65]

And what of men of color, and those who were enslaved? One of the most affecting images of the eighteenth century posed that very question. Produced and distributed as a popular medallion by Josiah Wedgwood, the image was ordered originally to serve as the seal of the Quaker-led Society for Effecting the Abolition of the Slave Trade in London in 1787. And while the depiction of

"Am I Not a Man and a Brother?" Anti-slavery medallion, produced at the Wedgwood Manufactory, Staffordshire, England, 1786–1787. Photograph © 2023 Museum of Fine Arts, Boston. Bequest of Mrs. Richard Baker.

a supplicant and kneeling Black man in manacle and chains may strike the modern viewer as projecting an image of submission, it was intended to appeal to eighteenth-century sentiment, fostering a sense of universal brotherhood. Were not Black men, too, created equal by God? Were not all human beings God's children?

Quakers, unlike so many others, answered in the affirmative in the eighteenth century, upholding the truth of the Christian proposition that we *are* our brothers' keepers. There were Quakers in Philadelphia, the city of brotherly love, and there were readers of Buffon there, too, as elsewhere, who were more discerning than Thomas Jefferson. After having read his *Notes on the State of Virginia* and noting its departure from Buffon's account of the likeness of original creation, David Ramsay wrote to the author of the Declaration of Independence, "I admire your generous indignation at slavery; but think you have depressed the negroes too low. I believe all mankind to be originally the same and only diversified by accidental circumstances." Ramsay referred to the now infamous passage in which Jefferson broached "as a suspicion only" the thought that "the blacks, whether originally a distinct race, or made distinct by time and circumstances, are inferior to the whites in the endowments both of body and mind." That "suspicion" would go on to receive "confirmation" by what passed for the cutting edge of racial science in Europe and America in the nineteenth century. But in the eighteenth century, as Jefferson acknowledged, there was still considerable doubt.[66]

Did that doubt not trouble him? And if so, how did he and other enlightened Americans in the eighteenth century overcome the seeming contradiction, so apparent to us today, between the proposition that "all men are created equal" and the exclusion of men who were black or brown, or, as Jefferson put it, "red"? The simple answer to the first question is that Jefferson, like many others, most certainly was bothered by doubt. And not only because he was the father of mixed-raced children, or because men of color took pains to assert their own equality in the eighteenth century by word and by deed. But above all because the proposition that "all men are created equal" was, as Jefferson well knew, one of the harmonizing sentiments of the day, a Christian commonplace for centuries, and one newly reaffirmed by the modern monogenetic science of Buffon. Ramsay's was far from the only hostile reaction to Jefferson's lines—Federalists even accused him of blasphemy! Jefferson was opinionated and thick-skinned. But he knew enough to know that to deny Black men the original equality of creation was a proposition that admitted of doubt.[67]

But as for the seeming contradiction, it was no contradiction at all—at least not when considered in context and in terms of the materials with which equality in the eighteenth century was reinvented and put to work. The proposition that "all men are created equal" had aged in Stoic philosophy, Roman law, and Christian theology in the fullest acknowledgment of slavery. Manifold exclusions had always been central to both these and the republican traditions upon which Jefferson and the Founders drew. In the eighteenth century, further conceptual resources were developed—including Buffonian science, the progress of civilization in conjectural history, and theories of merit and the rule of the best—that reinforced the inequalities of the world and further reconciled them with the equal creation of men. A world where all men were created equal was a world where some nations prospered and others lagged behind, where some accumulated wealth, status, power, and prestige by virtue and talent, while others did not, where men presided over women and masters over slaves, and where natural aristocrats vied to replace the aristocrats of old. It was a world, in short, that created inequality from equality itself.

Which takes us back to that ubiquitous symbol of eighteenth-century equality, the triangle of the Masons, and Simitière's gloss of "E pluribus unum" for the new nation's brothers and friends. The Masonic lodges, in fact, in both the New World and the Old, were central laboratories for the age's reinvention of equality. Cosmopolitan in their conception, like Simitière's original proposal for the Great Seal, they took in different peoples of the peopling sort in urban centers throughout the Atlantic world. And yet, with only some exceptions, in France, Germany, and the Hague, those fraternities were, as the word implies, overwhelmingly male, and exclusively so in the United States. And although there were Black Masonic lodges in the eighteenth century, the most famous of them organized in Boston by the revolutionary Prince Hall, the brethren seldom mixed.

People of different religious denominations might join—religious toleration was a respected Masonic value—but they were almost always of Christian background, if not always of unwavering Christian belief. And while social standing varied to some extent—in England and on the Continent the nobility joined in considerable numbers—on the whole brothers were of the middling to prosperous sort, men of property and some wealth who were, or who aspired to be, social betters.[68]

Yet within the relatively circumscribed confines of the Masonic Temple or Hall, brothers helped to fashion a new order for the ages, building like the great builders of the pyramids and the cathedrals

Brother Prince Hall, founder of the first Black Masonic lodge in the Americas. Hall penned a petition to the Massachusetts State Legislature in 1777, signed by other free Black men, demanding emancipation of the enslaved and appealing to the natural rights "bestowed equalley on all mankind." The New York Public Library / Art Resource, New York.

from whom they claimed to descend. As one of Masonry's leading historians affirms, "Within the selected and closed 'temple,' masonic men [were] among the first Europeans to be deemed equals" and to self-consciously negotiate their (in)equality. That was true in America as well. The carpenter's level that brothers wore on their breast served them well, for in the confines of the lodge, "all Masons, are as Brethren upon the same Level," as James Anderson's *Constitutions of the Free-masons* (1723) declared. The work, one of the oldest of the Masonic constitutions, was first published in London, but it was reprinted in 1734 in Philadelphia by Benjamin Franklin, the very year he became a grand master in the city's St. John's Lodge.[69]

Despite his elevated title, Franklin knew that under the watchful eye of providence, members were to treat one another as equals, putting aside differences of status, rank, origin, and power that prevailed elsewhere. Working together, they drafted constitutions and rules of law, they voted and debated, and they put in place the values and norms of a civil society. In short, as another early Masonic constitution put it, this one from France, the lodges were places where "the sweetness of Equality, of support, of mutual aid," could be acknowledged and lived.[70]

Masons looked after one another in networks providing insurance and charity. And they constantly invoked the language of brotherhood and fraternal friendship, using alcohol in considerable quantities to strengthen the bond. It is altogether fitting that America's first Masonic lodge was founded in a tavern, the Bunch of Grapes in Boston in 1733. As in England, where early Masons often met in pubs, in America the brothers raised glasses and drank lengthy toasts, with hands draped about each other's shoulders, singing boisterous songs.[71]

That image of backslapping male bonding evokes the modern American collegiate fraternity as much as the fraternal order of the eighteenth century. But it is a useful reminder that the Masons, like any other private club, operated from the beginning according to a dynamic of exclusion and inclusion. The language of fraternity and friendship reinforced that dynamic, marking off differences from those outside while also masking, in the suspended disbelief of the lodge itself, those within.[72]

We might, it is true, ask just how suspended that belief ever really was. In Europe, historians have argued, rank was seldom truly forgotten. The elaborate hierarchies of the Masons, moreover, with their ascending grades and orders culminating in the rank of "worshipful master," reinforced a language of distinction even as they denied it. One American Mason put it well, writing that the order "admits of no rank except the priority of merit, and its only aristocracy is the nobility of virtue."[73]

One man's merit can seem another man's privilege. And that was no doubt how it came to appear to many who stood outside the temple walls. The order of brothers, in the end, was an exclusive club: not all could gain admission. And what was true of the Masons was true of the nation at large. To be admitted as a member, one had to belong. Working out just who precisely that was would prove an enormously difficult task, one that is still ongoing. But in the eighteenth century, many, indeed the great majority, were in society but not fully of it. And while that realization led some to fight for inclusion as full citizens, contesting the equality of the equals, others opted out. When the Black brothers of Prince Hall's African Masonic Lodge were rebuffed in their efforts to join their white brethren as friends, they were told by a sympathetic white clergyman that "the truth is, [the whites] are *ashamed* of being on *equality* with the blacks." Hall turned his energy to returning his people to Africa, where, as he said, people of color could finally "live among equals."[74]

Many of even the most enlightened and well-intentioned whites in the United States were coming to agree, embracing movements to "repatriate" Blacks to Africa in an effort to solve the dilemmas of slavery at home. Much the same logic was extended to Native Americans, who, like other people of color, were segregated when the difficult work of integration broke down. On reservations they could be, at best, like African Americans in Africa, "separate but equal." But they would not be fellow citizens or brothers in the evolving order of the United States, and they would not be friends.[75]

7

LEVELING

The Scythe of Equality and the French Revolution

The French revolutionaries contrived many names for their heady contraption. *La guillotine* they called it eponymously at first, after the man who proposed that it be adopted and built by the French National Assembly, Dr. Joseph-Ignace Guillotin. That was October 1789. But the machinery of government moved slowly. The first working prototype was only erected and put to use in the spring of 1792, at which point observers grew more creative. The "national cleaver," they dubbed it, or "the national razor," and then, as France proclaimed itself a republic that September, and in the following January sent its most celebrated victim, King Louis XVI, to the blade, it became the "axe of the people," the "axe of the law."[1]

To one of its more enthusiastic proponents, the radical journalist Jacques-René Hébert, the instrument's power to mete out justice and retribution instilled a kind of holy terror. "Saint Guillotine" was his innovative term for the device: punisher of traitors, keeper of the law. And though Hébert was an atheist, who would himself be offered in sacrifice to the saint in 1794, others seem to have shared his quasi-religious awe for the invention, invoking it as the "celestial guillotine," the "holy guillotine," or even praying to it in a kind of sinister litany: "Saint Guillotine, protectress of patriots, pray for us! . . . Holy Guillotine, deliver us from tyrants!"[2]

"Natural Equality Among the Three Orders." Anonymous engraving, 1789. The banner proclaims "Tremble Aristocracy," and the severed heads cut down by the scythe back up the warning. Bibliothèque Nationale de France.

"The Dagger of Patriots is the Axe of the Law." Engraving by Jean Baptiste Louvion, Paris, 1793 or 1794. The caption at the bottom reads, "Traitors, look and tremble, [the axe] will not cease its activity until you all have lost your lives." Bibliothèque Nationale de France.

Yet of all the labels to appear during the French Revolution, one is most revealing, both of the guillotine's initial conception and of its lasting associations. To enemies and friends alike, it was known as the "Scythe of Equality." Leveler of kings and aristocrats, it struck at pretension, cutting men and women down to size. It was a weapon of the weak who made themselves strong, aiding the lowly in their efforts to raise themselves up, punishing those who dared to rise above the rest. As a popular ditty of the revolutionary shock troops, the *sans-culottes*, intoned in 1793, echoing, with violent overtones, Jesus's call in Matthew 23:12 and Luke 14:11 to humble the proud and exalt the lowly:

We must shorten the giants	Il faut raccourcir les géants
And raise the small to their heights	Et rendre les petits plus grands
When we are all at the same level,	Tous à la même hauteur,
Then we will have true happiness.	Voilà le vrai bonheur.

Niveler (to level) and *niveleur* (leveler) were neologisms in French. They appeared at the time of the revolution in a nod, initially, to the hedge-trimming English Levellers of the seventeenth century, but with precedents stretching all the way back to the Old Testament and the thinking of the Romans, for whom the verb *aequo/aequare* meant both "to level" and to "equalize." But the French terms soon took on distinct associations of their own. As a dictionary of revolutionary neologisms put it in 1796, a "leveler" was a "synonym for a planer, an equalizer, a guillotiner, or a Jacobin [*aplanisseur, égaliseur, guillotineur, jacobin*]." There were other ways besides the guillotine to level the plane, of course, other ways to "render equal." But the scythe captured nicely what both contemporaries and posterity alike considered the process at its most extreme.[3]

Admittedly, to invoke the guillotine as an image of equality may seem perverse, as if one were seeking to reduce the revolution's highest ideals to the bloodshed that accompanied it. There are, after all, less gruesome images from which to choose. In their iconographic enthusiasm, the revolutionaries experimented with a great many of these, representing equality as a chaste young woman, the "patroness of the French"; as a voluptuous goddess, replete with the cornucopia of bounty or the *fasces* of justice; or as a simple worker, intended to replace kings and queens on the chess boards and playing cards of old. The equilateral triangle with the carpenter's plumb, moreover, which had captivated Freemasons across the Atlantic world in the eighteenth century, continued to be invoked throughout the French Revolution as a ubiquitous symbol of leveling equality, the tool by which uneven surfaces could be made just and true. It was picked up as well in the French colony of Saint-Domingue, where the French Revolution spread to become a mighty revolution of its own. The formerly enslaved and mixed-raced people there asserted their place as equals in the world, and in doing so gave birth to the first successful slave revolt in history

"The Patroness of the French," 1794. Engraving by Pierre Guillaume Alexandre Beljambe. Equality presented as a young woman, with the equilateral triangle and plumb bob. Bibliothèque Nationale de France.

and the independent nation of Haiti. Finally, the French *tricolore*, the three-colored flag of red, white, and blue, could readily evoke the middle term of the great revolutionary trinity, *liberté, égalité*, and *fraternité*. Lily-white was chosen when the flag was conceived in 1789 as the color of the Bourbon kings; red and blue represented the colors of the city of Paris. But after Louis XVI was sent to the scythe in that great symbolic act of leveling, his beheading, the royal color went out of fashion. The white of the flag, some made haste to suggest, represented equality in its purity, while liberty and fraternity waved with red and blue.[4]

Equality then, as ever, was multivalent. It was also essentially contested, not least by the revolution's more determined opponents, who did in fact seek to stain the revolutionaries' highest ideals in blood. Depicting revolutionary attacks on hierarchical privilege as a threat to the social order, they implicated claims

Playing card showing equality in the image of a free Black man, 1790s. Other cards in the same series depict ordinary workers and citizens as equality. Bibliothèque Nationale de France.

to equality directly in the violence from the start. The scythe of equality, in their view, was luridly reminiscent of the figure of death who had haunted the European imaginary with his iconic blade since the Middle Ages. The guillotine brought new meaning to the old Christian adage that death was the great equalizer. And it made earlier attempts at leveling seem mere child's play by comparison. Subsequent understandings of equality would be profoundly marked by the turn to violence, as well as by the conclusion that many drew that liberty and equality were necessarily opposed. As Edmund Burke observed already in 1791, "Those who seek to level never equalize." Coercion, in his view, was a constant, and so the inevitable companion of egalitarian movements, which merely sought to replace old hierarchies with new forms of domination and power.[5]

More so than its other revolutionary representations, then, the image of equality as the scythe of Dr. Guillotin made a powerful and lasting impression. In a manner of speaking, it stuck in the head. But if the image of the guillotine captures well a certain counterrevolutionary portrayal of revolutionary equality—militant, vengeful, leveling down to the stump—it does not reduce to it. For also evident in its gleaming surface is a reflection of the fierce resolve and determined idealism of the revolutionaries themselves, who did not flinch from shedding blood in pursuit of their aims, and who knew that remaking the world would not happen of its own, without opposition from the lords of old.

That remaking had a destructive side, to be sure, but a constructive one as well. Observers must take care to not let the one occlude the other, lest the glint of the guillotine's blade blind us. For only by considering the uplift and the cutting down together can we fully appreciate what was most extraordinary, and at the same time most ordinary, in eighteenth-century terms, about the conceptions of equality that were entertained and put into practice in France and its former colony of Saint-Domingue amid the revolutionary upheavals that began in 1789. And only by considering them together can we understand how equality was severed in the public mind from liberty, its age-old companion and friend.

When the good doctor Guillotin assumed the speaker's rostrum in the French National Assembly in October 1789 to propose a broad package of legal and penal reforms, he did so with the enlightened authority of a physician and experimental scientist who had collaborated with the likes of Benjamin Franklin and the chemist Antoine Lavoisier. He also possessed the credentials of a longtime Freemason. He was the worshipful master of the "Lodge of Brotherly Concord" in Paris, no less, and a member of the famed "Lodge of Nine Sisters," where he had delivered an oration at the induction of Voltaire in 1778, while brother Franklin supported the great philosophe's arm. An elected representative of the Third Estate, Guillotin applauded the conversion of the Estates General into a legislative body tasked with writing a new constitution for France in June 1789. He welcomed the storming of the Bastille in July, the renunciation of feudal and seigneurial privileges on the

The three estates (clergy, aristocracy, and people) are leveled by a figure holding both a carpenter's level and the *fasces*, a common revolutionary symbol signifying equality and fraternity, 1789. Musée Carnavalet, Paris.

night of August 4, and the Declaration of the Rights of Man and of the Citizen several weeks later. The latter document declared, in its very first article, that "men are born free and equal in rights," while Article 6 made clear that "all citizens" were equal in the eyes of the law and that "all public dignities, offices, and employment" would be open on the basis of ability alone. The only cause for distinctions among citizens would henceforth be "virtue and talent" or the needs of society itself ("common utility").[6]

All that was very much in keeping with ideas about competition, merit, and civic equality that had circulated in the American republic and the Atlantic world in the eighteenth century. Together with further provisions for ensuring the sanctity of property ("an inviolable and sacred right") and the freedom of speech, belief, and action, the liberties and equalities spelled out in the French Declaration were in fact broadly consistent with those enshrined in the documents of the American Revolution. The correspondence is hardly coincidental. Not only did the Declaration of Rights of Man and of the Citizen partake of common Enlightenment assumptions, but its drafters consulted closely with American advisers, including Thomas Jefferson, who was on hand as US ambassador to France in 1789, and American precedents, such as the sundry state constitutions and bills of rights drafted in the New World. And while there were undoubtedly important differences—not least the French Declaration's universal pretensions and scope—there were also enough similarities that observers on both sides of the Atlantic could see the light of the American Revolution shining brightly in France. The same spark that had "kindled a blaze" in the New World, leaving "despotism in ashes," was now, the Welsh-born Presbyterian minister and moral philosopher Richard Price observed, "warm[ing] and illuminat[ing] France."[7]

Certainly that common light could be detected in Guillotin's proposal, which shone with the reason and humanity of the eighteenth century. The doctor himself did not invent the instrument created in his name—the honor belongs to the eighteenth-century

French surgeon Antoine Louis. Nor, ironically enough, was Guillotin a proponent of capital punishment. But if people must be condemned to death, he reasoned, let it be equal and humane. In the Old Regime, only aristocrats possessed the privilege of a quick and painless death for capital crimes: the executioner severed the heads of the convicted in a single blow with a sword. But in the New Regime there would be no privileges and private laws. "The same offenses will be punished in the same manner whatever the rank or estate of the guilty party," Guillotin affirmed. And "in all cases where the law pronounces the penalty of death, the punishment will be the same. The criminal will have his head cut off." As Guillotin's colleague in the National Assembly, Monsieur Guillaume, observed in support of the legislation, its overwhelming purpose was "to render men equal before the law, as they are in the eyes of the Supreme Being." The guillotine, quite literally, was an instrument conceived to strike down privilege and level up the lowly so that all might die with the same dignity.[8]

If equality could be brought in this way to the end of life, so too should it grace the beginning. In March 1790, the French, like their counterparts in North America, took steps to abolish primogeniture and the "unequal division [of estates] on the basis of the quality of persons," so that the children of families would not automatically be treated unequally in birth and inheritance. The provision was extended to women the following year. In June 1790, the revolutionaries abolished hereditary nobility, outlawing the use of titles and aristocratic distinctions, a practice which, as the liberal noble Charles de Lameth acknowledged, "offends the equality that forms the basis of our constitution." The move was of a piece with legislation passed several months earlier extending the full rights of citizenship to Protestants, and with them to actors and executioners, previously barred on account of the common indignity of their professions. Further decrees, passed in 1790 and 1791, granted Jews of Sephardic and then Ashkenazi origin equality as citizens of the nation.[9]

In the one set of cases, the revolutionaries "leveled downward," removing special privileges and private laws that granted higher standing to the well born; in the other, they "leveled up," raising those who had been discriminated against to the equal status of citizens. As one of the most important revolutionary newspapers, the *Revolutions de Paris*, proclaimed on its weekly masthead from its very first issue, published just two days before the taking of the Bastille, "The Great only appear great because we are kneeling. Let's stand up!" The revolution aimed to help people to their feet. It was a summons to rise.[10]

Of course, there were exceptions. If the measures outlined above were broadly consistent with similar laws passed in the American republic, the French revolutionaries' early understanding of equality was "typical" in another respect. Bound up in a dynamic of inclusion and exclusion, it did not apply equally to all.

That was evident from as early as January 1789, when the abbé Emmanuel-Joseph Sieyès, in the single most influential pamphlet of the revolution, *What Is the Third Estate?*, likened the two privileged orders of the First and Second Estates, the clergy and the aristocracy, to a kind of parasite or "malignant tumor" on the body politic that would have to be "neutralized" to allow the body to live. A member of the clergy, Sieyès was by rights a member of the First Estate himself. But he renounced that privilege to stand with the Third Estate, the majority of the people. The other two orders, he charged, saw themselves as a "race apart." The accusation echoed an assertion Sieyès had made in his very first published work, the *Essay on Privileges* of 1788, where he noted that "the privileged class look upon themselves as another species of beings." Those who claimed to be higher than ordinary humanity must renounce such pretensions or be excised from the nation as enemies of the people.[11]

Sieyès was quick to broach other exclusions, limiting the "equal" rights of women, children, and foreigners, along with those of beggars, vagabonds, and the propertyless poor, to say nothing of "domestic servants, or anyone dependent on a master," which is to say the enslaved. And while he might castigate aristocrats and members of the clergy for thinking themselves a race apart, elsewhere he speculated on the numerous gradations of reason that divided humanity into different races and types. He even considered, in an extraordinary early fantasy of state-sponsored eugenics, the possibility of breeding a new species of anthropomorphic beings, somewhere between humans and apes, to free French workers of the manual labor that in his view degraded them to the level of "human beasts." As one pioneering scholar, William Nelson, has put it, "new citizens," in Sieyès's vision, would require "new slaves."[12]

In the meantime, Sieyès took it for granted that "political liberty, like civil liberty, has its limits." The thought would form the basis of the National Assembly's crucial decision, in late September 1789, to distinguish between "active" citizens, who had the right to vote and hold office, and "passive" citizens, who were merely subject to the law. The distinction was based on gender (all women were categorized as passive) along with income and wealth: the law required that citizens meet a minimum tax threshold to vote, and a still higher one to serve as electors or to hold office. The latter group constituted only about seventy-two thousand in a country of close to twenty-eight million.[13]

The point of these observations is not to stand in condemnation of the eighteenth century for falling short of the values of the twenty-first. Indeed, by the standards of the time, the French voting law was inclusive, extending suffrage to just over half the male population. The point, rather, is to draw attention to a dynamic that we have seen play out repeatedly: the assertion of equality invariably depends upon assumptions of inequality, and most often generates new inequalities in the process.

In Sieyès's case, equality was ultimately linked to the capacity for reason and virtue, a capacity that he believed was dependent on cultivation through education and the enlightened leisure afforded by sufficient wealth. Those could be expanded, certainly, but where they were not, palpable distinctions between human beings remained. The passive citizens he associated with the uneducated multitude were effectively, in his view, "instruments of production" or "working machines," as he put it in his copious notes on the subject. He believed they were incapable of the rational reflection necessary to conduct social and political affairs.[14]

In a candid moment in *What Is the Third Estate?*, Sieyès commented that, "in general, men always have a strong liking for reducing everything superior to them to a state of equality; in this they display themselves as *philosophers*. The word becomes odious to them only when they notice that their inferiors have the same principles." Sieyès, by that criterion, was a philosopher. For although he punctured the pretensions of the First and Second Estates to rule by virtue of their spiritual condition or aristocratic descent, he put in place other criteria that could be used to draw distinctions with those "inferiors" claiming equality from below. If, as one authority observed, "the equality for which the century showed a predilection was that based on the presence of reason in every human individual," Sieyès denied its full development to wide swaths of the population.[15]

The move highlights the precarity of establishing human equality on any trait—whether reason, as in Sieyès case, or virtue, sanctity, or good standing before the law—that admits of gradation or degree. For that allows "philosophers" to draw distinctions between those who have more or less, establishing "degrees of humanity" in the common human family. The eighteenth century was good at drawing such distinctions, and separating by degree.[16]

The case of women during the French Revolution illustrates well how humanity, and human equality, can be spliced. Bold voices for centuries had entertained the thought that women were fully men's equals in their capacity for reason, echoing the sentiments of pioneers such as Christine de Pizan or Marie Le Jars de Gournay, whose *De l'égalité des hommes et des femmes* (1622) made that case explicitly. But it was the late seventeenth-century Cartesian philosopher and cleric François Poulain de la Barre who grounded the case philosophically. The mind, Poulain asserted, had no sex. His assertion and the Cartesian reasoning behind it were picked up in the succeeding decades in an Enlightenment philosophical literature, and given expression in works such as *Woman Not Inferior to Man: Or, A Short and Modest Vindication of the Natural Right of the Fair-Sex to a Perfect Equality of Power, Dignity, and Esteem, with the Men* (London, 1739), attributed to Lady Mary Wortley Montagu, or the anonymous *Female Rights Vindicated: Or the Equality of the Sexes Morally and Physically Proved* (London, 1758). The titles of such works alone spoke for their convictions, and together they testify to an important feminist current in eighteenth-century thought. These writers critiqued the strictures of institutionalized marriage, pressed the necessity of women's education, and pointed out the "civilizing" role of women in society.[17]

And yet, as a wealth of scholarship has also demonstrated, incipient assertions of the equality between men and women were countered by new, and equally modern, medical, physiological, and biopsychological claims alleging their essential difference. The cutting edge of eighteenth-century science, in fact, particularly in its second half, aimed to show how sex permeated not only the mind, but every "bone, muscle, nerve, and vein" of the body, yielding accounts that emphasized fundamental distinctions between men and women, even when they counseled complementarity.[18]

Such medical and physiological arguments were reinforced by broader cultural claims, notably those of Jean-Jacques Rousseau, who, for all his passionate writing on behalf of the equality of men, developed a stark contrast between the sexes in his later work, after earlier defending the equality of the sexes. Together with an evolving republican tradition, which emphasized masculine virtue and the male-dominated public sphere, Rousseau's thinking provided the blueprints for an ideology of separate spheres, in which women were consigned to the domestic realm and men charged with responsibility for business and public affairs. It is with good reason that the prominent early feminist Mary Wollstonecraft targeted Rousseau in particular in her *Vindication of the Rights of Women* (1792), noting that the most "virtuous equality will not rest firmly . . . if one half of mankind be chained to its bottom by fate." Despite Wollstonecraft's protest, fraternity in France, as in the United States, was most often just what its name implied, a sentimental bond between brothers, with mothers and sisters urged to attend to family matters at home.[19]

Those novel eighteenth-century arguments allowed the French revolutionaries to conceive of women, along with other targeted groups, as "in society, but not of it," vital to the life of the nation in their domestic capacities, but not essential to its active political life. Largely excluded from the body politic, they were denied the equality extended to men. The Declaration of the Rights of Man and of the Citizen was aptly and precisely named.[20]

To be sure, many revolutionary women (and some revolutionary men) contested those claims of exclusion. The Marquis de Condorcet was one prominent voice who did so publicly throughout the revolution, pressing the case for female citizenship while denying the alleged inferiority of their reason. Why were women any less capable of "exercising their rights" than men? he challenged. Because of their bodies? To claim that pregnancy or the menstrual cycle were just grounds for exclusion was as absurd as concluding that men with seasonal gout should be denied full rights.[21]

Women made their own efforts to demonstrate their equal capacity. Indeed, even as they were refused the label of active citizens, they played active revolutionary roles. They wrote and published journals, newspapers, books, and plays. They organized petitions and took part in the meetings of sections and clubs, such as the Cercle Social (Social Club) or the Société Fraternelle des patriotes de l'un et l'autre sexe (Fraternal Society of Male and Female Patriots). And they repeatedly took to the streets and galleries in applause and protest. In one of the most celebrated events of the revolution, women marched en masse from Paris to Versailles in October 1789 and invaded the palace of the king and queen, forcing the royals to accede to their demands and return with them to Paris. They were accompanied and flanked by (male) soldiers, but the action allowed wits to say of women what some said of the ordinary people who had seized the Bastille: surely they were France's truly *active* citizens![22]

Such claims, moreover, were pressed at the highest levels of state. Marie Madeleine Jodin, a former actress and friend of the French encyclopedist Denis Diderot, declared, in a December 1790 petition to the National Assembly urging full citizenship for women, "Sirs; we are not, on this earth, a different species from yours. The mind has no sex, any more than does virtue." In March 1791, another petition, written by the activist Pauline Léon and signed by three hundred persons, demanded the equal right to bear arms. And in September of that year, the playwright and constitutional monarchist Olympe de Gouges penned her famous Declaration of the Rights of Woman as a supplement to the Declaration of the Rights of Man. De Gouge's work closely tracked the original, highlighting its glaring absences and exclusions. "Considering that ignorance, neglect, or contempt for the rights of woman, are the sole causes of public misfortunes and governmental corruption, they have resolved to set forth in a solemn declaration the natural, inalienable, and sacred rights of woman," the preamble declares. Article 1 proclaims, "Woman is born free and remains equal to man in rights," and the document continues throughout in that vein. In a poignant addition, given that she herself would be sent to the guillotine in 1793, de Gouges observes, "Woman has the right to mount the scaffold, she must equally have the right to mount the tribune."[23]

Such assertions were not without their consequences. Perhaps most importantly, they helped to create "women" as a distinct political category in ways they had never been before. They also led to more immediate, concrete gains, including the right to divorce and to share equally in inheritance with men. Yet arguably the most direct consequence was to induce a "backlash," in what would prove a recurrent historical response. Decrying the "unnatural" influence of women in public life, French men poured scorn on "viragos" and those "monsters" who chose to "renounce their sex." In October 1793, the republic outlawed female membership in political clubs and began to persecute politically active women. And the radical Jacobin constitution of that year, which countenanced active citizenship for all males, refused to consider the prospect for women. No less than in the cases of England and the American republic, the French social contract was a "sexual contract," constitutionally established on the differences attributed to women's bodies and minds.[24]

If the exclusion of women was thus constitutional in both senses of the word—and so constitutive of revolutionary equality as it played out in France—much the same can be said with respect to the enslaved and people of color. Here again the French adhered closely to their Enlightened American counterparts, conceiving equality above all as the equality of white men. That conception was facilitated by the fact that, although the French Empire in the eighteenth century enslaved well over one million Africans in brutal plantation labor, chiefly in the Caribbean colonies of Martinique, Guadeloupe, and above all Saint-Domingue, there were very few in metropolitan France itself. According to legal convention and national myth, in fact, there were "no slaves in France" at all. In practice, there were always some, brought to the metropole with their white masters throughout the eighteenth century. The numbers were small, probably no more than a few thousand at a time, but their presence produced anxieties nonetheless, leading, in the 1770s, to the formation of a special set of laws known as the "Police des Noirs," tasked with tracking, regulating, and overseeing the "Blacks." Largely reflecting the practices of white planters in the colonies, who had instituted increasingly byzantine laws to regulate the lives of the enslaved and free people of color, the Police des Noirs focused chiefly on measures of surveillance, establishing a census of Black and mixed-race people in France, and instituting the first formal system of identity cards to monitor their comings and goings.[25]

The Police des Noirs reflected anxieties about the very presence of people of color in France, and gave rise to fears that they would "taint the blood" and "disfigure" the population. On the whole, the legislation, as one of its most recent students observes, "was an attempt to reassert the exclusion of enslaved people from the population of metropolitan France, taken as a social, political, and biological collective body." And while it is true that the emergent notion of race was not the "master concept" in this exclusion that it would become in the nineteenth century, it is also clear that there was "a correlation between racialization and inequality" with new anthropological and natural-historical ideas of how people of African descent fit into the natural order marshaled to emphasize their essential backwardness, barbarism, and degeneration. Thus, it was perfectly possible to concede, with the influential French naturalist Buffon, that all of humanity was of one species, while at the same time having recourse to theories of environmental exposure or stadial development to emphasize how some peoples were less advanced. The upshot, as the late Haitian intellectual Michel-Rolph Trouillot once put it, is that "non-European groups were forced to enter into various philosophical, ideological, and practical schemes," all of which "assumed and reasserted that, ultimately, some humans were more so than others." In France, in short, as elsewhere, the color of equality was overwhelmingly white.[26]

Of course, just as there were dissenters from the gathering scientific consensus regarding women's essential difference, there were those in France who contested attempts to relegate the nonwhite populations of the world to lower rungs of humanity. Condorcet and others addressed Black men and the enslaved as their "brothers," judging that "nature" had given them "the same spirit, the same reason, the same virtues as whites." Others condemned

European justifications for empire, and the Société des Amis des Noirs (Society of Friends of the Blacks), of which Condorcet and the revolutionary Jacques Pierre Brissot were founding members, and similar groups worked in the final years of the Old Regime to curtail (though not to end) the slave trade. Drawing on English and American abolitionist ideas, representatives of the group appeared before the National Assembly in 1790 to urge just that. As Condorcet and allies such as the abbé Henri Gregoire recognized, slavery sat as uncomfortably with the universal pretensions of the Declaration of the Rights of Man and of the Citizen as it did with the ideals of the American Declaration of Independence.[27]

Efforts to deny citizenship and rights to free mixed-race people (*gens de couleur*) were even more fraught. There were some thirty thousand of the latter in Saint-Domingue alone, property-owning and often possessing slaves. From the time of the calling of the Estates General they had argued their case in Paris, addressing the National Assembly in August 1789 to demand the very same liberty and equality invoked in the Declaration and bestowed on white men. There was support for their position among certain deputies, which only grew with news of the idealism of individuals such as Vincent Ogé, a man of color who returned to Saint-Domingue from Paris in late 1790 to lead an insurrection in support of the rights of *gens de couleur*. The insurrection was brutally suppressed, with Ogé and his followers tortured and executed in public, generating sympathy for their cause. Yet sympathy among the deputies for the slave-owning white planters and their representatives proved even stronger. The latter would brook no compromise with men of color. As a consequence, the National Assembly largely prevaricated on the question of granting citizenship across color lines, making only a small concession in that direction in the spring of 1791, when the so-called Rewbell amendment of May 15, 1791, named after the deputy Jean-François Rewbell, extended full political rights to free men of color *whose parents had both been born free*. The number of people affected by the amendment was tiny, and of course it did nothing to change the situation of the roughly five hundred thousand African slaves in Saint-Domingue. But the symbolism was still powerful enough to provoke a white revolt in the colonies, which succeeded in forcing the deputies to undo the amendment in September 1791.

By then, however, the situation on the ground had changed dramatically. A massive slave uprising that broke out in late August eventually succeeded in abolishing slavery in Haiti altogether. Full political rights were granted to *gens de couleur* on March 28, 1792, and eventually there was a general emancipation. That it was the uprising that made all the difference is underscored by the fact that the number of enslaved people imported into the colonies actually *increased* in the first two years of the revolution, between 1789 and 1791. Even for the most progressive "friends of the Blacks" in France, the abolition of slavery in the near term was effectively

"Mortals Are Equal. It Is Not Birth but Virtue That Makes the Difference," 1794. Beneath an equilateral triangle, the goddess Reason levels a white man and a Black man, who holds a copy of the Rights of Man and of the Citizen and the decree of May 15, 1791, while the demons of aristocracy, egoism, and discord flee. Bibliothèque Nationale de France.

"unthinkable," as was full liberty, equality, or fraternity for African subjects in the empire. That the enslaved and people of color succeeded in winning their freedom regardless, despite determined resistance and overwhelming odds, is a testament to their courage, tenacity, and acumen. But we should not kid ourselves that Haitian independence was somehow the magical consequence of the spread of Enlightenment ideas or the spirit of 1789. In very real ways, Haitian independence was achieved despite them.[28]

Which is not to deny that Haitian actors and "Black Jacobins" made use of, and even embraced, Enlightenment ideals when it suited their purposes, any more than it is to deny that French revolutionaries played a crucial role in the eventual, if short-lived, abolition of slavery. The brilliant, charismatic Toussaint Louverture, who gradually emerged as the galvanizing leader of the Haitian Revolution, made that allegiance explicit when he declared, famously, to would-be followers on August 21, 1793, "Brothers and friends, I am Toussaint Louverture. . . . I have undertaken vengeance. I want liberty and equality to reign in St. Domingue. I am working to make that happen." Louverture, at the time, however, was fighting for the Spanish *against* both the royalist and counterrevolutionary planters in Saint-Domingue and the representatives of the French republic, who were desperately trying to hold the empire together.[29]

Louverture would not go over to the French for close to another year. But in the meantime, pressed by the force of circumstances and the demands of war, the French government made good on a general emancipation proclamation issued on the ground by the republican commissioner in Saint-Domingue, Léger-Félicité Sonthanax, on the very same day as Louverture's own declaration. Sonthanax was an abolitionist of principle who married a woman of color. But his proclamation was all about expediency. Battling counterrevolutionary planters, as well as the Spanish and the English, he and his republican allies needed the strength of arms of the formerly enslaved for the very survival of the French colonies in the Caribbean. In exchange for their support and military service in what were known as "legions of equality," they were granted full citizenship and admitted to the protections of the rights of man.

Even though Sonthanax's actions were shaped by contingency and military necessity, they are no less affecting for that. Extended in the following months, they were ratified on February 4, 1794, by the French National Convention, which declared, in the presence of three representatives from Saint-Domingue—the Senegalese-born and formerly enslaved Jean-Baptiste Belley; the free man of color Jean-Baptiste Mills; and Louis-Pierre Dufay, a self-described white "commoner"—that "all men living in the colonies, without distinction of color, are French citizens and enjoy all the rights of the constitution." It was a historic and unprecedented decree, and it led to the inspiring, if short-lived, spectacle of integration, with representatives in France celebrating the demise of the "aristocracy of the skin" and declaring that equality was "consecrated" among them. A great celebration at Notre Dame Cathedral and in other parts of the country followed. Belley, Mills, and Dufay served together in the convention as deputies, and for the next several years, there were experiments in France without precedent anywhere in the Atlantic world, including the establishment of an elite boarding school in Paris, the National Colonial Institute, to integrate the children of Black, mixed-race, and white citizens from the colonies, and the promotion of extraordinary figures such as Thomas-Alexandre Dumas, the son of a French nobleman and an enslaved woman from Saint-Domingue (and the father of the famed novelist Alexandre), who would become in the 1790s the commanding general of the Army of the Alps and a celebrated revolutionary hero.[30]

Meanwhile, back in Saint-Domingue, Louverture affirmed his own military bona fides after realigning with France, gradually consolidating control over the island in the name of the French republic. In his army, Blacks, whites, and men of color fought together "like brothers, born of the same mother," Louverture claimed, insisting that this "is what we call equality." At the same time, the French republican commissioner Victor Hugues was busy liberating slaves in Guadeloupe, and soon, throughout the Caribbean, employing a guillotine brought expressly from France to serve as the scythe of equality in the New World in an attempt to eradicate the recalcitrant defenders of the Old.[31]

These were dramatic events, and they have given rise in recent years to a great deal of scholarship on the Haitian experience, which has yielded, in turn, a powerful interpretation that bears directly on the question of equality. That interpretation credits Haitian actors with fully realizing the potential of the universal ideals that Europeans had announced but never extended as such, drawing out the implicit promise of liberty and equality for all. By forcing Europeans to abandon the exclusions that accompanied their own declarations of rights, and so to make good on the assertion that all men are created equal, people of color and the formally enslaved thus radicalized the French revolutionary message, fulfilling its latent potential and "inner logic."[32]

There is much to be said for that powerful view, which is based on a wealth of careful and well-intentioned scholarship that aims to restore dignity, agency, and universal significance to people whose achievements were largely forgotten for far too long outside of Haiti itself. And yet it has been pointed out recently in an equally powerful critique that this interpretation tends to relegate the Haitian role to one of realizing or completing European universals, drawing attention away from what was specific and unique to the Haitian case, which was as much about achieving autonomy from domination as it was about realizing the rights of man.[33]

It also risks exaggerating the extent of the lessons learned, both within Haiti and abroad. After France attempted to reimpose slavery in the colonies under Napoleon in 1802, and tricked and captured Louverture, who died in a French prison in 1803, Haitians eventually did achieve their full independence at the cost of enormous and bloody sacrifice. But as the Haitian Declaration of Independence of January 1, 1804, makes clear, Haitians were in no mood to further countenance the "pitiful eloquence" of the "official proclamations" of the French, by which they had been deceived and "defeated" repeatedly since the beginning of their revolution. Like the emancipation decree of 1794, the Declaration of the Rights of Man and of the Citizen appeared, in retrospect, more a deception to be discounted than a set of aspirations to be fulfilled.[34]

The Haitian Constitution that followed in 1805 did invoke humanity's equal standing "in the presence of the Supreme Being" and the equality of all Haitians "in the eyes of the law." And these and other articles do clearly reflect the influence of the French and American examples, even though the Haitian revolutionaries' use of Creole phrases (such as *Te moun se moun*, "Every person is a person") hint at underlying African resources for conceiving common humanity as well. What is not in doubt is that the revolutionaries definitively abolished slavery on Haitian soil, and they outlawed legal distinctions between Blacks and *gens de couleur* despite lingering tensions between them.[35]

Still, beyond the overthrow of white domination, it is not at all clear that "equality" was the Haitian Revolution's primary goal. It certainly wasn't its result. For their sacrifices on the battlefield, Haitian women may have earned the dubious distinction of being executed by the French as combatants, just like men. But no more than French women who were sent to the guillotine did they win civil or political equality in the postrevolutionary state. And despite ideals of independence for small-scale cultivators and farmers, Haitian landowners reimposed the coercive plantation economy after independence to keep the sugar flowing, perpetuating inequalities between rich and poor that stand to this day. Finally, as is well known, the authoritarian temptation already evident in the consolidation of power under Louverture was made brutally apparent in the aftermath of liberation, when the "Louverturian state" flourished in the context of civil war and military dictatorship. The revolution that grew out of the slave uprising, as one leading scholar notes with arguable exaggeration, was "authoritarian from beginning to end," and the politics of Haiti's founders, whether Louverture, Jean-Jacques Dessalines, or Henry Christophe, "unapologetically dictatorial."[36]

The Haitian revolution was about many things, but it was not about democracy. And while it undoubtedly proved to Black men and women that they could contest white domination, equality did not prove to be its legacy. Napoleon failed to reimpose slavery in Saint-Domingue, but he did so successfully in Guadeloupe. In Martinique, it never went away, thanks to the efforts of occupying British forces. And in French Guyana, the guillotine-wielding Victor Hugues, once an agent of manumission, was tasked with returning slaves to their "rightful" place in the fields.[37]

As for the "unthinkable" revolution in Haiti itself, Europeans and North Americans quickly did their best to forget. Outside of the Caribbean, and with the important exception of underground networks of people of color in Latin America and the United States who worked to keep the memory of the Haitian Revolution alive, the ultimate legacy of that great event in the history of human rights was to demonstrate the power of erasure and silence. Covered over and forgotten, the Haitian Revolution did almost nothing, sadly, to undo the comfortable exclusions of Europeans and Americans. In the history of equality in the West, it was rendered, until very recently, a nonevent.[38]

I have insisted on the revolution's exclusions—on the ways in which the French revolutionary understanding of equality, like the American one, was constituted and constrained by its exceptions—in part because a powerful tradition of commentary has long emphasized the opposite, envisioning the advent of equality in France as the beginning of a process destined to expand and spread around the world. That tradition dates to the French Revolution itself, when it was first articulated with great eloquence by Condorcet, who envisioned, while in hiding during the Terror, the future progress of the human spirit. "Our hopes regarding the coming state of humanity," he announced, "may be reduced to three principal points: the destruction of inequality among nations; progress toward equality within each people; and finally, the real perfection of man." Condorcet included women, too, in his vision of the future, insisting that, like inequalities of birth, inequalities of wealth, education, and the accidents of life were destined to "diminish continually." "It is easy to prove," he added, commenting specifically on material conditions, "that fortunes tend naturally toward equality, and their excessive disproportion either would not exist or would promptly cease if civil laws did not establish artificial means of perpetuating and combining them." Those prognostications were given further weight by powerful interpreters in the nineteenth century, liberal, socialist, and republican, who likewise saw the French Revolution as but an early iteration of expanding human equality that eventually would encompass the world. "The gradual development of the equality of conditions," Tocqueville proclaimed on the strength of both the French and American examples, was "a providential fact," its spread at once "universal and durable."[39]

Influential students of the French Revolution in our own time have elaborated on these perspectives, interpreting its course as driven by the "limitless desire for equality," which progressed from demands for legal equality to political equality to equalization of material conditions, prefiguring in this way the struggles of the nineteenth and twentieth centuries. If equality in this conception was a seminal and germinating force, one that possessed its own "fecundity," energy, and motive direction, others have described it using the metaphor of gravitational descent, with rights flowing outward and downward from on high, like water trickling over a "cascade" to reach ever wider segments of the population. Finally, as we have just seen, a number of influential commentators have given Haitian actors a central place in such theories, arguing that it was they who drew out equality's "already built-in potential."

The metaphors differ, but the narratives converge around what the political theorist Anne Phillips describes as an "inner logic story," in which equality is conceived as a self-actuating principle, working itself out over time.[40]

In all of these accounts, equality is presented in strikingly idealist and teleological terms, as if it were gradually, yet inexorably, spreading across the globe according to some powerful necessity, overcoming barriers one by one. Others, like the influential economist Thomas Piketty, present the spread of equality less as a logical necessity and more as an empirical fact, a "tendency," a "long-term movement," a steady "march." Passing through "successive stages," equality may be temporarily thwarted or turned aside, but it possesses a driving momentum of its own. In truth, however, the history of equality defies such optimistic assessments, and shedding them can help us to better recognize and comprehend the actual uses to which discourses of equality have been put.[41]

We should be cautious, then, about seeing French revolutionary equality as the font of an overflowing pool cascading into the future. But what, then, was its legacy, and in what ways did it depart from the broader American and Enlightenment notions of equality from which it drew and with which it shared so much? Part of the answer lies in the emotional intensity with which French actors imbued the notion of equality, which became in their hands as much a feeling as an abstract principle, a sentiment as much as an objective assessment of actual conditions.

To be sure, ideas of equality had long possessed an affective dimension. Montesquieu said it well when he described virtue in a republic as the "*love* of equality." It was a "feeling," he insisted, "and not a consequence of knowledge." And insofar as republican equality was coupled with fraternity, just as Christian equality was coupled with charity and love, notions of friendship and familial belonging were bound up with the common standing of equals from early on.[42]

Yet the French revolutionary passion for equality, and the corresponding hatred of inequality, were singularly intense, the product in part of an affective and sentimentalist revolution carried out over the course of the eighteenth century. And the herald of that revolution in sentiment was none other than Jean-Jacques Rousseau, a man who knew both the privileged and the poor, and who had served in his youth as an apprentice, a footman, and a valet. He developed a deep and instinctive sense of the humiliations suffered, and the resentments nursed, by those in subaltern positions, and he channeled that sentiment into his writings. To a greater extent than any other writer of his time, Rousseau invested equality with a powerful moral and emotional valence, restyling an older Christian language that linked equality to natural goodness, while inspiring a corresponding revulsion of inequality as the symptom and cause of moral and political decay.[43]

But Rousseau also thought deeply about a question that vexed the French revolutionaries from the start: Just how might a society already corrupted be transformed into one that was not? In the French case that meant transforming a feudal and aristocratic order based on legal privilege and vast disparities in social standing, wealth, and political power into an entirely new regime. The challenge was daunting, much more so than the one faced by the American revolutionaries, who departed from social circumstances that were broadly equal for the free white male population, and who sought to recover rights and liberties, many of which they believed to have been usurped but that they had already known, the oft-invoked "rights of Englishmen." The rights of the French Declaration, by contrast, were largely aspirational, creating a predicament that one eminent authority has summarized in a simple, if imposing, question: "How could liberty, equality, and fraternity be instituted before the French had any real experience of them?"[44]

Rousseau had entertained just this question in *The Social Contract*, a book that was conceived in certain respects as a natural sequel to the *Discourse on the Origin of Inequality*. Whereas in the

Discourse he provided a seductive vision of what human beings had been like in their uncorrupted state, in *The Social Contract* he sought to envision how human beings could be made equal in society. There could be no going back to our lost innocence, Rousseau maintained, and so the undertaking would require a frontal assault on the human selfishness and pride that he identified as the cause of inequality and invidious distinction. Simply put, human nature would have to be changed, with men and women reeducated and regenerated so as to be able to live together as equals. And in order for an "emerging people" to accomplish that, "the effect would have to become the cause." Put another way, the very values that the new regime should seek to produce in its citizens—the elevation of society over individual self-interest and self-love, and the true cultivation of liberty, equality, and fraternity—would need to be instilled as widely as possible from the outset. And that was a task, Rousseau stressed, that could be accomplished through neither coercion nor simple rational persuasion. The citizens must be persuaded by other means.[45]

Scholars have long debated what such nonrational and noncoercive persuasion might entail. But clearly what eighteenth-century observers called the "passions"—affect or feeling—were a crucial element. Rousseau well understood their power to move and persuade, and he also understood that religion was an indispensable means of channeling them, because it moved the heart more than the head, creating intense feelings of common belonging and devotion. It was precisely for that reason that the founders of nations had invariably appealed to the gods to consecrate their earthly communities, a point that Rousseau developed in the famous penultimate chapter of *The Social Contract*, "On Civil Religion." Noting there that Christianity had done more to weaken society than to strengthen it, he proposed instead "a purely civil profession of faith," whose primary function would be to strengthen "sentiments of sociability" among citizens. A civil religion would further the work of rendering society sacred.

It would make equals of men by making them feel and desire alike.[46]

The French revolutionaries, of course, were never guided solely or exclusively by the thought of Jean-Jacques Rousseau, whose legacy in any case was always contested. Yet his influence was undeniably important—evident, among many other places, in the Declaration itself, with its reference, in Article 6, to law as "the expression of the general will." This was a direct allusion to *The Social Contract*, which was republished in some thirteen editions during the early years of the revolution, including in a pocket-size edition for soldiers. But more to the point, the revolutionaries fully understood the dilemma he spelled out there: the need to regenerate human nature, to purge it of the defects acquired over centuries under "despotism" and "slavery." And they fully understood the importance of investing that project with an affective and quasi-religious urgency.[47]

In a move singled out by nineteenth-century commentators on the revolution, including Tocqueville and Émile Durkheim, and then reaffirmed by some of its most perceptive scholars in our own time, the revolutionaries undertook nothing less than a "transfer of sacrality," investing their social creations, their institutions, and their beliefs with a sacred significance formerly reserved for the Christian religion itself. Played out in a dazzling variety of festivals, rituals, and rites, this consecration of the social had the effect of throwing every aspect of social life into question. As the Old Regime gave way to one that was new, everything—from laws and conventions to social mores and customs—was examined as potential carriers of the noxious habits and values of old. And as the past was purged, new values were put in their place as prophylactic and cure. In this way would the effect animate the cause.[48]

And so equality occupied a central place not only in revolutionary rhetoric but in the emotional register of the revolution—a fact that contemporaries, no less than later observers, were quick to note. When the politician and man of letters Pierre Louis Roederer, an active participant in the revolution from the time of the Estates General through the reign of Napoleon, sought to take stock of what he described as "the spirit of 1789," he placed equality at its center. The "desire" that "determined the first outbreak of the revolution," he noted, that "roused its most violent efforts, [and] obtained its most important successes" was "the love of equality." Similarly, Jacques Necker, Louis the XVI's popular minister of finance, who fled the revolution not long after it began and devoted his energies to opposing it, remarked with distaste, in early 1793, that "among the diverse metaphysical principles that serve in our time to stir up the world, the most remarkable, the most important and, by the extent of its influence and the diversity of its connections, is, I have no doubt, the principle of equality as it has been understood and interpreted by the new legislators in France." Necker spoke here of equality as a "principle," but he was clear about its impact on "sentiments," noting that the revolutionaries inspired an "enthusiasm" for "all ideas of parity, equality, and absolute leveling." In that sense, equality was not only, as a modern scholar observes, the "central tenet" of the revolutionary "credo," the inverse of the old society and the condition and purpose of the new, but a motivating passion bound up with what contemporaries described again and again as the revolution's giddy and intoxicating spirit, a kind of boundless energy and joyous devotion to the possibility of revolutionary renewal and the coming together of the nation in *fraternité*.[49]

Equality was a crucial part of that sentiment, and the paroxysms of feeling it induced helped accommodate and overcome the many actual differences—in wealth and social standing, in education and occupation—that otherwise divided "equals." The Calvinist pastor and republican representative to the National Convention Jean-Paul Rabaut de Saint-Étienne explained this nicely when he observed, in an article titled "On Equality" in the revolutionary newspaper *Chronique de Paris*, in June 1793, that what was meant by the term was "a state of society in which all men live together as brothers, so that inequality of wealth and conditions disappears before the feeling of fraternity and concord that dominates and covers everything." Insisting that no government could ever eliminate "inequality of wealth," he described the main task of the "politics of equality" as the promotion of the "equality of affections."[50]

Rabaut's words underscore the crucial importance of fraternity in revolutionary rhetoric and experience, for it was fraternity—in the army, in the clubs, among the *sans-culottes*—that induced feelings of common belonging and purpose among disparate peoples, reinforcing the reciprocity of dignity and respect that was the aim of the "equality of affections." Brotherhood was a common theme among eighteenth-century republicans and Freemasons, and it played a role in America, as we have seen. But the French invoked *fraternité* with an even greater insistence in their revolution than the Americans did in theirs, in part because they were unimpeded by the awkward necessity of stoking animosity toward "British brethren," as the Declaration of Independence described the colonists' erstwhile kin. The central republican and Enlightenment category was freer to flourish in France, where it was continually invoked to reinforce the affective ties of the community of equals staked out in the social imaginary. Fraternity and equality worked together, as Rabaut explained, to foster the concord that dispelled genuine differences of wealth and condition.[51]

To feel oneself the equal of another—just as good in a basic sense as anyone else—was accomplished at the level of sentiment and often in defiance of objective conditions. That fact helps to explain why material considerations never loomed as large in the revolutionaries' understanding of equality as is sometimes supposed. To be sure, material considerations were real, and it is an important consequence of the French Revolution that it put them on the map, raising the question of whether equality should be extended to the economic realm in ways that would resonate into the nineteenth and twentieth centuries. That was, above all, the case during the radical republican phase of the revolution from 1792 to 1794, when popular movements in Paris pressed the issue of whether rights should be "social"—extended, that is, to provisions of welfare (*bienfaisance*)—and the Jacobins debated whether the state had an obligation to ensure them. Some replied vigorously in the affirmative, seeking to satisfy rights to education, work, and basic subsistence, while drafting plans for pensions for widows, the aged, and the infirm. Others broached schemes of tax and inheritance reform and took steps to institute price controls (the "Maximum") to limit the cost of basic necessities such as bread. And the very fact that the revolutionaries began by expropriating the vast landholdings of the church, which they sold off, while doing the same with the commandeered estates of émigré aristocrats, gave credence to fears that they intended to level all. In large part because of those expropriations, wealth inequality during the period between 1789 and 1810 did in fact decline, if not dramatically.[52]

Yet the Jacobin state was never a welfare state; nor did it offer a sweeping "New Deal" as a model for the future. And that is not only because its egalitarian aspirations were thwarted by war and circumstance, lack of funding and time. In fact, its aims, like those of eighteenth-century republicans more generally, were limited from the start.[53]

It is certainly true that, like republicans elsewhere in the Atlantic world, the Jacobins insisted on frugality, moderation, and balance in economic affairs, and spoke of the desirability of removing "disgraceful" opulence and extreme inequalities of fortune. Yet their defense of private property rights, if sometimes debated, was principled and consistent nonetheless. It is altogether telling that on March 18, 1793, the Jacobins imposed the death sentence for anyone even proposing a *lex agraria* aimed at land distribution, "or any other law subversive of territorial, commercial, and industrial properties." They emphasized repeatedly, as Rousseau himself had done in *The Social Contract*, that the word "equality" "need

not mean . . . that degrees of power and wealth [were] to be absolutely the same." Robespierre was clear on the matter, concluding
that "equality of ownership is fundamentally impossible in civil
society." It was, he insisted in 1793, a "chimera."[54]

Despite fledgling initiatives, then, and the hopes and dreams
of some, redistributive justice was never the French Revolution's
overriding goal, even during its most radical phase. But the revolutionary spirit cultivated, nonetheless, a vital, existential sense
of *lived* equality. And while that was evident already in 1789, it
was the later, more radical phase of the revolution, in 1793 and
1794, when the passion for the experience of equality burned most
intensely. This was the period that would sear itself in the minds
of future generations, a time when equality was seemingly sought
in all places and applied to all things. And while the French in
practice remained very far from achieving that end, the sheer scale
of their ambition was impressive. As if in acknowledgment of the
ubiquitous carpenter's level of revolutionary iconography, with its
Christian associations of equality under God, the revolutionaries
took the measure of all things, not excepting even time and space,
in an effort to make them level and true.

"Time opens a new book in history, as simple and majestic
as equality," Charles-Gilbert Rome observed in his report for a
new revolutionary calendar in 1793. "It must engrave with a new
and vigorous instrument the annals of regenerated France." The
calendar year would be divided into "twelve equal months," and
each month would be divided into "three equal parts" of ten days.
The dating itself would begin from September 22, 1792, not only
the first day of the French republic, but also the "true autumnal
equinox," when the sun crosses the equator and day and night are
of equal length.[55]

Time was thus duly proportioned. It would also be marked
to commemorate the special place of equality in its evolution.
As the Jacobin official Joseph-Marie Lequinio proposed, every
year on 10 Frimaire—January 21, according to the old Christian

calendar—the French would celebrate a great national holiday in equality's name. The date was significant, for it was on January 21, 1793, when the "last henchman of royalty," Louis XVI, was dispatched by the scythe. The man whom counterrevolutionary caricaturists hailed as the "martyr of equality" was conceived by the revolutionaries themselves as a tyrannical patriarch, brought low by a band of patricidal brothers who had recovered their "original democratic equality." The day of Louis's death was a symbolic reversal, and in the revolutionaries' opinion, a cause for rejoicing. "Nothing should be given over to domination, but only to fraternity," Lequinio insisted. On that day, as at all revolutionary festivals and celebrations, men should be reminded that they stood on the same plane.[56]

In Lequinio's view—and he was not alone—equality was thus a principle that should order space as well as time. Already, early in the revolution, legislators had taken that notion to heart, redrawing the map of France so that its many departments would be more equal in size, population, and shape. And now, at every revolutionary festival, Lequinio counseled, citizens should gather in circles so that they faced one another at all times, with the people's "regularity, force, and equality" on constant display to itself. Visionary architects likewise experimented with amphitheaters and theaters in the round, in order to minimize inequalities of lines of sight, while festival organizers favored large open spaces, where "equality could be conveyed by horizontality and freedom by the lack of boundaries." The vertical was to be distrusted. One zealous patriot even suggested that leveling should apply to the earth. "What is a mountain," he cried, "if not an eternal protest against Equality?" Others looked suspiciously at bell towers, which soared into the sky. "Their domination over other forms of building seems to have contradicted the true principles of equality," the city government of Paris observed on 22 Brumaire, Year 1, inviting good patriots to destroy them.[57]

However outlandish, such proposals speak eloquently to the scope of revolutionary ambition as well as to its more performative aspects, which were fully on display in the revolutionary festivals and banquets. There the people dramatized and celebrated their regeneration, singing, dancing, and feasting as they performed "the advent of the reign of equality." There the rich might be made to stand and serve the seated poor in rites of reversal resonant of charivari. And there all might break the "bread of equality" (*pain d'égalité*) as *co-pains*, as friends. Combining the pure white flour of the wealthy with the cheaper, coarser grains consumed by the poor, the bread of equality was egalitarian fare, balanced and nutritious, served out in equal measures.[58]

To break bread with friends and to raise one's glass in fellowship and good cheer were the ultimate gestures of fraternity, and fraternity was central to these revolutionary gatherings, just as it was central to the other two terms in the revolutionary trinity. But to toast them together was not only a proud and defiant assertion of one's shared and equal status, it was also a thinly veiled challenge to anyone who might dare deny it. Fraternal equality was a summons to come together; it was also a threat to those who kept apart.

No revolutionary group toasted louder and more menacingly in this respect than the *sans-culottes*, the primarily urban artisans who served as the most faithful devotees of the "cult of equality." They were the French equivalent of the Athenian "middling men" or the Spartan *homoioi*, assertively plainspoken and ostentatiously unaffected in their republican virtue and moderation, ready at every moment to enforce and defend revolutionary ideals. As their name implies, the *sans-culottes* spurned the fancy knee-breeches (*culottes*), powdered wigs, silk stockings, buckled shoes, and other finery favored by the elites of the Old Regime. The *sans-culottes*, in a word, wore pants. Evincing a frugality and simplicity in manners and dress, they wore their hair naturally, which is to say long, often with a "liberty cap," or *bonnet rouge*, once the emblem of the freed slave in ancient Rome and now a sign of revolutionary conviction and militancy in the service of *liberté*, *égalité*, and *fraternité*.[59]

The *sans-culottes*, like other revolutionaries, were supremely aware of the politics of dress. That awareness led to occasional calls for a national costume to efface distinctions signaled by clothing. But the *sans-culottes* preferred to equalize through their speech and comportment, affecting frankness and unflinching self-respect. No doffing of hats, no kissing of hands. "Citizen" (*citoyen* or *citoyenne*) was their preferred form of address. They refused to call others *Madame* or *Monsieur*, and even tried to proscribe the polite form of address in the French language used to signal deference and respect on the logic that "the eternal principles of equality forbid [it]." Whereas earlier patriots had attempted to abolish such offending words as "master" and "obey," the *sans-culottes* assailed the hierarchies embedded in the laws of grammar itself, sending petitions and delegations to the National Convention in 1793 and 1794 urging the obligatory use of the informal *tu* form of address and the abolition of the formal *vous*. This would lead, they asserted, to "less pride, fewer distinctions, less ill-feeling, more obvious familiarity, a greater sense of fraternity: consequently, more equality."[60]

The *sans-culottes'* effort to purge language of its hierarchical traces was of a piece with the broader revolutionary effort, initiated with the advent of the republic in late 1792, to rid France of all references to the stratified world of old, whether of kings and aristocrats or the scions of the church. As part of that effort, the revolutionaries changed the names of tens of thousands of streets, towns, and squares across France, with equality figuring centrally in the rebranding. The little commune of Pagny-le-Château, for example, in eastern France became Château Égalité, and Le Château itself, a small town on the Île d'Oléron, was renamed Cité-de-l'Égalité, or simply Égalité for short. Montrichard in the Loire Valley became Montégalité. The unfortunately named Port Louis in Brittany became Port-d'Égalité. Saint-Quentin was rechristened Égalité-sur-Somme. Avesnes-le-Comte in the north became Avesne-l'Égalité, and Saint-Léger-sous-Margerie became Égalité-Bonne-Nouvelle, proclaiming the good news of the new gospel.[61]

Such changes applied even to the names of slave ships, one of which was christened *L'Égalité* and sent out to Africa from Nantes in 1792, only to be seized off the Gold Coast by the British in 1797.[62]

Meanwhile, back in France, countless avenues, tributaries, streets, and squares were also renamed to fit the times. The fate of the rue de Condé in the 6th arrondissement in Paris was typical. Named after the great princely house of Condé, it became, in 1792, the rue de l'Égalité, of which there were many in France, as well as in faraway Saint-Domingue. The following year, the Place Royale in Lyon was renamed the Place de l'Égalité, and the equestrian statue of Louis XIV that once stood there was toppled, the guillotine put in its place. Back in Paris, Philippe, Duke of Orléans, changed the name of his palace, Louis XIV's birthplace, the Palais Royal, to the Palais Égalité, an oxymoron if there ever was one. He then styled himself Philippe Égalité. As a representative to the National Convention, Philippe voted for the death of his cousin, Louis XVI, but his radical posturing could not, in the end, overcome the fact that he was a prince of blood and heir to the throne, as well as one of the richest men in France. His grandson Louis-Philippe became king of France in 1830, but he himself was sent to the guillotine on November 6, 1793. Others who saw the light, and were legally registered at birth in that year, escaped the scythe; steel was used only to cut their umbilical cords. Behold little Victorine Constitution Liberté Égalité, born on July 10, 1793; or August Égalité of Abbeville; or Angélique Égalité of Châteauroux. Like Nicolas Égalité, an abandoned child christened by his patriotic, if unimaginative, caregivers, who found him on the rue de l'Égalité in Avranches, they were marked by revolutionary equality directly.[63]

The remapping and renaming of space, time, and the people and places of France, like the effort to purge the language of hierarchical accretions or strike down bell towers for their vertical audacity, were spectacular gestures, designed in part to create spectacle. They aimed to affect all manner of revolutionary experience, shaping the sights, sounds, feelings, and even tastes of a regenerated people who would learn to break the bread of equality together. Like the countless busts and engravings of the goddess Equality, or the lines of the revolutionary primers and songs intended to instill in schoolchildren the knowledge of their equal rights, the many elements of the revolution flooded into homes and public squares across France, popularizing and sacralizing equality in the process. "Sacred equality, eternal symbol of creation, first law of nature, and first law of the Republic," intoned the culminating station of one of the great revolutionary festivals held on August 10, 1793, to commemorate the anniversary of the fall of the monarchy. "Saintly equality," "holy equality," the words were forever on the lips of its proponents in testament to its renewed, and newfound, sacred status. Arguably, equality has never lost that status. And that may be one of the revolution's greatest legacies—the sanctification of equality as an aspiration and ideal, synonymous with justice and virtue.[64]

But to sanctify is to draw boundaries with the profane, and to uphold equality with sacred enthusiasm is to invite stigmatizing the unregenerate, those who would spurn its sacred norms. It was not lost on contemporaries, above all the revolution's opponents, that the high point of revolutionary proselytism on behalf of equality coincided with the violent movement of the scythe. Many believed there was a connection, and while the causes of the Terror are certainly many and complex—ranging from the threat of armed counterrevolution to the accumulation of social grievances to the fear of conspiracies and plots—that belief was surely not entirely wrong. For if one way to create a virtuous people fit for equality is to educate and reform, another is to purge the corruption and excise the decay and rot. The leveling mechanism of the guillotine aimed to do just that, targeting those who refused equality's embrace, separating the good from the bad. Fraternity or death! Equality or death! Fratricide for those who refused the loving

Equality, Fraternity, or Death! From the frontispiece of the counterrevolutionary *Dictionnaire des Jacobins vivans* (Hamburg, 1799). Note the guillotine blades hanging from the crossbones.

fraternal embrace! The guillotine would cut away the perverse and the stubborn, all those who insisted on clinging to the values of the former regime and conspiring to bring them back.

Those who did so were described as "aristocrats." But the word had long lost its precise sociological meaning. Sieyès asserted early on that aristocrats were a "malignant tumor" on the body of the nation, and over the course of the revolution an "aristocrat" became anyone suspected of plotting against the New Regime. Aristocracy was simply the "reverse of equality." Which meant that the majority of the guillotine's "aristocratic" victims were neither lords nor ladies, nobles nor priests, but ordinary people caught up in the conflict and accused of thwarting revolutionary aims. Those who were leveled were not, on average, taller than the rest. They were simply suspected of seeking and scheming to rise above.[65]

And so, if, as Plato remarked, "equality produces amity," forging the affective ties that bind together bands of equals, so, too, as Aristotle observed, is the "passion for equality" at the "root of faction." The two observations complement one another, and in the case of the French Revolution they worked together in a way that illustrates nicely a proposition and general rule affirmed by modern psychologists: namely, that "the more intense the social threat," real or imagined, "the greater the social bonding." By invoking the revolution's enemies both real and apparent, its leaders sought to rally equals and friends.[66]

In the very short term, at least, that strategy was brutally effective, rallying the country to defeat enemies at home and abroad. But the human cost was enormous, the violence spectacular, and it had the effect of staining revolutionary equality in blood. The Terror aimed to terrorize, and in that it succeeded wildly, sending waves of fear, and then horror and revulsion, across France and around the globe.

For many, the image of equality shone in the guillotine's blade. Its steely light drew renewed attention to the warnings of those, like Montesquieu, who had cautioned on the example of the ancients against leveling and what he called the "spirit of extreme equality." It also prompted new examination of the relationship between liberty and equality. Although republicans on both sides of the Atlantic had long argued that the two were not only compatible, but closely aligned, in the aftermath of the Terror and the "Atlantic Thermidor" that followed, liberty and equality were pulled apart and cast in opposition. The pursuit of equality, it seemed, had trampled liberty underfoot. Erstwhile supporters of Robespierre were making that point soon after they had deposed him. As one such figure, the Thermidorean François Boissy d'Anglas, explained in 1795, while defending his proposal for a new constitution for France, "the illusionary principles of absolute democracy and limitless equality are unquestionably the most dangerous obstacles to true liberty." They had led to the "tyranny" of France. Classical liberals and conservatives repeated the point throughout the following century. It would be the great theme of Alexis de Tocqueville, for whom the advent of democracy and the equality of conditions threatened a new type of oppression so great that the "old words 'despotism' and 'tyranny' will not do." Socialists and Marxists countered that it was pursuit of individual liberty, by contrast, that eroded equality and led to the oppression of the many by the few. In either case, liberty and equality, so long conceived as inextricably linked, were sundered. Whereas Rousseau had insisted of equality that "liberty cannot exist without it," in the revolution's aftermath, it seemed, they could only exist apart.[67]

La Liberté et l'Égalité unies par la Nature

"Liberty and Equality United by Nature," engraving by Louis Charles Routte (Paris: Potrelle, 1795 or 1796). Although the French Revolution sought to unite liberty and equality, many in its aftermath believed that the revolutionary experience exposed the natural opposition between the two. Bibliothèque Nationale de France.

To see equality through the prism of the Terror, then, was distorting. The revolutionaries' zeal for equality looked more like a fit of madness wrought by passion, a frenzied illusion. "Absolute equality is a chimera," Boissy d'Anglas insisted. The reference to that destructive, if mythical, beast of Greek lore—part fire-breathing lion, part serpent, part goat—was invoked repeatedly in the years to come. And as observers looked back on the eighteenth century in an effort to discern signs and warnings of the coming catastrophe, they found the chimera lurking in warning in surprising places.[68]

"The chimera of equality is the most dangerous of all beliefs in a civilized society," Denis Diderot had observed in a work sometimes cited as a primer of revolution, the *Histoire des deux Indes* (History of the two Indias), cowritten with the abbé Guillaume-Thomas Raynal. "To preach this system is not to recall its rights, it is to invite the people to murder and pillage; it is to unchain domestic animals and to turn them into wild beasts." Similarly, Voltaire had explained in 1772 that "the so-called equality of men, that some sophists have made fashionable, is a pernicious chimera." Rousseau put his readers on guard in *The Social Contract* that the kind of equality that would ensure "that no citizen should be so rich as to be capable of buying another citizen, and none so poor that he is forced to sell himself," would be written off by its opponents as a "speculative chimera." It now was. Even Robespierre himself had used the term, describing the equality of ownership in 1793 as just that mythical beast. But no matter. He was guilty of conjuring it all the same. In the wake of his death, "that chimera, absolute equality," became a cliché, applied liberally and broadly not only by counterrevolutionaries in France, but by all those across Europe and the New World seeking to mark their distance from the revolution's excesses.[69]

Napoleon was among them. He may have proclaimed "careers open to talents," and in his plebiscites allowed the people to vote. He may have left the word "equality" chiseled on the buildings of France, alongside "liberty" and "fraternity," just as he retained the *tricolore* flag. But his entire regime was a rebuke to radical efforts to extend the equality of conditions. He recalled the aristocracy of old, though without restoring their privileges, and created a new one to stand beside it. He reinstated slavery in the empire, and made women once again the property of men. And he proclaimed himself an emperor on the model of Caesar. As he and his propagandists made clear, once the revolutionaries had departed from the safer ground of the equality of merit and legal equality for men, they had summoned a monster of conflicting parts, creating an illusion and a lie.

Ironically, some of the revolution's most radical heirs in the nineteenth century—socialists, communists, and Marxists—came to agree. In their view, too, the equality of the French Revolution, like that of the United States, was a conjuring trick, and must be revealed as such. By exposing the deception, some aimed to make equality more real. But others, Marx and Engels among them, worked to expose equality itself as a dangerous myth, no more practicable than the "crude leveling" of utopian fantasy. Equality, they argued, was an illusion that must give way to class struggle and the concrete realities of the final revolution to come.

PART III

PART III.

8

ILLUSION

From Each According to Ability,
to Each According to Need

"Equality . . . is only a chimera in the eyes of men depraved by the love of riches and power," Filippo Buonarroti observed in a footnote to history. It was a footnote to *his* history, first published in French in 1828, of the "Conspiracy for Equality" of François-Noël "Gracchus" Babeuf and his fellow "equals." Buonarroti, a Tuscan nobleman by birth and a "professional revolutionist" by occupation, had taken part as an equal himself in the conspiracy, a stillborn effort to revive the rule of the Jacobins in Paris in 1796 and to redistribute land in a sweeping agrarian law that earned "Gracchus" his classical cognomen. Put down before it even got going, the conspiracy proved a failure, with Babeuf carted off to the guillotine and Buonarroti imprisoned. Contemporaries dismissed the plot as a retrograde step, a futile effort to bring back the dreaded politics of Robespierre and the *sans-culottes*, whose memory many were eager to forget. But now, over thirty years later, Buonarroti succeeded as historian where he had failed as conspirator, effectively recasting the forgotten episode as a portent and new beginning. The historian would serve as prophet of the past, herald of a new dawn. And in so doing, he would recall equality from the land of mythical beasts. Equality, Buonarroti affirmed, was no chimera and no illusion. It was real, and real equality was what the world demanded.[1]

Buonarroti pressed this urgent message throughout the text. But it came across most clearly in a key "justificative" document included in the history to emphasize the prescient aims and intentions of the conspirators. This was the "Manifesto of the Equals," published anonymously in Buonarroti's book for the very first time, though likely written by the atheist, revolutionary, and early socialist Sylvain Maréchal in 1796. Its message was straightforward. The people of France, like all human beings, were equals by nature, though for centuries they had been forced to live as slaves, denied the very thing that philosophers, priests, and rulers had promised them again and again:

> Everywhere and at all times men were lulled with beautiful words; at no time and in no place was the thing itself [equality] ever obtained along with the word. From time immemorial they hypocritically repeat to us: *all men are equal*; and from time immemorial the most degrading and monstrous inequality insolently weighs upon the human race. . . . [E]quality was nothing but a beautiful and sterile legal fiction. And now that it is called for, with an even stronger voice they answer us: be quiet, you wretches! Real equality is nothing but a chimera; be satisfied with conditional equality; you're all equal before the law. What more do you want, filthy rabble?

Like their predecessors in classical antiquity, Christendom, and the republican United States, the French revolutionaries paid lip service to the claim that all are created equal, while denying the thing itself. But if revolutionary equality was thus exposed as a "chimera," real equality was nothing of the sort. And the French revolutionaries, for all their failings, had hastened that realization. Babeuf's conspiracy made it plain. "We want *real* equality or death," the manifesto proclaimed. "*This is* what we need. And we'll have this real equality, at whatever the cost." More than just a word or an appeal to abstract rights, real equality must be something palpable that one could see and share and touch. "We want it in our midst, under the roofs of our houses." Equal people should have equal things, sharing "common property" and "the community of goods," which would be parceled out in the "Republic of Equals" to come. The French Revolution was nothing but the precursor to another revolution, "one that will be greater, more solemn, and which will be the last."[2]

Buonarroti's history was thus as much about the future as it was about the past. Widely translated in a Europe experiencing the first social changes of industrialization while still in the grips of the conservative reaction to the French Revolution, it struck a nerve. Friedrich Engels and Karl Marx, among others, would later hail the text as a seminal contribution, praising Buonarroti for having "reintroduced" the "communist idea" into France. And while their praise was largely self-serving, and ultimately dismissive of a type of early socialism they regarded as leveling, unscientific, and crude, it nonetheless registered the work's transitional importance, even as it passed over a central tension at its heart. That tension—between the real equality of the future and the illusory equality of the present and past—would play out in their own work too, bequeathing a mixed message not unlike the one they decried in their bourgeois and liberal opponents. Equality was specious, they came to believe, deceptive and falsely alluring. And although many socialists continued to see it on the horizon, Marx and Engels cautioned that their vision was an illusion.[3]

It is tempting to see Buonarroti's invocation of equality, and particularly social and material equality, as a natural progression, part of the cascade that spilled over from the first rights claims of the French Revolution to encompass civil, political, and ultimately economic ground. In certain respects it surely was. Buonarroti presented it as such, as did Babeuf, whose own extreme Jacobinism was a clear extension of the most radical calls for social equality uttered, if never fully acted upon, between 1792 and 1794. Many other self-described "socialists" would reaffirm those connections in the following years. The French radical Pierre Leroux, for example, among the very first to coin and employ the word "socialism" in the early 1830s, made precisely that connection in his 1838 book *De l'égalité* (On equality). "We are between two worlds," the epigraph proclaimed, between "a world of inequality that is finishing and a world of equality that begins." In embracing the dogma of equality bequeathed by Rousseau, the French Revolution had revealed the sacred future. The task now was to usher it in.[4]

Such connections would be drawn throughout the nineteenth century, and even more insistently in the aftermath of the Bolshevik Revolution of 1917, when observers linked the French to the Russian Revolution while embedding equality claims firmly in the socialist tradition that ostensibly connected the two. On this view, socialism was but the natural extension of the egalitarian impulse that drove the French Revolution from the start. As one historian has summed up the logic, "Socialism originates in a moral idea—equality—and culminates in a practical program—the end of private property and the market."[5]

There can be no denying that equality did come to play a central, if complicated, role in socialist thought, and that many of its early partisans, including Buonarroti, saw themselves as taking up where the French Revolution left off. Yet such continuities can be deceiving. For if it is true, especially of more recent times, that "there has been wide agreement that equality should be regarded as a key socialist value, perhaps even *the* socialist value," that wasn't always so. Indeed, the central place of equality in modern socialist thought has obscured the ambiguous place it occupied at its origins, and that it long continued to play among its Marxian successors. Simply put, as one leading critic affirms, "socialism did not arise from a concern about equality"; in many ways it entailed its rejection. And even those early socialists who did embrace the "dogma" of equality bequeathed by insurrectionists such as

Buonarroti and Babeuf did so by transforming it, in the process, into something that the older atheists would not have fully recognized. Socialism, in their handling, became a kind of religion, or substitute for religion, in which the older Christian beliefs about equality and fraternity enjoyed a newly enchanted place.[6]

Consider first the theme of equality in the writings of Henri de Saint-Simon (1760–1825), widely regarded as among socialism's most important early prophets. Saint-Simon was born an aristocrat in the Old Regime and fought alongside Lafayette as a young man in the American War of Independence. An initial enthusiast for the French Revolution, Saint-Simon grew increasingly skeptical of its radical turn and was imprisoned during the Terror, in part for an oddly conceived plan to purchase Notre Dame Cathedral and sell off its materials for profit. Despite the failure of that visionary scheme, he lived to dream others, coming to see modern science and industry, as opposed to revolutionary insurrection, as the true agents of progressive change. Both depended, he believed, on the outstanding achievements of the few, which would redound to the benefit of the many when society was properly organized to care for all its members. Convinced of the need to improve the social and material circumstances of the "poor and the most numerous," Saint-Simon was no less convinced that equality was a specious route to that end.

In his very first published work, in 1803, Saint-Simon decried, like so many in the aftermath of the Terror, "the appalling atrocities that resulted from the application of this principle of equality." The French Revolution's excesses were the "natural result of putting power into the hands of the ignorant," he wrote, both in France and in the conflagrations it sparked abroad. With a casual racism and assumption of European superiority that was not uniform but hardly uncommon in early socialist circles, Saint-Simon called attention to what he regarded as the hopelessly naïve extension of "principles of equality" to Blacks (*les nègres*). He believed that if the revolutionaries had consulted with "physiologists," they would have understood that the Black man "was not susceptible, given his makeup, to an equal education, nor of being raised to the same level of intelligence as the European." The social and industrial order of the future would make no concession to ignorance or race, he said, but would be organized to empower originality, creativity, and intelligence.[7]

Saint-Simon envisioned a hierarchically ordered society divided between three principal classes. At the top would be the so-called industrials (*les industriels*), comprising the scientists, artists, technicians, and entrepreneurs who would play a leading role in furnishing the intellectual capital and leadership of the new society. They would be followed by an ample class of proprietors, and then, at the bottom of the social scale, by those whom Saint-Simon described as the "surplus of humanity," members of the most numerous class, who currently "rallied to the word equality." The word, clearly, was misconceived, according to Saint-Simon, for those aspiring to equality would not be equal in the new world to come. Nor would they lead, even if they would certainly benefit from the marvels of the new social order. Science and industry would be harnessed to free humanity's surplus from the drudgery and hardship that now characterized life for the great many.[8]

Saint-Simon's vision of a new "industrial system" admitted no formal privilege on the basis of hereditary nobility or birth. Having renounced his own aristocratic title during the French Revolution, he never sought to reclaim it. He also was sensitive, despite his racial prejudice, to the plight of women, broad-minded in his efforts to think outside the strictures of established gender roles, and in fact his followers developed an explicit Saint-Simonian feminism in the 1820s and 1830s that garnered adherents in Europe and the New World.[9]

Still, the new industrial order would not vaunt equality. Saint-Simon's future was a technocratic one, in which spiritual and intellectual elites led society for its overall benefit, and would accrue profits and status accordingly. A popular slogan of the Saint-Simonians encapsulated their view of redistributive justice:

"To each according to his ability, to each according to his works." People would get what they deserved.[10]

Thus, Saint-Simon and his acolytes coupled concern for the poor and downtrodden with a hierarchical view of society that aimed to enable individuals to realize themselves in keeping with their natural abilities, while casting a generally negative view of equality as "a principle at odds with human organization" and human nature. "Saint-Simon tells you that men are unequal," one disciple declared in summarizing the master's thought for all those "partisans of equality," who might be skeptical. "But he tells you as well that they will only be distinguished by their power of love, of science, and of industry. Isn't that what you want?" According to this view, equality may have played a positive role in deposing the feudal order of the Old Regime, but it had since become an impediment to progress. As one of Saint-Simon's leading students, and a social visionary in his own right, Auguste Comte, observed, "When the dogma of equality had achieved the overthrow of the old polities, it could not but become an obstacle to any reorganization. . . . [M]en cannot be made equal, because they are not equal or even equivalent." Comte insisted that all had a right to expect from society "the fulfillment of the conditions necessary to the natural development of one's personal activity." But beyond that, human beings possessed no identical rights at all, for the plain reason that we are all very different. "The simple physical inequalities that fix the attention of superficial observers are much less marked than intellectual and moral differences," Comte continued, "and the progress of civilization tends to increase these more important differences, as much as to lessen the inferior kind." It followed, in Comte's reckoning, "that applied to any assemblage of persons" in an advanced state of development, "the dogma of equality becomes anarchic."[11]

That other influential visionary of early socialism, Charles Fourier (1772–1837), expressed similar reservations throughout his adult life about what he described as equality's "illusions," even if he did confess to having "shared these illusions in 1789" as a young man. The son of a successful, if unschooled, cloth merchant, Fourier began his own professional life as a traveling salesman, and he quickly shed these childish illusions. In his first major work, *The Theory of the Four Movements*, published in 1808, he acknowledged that "yesterday academic arguments about equality toppled thrones, altars, and the laws of property." But after "the catastrophe of 1793," such illusions must be dispelled. The point was no longer to tear down society, but to set it aright.[12]

Equality would have no place in his new social edifice. It was, he concluded, "a political poison," a "social poison," that dissolved and infected communal ties, exacerbated envy, and directly contradicted human desires and needs. Equality was inimical to happiness, he believed, not only because it went against our natural inclination— "man being by instinct," as he elsewhere observed, "an enemy to equality and inclined toward a hierarchical or progressive regime"— but also because human character thrived on contrast, difference, and productive rivalry. Men and women were motivated by distinct and diverging passions, of which there were twelve principal kinds, ranging from those oriented strictly toward the five senses, such as the desire for sexual gratification, material luxury, or the pleasures of food, sound, or sight, to those that engaged the soul, including friendship, ambition, love, and parentage, to those that sought variety, competition, and community. In Fourier's account, the twelve passions combined in different people in different ways, yielding precisely 810 different basic character types. The details of his taxonomy are elaborate and arcane, and have often been ridiculed for their idiosyncratic flights, which one scholar likens "to the fantasies of someone on an LSD trip." But the basic insight was clear: that human beings varied tremendously in their needs. To treat them alike in leveling sameness was folly. Equality was fundamentally misconceived.[13]

No less devastating to genuine human flourishing in Fourier's account were the social structures of "civilization," which needlessly suppressed healthy human appetites and continually set them at odds. However idiosyncratic many of Fourier's views, his critique of contemporary society was trenchant. So-called free competition created endless strife, resulting in triumph and riches for some, misery and destitution for others. Current religious convictions and family structures stifled sexual gratification for men and women alike, and the general (dis)order of society was such that there was no rational correspondence between passion and fulfillment, character type and calling. Work for the great many was drudgery, often brutalizing and degrading, and social interaction yielded conflict and opposition rather than self-realization and complementary reward.

The solution, in Fourier's view, was to organize society in a more rational and harmonious way, so that human beings could harness their collective energies and satisfy their passions, working pleasurably together in activities that aligned with their proclivities and needs. The right ordering of society was crucial to human fulfillment because individual passions could only be adequately expressed and satisfied in harmonious "association" with others. Fourier imagined self-contained communities, what he called "phalanxes" (from the Greek and Roman military unit of tight formation), that would serve as the advance guard of the new Harmony to come. Bringing together all 810 basic personality types in a collective unit of some 1,500 to 1,600 people, the phalanx, or "phalanstery," as its emblematic living hall was known, would comprise people of different fortunes, ages, characters, and areas of knowledge, with the goal of providing ample opportunities for diverse social and sexual connections, as well as a healthy degree of cooperation through competition in the collective pursuit of luxury, wealth, and pleasure. There would be private property and different social classes, with profits divided according to contributions of talent, labor, and capital. But though, as Fourier insisted, there would be "no equality in Harmony"—there would be togetherness and common purpose, unity in association. In the future, human beings would be free to realize themselves in keeping with their particular desires and needs. The collective result would be extraordinary. When the globe was properly organized to maximize human potential, Fourier forecast "37 million poets equal to Homer,

37 million geometricians equal to Newton, 37 million dramatists equal to Molière, and so on through all the talents imaginable."[14]

It was Fourier's vision of how a new society could fully realize human potential while granting them the prospect of varied fulfillments in keeping with their aptitudes and tastes that would prove particularly compelling to Engels and Marx. The latter's famous reverie in *The German Ideology* (1845–1846) about how life under communism would "make it possible for me to do one thing today and another tomorrow, to hunt in the morning, fish in the afternoon, rear cattle in the evening, criticize after dinner, just as I like, without ever becoming a hunter, fisherman, shepherd, or critic," owed directly to Fourier. Fourier's critical reflection on contemporary society, and his enticing vision of cooperative fulfillment in the phalanx, also yielded several real-world attempts to put his theories into practice, including the founding of a number of Fourierist communities in the 1840s in the United States.[15]

Nor was Fourier the only early utopian to find acolytes in the New World. Another was the Welsh-born industrialist Robert Owen, who showed himself less critical of the "illusion" of equality than his French counterpart. Owen described his model factory town in New Lanark, Scotland, along with the short-lived experiment in communal living at New Harmony, Indiana, in the United States, as "Communities of Equality." A self-made textile manufacturer whose father was an artisan, Owen trained initially as a draper, viewing the early displacements of the Industrial Revolution firsthand. He came to regard the toll they took on the working population as a scathing indictment of contemporary society. Deeply influenced by British Enlightenment doctrines and the tradition of radical Protestant dissent, Owen developed a strong belief in the power of the environment to shape human character. The vastly unequal privileges, property holdings, and educational opportunities of Great Britain, he said, had created an immoral and selfish society, along with conditions inimical to human progress. To change human character, social conditions needed to be changed. As Owen stressed in a speech to the residents of New Harmony, not long after he had addressed the United States Congress in 1825, "Equal rights, property, and means of improvement and enjoyment" would be fostered among all so that "the evils of the old selfish, individual system" could be buried. A spirit of cooperation would replace the vicious competition of laissez-faire, and a shared community of goods would displace the inequities of a regime of private property. Owen acknowledged that in the short term, even in a select community such as New Harmony, a certain degree of "pecuniary inequality will be unavoidable." But he looked forward eventually to "the arrival of that period, when there shall be no artificial inequality among the whole human race," including, it should be stressed, between men and women, who would enjoy exactly the same rights in the new world to come.[16]

But if "artificial" inequalities—those based on class, station, gender, education, or wealth—were to be abolished, not all would be alike. Whereas eighteenth-century authors were often quick to emphasize human similarities, Owen, like Fourier and Saint-Simon, stressed human difference. It was evident from the beginning, he said: "No two infants have ever yet been known to possess, at birth, the same proportions of physical, intellectual, or moral elements." And natural differences and capacities, he insisted, were extensive, and must be considered along with the "natural inequality of different age and experience," which Owen regarded as the only legitimate forms of "inequality and condition." They were, in his view, indispensable "to preserve order and harmony in society." While, to be sure, a more just system of opportunity and education would inevitably narrow the chasms of possibility that now divided the experience of the rich and the poor, more equal opportunities would never efface human differences entirely. That was only for the good, as the "endless variety in the compound of the original elements of human nature in the individual," Owen said, resulted in the rich tapestry of humanity that he believed redounded to collective happiness. A more just society would develop the unique capacities of each to the overall benefit of all, drawing out human capacities that had long been stifled for the vast majority of men and women on the planet and allowing them to realize their full potential.[17]

Thus, even as he admitted, like Fourier and Saint-Simon, the extent of human difference, Owen hoped to a greater degree than they did to shape nature through nurture, fostering "as much equality as can be advantageously introduced into practice during the change from the old habits to the new." That said, he acknowledged that "existing feelings, arising from inequality of education and condition," would slow the emergence of the new society—and in the aftermath of the failure of the New Harmony experiment in 1827 and further setbacks in England in the 1830s, that acknowledgment deepened. In an open letter dedicated to the governments of Great Britain, Austria, Russia, France, Prussia and the United States, written in 1841, Owen called on the major powers of the "civilized world" to hasten the advent of the "Millennium" by way of "transition colonies" that would divide populations into four principal classes: "hired laborer or servants"; mechanics, artisans, and "superior kinds of servants"; tenants; and finally, a fully "independent class" that would show the way of the future. When this state of transition might give way to full equality, Owen did not say.[18]

Owen's use of the term "Millennium," however, is revealing of his vision of the end. It was not a metaphor, but a literal description of the onset of the "universal love, charity, and harmony" that would follow from the embrace of what he began to call in 1830 "the New Religion." This would be a religion unlike any the world had known, a religion stripped of the mystery and fear that prevailed in humanity's extant faiths. It would be a rational religion, a religion of nature and science, whose precepts accorded perfectly with the teachings of Owen himself, which he described with scant modesty as the "second coming of truth." As such, it would replace the "first great truth" long taught by the world's sages and prophets. Those men, he said, had revealed that there could be no "peace on earth" until men and women were "trained to love one another as they love themselves." But that kind of society had not yet been realized, and the reasons for that failure had been "hidden until now in impenetrable darkness." Only Owen had grasped them, showing how overcoming social injustice, ignorance, and inequality could "alone create universal charity and universal love." He was thus paving the way, he said, for "happiness from birth to death, for all."[19]

Notwithstanding its direct invocation of Christian charity and love, Owen's "New Religion" was overtly hostile to the practices of the established Christian churches and revealed religion more generally. In that respect, it was not unlike the corresponding views of Saint-Simon and Fourier, who both frequently excoriated the Catholic Church. Fourier, for his part, added noxious references to Jewish merchants and "the Jew." His writings are marred by a casual antisemitism not uncommon among nineteenth-century French socialists.[20]

Yet, like Owen, both Fourier and Saint-Simon recognized that the problem of religion was pressing in postrevolutionary Europe, and all the more so given the churches' historical failures and compromises. Collectively their work responded to what they perceived as the spiritual crisis of the age, opened up by the French Revolution's assault on Christianity and its failure to replace it with a viable form of civil religion. The religious history of Europe in the first half of the nineteenth century and the origins of socialism are inseparable, even if they have been frequently viewed apart.[21]

Thus, in a bid to provide a new locus of spiritual authority, Saint-Simon devised what he described in his last major work as a "new Christianity," whose two main tenets—universal brotherhood and an effort to ameliorate the condition of the poor—he regarded as a distillation of the "true spirit" of the Christianity of old. Fourier, similarly, whose criticisms of the "decrepit" Catholic Church and Christian attitudes toward the body were unsparing, nonetheless maintained that "John the Baptist was the prophet, precursor of Christ. I am the prophet, post-cursor, announced by him and completing his work of the rehabilitation of men." He put forth what he likewise described as a "new religion," and, in the *Nouvelle monde industriel et sociétaire* (The new social and industrial world) of 1829, he devoted considerable space to showing how his message was consistent with that of the New Testament rightly understood. One of his leading disciples, Victor Considérant, reaffirmed the point, insisting that Fourier's teaching was "quite simply the realization of Christianity in society."[22]

However outlandish on its face, that comment was indicative of a broader current among early socialists, who presented their teachings as the true fulfillment of Christianity. Some even made bold to rescue equality from the disdain of Saint-Simon and Fourier and to reclaim it from the insurrectionary heirs to Babeuf and Buonarroti. In doing so, they presented socialism and communism as natural extensions of the genuine teachings of Jesus, further sacralizing equality as a goal of social justice and human redemption.

Assertions to that effect—that the various new religions of the nineteenth century represented the fulfillment of Christianity's original promise of equality—were surprisingly widespread among socialists in the 1830s and 1840s, above all in France. But in England, too, Chartists pushing for universal manhood suffrage could stress that "our Savior . . . uniformly denounced riches and advocated equality in all things"; and in Germany and Switzerland, too, the tailor Wilhelm Weitling and his communist followers made equality's Christian underpinnings a central theme. Claiming to revive and regenerate the idealism of a faith that the historical churches had betrayed, such figures presented themselves as the true heirs of the Christian dispensation for the poor. Jesus himself, they reminded their followers, was a simple artisan, at ease among workers and peasants, a resolute defender of the marginalized and oppressed. His unconditional love excluded no one. It was in that context that socialists often invoked assertions of equality, fusing their "science" to a message of universal charity. As the self-described "Christian-socialist" and onetime Saint-Simonian Philippe Buchez observed, "The Christian era will not have reached its culmination until it realizes the equality that the earliest Christians proclaimed as the keystone of their dogma." The French Revolution, he argued, had been in large part a rebellion against the church for having abandoned its foundational egalitarianism. Socialists were now working to recover and redeem it.[23]

Pierre Leroux, similarly, presented the efforts of nineteenth-century socialists as consistent with those of the earliest Christians. In a long work on the "democratic origins" of the Christian faith, he took pains to show that Christian communities were originally consecrated on principles of democracy, with bishops elected by the people to do their bidding and represent their will. Only later was that democratic impulse suppressed by the popes and the rule of priests. And while he stressed that the modern doctrine of equality was ultimately a recent creation—the product, in large part, of Jean-Jacques Rousseau's own idiosyncratic engagement with Christian ideals—he also insisted that Jesus himself had been a social revolutionary who assailed human hierarchies. Pointing to Jesus's connections to early Jewish sects, Leroux maintained that he had learned to despise riches from the Essenes, and to advocate the community of goods that was then embraced by his first disciples. It is revealing that in his work on equality, De l'égalité, Leroux invokes Jesus some fifty times, describing him as the "destroyer of castes."[24]

The equality that Buchez and Leroux thus drew from the Christian tradition went beyond any simple moral, or even civil and political, equality. Theirs extended fully to property and possessions, and as such it militantly assailed the material inequalities of contemporary society that in the capitalist economies of the 1830s and 1840s were becoming more and more apparent. As Buchez put it, "As long as material inequality exists among men, the only sentiment which can provide the proper basis for social morality, as for individual morality, is the desire to wipe out that inequality." Likewise, Louis Blanc, the socialist theorist and politician who affirmed that the "task of our own epoch is to breathe life back into religious sentiment," assailed the "murderous inequality" wrought by a social and economic system based on competition: "With competition, there is no equality, because it is nothing but inequality in motion. With competition, there is no fraternity, because it is a form of combat." In Blanc's view, the revolutionary trinity of liberty, equality, and fraternity was firmly embedded in the message of the gospels.[25]

The utopian leader Étienne Cabet fully agreed, though he pressed the radical reading of the gospels even further than Blanc, arguing that Christianity and communism were one and the same. A fascinating figure in this regard, and an influential one, Cabet more than any other early socialist seized on the word "communism" and popularized it to denote a new kind of communitarian association that would abolish private property altogether while creating the conditions of shared abundance. A lawyer by training, though his father was a cooper, Cabet served briefly as a government official and then as a representative in the Chamber of Deputies during the constitutional monarchy of the French king Louis Philippe, before being forced into exile in Great Britain from 1835 to 1839 for his increasingly radical views. There he was introduced to the work of Owen, and read deeply in Saint-Simon and Fourier, among others.

Combining Owen and Fourier's vision of model cooperative associations with the confidence in the power of science and industry of Saint-Simon and the radical egalitarianism of Buonarroti and Babeuf, Cabet gave it all the blessing and imprimatur of scripture. "Yes, Jesus Christ is communist," he affirmed in concluding his long treatise *Le vrai Christianisme suivant Jésus-Christ* (True Christianity according to Jesus Christ) of 1846. "The Christianity of the apostles, of the first Christians, of the fathers of the church is communism." Christianity extended the call for social justice of the early Hebrew prophets, and John the Baptist announced what that would entail: "Every valley shall be filled in, and every mountain and hill shall be made low" (Luke 3:5). In Cabet's reading, John's words were a statement of leveling intention, and Jesus attempted to follow through. Everywhere he proclaimed "fraternity, equality, and liberty" among the people, condemning riches and embracing the poor. A revolutionary, a propagandist, a "worker, a proletarian," Jesus ushered in a model of a new and perfect social organization based on universal love. Even if the son of man never systematically explained the content of his "social and political equality," such "Equality," Cabet assured his readers, capitalizing the word as he often did, was "a necessary consequence of fraternity." The gospels breathed it on every page. And although their true teaching and example had long been suppressed by corrupt churches and grasping priests, the conditions of the world were ripe for their recovery, extension, and fulfillment. All men—and all women, too—could rejoice. "As much as Jesus, and more than any other reforming movement," Cabet insisted, "our communism wants to liberate woman, recover her natural rights, her equality, her education. Our communism demands justice for all."[26]

Cabet, in fact, had already provided a vivid portrait of what the recovery of Christian communism would entail in his best-known work, the utopian novel *Voyage en Icarie* (Voyage to Icaria), first published anonymously in London in 1840 and subsequently reprinted throughout the 1840s and 1850s. Icar, the founder of Icaria, "constantly invokes the name and words of Jesus Christ in favor of equality, fraternity, and . . . the community of goods," and the inhabitants of Icaria live to put them into effect. Without strife or conflict, misery or vice, Icaria is a harmonious place, devoted exclusively to the needs of the people. Popular sovereignty holds sway there along with total democracy, but there are no politics as such and no political parties. A single newspaper provides the news. Indeed, from a twenty-first-century perspective, Icaria is run with a disconcerting degree of homogeneity and authoritarian control: everything from food to housing to education is mandated and administered. The inhabitants even dress alike.[27]

Yet the image of ease and egalitarian fairness on view in the novel was apparently no less appealing to contemporaries for that. For uniformity and sameness yielded an "equality of abundance," a modest luxury that banished not only mansions and private carriages, but also prisons, brothels, and almshouses, guaranteeing a consistent level of comfort for all. And although all citizens are required to work, the most onerous tasks are performed by the marvels of modern machinery, with accommodations made for individual capacity. Whereas Saint-Simon had vowed to give "to each according to his ability, to each according to his works," Cabet emphasizes instead the varying responsibilities and needs of the inhabitants. As the epigraph to the 1845 edition of the novel (and all subsequent printings) declared on the title page: "To each according to their needs. From each according to their capacities" ("A chacun suivant ses besoins. De chacun suivant ses forces"). Louis Blanc reversed the order of the phrases but maintained the same general sense, noting, in his *Catéchisme des socialistes* (Socialist catechism) of 1849, "From each according their faculties, to each according to their needs" ("De chacun selon ses facultés, à chacun selon ses besoins").[28]

Like so much in early socialism, the phrases have revealing religious resonance, echoing, in the formulations of Saint-Simon, Cabet, and Blanc, various passages in the Bible, from which they were ultimately drawn. Blanc, in fact, explicitly attributes divine authorship to his slogan, noting, "Equality is but proportionality, and will not genuinely exist until each WILL PRODUCE ACCORDING TO HIS FACULTIES AND CONSUME ACCORDING TO HIS NEEDS, according to the law, which is, as it were, written by God himself into the [social] organization."[29]

But even more revealing than its religious provenance is the tension the phrase highlights in evolving socialist understandings of equality. For, on the one hand, the words in the slogan embraced by Cabet and Blanc frankly acknowledge the same natural inequality of ability that Fourier and Saint-Simon highlighted. Each will provide what they can, according to their unequal abilities, and be provided for in keeping with their unequal needs. But whereas Fourier and Saint-Simon used natural inequality as the justification for unequal rewards, Cabet and Blanc placed the emphasis on the added duties and responsibilities incumbent on those who had more. As Blanc explained in the first edition of *Organisation du travail* (Organization of labor) of 1839, "The day will come, when we will acknowledge that he, whom God has endowed with more strength, or greater intelligence, must do more for his fellow men. . . . For the inequality of capabilities has for its goal, not the inequalities of rights, but the inequalities of duties."[30] Those who need shall be satisfied, and those who have shall offer more. But what will they receive? Do unequal contributions imply unequal rewards? Or does unequal work demand equal pay? In early editions of the text, Blanc held back from suggesting "absolute equality"—that is, paying all alike, regardless of productivity or output. In a later version, he did so explicitly, only to withdraw the proposition in the face of popular protest when the experiment was put into effect briefly among worker cooperatives during the Revolutions of 1848.[31]

Cabet, by contrast, embraced the logic openly, and on biblical authority no less, invoking, in *Le vrai Christianisme*, Jesus's "Parable of the Workers in the Vineyard," recounted in Matthew 20. Jesus speaks there of an owner of a vineyard who paid out equal wages to all who worked in his fields. When some workers complain that those who were hired late in the day worked only one hour, but had been made "equal to us who have borne the burden of the work and the heat of the day," the landowner replies that he has done them no injustice. "I am not being unfair to you," he insists. "Didn't you agree to work for a denarius? Take your pay and go. I want to give the one who was hired last the same as I gave you." For Jesus, the conclusion to be drawn is general: "The last will be first, and the first will be last." But for Cabet it is also more specific. "Jesus wants the workers to be equal," he explains. "He wants equal pay" (*égalité du salaire*). Those who don't desire such an outcome are simply "not Christians."[32]

That they were not Christians, Marx and Engels, like the vast majority of their followers, stridently maintained. But that they were communists, they rarely denied. And as Engels complained in a long article on the varieties of European socialism first published in Robert Owen's journal, *The New Moral World*, in 1843, communists, at least in France, were decidedly of the faith: "It is, however, curious, that . . . the French Communists, being a part of a nation celebrated for its infidelity, are themselves Christians. One of their favourite axioms is, that Christianity is Communism, '*le Christianisme c'est le Communisme*.' This they try to prove by the bible, the state of community in which the first Christians are said to have lived, etc."[33] Engels went on to assert, arguably with good reason, that Christian communists read their Bible too selectively. But what he and Marx refused to consider was whether the "religiosity" of socialism's origins might have continued to influence their own species of faith. They also obscured, for the time being at least, the question of whether they hoped to make all workers equal and pay them the same, as Cabet's Jesus counseled, or individuals should instead be rewarded, as Saint-Simon proposed, according to their works. Were men and women created equal, or were they not? And could they be made so in the society to come?

Marx and Engels would provide a complex answer to those questions in due course, but already the astute Pierre-Joseph Proudhon, their onetime friend and later antagonist, perceived the stakes. As he noted in his 1840 *What Is Property?*, "Communism is inequality." By that he meant that "communism is the exploitation of the strong by the weak." Whereas in regimes based on private property, "the inequality of conditions is the result of force," he noted, "in communism the inequality of conditions comes from making mediocrity of talent and achievement equal to excellence." Communism, Proudhon concluded, was "oppression and slavery," for it must inevitably constrain ability and flatten needs while oppressing individual liberty and choice. Opposed to the "free exercise of our faculties," it violated not only the "autonomy of the conscience," but equality itself, "by rewarding equally labour and laziness, skill and stupidity, and even vice and virtue."[34]

Cabet, who was likely one of the main targets of this attack, essentially rested his rebuttal on the belief that the suppression of private property would bring about the end of egoism. Like Rousseau, and so many Christians before him, he regarded self-love as the great barrier to charity and full human equality. And also like Rousseau, and Owen too, he believed that changing social relations would induce a change in human nature. With the onset of universal love, it would be possible to give according to abilities and to accept according to needs without resentment, envy, or constraint. The strong would aid the weak willingly while embracing their equal lot.

Thus, whatever the doubters might say, Cabet regarded the future with optimism. Real equality, he declared in the preface to *Voyage en Icarie*, was no "chimera"; it was "realizable and possible." Indeed, to an even greater degree than the insurrectionary socialists in the tradition of Buonarroti and Babeuf, who regarded the armed takeover of the state by a vanguard minority as the prerequisite for equality's triumph, Cabet saw the spread of equality as inevitable, a process that was happening on its own. In a long "*coup d'oeil* of the history of humanity" included toward the end of the volume, he endeavored to map the slow but ineluctable progress of equality over time. The seed had been planted in humanity's infancy thousands of years in the past and had steadily grown and expanded. Cabet followed its gradual development through the ancient world and the flowering of Christianity, then through the Reformation and the English, American, and French Revolutions. Since that time, he said, the progress of industry and production had only given it further impulsion. He emphasized the point by quoting the observations of a litany of social observers sensitive to the evolving fortunes of equality. The evidence was clear: "Providence has decided that equality will triumph." A new era was dawning, and it would be radically different from anything the world had known. For if the recorded past of the world so far revealed nothing but an endless series of "troubles and disorders, vices and crimes, wars and revolutions, torment and massacres, catastrophes and calamities," the reason was altogether clear: "The more that we study history, the more we are profoundly convinced that *Inequality* is the cause." Remove it, "suppressing the cause, by substituting equality for inequality," and men and women would flourish like never before.[35]

With its sweeping metaphysical account of the course of human progress, its stark contrasts between the fallen world of old and the new world to come, and its repeated assertion that socialism marked the final fulfillment of the original Christian promise of universal love, Cabet's thought was of a piece with the other major movements of early socialism. Eschatological and chiliastic, these movements offered new religions and substitutes for religion to address the spiritual crisis of the age. And although they provided conflicting accounts of human equality, and of the kinds of social and economic relations the future would entail, they succeeded nonetheless in infusing the egalitarian ideal with an almost magical resonance. Leroux expressed this nicely when he observed that equality was "at once a dogma and a commandment," a "divine law anterior to all laws, and the basis upon which all laws must be derived." Sacralizing equality, he and others enhanced the profound emotional and redemptive associations that Christians and French revolutionaries had bequeathed to the concept and the word. To Leroux and Cabet, equality was nothing less than the final destiny of humanity and the solution to its tortured and troubled past.[36]

But how to hasten its arrival? The majority of the utopian socialists had favored the formation of small, ideal communities to model and prepare the way. Cabet, who spurned all talk of armed insurrection on Christian grounds, was no exception. In 1848 he sailed from France with some 1,500 loyal followers with the intent of forming an actual Icarian community in the United States. The experiment, like the American ventures of Owen and Fourier, proved short-lived.

Plagued from the start by insolvency, infighting, and disease, the effort seemed to give credence to the warnings of Proudhon. It ended in failure, with Cabet himself dying of a stroke in St. Louis in 1856.

Yet the very presence of such men in the New World underscores the fact that the United States continued to figure in the European imagination as a promised land of equality's future, or, conversely, as a specter of where equality might lead. It is revealing in that connection that Cabet could cite Tocqueville in support of his assertion that Providence was guiding equality's fate, paraphrasing the celebrated author of *Democracy in America* to the effect that "democracy and equality progress by the will of the sovereign master: to attempt to stop them would be to fight against God himself." Tocqueville had indeed come away from his travels in the American republic in 1831–1832 convinced that equality was an ineluctable, even providential force. But he gave voice to that conviction with a considerable measure of dread. The book was written, he said, "in the grip of a religious terror." Other European observers expressed their fears with even greater measures of horror and derision, decrying what they regarded as the leveling chaos of democratic governance, the absence of greatness, the confusion of ranks, the vulgarity and insolence of the American people.[37]

More sympathetic voices, meanwhile, pointed with reason to what that other great observer of democracy in America, Harriet Martineau, described in 1837 as the great contradiction between principles and practices in the treatment of women and slaves. She predicted, however, that such contradictions could not stand, and that the denial of the "equal rights of both halves of the human race" would soon be a thing of the past. Little more than a decade later, Harriet Taylor saw cause for cautious optimism. A flurry of women's conventions in the United States, she noted, in a celebrated essay in London's *Westminster Review*, was pushing the question of the "enfranchisement of women," and of "their admission, in law and in fact, to equality in all rights, political, civil, and social," in ways that would ultimately redound to the benefit of Europe and humanity.[38]

It was, in fact, in the very year that Cabet sailed for the New World (1848) that Elizabeth Cady Stanton, Lucretia Mott, Frederick Douglass, and a host of like-minded individuals met in Seneca Falls, New York, to issue their famous Declaration of Sentiments, whose opening line consciously echoed the Declaration of 1776: "We hold these truths to be self-evident; that all men and women are created equal." The feeling behind that sentiment was growing, and it merged with currents flowing back and forth across the Atlantic that deposited a series of charged "questions" on the shores of the American and European public spheres. The so-called "woman question" was of a piece with other central interrogations of privilege and right, including the "labor question," the "social question," the "slavery question," and the "democracy question," that bore directly on issues of equality as they took shape at midcentury.[39]

But while Cabet and others sought to answer these questions in vanguard communities on American soil, and while Americans themselves debated them in their households and public fora before taking them to the battlefields of the Civil War, others in Europe sought to force the issues by still another means: revolution. Only weeks, in fact, after Cabet set sail from Le Havre for the United States, Paris erupted, in late February, in what proved to be the first of a series of uprisings across Europe that are now referred to collectively as the "Revolutions of 1848." All of them pushed for the expansion of the suffrage and for greater political inclusion, challenging monarchies with liberal, republican, and democratic demands. All of them dramatized the social question and the plight of urban workers. And in France, leading socialists, such as Louis Blanc and Auguste Blanqui, played a central role. Yet despite some significant victories, including the introduction of universal manhood suffrage in France and the definitive abolition of slavery in the French Empire, the revolutions were met across the continent with repression and reaction. Erstwhile socialists and communists were driven underground or into hiding. And the calamitous crackdown that ensued forced a profound reexamination of socialist doctrine and tactics. It was in the years that followed that Marx and Engels consolidated their understanding of "true" scientific socialism, casting a critical and often dismissive eye on the socialists who preceded them, and revising their understandings of equality accordingly.

Even before the European Revolutions of 1848, Marx and Engels were marking their distance from the utopian socialists. Resident in Paris, where they met, from 1843 to 1845, and then in Brussels until 1848, they read deeply in the French socialist and communist writers. But when they were tapped in 1847 to write a theoretical statement for the newly formed Communist League, a corresponding society of German émigré radicals and revolutionaries formerly known as the League of the Just (Bund der Gerechten), they seized the opportunity to impose doctrinal uniformity and to set their own evolving theoretical positions in opposition to what they regarded as the false routes and deviations of others. The result was what we know today as the *Communist Manifesto*, written in Brussels and first published in London in early February 1848, before the initial uprisings of the revolutions of that year and thus bearing no direct connection to them.

The pamphlet aimed simply to enlighten the people, giving workers a sense of what true communism entailed and of the place of the proletariat in the developing class struggle. Its third section was devoted to warning against ersatz doctrinal forms, such as "Reactionary Socialism," "Conservative or Bourgeois Socialism," and what Marx and Engels termed "Critical Utopian Socialism and Communism." They included the writings of Owen, Saint-Simon, Fourier, and Cabet among the latter, and while they credited them with concern for the interests of the working class at an early stage of its development, they dismissed their overall programs as "fantastic" and their social analysis as misconceived. "They still dream of experimental realization of their social utopias, of founding isolated *phalanstères*, of establishing 'Home Colonies,' or setting up a 'Little Icaria'—pocket editions of the new Jerusalem, so many 'castles in the air.'"[40]

In the aftermath of 1848, that skeptical message fell on fertile ground, as the sporadic risings of workers and democrats across Europe were put down along with the short-lived revolutionary measures conceded on their behalf. A new era of reaction ensued, stifling the hopes of the previous era. At the same time, surprisingly resilient capitalist economies marked what in many respects was the nadir of European socialism from 1850 to 1870. It was in that period conducive to toughminded views that Marx and Engels consolidated their own scientific theories while redoubling efforts to distinguish them from their "utopian" predecessors. The effort, which culminated in Engels's *Socialism: Utopian and Scientific* of 1880, was largely successful, and it enabled the two men to cover their tracks with respect to the debts they owed to the early socialists, and for generations of scholars to reproduce uncritically their categorical distinction between "utopian" longings and Marxian "science."[41]

In the past several decades, however, that distinction has broken down with the full realization that Marxism was no more scientific than its immediate predecessors, and no less utopian in its ultimate longing for universal social transformation. The realization has permitted a fuller understanding of the connections between socialisms early and late and the continued religious impetus that bound them. Despite vehement protests to the contrary, Marxism, no less than early socialism, was shaped by a common religious genesis, and should also be understood as an effort to "complete and replace" Christianity. Replete with a teleology derived ultimately from Christian theology, a metaphysically conferred calling and vocation for the downtrodden and exploited, a millenarian and apocalyptic vision of the end of history, and, in due course, a cult of martyrs and saints doing battle with transgressors and apostates, Marxism offered at once a religion and a replacement for religion no less utopian than those proposed by the pioneers it so derided.[42]

And what of the place of equality in this new creed? If Marxism, as Lenin observed, paraphrasing Engels, was the consummation of "classical German philosophy, classical English political economy, and French socialism combined with French revolutionary doctrines in general," then it should not be surprising that it reflected the ambivalence and tension of its (French) socialist and revolutionary roots. The *Communist Manifesto*, for its part, makes no mention of equality, save for a dismissive reference to the "social leveling in its crudest form" (*eine rohe Gleichmacherei*) born of the French Revolution. And in fact, the discussions that animated the Communist League's predecessor, the League of Justice, in 1845–1846 expressed a worry about the stultifying effects of the communism of Cabet and his Christian counterpart in Germany, Wilhelm Weitling. The league's director in London, Karl Schapper, insisted that "equality should mean equal opportunity, not equal consumption or equal enjoyment," and emphasized that true communism must grant a greater role for individual freedom and self-development. It is likely that Engels and Marx's inclusion of the ringing final line of part two of the *Manifesto*—"In place of the old bourgeois society, with its classes and class antagonisms, we shall have an association, in which the free development of each is the condition for the free development of all"—owes in part to Schapper's insistence. But its emphasis on individual self-realization is of a piece with Marx's other writings from the 1840s, where he makes clear that "only in community with others has each individual the means of cultivating his gifts in all directions."[43]

Marx's emphasis on individual self-realization makes no mention of equality, and in fact it presupposes inequalities insofar as individual abilities, needs, and conditions will necessarily vary. To fully cultivate each person's individual gifts would require, as one scholar puts it, "qualitatively different and quantitatively unequal" treatment of individuals. The sentiment echoed the judgment of Saint-Simon and Fourier, and the broader post-French-revolutionary concern that to insist too strongly on equality of treatment, in the face of diverse human capacity and need, was to risk leveling oppression. In that view, which was shared by liberals such as Tocqueville, equality and liberty were dangerously at odds.[44]

Marx's seeming preference for liberty over equality was not the only point of commonality between men who were otherwise very much opposed in their ideas. Although Tocqueville looked to the United States as the image of the democratic future, even while warning that its people's "ardent, insatiable, invincible passion" for equality posed a threat to liberty, and risked facilitating a new kind of despotism, he also cautioned that the forces of American industry might well "lead men back to aristocracy." In an analysis in the second volume of *Democracy in America* (1840) that echoed Adam Smith's famous warning about the debilitating effects of the division of labor on individual workers, Tocqueville pointed out how intense focus on repetitive tasks limited and constrained the mind. "What should we expect of a man who has spent twenty years of his life making pinheads?" Tocqueville asked. "As the principle of division of labor is more thoroughly applied, the worker becomes weaker, more limited, and more dependent." The human cost of modern productivity was potentially great. At the same time, the profits that accrued to those who owned the means of production were vast. Tocqueville warned of the emergence of a new kind of "manufacturing aristocracy," unconstrained by the ties of obligation and noblesse oblige that had moderated the landed aristocracies of old. "Today's manufacturing aristocracy, having impoverished and brutalized the men it uses, abandons them in times of crises," Tocqueville pointed out, adding, "All things considered, I believe that the manufacturing aristocracy that we see rising before our eyes is one of the harshest that has ever existed on earth." Although Tocqueville immediately qualified that assertion, judging that its power was still limited, he nonetheless warned ominously that "if permanent inequality of conditions and aristocracy are ever to appear in the world anew, it is safe to predict that this is the gate by which they will enter."[45]

What Tocqueville regarded as a mere risk was in the view of Marx and Engels a certainty. Yet their general concurrence points out how observers of very different political persuasions could view the conditions of capitalist economies in the crucial middle third of the nineteenth century with alarm. We know now, in fact, from recent studies of economic history, that inequality in the period between 1800 and 1860 was growing at a considerable rate in the American republic, with the consequence that "Tocqueville's famous warning proved even more broadly current than he predicted." In Europe, too, the concentration of ownership grew for much of the nineteenth century, widening inequalities of wealth. And while it is also true that workers' wages gradually rose as well, contributing to an overall improvement in living standards and belying Marx and Engels's predictions of the proletariat's increasing immiseration, the fact remains that, much as in our own time, the gap between the rich and the poor was widening. In that respect, both Tocqueville and Marx were right to be concerned about the social and political costs of the growing division.[46]

But it was there that commonalities end. Tocqueville believed in the capacity of liberal democracy to right itself; Marx believed that it was fatally flawed. Tocqueville viewed the emergence of a new aristocracy of riches as a possibility to be forestalled; Marx believed it was capitalism's necessary consequence, and that it would only worsen with time. And whereas Tocqueville believed that an increasing equality of conditions was the natural consequence of liberal democracy, Marx believed that equality to be a lie. Indeed, if his dismissals of crude "social leveling" hinted at the reservations about equality expressed by early socialists such as Saint-Simon and Fourier, his critique of liberalism entailed a full-frontal assault. Liberal equality, for Marx, was a specious and misleading abstraction. In a word, it was an illusion.

That, in fact, is Marx and Engels's most common figure for describing equality. Part of the mystifying complex of bourgeois ideology, equality in their view was of a piece with the other abstract rights granted to man and the citizen by the revolutions of the long eighteenth century. Ostensibly universal, those rights served in practice to mask the "real" social and economic relations they obscured in civil society, where actual "human relationships and conditions" prevailed. As Marx aimed to show in his early essay *On the Jewish Question* (1844), via a close analysis of documents from the American and French Revolutions, bourgeois "liberty" was in truth a cover for egoism, a license to exploit others in keeping with the law. Equality as a right of man was similar. It is "only the equal right to liberty described above, namely that every man is equally regarded as a self-sufficient monad." "Equality," Marx continued, alluding to the French revolutionary Constitution of 1795, "consists in the fact that the law is the same for all, whether it protects or punishes." Though he did not develop the thought in this particular instance (elsewhere he did), the criticism echoed G. W. F. Hegel's critique of Roman law, which treated all citizens alike in the abstract while remaining willfully blind to their objective differences of wealth, status, and power. The law in the bourgeois regimes of liberal capitalism did the same, covering over the inequalities hidden in equality's name. The Nobel Prize–winning French novelist Anatole France would later sum up the spirit of the critique when he observed that "the majestic equality of the laws . . . forbid the rich as well as the poor to sleep under the bridges, to beg in the streets, and to steal their bread." The law, like all emanations of bourgeois ideology, in Marx's view, merely reinforced the existing relations of class exploitation.[47]

Thus, equality as it had emerged as a value at the time of the American and French Revolutions was not only an illusion, perpetuating false consciousness, but also served as a dominant "form of estrangement," further alienating us from our true selves and from our natural connections to our fellow human beings, what Marx termed our "species-being."[48]

Labor and exchange as practiced in capitalist societies had precisely the same effect. In a celebrated analysis in the first chapter of *Capital* (1867), Marx drew that connection explicitly in a discussion of Aristotle's treatment of justice and equality in Book 5 of the *Nicomachean Ethics*. Aristotle notes there the remarkable equalizing effect of exchange networks and the role of money in carrying it out. For how is it, he wonders, that we can express the equal worth of qualitatively different things as we do in virtually every relation of exchange? We judge, to take the example of Aristotle invoked by Marx, that five beds are equal to one house. But what is the "essential identity" that unites these things, which are otherwise so different and distinct? Wherein does their equality lie? Aristotle asserts, in a passage Marx cites (in the Greek original no less), that "there can be no exchange without equality, and no equality without commensurability." And yet in Marx's view, Aristotle here "falters," unable to admit that "such unlike things can be commensurable, i.e., qualitatively equal." And so, Marx continues, Aristotle attributes the equation to "something foreign to the true nature of things," hitting upon an expediency and "makeshift for practical purposes." That makeshift is money, which "serves as a measure that makes things commensurable and so reduces them to equality." Money, in Aristotle's words, was "the measure of all things."[49]

In Marx's view, that was a mystification that had only become more prevalent under the conditions of advanced capitalism, which related all things and all people through the currency of exchange. It was in part for that reason that some could think of money itself in the nineteenth century as the "great apostle of equality" or "the great leveler," which simplified and replaced older distinctions drawn between people on the basis of birth, honor, title, connection, or status. Marx himself refers to capital as a "leveler, since it insists upon equality in the conditions of exploitation of labor in every sphere of production." But of course, as that quotation indicates, capital was simultaneously the source of invidious distinctions in societies judging money to be the ultimate measure of human worth. Since the late seventeenth century, in fact, a nascent life-insurance industry had begun to quantify the value of a human life—and slave traders had conducted such calculations for far longer still. Indeed, it was precisely slavery and the attendant assumption of natural human inequality that in Marx's view had blinded Aristotle from what in fact was the true "homogeneous element," the "common substance," that equalized houses and beds. "And that is," Marx revealed, "human labour." Here was the "secret of the expression of value, namely the equality and equivalence of all kinds of labor." It was the reality of work, not the abstraction of money, that made things truly commensurable: the hours of labor that went into beds and houses that could make five equal to one. That was a "truth," in Marx's understanding, that Aristotle did not comprehend because of the "historical limitations inherent in the society in which he lived." And that truth could not be "deciphered until the concept of human equality had already acquired the permanence of a fixed popular opinion [prejudice]."[50]

However elliptically expressed, the implications of that insight were profound. For Marx was reaffirming a thought he had seeded in his earliest writings—that equality, like all ideological values, was a belief tied to a specific phase of historical development, the expression of a narrow and timebound class interest masquerading as universal truth. It was, he and Engels observed in *The German Ideology*, the "illusions of the era" (*die Illusion dieser Epoche*). And while he granted elsewhere that the spread of the "prejudice" of equality since the eighteenth century had enabled the revelation of the "secret" of the universal value of exchange—allowing contemporaries to see that human labor power is embedded in all commodities and services—he also implied that the value of that prejudice was short-lived. Beliefs were tied to their moment of historical development, which operated dialectically through opposition, destruction, and creative synthesis. Having permitted the revelation of the labor theory of value, and assisted the bourgeoisie to overthrow feudalism, the "prejudice" of equality had served its historical purpose. It was in that sense that Marx described equality, cryptically, in his *Economic and Philosophical Manuscript of 1844*, as communism's "groundwork" (*Grund*) and "political justification" (*politische Begründung*). It was now destined to be transcended.[51]

Engels later made precisely that point in his long work the *Anti-Dühring* (1877), which attacked the "vulgar" socialism of the German philosopher Eugen Dühring. "The idea of equality," he notes there, "both in its bourgeois and in its proletarian form, is therefore itself a historical product, the creation of which required definite historical conditions that in turn themselves presuppose a long previous history. It is therefore anything but an eternal truth." Engels makes clear that equality is not just a bourgeois prejudice, but a proletarian one as well, widely received among the masses. Referring directly to Marx's comments in volume 1, Chapter 1, of *Capital* just cited, he continues, "And if today it [equality] is taken for granted by the general public—in one sense or another—if, as Marx says, it 'already possesses the fixity of a popular prejudice,' this is not the effect of its axiomatic truth, but the effect of the general diffusion and the continued appropriateness of the ideas of the eighteenth century." But prejudices, like illusions, would need to be dispelled.[52]

Two years earlier, in 1875, Engels had written to the prominent German socialist Auguste Bebel, urging just that. Bebel, a principal founder of the German Social Democratic Workers' Party (SDAP), continued, like other socialists, to employ the language of equality and pressed for its inclusion in the party program. But Engels made clear that he believed this was misconceived:

'The elimination of all social and political inequality,' rather than 'the abolition of all class distinctions,' is similarly a most dubious expression.... The concept of a socialist society as a realm of *equality* is a one-sided French concept deriving from the old 'liberty, equality, fraternity,' a concept which was justified in that, in its own time and place, it signified a *phase of development*, but which, like all the one-sided ideas of earlier socialist schools, ought now to be superseded, since they produce nothing but mental confusion, and more accurate ways of presenting the matter have been discovered.

Equality, as a one-sided relic of the past, had no place in the future, which would be devoted to the great historical task of overcoming class conflict. It would be superseded, in the revolution to come, when the bourgeoisie had been liquidated like the aristocracy of old.[53]

Bebel and his colleagues, however, including the influential German Jewish socialist Ferdinand Lassalle, were unmoved. The SDAP's inaugural program, issued in late May 1875 at the Thuringian city of Gotha, called explicitly for the end of "all social and political inequality" (*aller sozialen und politischen Ungleichheit*). Marx, who had earlier slagged off Lassalle as a "Jewish N—" in a letter to Engels charged with racial slurs, would have none of such vague talk, however, and in his well-known *Critique of the Gotha Program*, he made his opposition clear. One could speak of the abolition of distinctions based on class, he observed, but not of overcoming inequality as such. Marx consigned language of that sort, along with all talk of "equal right" and "fair distribution," to the dustbin of history. Those were concepts that "in a certain period had some meaning but have now become obsolete verbal rubbish," the kind of "trash" common among "democrats and French socialists," but not worthy of hard-headed historical materialists who could see the present and the future with more clarity.[54]

But what, precisely, should such open-eyed observers see? Marx foretold that the coming communist regime would unfold in two stages. In the first period, right after the initial demise of capitalism, and "still stamped with the birth marks of the old society," reward for work, "instead of being equal, would have to be unequal." That is to say that bourgeois norms of exchange would still apply. Given that "one man is superior to another physically or mentally and so supplies more labour in the same time, or can labour for a longer time," he would need to be rewarded accordingly. As Marx explained:

> This *equal* right is an unequal right for unequal labor. It recognizes no class differences, because everyone is only a worker like everyone else; but it tacitly recognizes unequal endowment, and

thus productive capacity, as natural privileges. It is, therefore, a right of inequality, in its content, like every right. Right, by its very nature, can consist only in the application of an equal standard; but unequal individuals (and they would not be different individuals if they were not unequal) are measurable only by an equal standard insofar as they are brought under an equal point of view.

In effect, Marx invoked here the standard of justice of Saint-Simon: to each according to his ability, to each according to his works. And given that human beings, in Marx's opinion, were as unequal as they were different, in the short run they would be rewarded accordingly.[55]

Yet if such "defects" were inevitable in the first or "socialist" phase of the revolution, in a higher communist phase, Marx assured readers, they would pass. The "enslavement" of the individual to the division of labor would be overcome, and the "antithesis" between mental and physical labor would be abolished. "After the productive forces have also increased with the all-around development of the individual, and all the springs of co-operative wealth flow more abundantly—only then can the narrow horizon of bourgeois right be crossed in its entirety." And only then, Marx affirmed, "[would] society inscribe on its banners: From each according to his ability, to each according to his needs!"[56]

In the final phase of communism, the dictum of Blanc and Cabet would be put into effect. Social classes would at that point be abolished, and thus a major source of the inequality characterizing the capitalist world would be removed. The bourgeoisie would be destroyed, and men and women would be equally free to develop their capacities through productive labor in conditions of abundance. The free development of each would be the condition of the free development of all. Yet, strictly speaking, there would be no equality beyond the (un)equal right to free development, only the unequal contributions that different (and so unequal) individuals would make to society and their different (and so unequal) needs. Anything else, in Marx's view, was an illusion left over from an earlier phase of historical development.

In his takedown of Proudhon, *The Poverty of Philosophy*, published the year before the Revolutions of 1848, Marx ridiculed the notion that "equality is the *primordial intention*, the *mystical tendency*, the *providential aim*" of society. The overcoming of class struggle, rather, was history's ultimate end, and that was not at all the same thing. There is no evidence whatsoever, in fact, that Marx envisioned the coming communist state as one of material equality or fairness. And while it may be argued that he would surely have wanted to limit inequality when it impinged on freedom as it did in capitalist states, equality was not the communist goal, and still less was the kind of leveling that Marx and Engels associated with the crudeness and excess of Babeuf and the early utopians, and invariably described in pejorative terms as *Gleichmacherei* or *Nivellierung*.[57]

That is not to say that Marxism, where it was implemented, had no egalitarian consequences. It certainly did, reducing Gini coefficients where they can be measured, and providing opportunities for workers, women, and other hitherto excluded groups. But no less than the other ideologies examined in this book, it generated and thrived on exclusions. Class enemies were everywhere, useful in binding comrades together and keeping them on guard. The "bourgeois" and the "capitalist" proved even more elastic than the "aristocrat" of the French revolutionaries, and Marxists found more efficient means than the guillotine of cutting people down. In that sense they surely engaged in leveling. But egalitarian distribution was not their goal.[58]

Marx's most important heirs understood such distinctions. Marx "takes into account with the greatest accuracy the inevitable inequality of men," Lenin observed in 1917. Mocking the "empty phrase mongering about equality" prevalent among his contemporaries, Lenin insisted, on the authority of Marx and Engels, that "the concept of equality is a most absurd and stupid prejudice *if it does not imply* the abolition of classes." "We want to abolish classes, and in this sense we are for equality," he acknowledged. "But the claim that we want all men to be alike is just nonsense"—the invention, as he put it, of "bourgeois professors" seeking to cast aspersions on genuine communists.[59]

Stalin, too, was doctrinaire in his interpretations, invoking Marx and Lenin together when he cracked down in the 1930s on equality mongering and what he considered excessive leveling (*uravnilovka*). It was necessary to pay skilled and unskilled laborers differently in the present stage of socialism, Stalin stressed, noting that "whoever draws up wage scales on the principle of equality . . . is at loggerheads with Marxism and Leninism." When, as Marx said in his *Critique of the Gotha Program*, the final stage of communism had been reached, Russians could live by the principle "from each according to ability, to each according to needs." But until then the principle to be followed tended more in the direction of Saint-Simon. "From each according to his ability, to each according to his work," was the subtle modification of the phrase that Stalin included in the Soviet Constitution of 1936. Men and women in the present stage of socialism would get only what they deserved—a truth that was made to apply to the millions of "enemies of the people" who were liquidated in the pursuit of a classless society under his reign.[60]

Still, the dream of equality did not disappear. Incubated by utopians in the nineteenth century, it served as a "central element" in the popular thinking that led up to the Bolshevik Revolution of 1917, which, like the French Revolution that preceded it, was "heavily saturated" in its early years with "ideas, words, symbols, and gestures denoting varying forms of equality." Despite Lenin's and Stalin's determined efforts to stamp out such bourgeois and utopian prattle, they could not entirely defeat the dream, which remained central to workers' movements in many parts of the world long after they were dead.[61]

It has been argued, in fact, that Marx himself, despite being "the denouncer of equality as illusion," remained the "prophet of its effective realization." Appearances to the contrary notwithstanding, Marx's philosophy, in that view, merely disguised its millenarian promise of deliverance in the language of science, while continuing to channel the utopian longing for equality expressed by all those, Christian or communist, who had come before, and by many who would come after. The utopian longing for equality, that is, remained the "psychological mainspring" of Marxism-Leninism even as Marxism-Leninism denied it, with equality itself, as another scholar has put it, continuing to serve, even where it was not recognized explicitly, as the "core moral ideal of all forms of socialism," which together insisted on the "primacy of equality in determining the just society."[62]

The thought is intriguing, if impossible to fully confirm. But it is given some credence by the long article on равенство (equality) published in the first edition of *The Great Soviet Encyclopedia* in 1940. The author, Iosif Kryvelev, was a scholar of religion, interestingly—a historian of Judaism and Christianity—who began by observing that "the equality of humankind has been a cherished dream of all workers and all the exploited" since class divisions first appeared on earth. After tracing the long history of the concept through its many "different forms" from antiquity to the present, Kryvelev took pains to echo Stalin's warning that "leveling in consumption and personal needs was a reactionary, petit-bourgeois absurdity." Inequalities remained in the Soviet Union as the "birth marks" of the capitalist stage of development. But as Kryvelev's final line promised, they would gradually disappear. "Soviet society is taking giant steps towards the construction of a just social order, about which the best minds of humanity have always dreamed—an order based on the equality of the people." At that very moment, however, other minds, to the west, of a *national* socialist persuasion, were working to thwart that construction, conceiving of the equality of the people, and the people's enemies, in very different terms.[63]

9

DOMINATION

The Equality of the Volk

Only two years after the Bolshevik Revolution of 1917, in Milan, Benito Mussolini formed the Fasci italiani di combattimento (Italian Fighting Leagues), a political movement made up largely of disgruntled fighters and veterans of World War I. The group grew out of the earlier Fascio d'azione rivoluzionaria (Revolutionary Action League), which Mussolini had formed in 1914 to bring Italy into the conflict on the side of the Allies. It would serve as the nucleus of the better-known Partito nazionale fascista (National Fascist Party) of 1921, which helped launch Mussolini to power in his infamous March on Rome the following year.

The central image and metaphor in the name of all these groups, and from 1921 a widely adopted emblem of the party, was the Roman *fascis* (or *fasces* in the Latin plural), a tight bundle of rods of sturdy elm or birch, often bound around the handle of an axe with a sharp, protruding blade. In the ancient Roman world, *fasces* were carried by the presiding attendants of Roman magistrates known as *lictors*, strong men tasked with accompanying high state officials in public to enforce the law. At once a tool and a symbol of Roman authority, the *fascis* could be used literally to beat transgressors or to decapitate by means of the axe. It represented the abstract force of justice as well as the very real authority of the state to administer violence.[1]

A mid-nineteenth-century depiction of Roman *lictors* and their *fasces* from Giulio Ferrario, *Costume antico e moderno* (Florence, 1843). © Florilegius / Bridgeman Images.

The *fascis* was also a symbol of the indissoluble bonds that tied citizens together. It had served the ancient Roman republic in that way, and the French revolutionaries employed it similarly, often with a *bonnet rouge* or an equilateral triangle and the ubiquitous slogan *liberté, égalité, fraternité*. Later, it was used in France as the official seal of the short-lived democratic republic of 1848, "one and indivisible," and in Italy it was employed primarily by left-wing groups until its Fascist appropriation. So, too, was it drawn on regularly in the United States, where it serves to this day to underscore the underlying values of American democracy. Visitors to Washington, DC, like visitors to countless state capitals across the country, will find it prominently displayed, flanking the speaker's rostrum in the US House of Representatives, or beneath the mighty hands of the seated emancipator in the Lincoln Memorial. The *fascis*, in short, is a symbol of intimate connection, of ties that bind, and as such, it has long been employed as a symbol of equality.

To think of the emblematic symbol of Italian fascism as a symbol of equality will likely be difficult for many readers. It is no less difficult to think of the German swastika as signifying what it

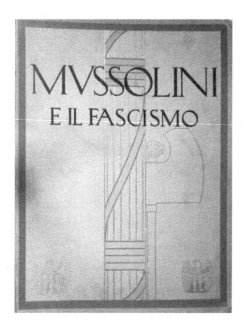

The cover image of an official book cowritten in 1929 by Mussolini and Augusto Turati with the *Fascist* symbol front and center. Universal History Archive / UIG / Bridgeman Images.

Antoine-Jean Gros, Allegory of the Republic, 1794. The figure's left hand rests on a carpenter's level with plumb line atop a *fascis*. Museum of the History of France, Versailles.

The statue of Abraham Lincoln at the Lincoln Memorial in Washington, DC, sculpted by Daniel Chester French in 1920. Lincoln's hands rest atop two *fasces*.

did for millennia in its original Aryan home: balance, harmony, and well-being, as the meaning of the root word in Sanskrit suggests (*svastica*, conducive to well-being). But part of the historian's task is to strip away the accretions of time to reveal meanings and associations that have been lost or obscured. And we have largely covered over and forgotten the languages of equality of the right-wing movements of the first half of the twentieth century—to such an extent that it is difficult to conceive that they were ever employed at all.[2]

Yet just as "freedom" and "democracy" have meant very different things to different people at different times, languages of equality have been widely employed and construed. It is well worth recalling those languages today, if only to better appreciate a phenomenon that is still very much with us: the affirmation of equality in the figure of domination.

The claim that appeals to equality figured centrally in the rhetoric and practice of the extreme Right in the first half of the twentieth century may seem, on its face, implausible, or even perverse. If the mental image of jack-booted thugs proclaiming supremacy in the streets doesn't counter the thought, then the gas chambers, with their explicit aim of ridding the world of alleged inferiors, surely will. Those searing images are reinforced by the words of fascists themselves. Mussolini, in a widely disseminated pamphlet, *The Doctrine of Fascism* (1932), cowritten with the Italian philosopher Giovanni Gentile, was seemingly categorical in his rejection of equality and democracy. "Fascism," the authors observe, "affirms the immutable, beneficial, and fruitful inequality of mankind," and it "denies, in democracy, the absurd conventional untruth of political equality." For his part, Hitler, with his incessant talk of subhuman peoples (*Untermenschen*) and the German master race was even more explicit, dismissing in *Mein Kampf* appeals to the "equality of all men, no matter what their race or color," as a Jewish lie. The inequality of peoples was fundamental to his thought, an unquestioned certainty and assumption.[3]

If that much is clear, so, too, should be the long suspicion of equality talk in conservative and right-wing circles, stretching all the way back to the eighteenth century. Enemies of the Enlightenment consistently railed against what they regarded as their opponents' rash attacks on natural human hierarchies and their naïve pursuit of "perfect equality." Edmund Burke's mocking dismissal of the French revolutionaries' "deceitful dreams and visions of the equality and rights of men" proved symptomatic of a broader counterrevolutionary critique spanning national and confessional divides. Well before Marx and his utopian socialist predecessors, conservatives were warning that revolutionary claims to equality were illusory and would only substitute an "aristocracy of the rich" for the aristocracy of old. Catholics joined with those deriding the "chimera" of revolutionary equality and its alleged leveling pretensions, claiming, like the Sicilian ex-Jesuit Sebastiano Ayala, that "the meaning that equality assumes today" was "opposed to the social order, absurd in its principle, and immoral in its application." They added their voice to those charging, with the Göttingen historian Christoph Meiners, that irreligious "prophets of equality" (*Gleichheitspropheten*) had precipitated the chaos and anarchy of the French Revolution.[4]

Meiners, as it happens, was an early advocate of scientific race theory, proposing, in his 1785 *Grundriß der Geschichte der Menschheit* (An outline of the history of mankind), that "Caucasians" were a separate and superior race. That crude and categorical assertion and the scientific pretensions surrounding it would be elaborated throughout the nineteenth century in works such as the Scottish ethnologist Robert Knox's best-selling *The Races of Men* (1850), and the French count Arthur de Gobineau's *The Inequality of the Human Races* (1853). Both argued, in Gobineau's words, that "racial differences are permanent," that "the human races are intellectually unequal," and that the "white or Aryan type is superior."[5]

Such views were hardly confined to the rightward end of the political spectrum. As European political hegemony expanded from roughly one-third of the globe's territory in 1815 to close to 85 percent in 1914, voices of all kinds embraced theories that purported to explain and legitimate that control. Initially, racial superiority was only one of a number of overlapping explanations, which ranged from differential accounts of human progress, with Europeans depicted as farther ahead on the universal ascent from barbarism to civilization, to justifications of Europe's civilizing mission, its *mission civilisatrice*. But in the second half of the nineteenth century, one can note a "hardening" of racial thinking, as well as the appropriation of the work of Charles Darwin, who was used to justify beliefs in evolutionary superiority and social and civilizational struggle. Darwin's famous "bulldog," Thomas Henry Huxley, openly affirmed the "natural inequality of men" in work aimed at debunking the "speculative chimeras" of Rousseau, and Darwin's cousin Francis Galton drew on his relative's theories to lay the foundations of the new science of eugenics. At the same time, "social Darwinist" accounts moved from the survival of the fittest within species to the survival of the fittest between peoples. And though, again, such theories were by no means the exclusive possession of conservative or right-wing voices, they did prove particularly attractive to those who were keen to exploit fears of racial mixing, pollution, and degeneration.[6]

They also combined well with the withering critiques of democracy and equality circulating toward the end of the nineteenth century, of which the work of Friedrich Nietzsche stands out for its impact and force. Nietzsche himself was generally disdainful of crude nationalism, racism, and antisemitism. Yet his thought unleashed an unsparing attack on what he considered to be the glib pieties of the modern age, which in their democratic and socialist idioms especially he considered decadent, puerile, and leveling. "The lie of the equality of souls" that moderns had derived from Christianity was a fraud, Nietzsche alleged, a source of resentment and rancor against the "aristocratic habit of mind." The politics of equality was the politics of the herd, redolent of lowliness, abasement, and an unhealthy sympathy with sufferers. The solution, he believed, was to cultivate once again a politics that extolled greatness. The "more one again permits the unique and unparalleled to raise their head," Nietzsche wrote, "the more one unlearns the dogma of the 'Equality of men.'" History, in his view, only progressed through the creative power of elites.[7]

Not long after Nietzsche, the Italian polymath Vilfredo Pareto sought to give greater precision to that general claim, arguing that elite rule was inevitable, even in the aftermath of regime change or revolution. Elites merely "circulated," he observed, swapping out one for the other. The two other celebrated "Italian" theorists of elites in the early twentieth century, Gaetano Mosca and the German-born Robert Michels, elaborated those claims. Like Pareto, they had read and were influenced by Nietzsche. And like Nietzsche, they were convinced that all societies, except the most primitive, were ruled by numerical minorities, whatever their legitimating ideologies might claim. As Mosca put it in 1896, the "dominion of an organized minority . . . is inevitable." Michels fully concurred, spelling out in 1911 his famous "iron law of oligarchy," the tendency of all parties and organizations, even the most ostensibly democratic, to come under the sway of the few.[8]

Without question, then, conservative and right-wing thinkers were often openly contemptuous of doctrines of equality, which they could cast aside as readily as Marxists in the figure of illusion. Rejecting assertions of equal rights and the equality of peoples, they defended power and domination as natural and life-affirming, dismissing equality as decadent and diseased. The nineteenth-century German antisemite and racial Darwinist Julius Langbehn summed up this position when he declared, pithily, "Equality is death, hierarchy is life."[9]

All that is familiar, and hardly surprising. Indeed, it helps form the background to the dominant image of fascism as an ideology organized "against equality," which in central respects it undoubtedly was. Much less appreciated, however, is the degree to which fascists developed their own languages of equality and put them to use to mobilize their followers in important ways. Countering what they regarded as the seductive and dangerous appeal of both liberalism and communism, they put forth an alternative vision of a classless society targeted initially at workers, as the very name of the Nazi Party, the National Socialist German *Workers'* Party (NSDAP), underscores. Fascists in Italy did the same. And right-wing forces across Europe mobilized new languages of equality to bind their peoples together on the basis of shared history, identity, and blood.[10]

Right-wing discussions of equality were seldom, if ever, universal. On the contrary, they founded claims to the equality of some explicitly on the inequality of others. The French right-wing intellectual Maurice Barrès put the matter succinctly at the end of the nineteenth century when he declared, in a pamphlet decrying the "armies of foreigners invading our country," that "the idea of the fatherland implies an inequality, but to the detriment of foreigners, not, as is the case today, to the detriment of French nationals." Equality, in a word, should be for equals, just as France was for the French. The hordes of immigrants "oppressing" French citizens, sullying French civilization, and "taking possession" of France's wealth, Barrès fumed, would need to be turned back.[11]

Populist, nationalist, and xenophobic, such rhetoric was invoked in different national settings across Europe and the Americas in the late nineteenth and early twentieth centuries. It has been described by one leading commentator as a "pathology," a "negative" version of the ideal of equality in its more positive and universal forms. Contemporaries, however, claimed with considerable force that they were merely owning and acknowledging the exclusions and oppositions that were present, though denied, in the equality talk of their opponents. The ostensibly more universal equality of liberals, democrats, and socialists, they charged, was a delusion and sham.[12]

Many developed that line of attack, but it was given its most sophisticated articulation in Germany in the aftermath of World War I by the New Right theorist, and later Nazi jurist, Carl Schmitt. In his *Crisis of Parliamentary Democracy*, first published in 1923, and then again with an added preface in 1926, the political and legal theorist called out what he saw as the fecklessness and abstraction of contemporary liberalism, particularly as embodied in Germany's postwar Weimar Constitution. Liberalism, Schmitt charged, and the "government by discussion" of mass parliamentarianism that was its issue, alleged the universal and absolute equality of all persons. But such abstraction was misconceived in a world of states; it reflected a vague humanitarian sentiment, not an actual politics or even a democracy. For "every actual democracy," Schmitt pointed out by way of contrast, "rests on the principle that not only are equals equal but unequals will not be treated equally. Democracy requires, therefore, first homogeneity and second—if the need arises—elimination or eradication of heterogeneity."[13]

Schmitt proceeded to point out how, in historical practice, that had always been the case. It was true of ancient democracies, such as

Athens, which excluded slaves and women, among others, and also of modern democracies such as Turkey, with its "radical expulsion of the Greeks," or the Australian Commonwealth, which restricted "unwanted entrants" through its immigration laws, ensuring on racial grounds that only the "right type of settler" was admitted. The United States and Great Britain, with their exclusions based on color, caste, and colonial possession, were hardly exceptions to this democratic pattern. They confirmed it. "A democracy," Schmitt asserted, "demonstrates its political power by knowing how to refuse or keep at bay something foreign and unequal that threatens its homogeneity."[14]

It followed, in Schmitt's reckoning, that "the question of equality is precisely not one of abstract, logical-arithmetical games. It is about the substance of equality [*die Substanz der Geichheit*]," about the thing that binds together equals as equals. What that common "substance" was, he conceded, could vary. For the ancients it had been *arete*, or civic virtue, whereas for the English radicals of the seventeenth century, it was common religious conviction. More recently, "since the nineteenth century," he contended, "it had existed above all in membership in a particular nation, in national homogeneity." But the common and underlying point was that "equality is only interesting and valuable politically so long as it has substance, and for that reason at least the possibility and the risk of inequality." Schmitt reiterated the point by stressing that precisely "because inequality always belongs to equality," democracies could readily exclude one part of the governed without ceasing to be democracies. Democratic regimes had always marginalized unwanted categories of people—barbarians, the uncivilized, atheists, aristocrats, counterrevolutionaries, slaves, and women, among numerous others. And in the current era, the legal forms of empire facilitated ever more creative exclusions. "Colonies, protectorates, mandates, intervention treaties, and similar forms of dependence" made it possible to govern a heterogeneous population without making them citizens. They could be held apart from the state.

The British Empire provided Schmitt with a perfect example. "If English democracy, universal suffrage, or universal equality" is spoken of outside the British Isles, Schmitt concluded, such talk was merely self-deception. "These hundreds of millions [of imperial subjects] in English democracy are just as unquestionably ignored as were slaves in Athenian democracy."[15]

That was the reality. But contemporary liberal regimes, as opposed to genuine democracies, seldom faced it. Modern mass parliamentary governance, Schmitt charged, was a "patchwork" affair, combining liberal and democratic elements to its own hypocrisy and confusion. The result was a liberal-democratic politics that was dishonest about its actual exclusions, blind to the "substance of equality" necessary to bind its peoples together, and naïve about the prospects of any genuine equality in a heterogeneous world. For to treat all human beings as political equals while according them universal rights "would be an equality understood only in terms of itself and without risk; it would be an equality without the necessary correlate of inequality, and as a result conceptually and practically meaningless, an indifferent equality." "Empty" and "insignificant," such naïve liberal equality would nonetheless have real consequences. For "substantive inequalities," Schmitt warned, "would in no way disappear from the world and the state" with the declaration that all were equal. They would merely "shift into another sphere, perhaps separated from the political and concentrated in the economic, leaving this area to take on a new, disproportionately decisive importance." "Wherever an indifferent concept of equality, without the necessary correlate of inequality, actually takes hold of an area of human life, then this area loses its substance and is overshadowed by another sphere in which inequality then comes into play with ruthless power." The "universal equality" of liberals was hypocritical, leaving in place the actual inequalities that divided human beings of flesh and blood.[16]

Schmitt surely exaggerated the degree to which modern liberal-democratic regimes were blind to their own exclusions.

The important nineteenth-century French republican theorist Lucien-Anatole Prévost-Paradol, for example, whom Schmitt himself cites disparagingly, called attention to how French equality in the metropole was predicated on inequality in the empire. And many Americans in the post-Reconstruction United States, like citizens in the white settler nations more broadly, acknowledged frankly that white equality excluded the equality of Blacks. Germans, including Schmitt himself, took notice, studying US racial and immigration law closely.[17]

Yet qualifications of this kind did nothing to detract from the rhetorical power of Schmitt's critique, which offered a right-wing counterpart to the Marxian charge that liberal equality was an "illusion" that masked the actual inequalities it served to condone. His forthright contention that equality must always be based on an explicit rejection of unequals opened up a populist space in which to exalt the "true" democracy and equality owed to the homogeneous people who shared a common substance. And his brief but chilling allusion to the "elimination or eradication of heterogeneity" as the need arose gestured to the mechanisms that right-wing regimes would employ to further the equality of the people in the years to come.

Schmitt, it is true, said relatively little in the *Crisis of Parliamentary Democracy* about race as the substance that might bind people together. He uses the word only occasionally in the text, and in fact remained skeptical throughout his career of racist biologism in ways that would eventually draw attacks by the Schutzstaffel, or SS, and compromise his own position in the Nazi Party. Yet his many references to homogeneous national belonging as the dominant substance of equality since the nineteenth century, and his further assertion that the "circle of equals" must be marked off from the nation's heterogeneous enemies both within and without, lent themselves naturally enough to racist construal and appropriation.[18]

Schmitt flirted with such construal himself. In his theoretical magnum opus of 1928, *Verfassungslehre* (Constitutional theory), for example, he invokes "ideas of common race," along with religion, belief, shared fate, and tradition, as among the crucial elements of substance that bind together peoples. He does suggest assimilation through legal means, along with deportation and immigration control, as ways of dealing with heterogeneous national minorities. But he also invokes "another method, which is faster and more violent: the disposal of the alien component by oppression, resettlement of the heterogeneous population and similar radical means." Regardless of the specific method chosen for guaranteeing homogeneity, however, the homogeneity itself was crucial. For in both formal democracies and regimes organized around a powerful leader who embodied the people's will, the "identity of ruler and ruled, those commanding and those following," was paramount.[19]

Schmitt spelled out that identity as the "absolute racial equality between the Führer and his followers" in his 1933 *Staat, Bewegung, Volk* (State, Movement, People), one of his first explicitly Nazi publications. It was there that he introduced the principle of *Artgleichheit*, without which, he stressed, "the National Socialist state could not stand, and its legal life would be unthinkable." The word had circulated in the writings of German racial theorists since at least the 1920s, and it would prove absolutely central in subsequent Nazi formulations. Literally it meant "equality of type," but the "type" in question was generally cast in terms of race, and set against its avowed racial enemies (*Artfremde*). And because it was invariably used in contrast to liberal equality (*Gleichheit*)—the abstract equality of citizens that served as a topos of the Weimar government—*Artgleichheit* constituted a clear and self-conscious keyword in an alternative discourse on equality itself. "National socialism," Schmitt exulted, "has the courage to treat unequals unequally and to push through the necessary differentiations." It was the principle of *Artgleichheit* that channeled that "courage" into law by spelling out the distinctions between unequal and equal, enemy and friend, the very basis of genuine politics in Schmitt's reckoning.[20]

But, just as importantly, *Artgleichheit* effected the mystical connection between Führer and *Volk*. Schmitt compared what he regarded as the new and unprecedented form of political rule represented by Adolf Hitler (*Führertum*) to earlier political forms, such as royal absolutism, in which the mystical body of the king represented the will of his subjects, or direct democracy, in which the sovereign people in assembly became present to itself without distinction between ruler and ruled. *Führertum* was unlike these older forms of political representation and identity, however; it went beyond them. For the Führer literally incarnated the *Volk*, channeling and diffusing its collective will. In what was likely a nod to the Catholic doctrine of transubstantiation, in which the host of communion is transformed into the body of Christ and then diffused throughout the people, Schmitt described *Führertum* as a "concept of unmediated present and real presence" (*unmittel-barer Gegenwart und realer Präsenz*), adding that it was based upon "absolute racial equality between the Führer and his followers." The Führer, in other words, did not *represent* the people, he embodied and became them, one and the same, while the people in turn were transformed into a unified community and followership (*Gefol-gschaft*). The Führer and his people were one, and the substance that allowed for that strange alchemy, connecting all together in unity and sameness, was the equality of type (*Artgleichheit*). Its product and consequence, in Schmitt's perverse reading, was the purest, most unmediated, and most imminent form of democracy the world had ever known.[21]

The concept of *Artgleichheit*, then, was of critical importance. It "permeates all legal considerations," Schmitt stressed, and it would be "especially necessary for the scientific jurists of the new German law to become aware of [its] power." A number of Schmitt's leading students and associates, including Ernst Forsthoff, Otto Koellreutter, Ernst Rudolf Huber, Heinrich Henkel, and Theodor Maunz, did precisely that, putting the concept to work as one of the central organizing principles of Nazi jurisprudence.[22]

In Schmitt's terms, the Nazi regime found the "courage" to treat unequals unequally and to base its own claims to equality on that foundational decision, attacking liberal universalism at its heart. As Wilhelm Stuckart, a key architect of the infamous Nuremberg Laws, and his collaborator Hans Globke observed in a formal commentary on the Reich Citizenship Law, shortly after its passage in 1935, "In the Weimar Constitution, so-called basic rights played a dominant role. Above all the principle of equality was most scrupulously guarded." In the new regime, by contrast, only racial comrades (*Volksgenossen*) could be citizens, and only the racially similar could be equals. All "persons of alien blood, and especially Jews," were necessarily excluded as enemies of type.[23]

Of course, it may well seem to observers in our own time, as it did in fact to contemporaries outside of Germany, including those who identified as fascists, that "race" provided a rather unstable substance on which to found a jurisprudence. Even for the most diehard Nazis, the term eluded fixed definition. Jurists and theorists made efforts at greater specificity, speaking in Byzantine terms of *Erbgleichheit* (hereditary equality) in reference to the racially identical and equal, who together constituted a *Volksgemeinschaft*, a homogeneous people, or a kindred community of blood (*Blutgemeinschaft*). Those equals of type were "racial comrades" (*Volksgenossen*), who inhabited a circle of equality, which was set off against all those enemies, foreign and domestic, who were excluded from its midst. Still, however often Nazi jurists claimed to be replacing the "abstract" equality of liberalism with the "concrete" equality of race, the "substance" of their foundation was inevitably squishy.[24]

Yet the racial "science" (*Rassenkunde*) of nineteenth- and twentieth-century Germany was widely credited and broadly received. And even those, like Schmitt, who balked at its more outlandish claims were adept at fashioning expedients to talk around it. In place of a biologically grounded Nordic or Aryan "race," they more commonly invoked the historical German *Volk*, shaped by common history, culture, language, and experience. And while hardliners in the so-called vitalist faction among the jurists insisted on the biological element that allegedly served as the marker of the equality of type, even they were quick to add emotional, historical, and voluntary elements. The concept of *Artgleichheit* was always political, as Schmitt knew better than anyone, and thus most useful in stigmatizing "unequals," whether Jews, gypsies, Slavs, or others in relation to the corresponding superiority of Germans.[25]

The Nazi jurist Ulrich Scheuner made plain the political under-pinnings of *Artgleichheit* in his 1939 article "The Idea of Equality in the Völkish Constitutional System." *Artgleichheit*, he observed, was not primarily a scientific concept, but a "political concept, whose primary function was to ground the unity and inner homogeneity and solidarity of the German people." Its "substance" could be detected not only in the "community of blood," but also in the "inner attitude and mentality" revealed by the loyalty and behavior of comrades. German belonging, in other words, was made by "disposition" and "conscious and willful commitment" in service to the Reich.[26]

Thus, even as he emphasized the racial or blood component of German equality, Scheuner acknowledged its emotional and political underpinnings. "Since the abolition of the classifications of the estates and social gradations handed down from the Middle Ages," he explained, "equality has formed the basis of our polit-ical and social life and is deeply rooted in the feelings of modern man." But its "content and meaning" varied in different times and political regimes. Equality eluded any "formal and universal defini-tion." And so it was crucial to specify what its "substance" entailed. Scheuner proceeded to repeat the clichés about how the equality of the contemporary German people should be set in contrast to the principle of equality of the liberal epoch and the Weimar Constitution. "For us," he wrote, "it is not an abstract equality of all human beings, not a denial of all qualitative differences between them that constitutes the essence of equality." He insisted, on the contrary, that "today's views on equal and unequal are based on the fundamental fact of blood differences between peoples, which makes the ethnic equality of species the decisive factor." But even as he did so, he acknowledged that the substance of equality was culturally and historically determined, the product of political decision and choice. To be an equal German was to be prepared to feel and declare oneself so, drawing the necessary distinctions between enemies and friends.[27]

That willful, affective, and ultimately political dimension of equality was even clearer in Mussolini's Italy, where, as Schmitt himself claimed in a 1936 article comparing the Nazi and Fascist regimes, "the problem of race is ignored." Recent scholarship has complicated that claim, showing that race was hardly ignored in Fascist Italy. Yet it is revealing that when a number of Schmitt's own writings, including *Staat, Bewegung, Volk*, were translated in Italy in the mid-1930s, Fascist commentators there largely rejected the racial and biological underpinnings of *Artgleichheit* spelled out in his work. And though, by the early 1940s, with Italy's increasing military dependence on Hitler, Italian Fascists had become more receptive to German racial doctrines and the accompanying virulent antisemitism, they never embraced it with the same enthusiasm. Prior to that point, in any case, the dominant tone was struck by Gentile, who argued that national belonging was spiritual and moral, not racial or biological.[28]

The same was true of the circle of equals. Unlike Nazi Germany, the Italian Fascist regime never elaborated a formal jurisprudence around the "equality of type," even if it was every bit as insistent on rejecting what it viewed as the spurious and hypocritical defense of abstract, universal equality so prevalent among liberals and social democrats. Indeed, no less than in Germany, the word "equality" was often employed as a pejorative, a synonym for sameness, mediocrity, and social leveling. "Abbasso l'eguaglianza!" (Down with equality!), mocked Filippo Marinetti, the Italian Futurist and author of the first Fascist Manifesto (1919), in his 1924 essay

"Futurismo e Fascimo." "In fact," he boasted, "I am equal to no one. One of a kind. Inimitable model."[29]

Marinetti's lines reflected a wider suspicion of the alleged homogenizing, leveling, and atomizing effects of the politics born of the French Revolution among those who rejected its assertion that all men were born free and equal in rights. That, as the leading Fascist ideologue Giuseppe Bottai observed plainly, was "a formulation we cannot accept." The principles of 1789 had encouraged a dangerous and deeply mistaken attempt to move from the equality of all persons to the equality of all things. And the language of individual rights had infected the politics of liberalism and all modern democratic regimes with a "fetishism" for constitutional charters and the presupposition that the isolated individual must be protected from the state. "All state systems of the liberal type," Bottai continued, "have this original flaw," and so they "consider the juridical order not as the space in which the life of social man is realized . . . but as the system of limits that defend the citizen from the state." From that mistaken conception, "the liberal state" had "degenerated into abstract atomistic democracy."[30]

And yet the French Revolution was not without its redemptive features. Gentile developed that point in his 1924 essay *Che cosa è il fascismo* (What is fascism), by quoting the words of the nineteenth-century Italian nationalist Silvio Spaventa:

> The modern state arises from the so-called state of law, which is to say, from that state in which all citizens feel and recognize themselves equal before the law. That equality, it can be said, is the fruit of the history of Europe up to the French Revolution. From that feeling of equality, a terrible need arises in the conscience of the multitude, for whom it is not enough to be equal before the law. They seek to rise up, to participate in the goods of life which, in centuries past, had been reserved only for the few.

To be sure, that "feeling of equality" and the "terrible need" it engendered had proved the source of manifold political errors since

1789, culminating in the perversions of communism. But that was largely because the feeling had been misdirected and misapplied. The feeling itself was authentic and should not be dismissed. As Mussolini and Gentile affirmed in *The Doctrine of Fascism*, "The Fascist negation of socialism, democracy, and liberalism must not be taken to mean that Fascism desires to take the world back to the state of affairs before 1789." Feudal privileges, like the dominance of the church and the division of society into castes and estates, had been abolished with good reason. Bottai, similarly, for all his criticism of the noxious spirit of '89, openly affirmed the French Revolution's importance as "truly one of the greatest events in the history of humanity," the source of the "modern spirit" of human agency, autonomy, and revolutionary change. Italian Fascists were revolutionaries, not reactionaries, he insisted. They had no desire to turn back the clock.[31]

Fascists could even imagine themselves continuing a project of populist and nationalist consolidation that the French Revolution had begun. As a popular German newspaper declared, implausibly, in 1935, "The demands for liberty, equality, and fraternity, with which the German worker was betrayed by liberal-Marxist demagogues, have become reality, thanks to National Socialism." The Italian Fascist ideologue Carlo Talarico developed the point at greater length in a work first published in 1933 treating the relationship between the French and Fascist Revolutions; it was republished in 1939 (and again in 1940 and 1942) with the official backing of the National Fascist Party under a new and revealing title: *Le due rivoluzioni: Dall'eguaglianza dinanzi alla legge all'eguglianza dinanzi al lavoro* (The two revolutions: From equality before the law to equality before labor). There, in a chapter devoted to the "Equality of Citizens," Talarico made clear that of all the causes that animated the French Revolution, "the oldest and most profound" was the "violent hatred of inequality." That was a legitimate sentiment, he said, and it had given rise, in the revolution itself, to high-minded ideals.[32]

And yet the equality of the French revolutionaries was merely an impression, a "virtual" equality, in Talarico's words, "not an equality of fact." It put in place a specious liberal and democratic system that legitimated egoism, enshrined individual property rights, and hid actual inequalities behind a universal facade, creating a new class of the privileged to replace the old. Talarico cited the influential Fascist philosopher Sergio Panunzio to stress how the doctrine of rights issuing from the French Revolution treated the individual as "the supreme reality and synthetic being of the universe," all while in truth atomizing and dividing the social whole. Ignoring "individual differences in personal merit or demerit, and the diversity of attitudes, actions, and conditions among citizens," the absolute equality of rights before the law issuing from the French Revolution created "real inequalities between the same individuals subjected to uniform treatment." Thus, although Talarico could praise the French revolutionary principle of equality for having "raised and pushed the destiny of humanity towards higher and more worthy goals," that principle had gone awry. It remained, for the second, Fascist revolution, to correct and complete it.[33]

But what would such a completion look like? In the second edition of his book, Talarico provided a quotation from Mussolini that served as the epigraph and basis of his new subtitle:

> The last century proclaimed the equality of citizens before the law—and this was a conquest of formidable scope. The fascist century consolidates this principle, and adds to it another, no less formidable: the equality of men before work understood as a duty and as a right and as a creative joy that must expand and ennoble existence, rather than mortify and debase it.
>
> Such equality does not exclude—on the contrary it requires—the very clear differentiation of hierarchies, from the point of view of function, merit, and responsibility.

The words are taken from a speech Mussolini gave in 1934 to the National Council of Corporations, one of the main Fascist corporate bodies, set up to mediate the concerns of capital and labor. They reflected, in part, Mussolini's early and lasting infatuation with the tradition of revolutionary syndicalism as it had evolved in both Italy and France. Mussolini, it bears repeating, began his career, like many other Italian Fascists, as a socialist, and had been drawn over time to revisionist thinkers who renounced Marxist dogmatism and the emphasis on class struggle in favor of social and economic forms designed to integrate the nation while making peace with private enterprise.[34]

One such thinker, the erstwhile anarchist and socialist Francesco Saverio Merlino, had argued that true socialism entailed "not the victory of one class over others," but the triumph of the general interest over the particular in the service of collective justice. Panunzio would later credit him with initiating the process of socialist revision that culminated in fascism, and it is noteworthy that Merlino invoked directly the "equality of men before the necessity of labor," an emphasis that the idiosyncratic French syndicalist Georges Sorel echoed. Sorel wrote a preface to the French translation of one of Merlino's major works, and he exerted a massive influence on Mussolini, whom he in turn admired. Imagining a mass movement harnessed by struggle, violence, and myth, Sorel wrote of independent labor organizations or syndicates that could provide "a real and justly organized equality" in place of a "purely ideal and utopian equality." In Italian Fascist rhetoric, the corporatist state they were constructing aimed to do just that.[35]

Mussolini's words, then, tapped into an early syndicalist concern with the place of labor in modern societies and the effort to elaborate an alternative corporatist account of social justice to replace the "decadent" ideologies of liberalism, socialism, and communism. They also resonated with a broad current of Catholic social teaching. Pope Leo XIII's 1891 encyclical *Rerum novarum* (On Capital and Labor) had emphasized the dignity of labor and the need to address the plight of the working classes, but also defended private ownership and rejected the Marxist doctrine that "class is naturally hostile to class." Subsequent Catholic thinkers followed the pope's lead, making the case across Europe for an organic community that mediated the needs of labor and capital alike while seeking to reconcile issues of hierarchy and equality. The resulting "vogue" for corporatism as an alternative and antidote to Marxism offered fertile ground for fascists seeking to develop their own model of a classless society to counter that of the Soviet Union. Pope Pius XI, for his part, offered cautious praise in 1931 for Mussolini's corporate experiments.[36]

But regardless of their specific genealogy, Mussolini's 1934 remarks on equality served as a touchstone for Fascist discourse on the subject. They were frequently invoked and repeated. Talarico stressed that they captured the underlying philosophy of the Fascist Labor Charter of 1927 (*Carta del Lavoro*), which, while maintaining private enterprise, sought to integrate workers organically into the nation not merely as "atomized" individuals but via associations serving the collective interest. This yielded what Talarico described as an "equality of categories" (*l'uguaglianza delle categorie*), the many different social and economic groups—whether industrial laborers or farmers, tradespeople or industrialists, shopkeepers or artisans—that made up the nation. Unlike liberalism or socialism, which set individuals and classes in conflict, armed with opposing interests, the corporate state claimed to resolve them through mutual enterprise and collective undertakings, doing away with class altogether. The result was what numerous Fascist ideologues called "true equality," which honored the value of all those who labored and sacrificed for the nation, but at the same time avoided the "fatal illusion of considering the alleged equality between men [to be] without limit or reserve." Such true equality, Talarico emphasized, echoing Mussolini, was not inconsistent with "absolute respect for hierarchical values in relation to capacity, functions, and responsibilities."[37]

Guido Bortolotto, the author of numerous books on corporatism, made a similar point in his 1939 *La dottrina del fascismo*

(The doctrine of fascism). "In our regime work has been placed on the same level as capital in conditions of true equality [*vera eguaglianza*]," he wrote, referencing Mussolini's claim that "the Fascist revolution has proclaimed the equality of all men before labor." Yet Bortolotto emphasized, at the same time, that "true equality" should not be confused with systematic leveling; rather, it was a question of "equalizing and balancing the elements" that made up the unity and totality of the nation. In that respect, what Bortolotto called (without racial signification) "homogeneity" was as crucial to social integration as equality. Whereas "equality signifies parity, equal grade, and equal level," he specified, "homogeneity signifies equal tone, equal type, equal imprint [*impronta*], and equal regime, but admits the hierarchy of values and grades." He offered as a concrete illustration of the distinction the case of a soldier equal to other soldiers, but homogeneous (and unequal) with respect to his commanding officers. Within the same unit or division, there were equals, who were at one and the same time superiors and inferiors. For Fascists, much the same was true of society as a whole.[38]

Martial metaphors were of course ubiquitous in fascist rhetoric, which sought to militarize politics at all levels. They are a reminder that for many World War I veterans, who made up such a crucial contingent of early fascist cadres, combat in the trenches had yielded a visceral experience of a kind of equality or classlessness in the face of death that transcended formal hierarchies between enlisted men and officers, even as it recognized their necessity and importance. The equality before labor could be likewise imagined as both the contributions of equals and the unequal contributions of comrades united by conviction and marshaled like an army, in which different ranks and units played different roles. What they shared was a common commitment, an equality of duty, even though the duties themselves necessarily varied. The French fascist and Nazi collaborator Marcel Déat put this nicely when he observed that "the existence of a hierarchy does not exclude equality of sacrifice." True equality, he maintained, "was a totality, in which each person can develop, a total man in a total society."[39]

In Germany, Scheuner elaborated a similar point in clarifying the "idea of equality" in the Nazi constitutional order. "The National Socialist conception of equality does not strive for the abolition of all barriers," he stressed, "like the leveling thinking of late liberalism, but recognizes essential differentiations within the national body in its political and professional structures." Those included the "fundamental hierarchy of leaders and followers, as well as the differences in task and position within the nation as a whole, which are based on the professional order." But the hierarchies themselves, Scheuner and his colleagues hastened to add, were justly ordered, based on capacity and merit, and culled through equal opportunity.[40]

Fascists could claim, with a certain plausibility, that they opened up opportunities for social mobility and leadership to men of different backgrounds and means, beginning with the two corporals Mussolini and Hitler themselves, who had served as simple soldiers in World War I. Fascism, they argued, was genuinely meritocratic, unlike its hypocritical predecessors and opponents, and so its hierarchies were just. Organized for victory, like efficient military machines, fascist societies were at once hierarchical and homogeneous, a unity of equals divided by rank. Like the *fascis* that served as their governing symbol, they were bound together as one.[41]

That, at any rate, was the rhetoric, which was invariably distorting, serving to deny or paper over genuine social cleavages in the name of national unity and the transcendence of class. Appeals to the equality of comrades, moreover, further reinforced the gender dynamics of the regimes, which, as was true of fascist movements more broadly, made a "perpetual fetish" of male prowess and virility. Italian Fascists, like German National Socialists, assailed the ambitions of the women's movement of the nineteenth and early twentieth centuries, taking explicit aim at efforts to secure female suffrage, family planning, and participation in the workforce.

Hitler decried the very idea of female emancipation as a Jewish and communist plot, and his ideological sympathizers across Europe made efforts to mobilize women for domestic service as wives and mothers in complement to men.[42]

The rhetoric, however, emphasized equality in difference, or equality in inequality. As Hitler's minister of propaganda, Joseph Goebbels, put it in a celebrated speech on German womanhood in 1933, "It is not because we see the woman as inferior but because we see her as having a different mission, a different value, than that of man" that the Nazi government "keeps women from direct involvement in daily politics." It was true that "men make history" and women "raise our young boys to manhood." But they nonetheless were working together "to rebuild the nation on its original foundations, to transform the life and work of the woman so that it once again best serves the national good of the *Volk*, and to eliminate social inequalities." Hitler, for his part, urged women "to be man's counterpart in these, our struggles on behalf of the *Volk* for freedom, equality, and honor." As in their conception of labor, Nazis imagined German women, like German workers, as part of an organic whole, homogeneous yet distinct, occupying an "equal" place in the national *Volk* community in roles that were necessarily different from those of men. And while it is true that, especially late in the war, the incumbencies of mobilization had unintended consequences, bringing women into the labor force and affording them enhanced responsibilities in various quarters, that was never the ideological intent. Fascist equality was decidedly male and homosocial, its bonds imagined as those of brothers in arms, with women on the home front. But they were united together in defense and domination of their common enemies.[43]

That those enemies, variously defined, were crucial to the elaboration of the distinction between equals and unequals, fascists rarely denied. Italians may have been less inclined than their German allies to cast those distinctions in purely racial terms, but they were no less vociferous in condemning "indifferent" universal equality as the fiction to be overcome. Antonino Pagliaro, the author of the long entry on "equality" in the National Fascist Party's *Dictionary of Politics*, first published in 1940, delighted in exposing how the plutocratic liberal state was "unable to satisfy the egalitarian aspirations of the masses," despite its lofty pretensions. The same was true of the Soviet Union, where the "strident economic as well as political inequalities" separating "the Bolshevik oligarchy from the great masses of workers" gave the lie to its meaningless ideals. In the one instance, liberals excluded the proletariat, while in the other, communists attacked the bourgeoisie. In both cases, the people suffered. By claiming only to make Italy equal for Italians, just as the Germans sought to make Germany equal for the *Volk*, Fascists and Nazis showed themselves to be truly *national* socialists. "Fascism," Pagliaro concluded, "has given new content to the aspiration for equality that is innate in the human heart."[44]

But what of that actual content? The question is fraught, and is caught up in the historiographically contested subject of right-wing welfare initiatives. That there was such a thing as fascist "welfare," scholars have come increasingly to acknowledge, with some calling attention to the "fundamental similarities" between the "New Deals" of Mussolini's Italy, Hitler's Germany, and Roosevelt's United States. In all of these instances, efforts to shore up the citizenry in the face of economic crisis and the Great Depression were carried out with an acute awareness of the challenge posed by the Bolshevik Revolution. And they led to broad experimentation with state-financed public works projects, tax innovations and insurance schemes, and various efforts at poor relief and domestic assistance. In the cases of Italy and Germany, those efforts further entailed explicit attacks on the liberal policies and institutions of their predecessors, along with rival socialist and social-democratic initiatives being put in place in the 1930s in countries such as Sweden.[45]

Yet Fascist and National Socialist welfare, like similar efforts in Francisco Franco's Spain, António de Oliveira Salazar's Portugal, or Getúlio Vargas's Brazil, as well as in other Latin American countries with populist regimes, was not simply reactive. The very idea of the strong or "total state" to which German and Italian ideologues aspired gestured to a role for government in virtually every aspect of national life. And while there was always considerable ideological variation within and between fascist movements, there was never a shortage of militants, especially in the early years before the war, for whom social welfare and the "social state" (*stato sociale*) were genuine organizing principles. "The factory worker and the tiller of the soil must be able to say: if I am actually better off today, I owe it to the institutions created by the fascist revolution," Mussolini insisted. It is revealing that one of his supporters, the statistician and eugenicist Corrado Gini, was the creator of what is still today the most widely used metric of national income inequality, the so-called Gini coefficient. His formulation points to an underlying interest in social and economic differences and the desire to work to reduce and contain them in the service of greater national unity.[46]

Hitler likewise spoke of the need to cultivate the "highest degree of social solidarity . . . for every member of the German race" as a way to better ensure its mastery over others. Although founded explicitly on a doctrine of inequality between peoples, the regime promised greater equality for the German *Volk*. The result was a paradox. As one scholar puts it, "Nazi social theory denied equality while at the same time asserting it."[47]

There is considerable debate over the degree to which Nazi social promises were actually fulfilled. But the promises themselves were "far reaching," and in certain cases, such as the Nazi program of quasi-compulsory national charitable assistance, the Winter Relief Fund (*Winterhilfswerk*), or the "Strength Through Joy" initiative, which subsidized holidays and recreation for ordinary Germans, the effort to make good on them was met with genuinely popular approval. Taken as a whole, fascist efforts were significant enough to leave a lasting imprint on European welfare initiatives in the postwar period. Prior to the end of World War II, at least, with the broad discrediting of fascism, they were more directly influential as models for Western countries than were those of the Soviet Union.[48]

Still, more often than not, there was a considerable gap between rhetoric and reality. The gap was the result of a wide variety of factors, ranging from corruption and incompetence, to the desire to placate big business at the expense of labor, to social Darwinist fears about coddling the "weak," to outright (and ample) hypocrisy. Fascist welfare initiatives, moreover, were always instrumental, designed to reward and encourage ideological support, punish transgressors, and facilitate social control. And they never aspired, even in theory, to widespread economic redistribution, or "leveling," of the kind that fascists invariably associated with their communist and socialist enemies. One historian's verdict on the egalitarian commitments of Mussolini's Italy—that "the regime failed to practice what it preached"—is largely true of the egalitarian commitments of fascist regimes more broadly.[49]

Thus, the purely material content offered to satisfy the "aspiration for equality" that Pagliaro and other ideologues described as innate in the human heart was in the final reckoning comparatively slight. Yet the weightier, if no less insidious, contribution was paid out in status rather than specie. Where equality was concerned, the fascist currency of exchange was above all psychological and symbolic, and here its ideologues made a lasting contribution, one that is still with us today.

Both proponents and opponents of fascism recognized A distinct psychological dynamic at work in its politics. One early and prescient observer was Hendrik (Henri) de Man, the Belgian Nazi collaborator and erstwhile revisionist socialist who served as the head of the Belgian Labor Party in the late 1930s prior to the German occupation. De Man was deeply interested in mass psychology and behavior, and in 1926 he examined those issues in the specific context of equality in a book, first written and published in German, with the title *Zur Psychologie des Sozialismus* (On the psychology of socialism). It was then quickly translated into French and other languages as *Au-delà du marxisme* (*Beyond Marxism*).[50]

Chapter 3 of the work is titled "Equality and Democracy," and the epigraph to the chapter, a quotation from Goethe, sums up its principal insight: "The most envious man is he who considers every man his equal." Treating the notion of democracy in its widest sense as the advent of mass politics, de Man argued that the conditions of life in advanced societies, with their egalitarian pretensions and various appeals to equal rights, created the yearning to reconcile principle with fact. That, more than any other ideal or goal, provided the motive force of socialism, which was propelled by "the need at once instinctive and immediate of the inferior classes to lessen social inequality." Their "feeling" was prior to any calculation of interests, and it was the product of a long historical development. But in practice, the "socialist claim to equality [was] the compensatory representation of an inferiority complex" that had gestated among working people for centuries.[51]

In de Man's view, modern Western societies had induced a peculiar and unprecedented psychological condition, an internalized "sentiment of social inferiority" in the minds of vast segments of the population who believed themselves to be the equals of others while at the same time feeling palpably that they were not. That condition was not simply the result of political injustice, or material exploitation, and it could take hold in even abundant societies, such as the United States. Indeed, to fully understand the condition, one must "go beyond a purely political or economic framework" to the level of psychology. And there one would confront a paradox at the heart of the modern individual: the presence of a deeply embedded envy, anger, and resentment coexisting with a conflicted admiration for one's social betters.[52]

Although he does not cite him directly, de Man's discussion of the frustrated longing for status in modern societies recalls Tocqueville's description of the way in which democratic institutions "awaken and flatter the passion for equality without ever being able to satisfy it in full." But whereas for Tocqueville, the "insatiable" passion for equality is a predominately energizing force, de Man presents it as emotionally and socially toxic. In place of the work of the French analyst of democracy, he draws on the Germans Nietzsche and Max Scheler, to focus on the resentment (or in the French favored by Nietzsche, *ressentiment*) produced when the longing for equality runs up against the inevitable reality of stratification. Because, de Man writes, "one always envies what one doesn't have," individuals in modern societies seethe with anger and resentment, which can easily express itself in the desire to lash out, to dominate, and to oppress. At the same time, however, that feeling was countered by another: the desire to be dominated. The Western individual's belief in equality, in other words, coexisted with a psychological yearning to be ruled by a "superior class." Like Robert Michels, whom he cites on numerous occasions, de Man believed that no society was possible without an elite—a proposition, he held, that was as true of America, with its pilgrim fathers and presidential heroes, as it was for the Soviet Union of Lenin and Stalin and their party apparatchiks. The "desire for equality and the need for inequality, far from being exclusive, conditioned one another," he said. They were "parallel phenomena," mutually reaffirming.[53]

Although de Man penned his analysis in 1926, while still in the socialist camp, he was already trading ideas in a fluid intellectual world of the kind that attracted Mussolini, whom de Man himself came to admire. Given his insights, it is not difficult to understand his later rightward drift. For although he proposed his own solutions to the dilemmas he identified, he had put his finger on a constellation of psychological forces that fascists understood and exploited with cunning. The human desire for status and equality, they knew, bred deep social resentment when unmet. But that resentment, and the rage that accompanied it, could be channeled via domination over others, and assuaged by symbolic means administered by the great leader on high. In that way would the desire for equality and the need for inequality be satisfied, responding at once to the human need for recognition, the desire for mastery, and the yearning to submit.

It was Hitler, above all, who proved to be the master manipulator of these combustible forces, which he channeled through his own personal rage. The same protean figure who could appear before the *Volk* as a higher being and godlike genius could descend to the level of the people and become one with them. He was, he continually boasted, a former construction worker, and a bohemian artist of humble origins. He sat in the front seat of his chauffeured car with his driver, kept a simple table, and freely used the informal form of address with associates (*duzen*). He was the *Volkskanzler*, the people's chancellor, the "little corporal," who had served as a common soldier in the war. And like all those whose worth had been overlooked and undervalued, he knew and voiced the resentment with which they seethed. Targeting the enemies of the people, the Jews and Slavs and *Untermenschen*, whom he blamed for keeping the people down, he vowed to put them in their place.

In this way did Hitler and the Nazis engineer what one historian has described as a "status revolution," displacing older figures of authority and bringing in new cadres to staff the machinery of the state, while distributing hundreds of thousands of medals, sashes, honorific titles, and distinctions to recognize and flatter the new men in society. In the Hitler Youth, the National Labor Service, the army, and other institutions, the Nazis aimed for a new kind of social relation. The official National Socialist newspaper, *Der Angriff* (The attack), expressed this well, noting in 1937, of the armed forces, "The uniform makes all men equal. The college teacher feels no different from the manual worker, and nothing stands in the way of the friendship between the medical student and the gardener's helper." That was, of course, an idealized picture, a form of propaganda, which left unsaid the simple fact that uniforms and their insignia can not only make men equal, but also highlight distinctions of rank. And yet, for that very reason, the statement captured perfectly the Nazi aim to transcend actual differences by an appeal to common belonging, keeping the desire for equality and the need for inequality side by side.[54]

Hitler repeatedly expressed that aim himself. "We have taken trouble," he observed at a mass rally in Saarbrücken in 1935, to look past the superficial, "to forget origin, standing, profession, wealth, education, knowledge, capital, and everything else that can separate people in order to pierce through to what can bring them together" as *Volksgenossen*, as "comrades of one people." Or, as he put it in *Mein Kampf*, "Equality is not based and can never be based on individual achievement," or the parity of material reward. Rather, it was possible only, he claimed, in the form in which "everyone fulfills his special obligations," in which "every individual does his best in his field no matter what it may be."[55]

Here, then, was an imaginary equality of a new kind, one that sought to transcend actual differences of rank and reward through a common appeal to national and racial belonging. That this appeal depended crucially on exploitation of the very kinds of paradoxical sentiments analyzed by de Man should be clear. Envy and resentment, inferiority and equality, domination and submission came together in a dangerous mix that was vital to fascism's success. But those very same ingredients were produced in abundance in all modern democratic societies.

It was the Dutch modernist writer Menno ter Braak who called this out most precisely. Unlike de Man, ter Braak was an anti-fascist who committed suicide rather than submit to the Nazi occupation of the Netherlands in 1940. But in a subtle and powerful essay first published in 1937 amid the rise of fascism in his own country, ter Braak drew even more explicitly than the Belgian on the category of resentment to reveal the inner workings of the Nazi machine. National Socialism, he observed plainly, was a doctrine of pure "rancor" and "*ressentiment*," which had liberated those sentiments from all previous constraints. Fascism, accordingly, appealed to "losers," but not simply to petty-bourgeois shopkeepers or down-and-out segments of the working class. Indeed, to look for the source of fascist resentment in injustice or penury alone would be misconceived, for in fact its sources were as varied as individual psychology. All those who nursed a grudge in some way—who felt aggrieved or resentful of the privileges, possessions, or status of others—were susceptible to the fascist appeal. Their numbers were considerable. "In reality, rancor is one of the most essential elements of our culture," ter Braak emphasized, "to which it is inseparably bound; it is ubiquitous."[56]

Ter Braak proceeded to analyze how the doctrine of fascism was inconceivable without hatred and the mystical fabrications of race, which found a precise object for the people's animus in the "eternal scapegoat, the Jew," though that object could easily be replaced by another. Shared hatred united the *Volk*, and it leveled them, too, after a fashion. "Rancor knows no status differences" when the common enemy is before it. In the same way, fascist appeals to a "higher equality" created the illusion of unity. For "equality, through the *Volksgemeinschaft*," ter Braak wrote, "is a slogan of *ressentiment*, which *in theory* tolerates not a single inequality, but thereby all the more serves in practice to disguise existing inequalities." Ter Braak described the cover of a pro-Nazi Dutch magazine, *Volk en Vaderland*, which portrayed a count and a farm laborer together with the caption "A single ideal unites [them]." That single ideal of the *Volksgemeinschaft*, with its appeal to the "fiction" of "the higher equality," would not be enough, ter Braack said mockingly, to induce the count to give up his title or to raise the farm laborer to the peerage. Their equality was one of shared contempt that would leave economic differences largely intact, whatever the handouts of the *Winterhilfe*.[57]

But if in this way ter Braak captured neatly the inner workings of the Nazi discourse on equality, status, and power, he hastened to add that the "losers" he described were by no means particular to National Socialism, which was itself but the "realization" and "perversion" of democracy and socialism, not their opposite. All were "bound together by the shared factor of *ressentiment*," the necessary by-product of any "culture which, like ours, features the tendency to grant everyone equal rights": "It is *equality* as ideal which, given the biological and sociological impossibility of equal human beings, elevates rancor to a power of the first order in society." Ter Braak hastened to add that democratic forms of government were preferable to the alternatives, and that the Nazis exploited the sentiments of rancor and resentment in particularly ugly ways. But his greatest insight was that those same sentiments were not some sort of fascist perversion, but a structural feature of democracy itself, which generated feelings of envy and resentment and then validated them in the name of equality. "This is the great paradox of a democratic society, in which rancor is not only present, but is also encouraged as a human right!" Where the belief in equality prevailed, resentment would find a place. With the consequence that democratic societies would always produce a steady stream of the very poison that could be used to kill them off. What ter Braak didn't say, but what was no less true, was that democratic regimes were producing a steady stream of resentment not only within their borders, but beyond them.[58]

10

BALANCE

Sovereign Equality and the Peoples of the World

As Allied troops stormed Berlin in late April 1945 and war in the Pacific still raged, representatives of the majority of the world's sovereign countries, along with over forty nongovernmental organizations, gathered in San Francisco to draft a document that would become the Charter of the United Nations. Signed by fifty of the original fifty-one member states in June, it entered into effect that October following ratification by the five powers of what would become the UN Security Council: the United States, the Soviet Union, Great Britain, France, and China.

The UN Charter grew out of a series of declarations announced by the major Allied powers as they attempted to clarify their war aims and to articulate a vision of a new international order to be implemented with the cessation of hostilities. It made clear in its second article that the United Nations was to be "based on the principle of the sovereign equality of all its Members." Legal scholars were quick to point out that just how the "sovereign equality" of nations was to be construed was far from clear, and still less was the status of colonized people and those placed in trusteeship by the victorious powers. But the charter went beyond merely asserting the formal equality of extant nations "large and small." It announced, in addition, the equal rights of human beings promoted "without distinction as to race, sex, language, or religion" (Article 1.3). Those commitments were stated even more forcefully in the Universal Declaration of Human Rights of 1948, which gave expression to the United Nations' loftiest ambitions. As Ramaswami Mudaliar, the Indian delegate at San Francisco, put it, the "fundamental human rights of all beings all over the world should be recognized, and men and women treated as equals in every sphere."[1]

That was a ringing and remarkable invocation, following as it did on decades of colonial exploitation and years of wartime atrocity. But the paradoxes at play in the spectacle of the Great Powers endorsing the equality of peoples they had long ruled, and in many places still did, was not lost on clear-eyed observers. W. E. B. Du Bois, for one, on hand in San Francisco as a representative from the National Association for the Advancement of Colored People (NAACP), called out the "twisted contradiction of thought in the minds of white men" who proclaimed universal rights while embracing the privileges of power that attended their countries and the color of their skin. Similar contradictions were inscribed in the institutions of the United Nations itself, which from the Security Council to the governing boards of the World Bank and the International Monetary Fund were conceived partly as victors' spoils, concentrated in Western capitals and constituted on highly unequal terms. For all its stated desire to combat the inequalities of the world, the United Nations also reflected and reproduced them, rendering the body a symbol of "both global solidarity and global injustice."[2]

That reality calls attention to the fact, pointed out by two leading scholars, that the "egalitarian language enshrined in the UN" was hard-pressed to fully acknowledge, let alone to deal with, "the very real inequalities—political, economic, racial—that persisted and deepened in the post–World War II period." It also begs the question of whether the circle of equals could ever really be global, or must rely on the substance of national belonging and the differences marked off by national frontiers. That question,

Two early prototypes of the United Nations emblem. Although the version in use today depicts an equidistant projection of the globe centered on the North Pole, the earliest versions produced by the team of the American architects Oliver Lincoln Lundquist and Donal McLaughlin depicted North America, the "host of the United Nations" and "center of the world," in the middle. In a slightly later iteration, the image was "centered on Europe," "more the epicenter . . . of the east-west world," Lundquist later recalled. UN Digital Library, ST/DPI/ORAL HISTORY(02)/L8. Reprinted with the permission of the United Nations.

which Carl Schmitt had raised pointedly between the wars, and which critics of empire and neocolonialism pressed further in their aftermath, took on added resonance in the postwar period with the proliferation of sovereign states at the very moment that Western nations themselves were pursuing the construction of robust welfare regimes that went some way toward reducing social and economic inequalities within their borders. Despite calls by some for the advent of a "welfare world," however, the postwar period saw the persistence and growth of inequalities between nations and peoples with precious little respite.[3]

Mudaliar's rousing call for the men and women of the globe to be "treated as equals in every sphere" proved difficult to carry out. The "dream of a fully global equality" may have been dreamed in this period, the product of an earlier proliferation of equality doctrines that were spread around the world in the first half of the twentieth century, as this chapter will explore at some length. The globalization of equality, however, did not lead to "global equality." That term, revealingly, only gained currency in the 1970s, and slowly at that, along with the gradual accumulation of data to measure the differences in income, wealth, and life chances of the world's nations and peoples. When the data trickled in, what the numbers began to show was that the run of equalization that economists now call the "Great Compression" for the better part of the twentieth century was experienced in much of the world outside the global north as a "Great Squeeze."[4]

"It has always been the way of the world that the weaker is kept down by the stronger," the Athenians acknowledged to the Spartans in the Peloponnesian War, admitting that they weighed the balance of justice differently in the world than they did amongst their equals at home. To the extent that the victors of World War II and their postwar allies could envision global equality at all, they tended to see it, similarly, as a function of forces to be weighed, and they counted themselves as weighing more than the rest. They thus imagined equality in the world in proportional terms. Long before 1945, it assumed shape for them in the figure of balance.[5]

The principle of "sovereign equality" proclaimed in the UN Charter drew on a long history that, like the notion of the equal rights of individuals, was bound up with the natural law theories of the seventeenth and eighteenth centuries. One of the foremost early exponents of the principle, the eighteenth-century Swiss jurist and diplomat Emer de Vattel, famously likened sovereign states to moral persons. As Vattel explained in his 1758 *Droit des gens* (*The Law of Nations*), building on the seventeenth-century foundations of predecessors such as Hugo Grotius and Samuel von Pufendorf, "Since men are naturally equal, and a perfect equality prevails in their rights and obligations, as equally proceeding from nature,— nations composed of men, and considered as so many free persons living together in the state of nature, are naturally equal, and inherit from nature the same obligations and rights."[6]

Nations, like individuals, were free and equal persons, inviolable within their boundaries, and equally subject to laws. But though equal, they were not alike. On the contrary, Vattel took for granted the many differences in size, resources, and military might that separated the nations of the world. "Power or weakness," he continued in a memorable line, "does not in this respect produce any difference. A dwarf is as much a man as a giant; a small republic is no less a sovereign state than the most powerful kingdom." Just as Roman law had once conceived all male citizens as equal in their formal abstraction, despite their vast differences in aptitude, power, and means, the law of nations looked upon individual states as equal corporate persons, equal in "dignity" no less, notwithstanding their many inequalities of fact.[7]

This was the condition that Thomas Jefferson, a close reader of Vattel, described in the Declaration of Independence as the "separate and equal station" of peoples accorded by the Law of Nature and Nature's God. It was through appeal to that equal station that he and his compatriots justified separation from the powerful British Empire, as Haitians did from France, and Latin Americans from Spain. A similar station would be claimed by the dozens of newly sovereign nations that emerged as postcolonial states in the aftermath of World War II. By that point, to be sure, understandings of the sovereign equality of nations had undergone considerable evolution, and they drew on differing rationales. But the general principle remained a foundational tenet of international law. Already in the early nineteenth century, the US chief justice John Marshall could affirm that "no principle of general law is more universally acknowledged than the perfect equality of nations." Legal authorities well into the following century affirmed the same.[8]

Sovereign equality was above all a juridical principle, and in theory it comprised a *formal* dimension, which granted nations equality before international legal organs and bodies of international law; a *legislative* dimension, which bound nations only to those laws to which they gave their consent, while making provisions for equality of voting in international bodies; and an *existential* dimension, which acknowledged the right of sovereign nations to exist in their territorial integrity and to choose the manner of their existence by fashioning their laws and forms of government free from outside interference. Ideally, sovereign equality was a guarantee of the domestic autonomy of states within their borders and of pluralism and diversity in the international system writ large.[9]

But theory and practice seldom perfectly coincide, and the principle of sovereign equality as it had developed since the early modern period was no exception. In theory, the so-called Westphalian system of states, said to have come into being when the Peace of Westphalia (1648) put an end to the European religious wars of the sixteenth and seventeenth centuries, gave birth to the sovereign equality that Vattel described, with its attendant principles of territorial integrity and nonintervention. But as historians have made clear, the Westphalian system is largely a myth, and even in Vattel's aspirational form, it admitted of numerous exceptions.[10]

More to the point, the European state system described by Vattel was predicated on what he called "the famous scheme of the political balance, or the equilibrium of powers, by which is understood such a disposition of things, as that no one potentate be able absolutely to predominate, and prescribe laws to the others." That balance of power, in turn, depended on "Great Powers" that could uphold and enforce it, putting their fingers on the scales as need be, but that were wont to violate the very principles of sovereign independence and nonintervention they allegedly upheld. The principle of sovereign equality, in other words, existed from the start in tension with the unequal prerogatives and privileges claimed by the strong.[11]

That was even more the case in the aftermath of the Napoleonic Wars, when the Congress of Vienna tasked the victorious states, Russia, Prussia, Austria, and Great Britain (and eventually defeated

France), with maintaining security on the European continent, intervening militarily when and where they saw fit. It was even more the case still as European powers trained their designs on the rest of the world in the great scramble for empire that characterized the long nineteenth century. The world "order" that emerged was enforced by mighty hegemons, who showed themselves far less respectful of the sovereign equality of peoples abroad than they did of those in their European midst. Indeed, by withholding from so-called tribes and territories the full standing of peoples, Europeans denied nationhood and thus sovereignty to much of the globe.[12]

It is largely for that reason that the principle of sovereign equality could take on a radical inflection when invoked either by subject peoples, struggling under empire to achieve their "equal station" in the world, or by less powerful countries anxious to guard their independence. At the Second Hague Conference of 1907, for example, an important early effort to lay the foundations for a permanent international court, the Brazilian delegate Ruy Barbosa emerged as a champion of small states in general and the Latin American delegations in particular, eloquently defending the principle of sovereign equality. Drawing, as did Vattel before him, on the analogy between the democratic rights of individuals and the rights of states as moral persons, Barbosa observed, "There are, no doubt, between state and state, as between individual and individual, differences of culture, of honesty, of wealth, of physical strength." But just as "civil rights are identical for all men," and "political rights are the same for all citizens," should they not be the same for all countries? "Well, then," Barbosa concluded, "sovereignty is the prime and elemental right of constituted and independent states. Therefore sovereignty signifies equality." Unlike a number of the delegates of the Great Powers, who argued that their role in the proceedings, their say in its deliberations, and their position in any standing international bodies they might create should be commensurate with their superior military and economic means, Barbosa pressed for a strict equality of states.[13]

In effect, Barbosa and his allies argued for what Aristotle had once described as "numerical equality," an equality of the things divided based strictly on the number of participants, in this case the sovereign nations themselves. Britain, for one, however, defended what Aristotle called "proportional equality," or an "equality of ratio," in which "unequals are treated in proportion to the inequality existing between them." In practice, that meant that nations would be weighed on the basis of their relative economic and military might. The balance of power should be measured accordingly, in this view, like the balance of pans on a scale. Equality was produced when equilibrium was achieved, when the pans were aligned. And that meant, as Vattel put it, that the many smaller and weaker nations would have to be counted "like so many weights thrown into the lighter scale," in order to offset the mass of the powerful. That was the way to achieve equality, keeping the international system in "political balance."[14]

The long-standing tension between a robust interpretation of the sovereign equality of nations and the privileges and prerogatives claimed by the Great Powers surfaced even more dramatically at the end of World War I, when those hoping for an equal station in the world found, if only briefly, an apparent champion in the US president, Woodrow Wilson. Wilson signaled repeatedly in the war's waning months his support for the "equality" and "self-determination" of peoples. Here, it seemed, was a leader of a newly emerging Great Power ready to use his authority not for narrow national self-interest but for the wider benefit of mankind. The advent of the Paris Peace Conference in 1919, accordingly, witnessed an extraordinary outpouring of expectation and support among colonized and stateless peoples, who fastened onto the US president their hopes and dreams for the end of imperial domination. The moment—this "Wilsonian moment"—seemed propitious. The tremendous carnage and upheaval of the war had led to the destruction of at least four sprawling empires—the German Empire of the Hohenzollerns, the Austro-Hungarian Empire of the Habsburgs, the Turkish Empire of the Ottomans, and the Russian Empire of the Romanovs—with the prospect of constructing new sovereign nations from their sundered remains. Many across Asia and Africa, conscious of their own sacrifices on behalf of the Allied war effort, allowed themselves to dream of their own independence.

Yet it quickly became apparent that self-determination did not apply to all. Although Wilson's vision never explicitly ruled out prospects for peoples of color, his well-attested racism and paternalism and the recalcitrance of the victorious imperial powers, who were in no mood to sacrifice their empires on the altar of sovereign equality, meant in practice that self-determination applied mainly to the white peoples of Eastern Europe.[15]

Western double standards were further exposed when the Allies, led by Great Britain and its white settler dominions together with the United States, squelched a motion, introduced by Japan, to insert a provision on racial equality into the preamble to the Covenant of the League of Nations. The so-called racial equality proposal was conceived with an eye to the plight of Japanese immigrant workers in Australia and New Zealand and on the West Coast of the United States, where they had long been the target of discriminatory laws and practices. But the proposal, which sought to forbid discrimination "either in law or in fact, against any person or persons on account of his or their race or nationality," quickly galvanized the support of nonwhite peoples around the world, precipitating what Du Bois described as a global outpouring of "colored pride."[16]

As sponsors of the proposal, the Japanese were in an interesting position. In 1894–1895 they had stood up to the West diplomatically, renegotiating the so-called unequal treaties forced upon them by Americans and Europeans earlier in the century, reclaiming full sovereignty and independence. Shortly thereafter, they astounded the world by defeating Russia in the Russo-Japanese War of 1905. That victory opened the way for Japan to expand its sphere of influence and to further its quest to join the Great Powers as an equal. It also floated the tantalizing prospect to many that the white nations of the world were not invincible. Having annexed Taiwan in 1895 after a successful war with China, Japan did the same again in Korea in 1910. And it was increasingly emboldened to assert its own claims to national and racial superiority, drawing at times on the same social Darwinist doctrines vaunted in the West to do so. Still, and in part for those very reasons, Japan occupied a position of prestige among many colonial subjects, who saw the country as a champion capable of standing up to the Western imperial powers.[17]

The defeat of the equality clause, together with the denial of self-determination, was greeted with widespread disillusion, which was only compounded as the United States and other nations doubled down on racially motivated immigration restrictions in the 1920s. It seemed clear that the Allied powers were intent on reinforcing what Du Bois had famously identified in 1900 as the global "color line" dividing the white nations of the world from the rest. In Japan the defeat left a deep scar of national shame and resentment that helped fuel revanchist policies toward the Allied powers in the years to come. And in other parts of the world, it crystallized a determination to challenge Western hypocrisy outright.

An immediate consequence was the eruption of nationalist and anticolonial campaigns. The year 1919 alone saw the emergence of the May Fourth Movement in China, devoted to national renewal and the reclamation of sovereign equality; Gandhi's nonviolent resistance movement in India; the March First Movement in Korea, fighting for independence from Japan; the 1919 revolution in Egypt and Sudan, against British occupation; and the convocation of the first Pan-African Congress in Paris in 1919, in support of the principle of African home-rule. In the years and decades that followed, the colonized and subjugated would force others to acknowledge that the high-minded principles espoused by Wilson could not so easily be contained.

An unintended consequence of the Versailles peace negotiations, then, was the energy and impetus they gave to anticolonial movements striving for self-determination and sovereign equality in different parts of the world. Fueled by the initial setback and disappointment, that energy merged with, and was often radicalized by, the revolutionary currents that flowed from the Soviet Union in the wake of the Bolshevik Revolution of 1917. And they were intertwined, as well, with a baffling array of new ideologies, including state socialism and revolutionary communism, secular and religious nationalisms, pan-Islamic and pan-Asian currents, and varieties of republicanism, fascism, and liberal democracy. The result was an intensification of the process of blending and hybridization long underway in the intellectual life of societies impacted by Western power. Interrogating Western ideals in the light of their own traditions, critical voices in those societies asked what was crooked and what could be made straight, what might be borrowed and what need be abandoned. The result was an explosion in creative thought around the equality question and a genuine globalization of the concern.

For it was not just doctrines of sovereign equality that spread in these years. As the Japanese effort to include a racial equality clause in the covenant of the League of Nations illustrates, consideration of the equality of nations could readily prompt consideration of the equality of persons that transcended national frontiers. The very use of the Vattelian analogy invoked by Barbosa and others, likening the personhood of nations to the personhood of individuals, invited such consideration. It was encouraged by other forces as well. One leading scholar has written of the "globalization of equality" in the decades between 1880 and 1940, as new doctrines of common humanity emerged in response to the strident assertion of scientific racism and white supremacy in the same period. Another invokes a phrase of the Indian activist and statesman B. R. Ambedkar to describe the emergence of a modern "faith in equality" that crystallized in this period and spread around the world.[18]

It was this same period, too, that witnessed the birth and consolidation of an international women's movement, channeled through such bodies as the International Council of Women, the

International Alliance of Women, and the Women's International League for Peace and Freedom. Spearheaded by elite actors from Europe and the United States, who very often shared a sense of cultural superiority of a kind that has been styled "feminist orientalism" or "imperial feminism," these groups nonetheless made overtures to the "women of the world" with pretensions to include "all races, nations, creeds, and classes." Over time, women from outside the Euro-American inner circle, and particularly from Asia, the Middle East, Latin America, and Africa, played a crucial role in challenging Western assumptions of superiority within these international networks, just as they challenged the assumptions of the superiority of men without.[19]

Anthropologists working in the footsteps of such pioneering nineteenth-century critics of scientific race theory as Frederick Douglass, Anténor Firmin, and the "grand old man of India" Dadabhai Naoroji also did their part, challenging prevalent assumptions of racial and cultural superiority by emphasizing the relativity of cultures. A key figure in this regard was the German Jewish émigré and Columbia University professor Franz Boas, widely recognized as the father of cultural anthropology. Boas did early fieldwork among Inuit and First Nation peoples in Greenland and Canada, and he and his many students labored over the course of his long career to undermine claims to racial superiority and to break down the distinction between so-called civilized and primitive cultures. Boas's arguments were not without an element of paternalism, but they still had the power to inspire men of the stature of Du Bois, who invited Boas to deliver the commencement address at Atlanta University in 1906. Boas's theme was the history of African civilization, which had been denied outright by Western scholars and categorically effaced to such an extent that even Du Bois declared himself surprised by Boas's revelations, "too astonished to speak." "All of this," he confessed, "I had never heard."[20]

The slow and arduous work of reclaiming the history of African civilization prior to the European conquest—which Firmin, among others, had begun, and to which Du Bois, among others, would devote enormous effort in the years to come—was underway. When the second Pan-African Congress met in London in 1921, gathering representatives of some twenty-six different groups of Black descent, it issued a manifesto, written by Du Bois himself, which began by declaring that "the absolute equality of races, physical, political and social, is the founding stone of World Peace and human advancement." Voices from the cradle of humanity thus registered a goal for humanity's future, and they would work in the decades ahead to push it along.[21]

It was in Africa, in fact, on the front lines of European empire, that another crucial figure, Mohandas Gandhi, cut his teeth as an activist fighting in the name of equality. Gandhi spent twenty-three years in South Africa as a young British-trained lawyer before returning to India in 1915, and it was there that he first formulated his principle of *satyagraha*, or truth-force, while perfecting the techniques of civil disobedience and nonviolent resistance that he would later use in India itself. Gandhi began by defending the rights of Indians in Africa, hoping to redeem the promise of equal British citizenship within the empire for Asians, if not initially, at least, for Africans; he ended by concluding that the promise itself was disingenuous. His 1909 work *Hind Swaraj* (*Indian Home Rule*) pressed the case for Indian independence and the need to combat, with all vigor, an insidious, internalized sense of subaltern inferiority.[22]

Human beings were equal, Gandhi affirmed, and in subsequent years he defended that proposition with growing conviction. In a 1927 speech, he asserted, "I believe implicitly that all men are born equal. All—whether born in India or in England or America or in any circumstances whatsoever—have the same soul as any other. And it is because I believe in this inherent equality of all men that I fight the doctrine of superiority which many of our rulers arrogate to themselves. . . . *I consider that it is unmanly for any person to claim superiority over a fellow-being.*"[23]

As the gendered language suggests, Gandhi's thought was not free of certain traditional assumptions about the proper roles of the sexes and male and female difference. "Men and women are of equal rank," he later declared, "but they are not identical." And although he fought to end practices that he deemed abusive or inimical to the well-being of women, such as the denial of education or female separation (*purdah*), Gandhi generally assumed, like so many men born in the nineteenth century, that a woman's role was largely complementary to that of the more active male partner. Nor, despite his compassion for social outcasts, did Gandhi fundamentally challenge the system of Indian caste, with its inherently hierarchical assumptions about social order.[24]

More radical in that respect was the other great partisan for equality in early twentieth-century India, B. R. Ambedkar. Ambedkar is best known as the independent nation's first minister of justice and the "father of the Indian constitution," which in its preamble vows to secure "equality of status and opportunity" for all, and later develops the "right to equality" at length. But he had risen to prominence as a journalist and activist. Born into a Dalit caste, he had pressed tirelessly for Dalit and broader human rights, and, indeed, the total "annihilation of caste," to invoke the title of his 1936 treatise of that name. In the 1920s, Ambedkar spearheaded a mass protest movement on behalf of untouchables, forming the Samata Sainik Dal (SSD, Soldiers for Equality) to serve as nonviolent shock troops in the cause. No less a defender of women's rights—to property, to education, to divorce—he has been hailed as the "messiah and emancipator" of Indian women. The fact that Ambedkar named one of his many newspapers and periodicals *Samata* (Equality) is altogether fitting, for, as he put it, "to protect human rights by professing not only social equality but political and economic equality" was central to his life's work. His commitment to equality, one scholar notes, was "axiomatic" and "unconditional."[25]

Both Gandhi and Ambedkar were thoroughly conversant in Western intellectual traditions as a product of their educations, and they drew on them freely. But the globalization of equality in this period—like that of other complex ideas—was never a question of the passive reception of Western ideals, but rather of their creative appropriation and reinvention in the many and varied laboratories of the world. Colonized subjects drew deeply on their own indigenous traditions, very often mining the rich legacy of the Axial faiths to generate "distinctive notions of equality," and "radically original approach[es] to the modern egalitarian imperative," whose histories are only beginning to be written. As they did so, they interrogated Western ideals while at the same time investigating their own traditions in a new light, "braiding" the two together.[26]

Thus Gandhi could invoke Henry David Thoreau, Leo Tolstoy, Plato, or the Quakers, reminding Christians, who were inclined to forget, that their "Great Master knew no distinction between a Jew and Gentile, a European or an Asiatic"—in short, that a "doctrine of equality" lay at the heart of the Christian faith. And yet his own thinking about equality was marked most profoundly by his sustained engagement with classical Indian and Hindu thought, grounded in principles of nonviolence (*ahimsa*) and a creative interpretation of the doctrine of *advaita* (nonduality or oneness), which, as he explained, was the "rock-bottom" upon which he built a foundation rejecting inherited or acquired superiority. Ambedkar worked in similarly creative and hybrid ways, adding to his close engagement with classical Indian texts, such as the *Bhagavad Gita*, a sustained dialogue with the Buddhist tradition, to which he eventually converted. The result, as Ambedkar explained, was that even in what seemed to be quintessentially European values, there could be found analogues and spiritual grounding much closer to home. "Liberty, Equality, Fraternity" encapsulated his social philosophy, he explained. But he derived them not from the French Revolution, but from "the teachings of my Master, the Buddha."[27]

Such creative synthesis was carried out by many, particularly in the fertile hybrid space of Indian socialism, which generated unique reflection on the subject of equality in the interstices of

Western and indigenous thought. But the process was by no means confined to India. Pan-Islamists in this period, in both India and throughout the broader Muslim world, reimagined Islam as a "global manifestation of human equality" that challenged racial and imperial prerogatives while stressing the plurality and equality of the *ummah*, the community of believers.[28]

In China, similarly, reformers canvassed the past and the present alike in search of tools to effect national and intellectual renewal and to counter the assertion of Western domination. Tan Sitong, for example, one of the first major philosophers of Chinese reform in the late Qing, turned, like Ambedkar, to the Buddhist tradition, in conjunction with Neo-Confucianism and Christianity, to envision a coming reign of benevolence and altruism (*Ren*) in fulfillment of the foundational Confucian virtue of that name. Buddhism, Confucianism, and Christianity, Tan wrote, despite their ostensible differences, all attempted "to transform inequalities into equalities." And as such, they offered guidance for the future.[29]

Tang's master, Kang Youwei, likewise envisioned a radical utopia on the horizon in eclectic terms. His "Great Harmony" (大同) was a reimagining of the Confucian utopia of the same name, but seen through the prism of a reconfigured blend of Neo-Confucian, Buddhist, and socialist thought. Racial differences would disappear through widespread racial mixing, Kang foretold; private property would give way to communal sharing; class differences would be abolished; and full gender equality would be achieved in education, politics, and marriage, where women would no longer be subordinate to men.[30]

To be sure, not all regarded the past with the same indulgence, viewing the Confucian inheritance as supple clay to be reworked to suit the times. The anarcho-feminist He-Yin Zhen patently rejected efforts by more moderate scholars to retool Confucian arguments in the service of women's equality. Confucian scholarship, she argued, citing a litany of classical texts, was an "instrument of male tyrannical rule" and had underwritten the oppression of Chinese women for over two thousand years. It needed to be scrapped in its entirety. Others, such as the anarchist and revolutionary Liu Shipei, turned outward, seeking confirmation for their own theories of natural human equality and China's social contract in the writings of Rousseau, who enjoyed a surprising, if idiosyncratic, vogue in early twentieth-century China.[31]

The various thinkers associated with the May Fourth or New Culture Movement of 1919 similarly sifted Western science and learning in the service of rejecting traditionalism and fostering patriotic renewal. In that they followed the inspiration of older figures, such as the celebrated intellectual and reformer Liang Qichao, another disciple of Kang, or that of his acquaintance and sometimes ally Sun Yat-sen. The two men had met in North America, and each took inspiration as exiles in Japan. Their views departed over the question of revolution, but they agreed wholeheartedly on the instrumental necessity of adopting Western technology and science and Western social and political doctrines in the service of national renewal.

Equality figured in their calculations as a means to foster national strength and to better cultivate the capacities of the Chinese people. "It is certainly a good thing that all schools of thought have come to be concerned about the problem of equality!" Liang observed in an essay arguing for the importance of expanding women's education. "Men and women are equally human—how is it that one works and the other does not?" Liang noted that the "idea of equality between men and women was first advocated in America," but had since been adopted in all nations seeking to maximize their human capital. It was thus not only just, but expedient, to grant women equal opportunities to learn and work in the service of the nation. Later, Mao Zedong would adopt a similar perspective, famously declaring that "women held up half the sky."[32]

Sun, for his part, adopted a similarly pragmatic view. The French slogan of liberty, equality, and fraternity, he argued, like Lincoln's description of democracy as government "of the people, by the people, and for the people," found its Chinese parallel in his own *San-Min-Chu-I* doctrine, on the "three principles" of nationalism, democracy, and livelihood (welfare). Together, the three principles constituted a "doctrine for national salvation," which aimed to promote China's "equal international status, equal political status, and equal economic status." By working to foster greater political and social equality at home, the Chinese would help to secure the country's permanent place in the world.[33]

In Sun's mind, equality was both an instrument and an end, at once a tool to further national renewal and social justice *and* the marker of China's rightful place among the world's nations. But just what that equality entailed was somewhat open-ended, as capacious as the wider appeal of his thought, which evolved over the course of his career, and his effort in the final years of his life to effect an alliance between the Chinese Nationalist Party he founded, the Kuomintang (KMT), and the Chinese Communist Party (CCP). On the one hand, Sun cautioned against leveling. Surveying the fortunes of global politics since the eighteenth century, he noted how a specious, if originally liberating, belief in natural human equality had taken hold, spread by Rousseau and others as a challenge to the hierarchies and "man-made inequalities" of divine-right kings. Yet once those kings had been overthrown, "the people began to believe firmly in the theory of natural equality and kept on working day after day to make all men equal. They did not know that such a thing is impossible." Only recently, in the light of science, Sun maintained, had people begun to understand that "there is no principle of natural equality" among human beings. And so to try to force such an equality upon human society would be to create a "false equality." To avoid these leveling consequences, Sun proposed instead a kind of equality of opportunity that would permit individuals of vastly different capacities to cultivate their natural endowments. "Real equality," then, was not "artificial equalization" (false equality), but free and equal opportunity, and its necessary result was meritocratic distinction. The "sage" and the "inferior man" would never be the same.[34]

False Equality

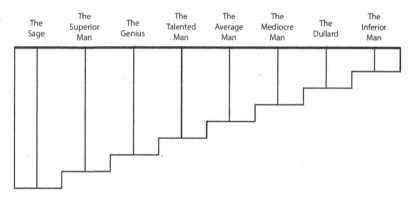

Sun Yat-sen used figures like these, drawn in chalk on blackboards, to contrast "False Equality" (above), which levels down from the superior position in order to make all equal, with "True or Real Equality" (below), which establishes a "baseline" of political status but then permits each to rise to their capacity for the overall benefit of humanity.

True Equality

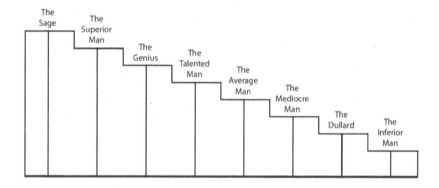

But if in these respects Sun sounded somewhat like a nineteenth-century liberal, he insisted, on the other hand, that equality, like liberty, must be tempered by the people's "democracy," which he took to be the "principle and motto" of the KMT. It was in the absence of that tempering force, Sun charged, that Europe and America had carried out so many evils in the name of the very principles of liberty and equality they espoused and so frequently "abused." Democracy was crucial to protect the people's rights, and it was consonant with the third of Sun's three principles, the people's welfare, or livelihood, which he likened to European socialism and communism while also finding precedents in Chinese history.[35]

Bringing together such diverse influences as Rousseau, Lincoln, Marx, and Confucius, Sun's eclectic thinking about equality, like his nationalism more generally, offered something for very different constituents. He was at once a hero to Mao Zedong, the future leader of the Chinese Communist Party, and to Chiang Kai-shek, Sun's successor as leader of the KMT, whose own constellation of forces included, alongside liberals and republicans, the members of the so-called Blue Shirt Society (BSS), officially known as the "Society of Practice of the Three Principles of the People," who modeled themselves on European fascists.

Those divergent allegiances point to the broader array of ideological temptations on offer in the colonized and subaltern world, which further complicated the reception and generation of discourses about equality. The dramatic success of the Bolshevik Revolution in 1917 quickly garnered admirers and imitators: in China, which saw the formation of the Chinese Communist Party in 1921; in South Asia, where the globetrotting revolutionary and intellectual M. N. Roy participated in the establishment of the Communist Party of India in 1925, after helping to found the Mexican Communist Party in 1919; in the rest of Latin America following the conclusion of the Mexican Revolution in 1920; in South Africa in 1921; in Korea in 1925; and in Vietnam in 1930. In due course, the same ideas were carried like spores around the globe.

As they descended and took root, Marxist ideas gave rise to new strains and grafts in their various national settings, often combining with other forms of socialism to evolve new forms of equality talk. Yet, for the reasons outlined in Chapter 8, we should be wary of assuming that "equality" sprouted up with Marxism as a matter of course. Even Mao spoke surprisingly little of equality, refusing to engage in the "empty phrase mongering" on the subject called out by Lenin. It is true that, like many Marxists, Mao identified equality between men and women as an important theoretical goal. And Maoist economic policies and efforts on behalf of ordinary peasants and workers undoubtedly had egalitarian effects, although these should not be overstated. Even the bloody and chaotic experiment in social engineering that was the Great Cultural Revolution was more destructive than constructive, uneven and partial. Aimed above all at purging the remnants of capitalism, its episodes of crude "leveling down" went against Marx's clear and consistent strictures on the subject. The point being that even where they had egalitarian consequences, Marxian-inspired movements around the globe were generally less interested in equality than is commonly assumed.[36]

That said, communism as an idea and the USSR as an inspiration gave powerful impetus to anticolonial struggles, which were inclined to see imperialism, as Lenin observed, as the "highest stage of capitalism." And insofar as they pushed for the downfall of both, while asserting the unity of the workers of the world, Marxists tended to support the equality and independence of colonized peoples with respect to their imperial overlords and oppressors, at least where they had not assumed power themselves.[37]

Ultranationalist movements of the Right did much the same. But unencumbered by the rhetoric of socialist and communist internationalism, they were freer to traffic not just in assertions of national equality, but to engage in an inverted national superiority. Whether Mongolian, Manchu, or Han, the Chinese for centuries had asserted the "sacred mandate" of divine preeminence in the international order, distinguishing between themselves (*hua*) and the less civilized foreigners or barbarians (*yi*), who comprised almost everyone else. The abstract notion of "sovereign equality," in fact, had no place in the conceptual space of imperial Chinese international thought. As British diplomats learned in the nineteenth century, there was no Mandarin word for it until W. A. P. Martin selected the sign *pingxing* (平行) (parallel/parallelism) as a rough equivalent in his Chinese translation of Henry Wheaton's influential *Elements of International Law* in 1864. The fiction of sovereign equality was then rendered doubly fictitious as Great Britain and other Western nations forcibly leveled the elaborate hierarchies of Qing diplomatic protocol, abolishing the kowtow and other signs of obeisance, while severely curtailing China's independence. It was only too easy for later Chinese nationalists to repurpose the distinction between *hua* and *yi* and to fling it back in the face of their vaunted Western "equals" in assertion of their own superiority.[38]

Hindu nationalists in the 1920s and 1930s invoked similar distinctions. Embracing the ideology known as *Hindutva* ("Hinduness"), first elaborated by Vinayak Damodar Savarkar in 1923, they attempted to enforce it through paramilitary groups such as the Rashtriya Swayamsevak Sangh (RSS)—a former member of which would later assassinate Gandhi in 1948. Like the European fascists and populists whom they openly admired, these groups appealed to a common identity by way of comparisons with alleged inferiors, foreign and domestic.

The Japanese did this on a much wider scale and with conscious recourse to racial science to justify their own claims to superiority within their growing empire. It has been argued that from the time of the Meiji Restoration in 1868, when references to equality first emerged as an apparent novelty from the West, appeals to a common Japanese national community (*kokutai*) under the emperor, to replace the highly stratified and aristocratic social order of the Tokugawa Shogunate, provided the "political premise for the idea of equality," predicated "on the basis of discrimination against foreigners." The line separating nationalism from racism is often thin, and in the Japanese case, as in so many others, it blurred. Belonging to the national community extended a promise of a certain kind of equality to those within it, but was based on the exclusion, and inequality, of those who were not.[39]

Latin American fascists and Arab nationalists trafficked in similar appeals, as did admirers of Mussolini and Hitler elsewhere, such as the Jamaican-born Black nationalist Marcus Garvey. Garvey pressed for racial purity, separatism, and African repatriation as a muscular response to his bitter recognition that "nowhere in the world, with few exceptions, are black men accorded equal treatment with white men." He urged his followers to "close ranks against all other races" and to pursue an equality of blood under charismatic leadership in a Black fascist state.[40]

Garvey's legacy and impacts are undoubtedly complex, and reception of his ideas was mixed. And yet such language is a reminder that varieties of fascism and militant populist nationalism were, like communism, global phenomena. As these ideologies circulated together among colonized and subaltern peoples, they only strengthened the polyglot chorus of voices calling for an end to Western imperial domination and due recognition as equals, at the very least. On that much, even sworn ideological enemies could agree.

And so it is somehow fitting that it was under the aegis of the two rival leaders vying for control of China in 1945, Chiang and Mao, that the country's representatives took up the defense of the racial equality clause first broached by the Japanese at Versailles in 1919. Fitting, and also ironic, given that Japan's forces had invaded and ravaged China, along with much of the Pacific, between 1937 and 1945. Now on the verge of an ignominious defeat, Japan was in no position to render petitions. It was the large Chinese delegation, led by the influential statesman V. K. Wellington Koo, who was then the Chinese ambassador to Great Britain, which pressed for a declaration of "complete racial equality" and "the equality of all states and all nations" at the Dumbarton Oaks conference in Washington, DC, in late 1944.[41]

The other Great Powers effectively resisted the effort, promising only to "promote respect for human rights and fundamental freedoms" while adhering to earlier endorsements of "the principle of sovereign equality of all peace-loving states." Still, the delegates were mindful of the fate of the Japanese proposal of 1919, and also of what NAACP representative Walter White called the "rising wind" of protest against white domination. When they convened again to draft the United Nations Charter in San Francisco, they found it harder to resist the logic of the representative from Iraq who pointed out that racial discrimination was a Nazi doctrine that should have no place in subsequent international affairs. The representative from the Philippines, Carlos Romulo, among others, reminded those assembled that, having joined in the effort to defeat the Axis powers, the world's colonized peoples were now "on the move," and so, as China insisted, the principle of the equality of races should be joined to the right of self-determination. The call was strongly supported by India, the Philippines, Haiti, and numerous countries and representatives from Latin America and Africa, along with associations representing people of color, such as the NAACP, and women from the great transnational organizations.[42]

In the end, cognizant of the fact that the world of 1945 was not the world of 1918, the Great Powers, with the support of the Soviet Union, acceded partially to these pressures, amending the language crafted at Dumbarton Oaks to endorse human rights and fundamental freedoms "for all without distinction as to race, sex, language, or religion," while reaffirming, in the preamble, the United Nations' support for the "equal rights of men and women and of nations large and small." That language was reaffirmed in the Universal Declaration of Human Rights, which recognized in its preamble, and in numerous articles of the text, the "inherent dignity" and "equal and inalienable rights of all members of the human family," as well as spelled out various social rights to food, health care, housing, unemployment insurance, and other social services. Such language reflected the long-term legacy of Enlightenment rights-talk, widespread revulsion at Nazi racial doctrine and the atrocities of war, and a growing consensus around the need to supplement civil with social protections. But crucial pressure had come from women's organizations, anticolonial activists, and representatives of the global south, who pushed in the face of Western intransigence for language acknowl-edging the equal dignity and worth of all human beings regardless of race or sex.[43]

These were victories, to be sure, and they would have been unthinkable without the global spread of equality talk in the previous decades. Yet, although the UN Charter reiterated the language of sovereign equality that had figured in the Allies' decla-rations from early on, it said little about the self-determination of peoples, which was mentioned only twice (in Articles 1 and 55), and subordinated in both cases to the overriding aim of securing "peaceful and friendly relations among nations." Western colo-nies and mandates were renamed "non-self-governing territories" and "trustees," respectively. But they were not abolished, and the victorious Great Powers secured their prerogatives in the United Nations, as they did elsewhere, claiming the special right to issue binding resolutions and exercise veto-power at the Security Council. As one leading scholar observes, "From the perspective of anticolonial critics and nationalists, 1945 was eerily reminiscent of 1919." The African American historian and Pan-African activist Rayford Logan was blunter, calling the charter a "tragic joke." It left at least "750 million colored and black folk inhabiting colonies owned by white nations," Du Bois bitterly observed. And though in the years ahead, between 1945 and 1960, some three dozen new states in Asia and Africa would achieve autonomy or independence from their colonial overlords, with dozens more following in the succeeding decades, self-determination and sovereign equality did not flow to them as an "inevitable outgrowth" of Westphalian or UN principles, but rather were claimed by anti-imperial actors themselves in the face of considerable skepticism and opposition, often through bloody force of arms.[44]

Still less did social and economic equality flow freely from the stewards of the United Nations or the wealthy countries of the world. On the contrary, the prosperous nations of the global north pursued their own egalitarian agendas, leaving their erstwhile subjects largely to themselves. In their myopia, they allowed themselves to believe that the world was becoming more equal, when in fact it was becoming less so.

It may seem surprising that the carnage and horror of two world wars should give way to optimism about the future of equality. But that, in fact, is what happened, in part because the wars themselves had powerful egalitarian effects. Although there is no necessary connection between warfare and more equal distribution, economists and social scientists make clear that the mass warfare of the twentieth century was one of the greatest leveling forces in history. It wiped out fortunes and capital through inflation and destruction, leveling wealth as it leveled cities. It justified powerful government interventions in the economy and confiscatory taxation at unprecedented rates. The direct impact of total war, moreover, was multiplied many times over by a number of related factors: state failure and social collapse, which reset the status quo and altered expectations for the future; transformative revolutions, such as that of Russia in 1917, with their vast expropriations of land and capital; and mass famine and pandemic, which added to wartime casualties, further gutting working populations and driving up the price of labor. Together, these forces, what the historian Walter Scheidel has called the "four horsemen of leveling"—war, revolution, state failure, and disease—combined to flatten inequalities on a truly unprecedented scale.[45]

But there was also a more constructive side to the leveling forces unleashed by the wars. If economists describe the period beginning in roughly 1914 as the onset of a "Great Leveling" or "Great Compression" that continued into the 1970s, reducing inequalities of income and wealth along the way, they also note that it was a time of "Great Redistribution," when reforming governments took active steps to improve the welfare of their citizens and to respond to hard-fought demands for social change. The "malign" forces of war and upheaval were complemented by the more "benign" effects of active political will. Redistributive tax and inheritance policies, as well as the provisions of the New Deal and emergent welfare states, were the consequence not only of the wartime ethos of shared sacrifice and solidarity, but also of long-term political struggles. In the aftermath of World War II, as economies rebounded and policy planners grew more ambitious in their efforts to build upon the fledgling welfare provisions initiated earlier, those struggles bore fruit.[46]

In retrospect, it is clear that the Great Compression was a unique, and perhaps anomalous, period in world economic history, and that it was due to an unlikely conjuncture of forces. But contemporaries were inclined to see their situation less as a historical exception than as foundation for things to come. This was the West's "social democratic moment," the "golden age of the welfare state," when a kind of welfare capitalism that for the most part eschewed the nationalization of industry, but put faith in government's capacity to direct the economy's commanding heights, came into its own. In country after country, the share of national income devoted to social security grew, with money lavished on pensions, health care, education, culture, housing, family assistance, and unemployment and disability insurance. And given that such initiatives were carried out in the context of a postwar economic boom—what Germans call the *Wirtschaftswunder* (economic miracle), and the French *les trentes glorieuses*, the thirty glorious years that followed the peace of 1945—there was money to fund them, meaning that growth and compression occurred together. The long dark night of war gave way to glimmers of a more optimistic view of the future, and a recovery of the hope expressed intermittently since the late eighteenth century that an expanding equality lay on humanity's horizon.[47]

Already in 1949, the British sociologist T. H. Marshall gave that renewed hope an early and classic formulation in the context of the construction of the British welfare state. Delivering the Alfred Marshall Lectures at Cambridge, he described "the modern drive towards social equality" as "the latest phase of an evolution of citizenship which has been in continuous progress for some 250 years." This was a confident articulation of the "cascade thesis," which noted that rights had spilled over steadily, if gradually, from the civil to the political to the social realms, and would continue to do so going forward. The Christian socialist R. H. Tawney agreed. In a 1951 epilogue to his book *Equality*, first published in 1931, Tawney expressed cautious optimism where earlier he had voiced doubt, observing "that a somewhat more equalitarian social order is in progress of emerging." A long-standing concern with economic egalitarianism on the British Left was finally, it seemed, gaining traction.[48]

From France, another celebrated sociologist, the public intellectual Raymond Aron, drew similar conclusions about the future of equality, albeit from a somewhat different perspective. Summing up the main points of a series of lectures he delivered at the Sorbonne in 1955–1956, Aron remarked, "I have shown that several basic tendencies are common to all industrial societies: for example the tendency to become middle class and to reduce the inequality of incomes." In charting that vision, Aron, like other so-called "convergence theorists" of the time, took account of both the Soviet Union and the West, which were in his view but "two versions of the same social type, progressive industrial society." Aron's prophet of the future, however, was not Marx, but Tocqueville, whose thought enjoyed an important revival in this period. Aron cited approvingly from the preface to *Democracy in America*, in which the French aristocrat posited an ineluctable movement toward greater equality of conditions. "Everyone's status is tending to become more similar," Aron observed, noting that the "democratic movement combined with industrial society would lead to an increase in the intermediate ranks" and a tendency "to a reduction in extreme inequalities," though not to the complete equalization of fortunes. The future, it seemed, was steadily becoming fairer.[49]

That sanguine outlook was reinforced by a number of reigning economic theories. The legacy of the British economist Maynard

Keynes, for example, buttressed the confident assumption that governments had acquired the power and expertise to manage economic life for social and political ends, curbing the swings of the business cycle and mitigating inequalities through social spending and taxation.[50]

That technocratic view was baked into welfare policy on both sides of the Atlantic. Yet one did not have to be a Keynesian to share the belief that the world could be made more equal. The Russian Jewish émigré economist and later Nobel laureate Simon Kuznets published in this period his pathbreaking 1955 study "Economic Growth and Economic Equality." Based on pioneering analysis of US income tax returns, the work showed that income inequality had fallen sharply in the United States between 1913 and 1948 from previous highs. Extrapolating from this data, Kuznets put forth the theory that economies in the early stages of industrialization experienced widening inequalities as a consequence of initial growth, which was invariably uneven. But as economies passed through successive stages, those inequalities would diminish as education, productivity, and technical expertise spread more widely in the population and allowed more and more people to partake of

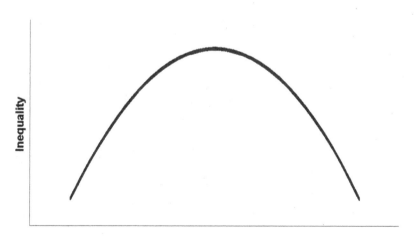

The Kuznets curve.

growth's benefits. Inequality, Kuznets concluded, followed a curve that looked like an inverted U (the "Kuznets curve"), first rising and then falling over time.[51]

With its comforting suggestion that economic development generated its own equalizing mechanisms, Kuznets's theory proved powerful and influential, not least because it helped to explain the apparent empirical finding that economies in the early stages of economic growth were generally less equal than the economies of their more developed counterparts, while at the same time assuring that the former would eventually "catch up" with the latter. Neoclassical trade theory offered a related assurance about the long-term benefits of free trade. Building on the insights of the important early nineteenth-century British economist David Ricardo, the theory held that commerce between rich and poor nations was mutually beneficial, owing to the law of comparative advantage, and that it would eventually lead to equalization across borders, with the poor once again catching up to the rich.

Such promises—with the attendant counsel to patience for countries in their early stages of economic growth—were central to the pervasive modernization and development theories so influential at midcentury. In these, the advanced nations of the world held up their own affluence and social welfare as the prizes to be achieved in due course by all those "latecomers" who would fashion themselves in their image. The American modernization theorist Edward Shils waxed eloquent on the subject in 1959, defining the 'modernity' to which the newly sovereign and equal nations in Asia, Africa, and the Middle East should aspire: "In the new states 'modern' means democratic and equalitarian, scientific, economically advanced and sovereign. 'Modern' states are 'welfare states,' proclaiming the welfare of all the people and especially the lower classes as their primary concern." Modernity, he continued, meant "the dethronement of the rich and the traditionally privileged from their positions of pre-eminent influence." It involved land reform, progressive income taxation, universal suffrage, and universal public education—all those things, in short, that Western nations had only recently attained. Shils captured the ideals of a host of prominent midcentury intellectuals on both sides of the Atlantic. Together they conceived of modernization theory as the "foreign-policy counterpart" to the welfare state, aiming, as Shils's colleague, the influential W. W. Rostow, envisioned, to make "the social democratic welfare state the final outcome of world history."[52]

Those aspirations were well intentioned, but they were never disinterested. To some extent they echoed the late imperial promises of colonizing nations that vowed to spread the benefits of welfare and civilization to their subjects in the empire. Certainly, modernization theory aligned closely with Western economic interests—facilitating trade, financing, and investment on favorable terms. Even more crucially, it served Cold War geopolitical interests. Economic growth and poverty reduction were seen in the West as the keys to strategic competition with the Soviet Union, and so the necessary condition for maintaining the global balance of power. To that end, the United States and its allies were ready to dispense aid, along with military assistance, as a prophylactic against communism. But all too often that meant doing business with regimes whose human rights records were compromised. And as for the lofty goals of social democratic welfare dangled at the end of history by the likes of Shils, developing nations would have to wait for modernity to arrive while markets and growth worked their magic.

Indeed, in what was styled "growthmanship," the United States and its allies aimed to demonstrate the superior performance of the Western capitalist model over communist alternatives. But that meant effectively sidelining near-term concerns about inequality and distribution. The German economics minister (and later federal chancellor) Ludwig Erhard put this nicely in 1958, noting "how much more sensible it is to concentrate all available energies on increasing the nation's wealth rather than squabble over the distribution of this wealth." John Kenneth Galbraith, the influential Harvard economist, remarked on the phenomenon in his 1958 book *The Affluent Society*, pointing out that amid postwar plenty "it has become evident to conservatives and liberals alike that increasing aggregate output is an alternative to redistribution or even to the reduction of inequality." At home and abroad, a rising tide would lift all boats.[53]

In the meantime, one needn't worry too much about equality; it would happen on its own. Galbraith pointed out strikingly "the decline of interest in inequality as an economic issue." Historians of economic thought have emphasized the same, noting that mainstream economists largely ignored inequality and distribution for much of the twentieth century. At the international level, above all, efforts to collect data and innovate measurement tools in order to understand global inequalities of income and wealth are recent developments, only undertaken seriously from the late 1990s and early 2000s, after initial forays at the United Nations in the 1970s.[54]

Thus, in the absence of hard data to suggest otherwise, these different economic theories—development and modernization theory, neoclassical trade theory, and the Kuznets curve—served to reinforce the shared belief that time was on equality's side. At home, the wealthy nations of the world nurtured that belief in the fog of their own affluence, looking confidently to the future. And abroad, the same belief allowed Western diplomats and statesmen to preach the virtues of free trade while arming elites in countries just beginning their processes of economic transformation with arguments that justified widening inequalities in the short term on the promise that growth would give way to a more egalitarian distribution in time. Well into the 1960s, in fact, many believed in good faith that the future was not far off. "The dominant Western temporality of international inequality," two experts on the period remark, "was that of a near-future equalization." If only developing nations could wait, the future would be upon them.[55]

Backed up by development aid from the United States and its allies and the influx of private capital, that argument, for a time, worked. The social scientist Albert Hirschman later developed a theory of what he called the "tunnel effect" to account for the near-term patience. When two lanes of traffic are blocked in a tunnel, the drivers in one lane will take heart initially as the other begins to move, confident that their own prospects will also soon improve. But if they continue to stay where they are, or only move slowly as the others speed ahead, they will grow frustrated. In Hirschman's view, that was an apt metaphor for welfare economics in the developing world, where incipient growth widened disparities that at first were tolerated, but then increasingly were not.[56]

Those stalled in traffic, moreover, watched—before too long directly on television—as not only their more fortunate fellow citizens, but the wealthy nations of the world, surged ahead, adding to their frustration and resentment. The temporality of the near future, they came to realize, was in truth a persistent "temporality of not yet." And as the world's poor, and the new sovereign nations they inhabited, grew tired of waiting for a more prosperous and equal tomorrow that never seemed to come, their advocates drew attention to the widening "gap" that divided the north from the south, frustrating efforts to fashion a more equal world.[57]

That chasm of a word came to figure centrally as a description of the gulf between rich nations and poor nations as postwar optimism gave way to a more pessimistic mood, evident from the mid- to late 1960s. Already in the 1950s, sporadic UN reports remarked on the "gap" in levels of income, wealth, production, and consumption with respect to developing nations, noting that it was "wider than before the Second World War," and growing more so. And although these early reports tended to be framed optimistically, dissident economists working at the United Nations were in the process of developing more critical perspectives.[58]

The two most influential were the Swede Gunnar Myrdal and the Argentine Raúl Prebisch, who served, respectively, as the executive secretary of the United Nations Economic Commission for

Europe and that of Latin America. From the late 1940s, Prebisch began to call the mainstream assumptions of development theory into question, arguing, in *The Economic Development of Latin America and Its Principal Problems* (1950), that Ricardian notions of the mutual benefits of trade were misplaced. In a lopsided world system in which the core wealthy nations controlled technology and advanced production and the peripheral nations provided only agricultural goods and raw materials, convergence was a mirage. In such a system, the poor nations of the globe would never "catch up."[59]

Myrdal likewise pointed to structural features in the global economy that stood in the way of convergence, arguing that current economic development would only "award its favors to those who are already well endowed and even to thwart the efforts of those who happen to live in regions that are lagging behind." Part of the solution, he began to argue as early as 1956, must be to extend welfare on a global scale. "*The concept of the welfare state, to which we are now giving reality in all the advanced nations, would have to be widened and changed into a concept of a 'welfare world.'*" That would require moving beyond national and even regional frontiers, such as the "protective rich man's club" being created by the process of European union. A "welfare world" would eventually require global governance—a "world state"—to fully carry it out.[60]

Myrdal's proposal was utopian, but its underlying analysis of the gap between rich and poor countries was clear-eyed and prescient. Within a number of years it was being echoed more widely. Pope John XXIII, like his successor Paul VI, made the "glaring economic and social imbalances" of the world a central theme of postwar Catholic social teaching. And the British-born development economist and policy adviser Barbara Ward, herself a committed Catholic, emerged as an important public voice calling attention to the gap between nations, as the title of her prominent 1962 book, *The Rich Nations and the Poor Nations*, makes clear. Ward stressed there, as Myrdal had in his own book, *Rich Lands and Poor: The Road to World Prosperity* of 1957, that a "revolutionary idea [was] now at work from one end of the world to the other: the revolution of equality—equality of men and equality of nations." "Men's passionate desire to see themselves as the equals of other human beings," she insisted, "without distinctions of class or sex or race or nationhood is one of the driving forces of our day." It was the "tap root of modern nationalism." "The whole United Nations," she added, "with its 'one state, one vote,' reflects this egalitarian nationalism[,] and the 'right to self-determination,' the most cutting edge of nationalism as old empires dissolve, is in essence the new peoples' claim to national equality with the older states." It followed that "the equality of nations one with each other," and the "equality of esteem and prestige which comes from not being run by other nations," was one of the "great drives" of the current world.[61]

Ward framed her discussion in the context of Cold War competition with the Soviet Union and Marxian efforts to recruit leaders among the dispossessed "in the name of equality." Like Myrdal, she worried that the gulf between the wealthy capitalist nations and the developing poor served as a powerful recruiting tool for Marxists. In a series of publications with revealing titles, such as *The Lopsided World* (1968) and *The Widening Gap* (1971), she pressed the point, urging the West to do more. Nor was she a lone voice. Yet, as her close friend, the president of Ghana Kwame Nkrumah, pointed out, there was a limit to what the developing nations should expect. "It has been argued," Nkrumah observed witheringly, "that the developed nations should effectively assist the poorer part of the world, and that the whole world should be turned into a Welfare State. However, there seems little prospect that anything of this sort could be achieved." Nkrumah's words reflected the realism of Africans who had heard grand promises before. In the last stages of empire, talk of "colonial humanism" and welfare for the members of the commonwealth had circulated freely, even as those proposals came to naught. Now, however, as the optimism about convergence of the 1950s gave way to the more pessimistic mood of the mid- to late 1960s, leaders of the new nations of what was being called the "Third World" sought to take matters into their own hands.[62]

That conception of the tripartite division of the globe, based on the analogy of the three estates of France, was first formulated in 1952 by the French intellectual and anticolonial activist Alfred Sauvy. If the wealthy West was the First World, and the Soviet bloc constituted the Second, the Third World comprised everyone else. And like the members of the Third Estate of old, they desired to be something. Indeed, as Ward recognized, they wanted to make themselves equals. That desire had long coursed through the anticolonial movements, and it accompanied the birth of the new nations from the start. As the Caribbean poet and intellectual Aimé Césaire noted acidly in 1955, in vowing to leave the "putrid carrion" of colonial society behind, "It is a new society that we must create, with the help of all our brother slaves, a society rich with all the productive power of modern times, warm with all the fraternity of olden days."[63]

Postcolonial leaders cultivated the egalitarian traditions embedded in native soil, and they drew creatively on those of others, all the while dreaming publicly of providing the benefits of abundance that the rich welfare states lavished on their own metropolitan citizens but had denied to their erstwhile imperial subjects. From Gamal Abdel Nasser's Egypt to Jawaharlal Nehru's India and in a variety of ideological idioms, leaders drew up lists and crafted constitutions that spelled out the social rights and protections they aimed to provide: the right to work and study, the right to health care and assistance in old age, the right to freedom from want. They spoke of material fairness and equality, both within their new societies and among the peoples of the world.[64]

Those conversations varied from country to country, of course, and they were marked by internal political contestation that could turn violent over issues of how best to achieve development and fulfill popular expectations. But the expectations themselves—to education, to health care, to housing, to food, to clothing, to necessary social services, to work and leisure—were continually raised, and not only by reforming leaders. The very same social rights were spelled out in Articles 23–26 of the Universal Declaration of Human Rights. Translated into over five hundred languages, it was there to be consulted.

Although in the end much of the talk of providing welfare for the peoples of the global south was aspirational—contingent on prospects for financing, development, and cooperation that all too often were severely lacking—the newly sovereign equals did register some notable successes. Sociologists point out that "vital inequality," which relates to overall life-chances and includes such variables as infant mortality rates and life and health expectancies, fell in global terms between roughly 1945 and 1990, owing to improvements in medicine and the delivery of vaccinations and basic health care. So, too, did "existential inequality," which is bound up with measures of autonomy, dignity, freedom, self-development, and respect. In both cases, the initiatives of newly independent nation-states, which aimed to educate their citizens and reaffirm their basic worth, clearly played a part. And one can point to the reduction of other global inequalities on indices of "Augmented Human Development" that measure more than just income and wealth.[65]

Third World nations also scored some successes vis-à-vis inequalities of income and wealth within their own borders. The Great Compression was not confined to the West. It extended to the Soviet sphere and China, where a combination of malign leveling forces and redistribution had their effect, as well as to countries such as India and Indonesia, even if it registered very little in Latin America, in sub-Saharan Africa, and in the Middle East, where inequality actually grew. But in all these places, distribution occurred at far lower levels of affluence, and often, as in the Soviet case, in ways that inhibited longer-term incentives and innovation, inducing eventual stagnation. And that is to say nothing of the tremendous human costs. In the Soviet Union and China, especially, but also in places such as Cambodia under Pol Pot, leveling came at a horrific price in blood. Elsewhere in the Third World, egalitarian poverty was seldom a great consolation for the lack of development, particularly when weighed against the evident imbalance of First World wealth and welfare.[66]

Still, the efforts to provide their citizens with something like the welfare provisions of the global north did create solidarities among the subaltern and a willingness to confront a world economic system that appeared set against them. "The consciousness of economic inequality," observed the first premier of Senegal, Mamadou Dia, in *The African Nations and World Solidarity* (1960), "align[s] the nations of Africa and Asia on the same battlefront against the West." Many shared Nkrumah's analysis of a neocolonial economic order put in place by the victors after World War II. Boxed out of a system whose founding they could not attend, postcolonial states knew only the "outward trapping" of sovereignty. "In reality," their economic systems and thus their political policies were "directed from the outside . . . through economic or monetary means." A similar complaint could be leveled at the countries of the Soviet bloc, seen as comparatively advantaged and just as inclined to meddle militarily and economically as the West. Others invoked a global class struggle between the "have" nations, which included the Soviet Union, and the "have nots," which included Maoist China. Permutations of "Third Worldism" varied, and they were always complicated by the shifting strategic calculations of the Cold War. But they shared a willingness to entertain radical critiques of the world economic system and the global balance of power. Recognizing that inequality was organized and enforced on a global scale, they pressed for a global response, endeavoring to remake the world.[67]

That idealistic project to remake the world culminated in the ill-fated effort to launch a New International Economic Order (NIEO) in the early 1970s. But its outlines began to coalesce considerably earlier, from at least the time of the 1955 Asia-Africa Conference at Bandung, Indonesia, which gathered representatives of twenty-nine

Third World countries to consider prospects for international solidarity and cooperation. The first four points of the ensuing joint
declaration made clear the desire to enhance sovereignty and
equality together through mutual cooperation in "recognition
of the equality of all races and of the equality of all nations large
and small." A similar aim helped guide incipient economic and
political federations in the Black Atlantic promoted by Nkrumah
and the eventual first prime minister of independent Trinidad and
Tobago, Eric Williams: the short-lived Union of African States
(1958–1963) and the West Indies Federation (1958–1962). And
it further informed the meetings of the Non-Aligned Movement
(NAM) that succeeded Bandung in the effort to make "equality
and mutual benefit" between nations a guiding principle of international organization.[68]

Such organization extended increasingly to the United Nations
itself, where the proliferation of sovereign states that attended decolonization meant that the Third World constituted a growing majority
in the General Assembly. With the sharper realization in the 1960s
of a "widening gap" that was leaving the developing nations behind,
UN agencies grew even more sympathetic to the analyses of Myrdal,
Prebisch, and the Saint Lucian–born UN development economist
Arthur Lewis, who served briefly as special adviser to Nkrumah in
Ghana, and in 1979 was awarded the Nobel Prize.

Nowhere was that sympathy more evident than at the UN
Conference on Trade and Development (UNCTAD), whose
founding secretary-general was none other than Prebisch himself.
It was Prebisch who coined the term "New International Economic
Order," in 1963, and throughout the decade he worked to elaborate the critique of neoclassical trade and development theory that
he and others, such as the German-born British economist Hans
Singer, had developed earlier. Prebisch helped build UNCTAD into
a clearinghouse for kindred ideas, including dependency theory, and
the later world systems theory, along with various Third World and
New Left critiques of neocolonialism and racial discrimination.

349

Crucially, at an organizational level, UNCTAD became the nucleus for a voting bloc at the UN General Assembly, the Group of 77 (G-77), that would spearhead the successful passage of the NIEO in 1974.[69]

The plan for the NIEO reflected these earlier aims and efforts. The official declaration adopted by the General Assembly called for the establishment of a "New International Economic Order based on equity, sovereign equality, interdependence, common interest and co-operation among all States." The NIEO would work to "correct inequalities and redress existing injustices, [and] make it possible to eliminate the widening gap between the developed and the developing countries." The declaration also called out the "vestiges of alien and colonial domination, foreign occupation, racial discrimination, apartheid and neo-colonialism in all its forms," flagging them as stubborn obstacles to progress. It further noted the injustice of the fact that although the developing countries constituted 70 percent of the world's population, they accounted for a mere 30 percent of the world's income. Finally, and most concretely, it put forth a comprehensive program of economic, legal, and political measures designed to strengthen the hand of the south in global governance and trade and to address inequalities vis-à-vis the north head on. Those measures ranged from laws governing the ownership and extraction of raw materials; to debt forgiveness, technology transfer, and import substitution; to ambitious proposals to foster cooperation among the poorer nations, especially by enhancing their capacity to affect pricing and the terms of trade through collective bargaining on the loose model of the union or cartel.[70]

With its overall aim to democratize global decision-making and redistribute income from world trade, the NIEO looked to some observers like earlier proposals for a "welfare world," and they described it as such. Myrdal himself, however, did not. Although sympathetic to the project, he sounded a generally gloomy note in his 1975 acceptance speech for the Nobel Prize, "The Equality Issue in World Development." "*The blunt truth,*" he acknowledged there, *"is that without rather radical changes in the consumption patterns in the rich countries, any pious talk about a new world economic order is humbug."*[71]

Humbug or not, the NIEO did represent what one authority calls the "most serious challenge to [US] global leadership" and the extant terms of world trade since World War II. Owing, moreover, to the initial support of oil-producing nations in the wake of the oil crisis of 1973, the NIEO provoked genuine hopes in the global south that together its countries could act with strength—and genuine fear among influential sectors of the global north that they would. That fear drove a forceful response, led by the United States on behalf of allies who understood the global (im)balance of power in more traditional, proportional terms.[72]

This was the moment of neoliberalism's rise, and the beginning of a successful "counterrevolution" that divided its opponents and countered their representation of a world shaped by domination and dependency with one of a self-regulating system that multiplied riches and distributed them rationally through the free circulation of capital and goods in global markets. That spelled the end of robust national economic sovereignty and the NIEO's dream of preferential treatment for the poor, and the rise of a new imaginary, no less utopian, of a perfectly free and fetterless world in which all nations and their peoples would compete as equals, while markets, pricing, and the laws of supply and demand guaranteed appropriate outcomes.[73]

That utopia of the global market was no respecter of national frontiers, and insofar as it acknowledged the sovereign equality of states, it did so in the interest of allowing giants to compete equally with dwarves. Yet as one Indian trade delegate demurred, in words that Aristotle would have approved of, "Equality of treatment is equitable only among equals." The nations of the world, and their peoples, clearly were not equals. The president of Tanzania, Julius Nyerere, made it plain. In a broad critique of the imbalances masked by traditional sovereign equality when considered without reference to resources, income, and wealth, Nyerere noted that "equality between nations of the modern world is only a legal equality—it is not an economic reality. Tanzania and America are not equal." In Nyerere's judgment, "the poor nations of the world remain poor because . . . they operate as if they were equals in a world dominated by the rich." No less than the two K/Carls, Marx and Schmitt, Nyerere understood that the language of equality served effectively as the basis for domination.[74]

The demise of the NIEO and the dream of a welfare world confronting global inequality are most often framed today in the context of the demise of the welfare state in the global north and the end of the Great Compression. With the elections of Margaret Thatcher, Ronald Reagan, and Helmut Kohl, one observer notes typically, "inequality was pushed off both domestic and international agendas," with the result that "justice claims based on the inequality of resources among states" steadily disappeared. That frame is not wrong. The neoliberals who assailed the welfare state were no less enemies of the welfare world, and the triumph of their economic policies did put an end to the Great Leveling. It was at this moment—the end of the 1970s and early 1980s—that income and wealth inequalities within the nations of the global north began to take off once again after the long run of redistribution and compression that began to take hold at the time of World War I.[75]

Yet that same frame can obscure an irony about the long-term fate of global inequality, masking a deeper tension between national and international welfare. For it was at this same moment, with the demise of the welfare state and the end of the Great Compression, that growing global inequalities of income and wealth between the world's people began to level off and fall. Whether that conjuncture was causal or coincidental is a matter of debate. Much of it owes to the economic resurgence of China and the so-called Asian Tigers, and the timing is not altogether clear. The calculation of global inequalities is an imperfect science, and charting the history of those inequalities, given the many gaps in the data, is more imperfect still. And yet, when taken up in earnest from the early 2000s, the measurement of global inequality revealed some interesting patterns.

Global income inequality began to rise in the eighteenth century with the beginnings of the Industrial Revolution and the so-called "Great Divergence," which opened up as first the United Kingdom and Western Europe, and then the United States and a smattering of their other former colonies, began to surge ahead of the rest of the world, leaving former economic powerhouses, including China and India, behind. Compounded by military conquest, imperialism, and protectionist trade policies, that overall upward trend can be demonstrated in data from 1820 onward. And

Global inequality between world citizens and its components, World, 1820 to 1992
The measure shown here is the mean logarithmic deviation.

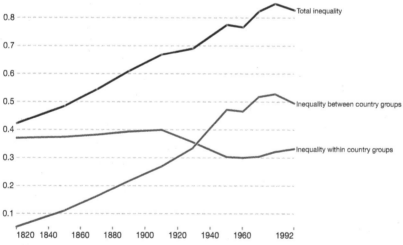

Source: Inequality Among World Citizens - Bourguignon and Morrisson (2002)   OurWorldInData.org/global-economic-inequality • CC BY

The long-term fortunes of global inequality. Source: Max Roser, "Global Economic Inequality," Our World in Data, 2013, https://ourworldindata. org/global-economic-inequality, citing François Bourguignon and Christian Morrisson, "Inequality Among World Citizens: 1820–1992," *American Economic Review* 92, no. 4 (September 2002): 727–744.

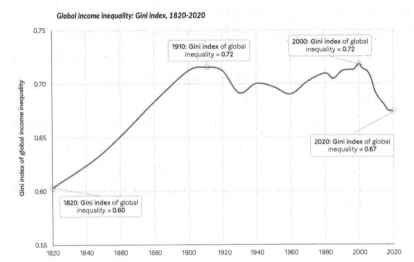

Global income inequality: Gini index, 1820-2020

1910: Gini index of global inequality = 0.72

2000: Gini index of global inequality = 0.72

2020: Gini index of global inequality = 0.67

1820: Gini index of global inequality = 0.60

Interpretation: *Global inequality, as measured by the global Gini coefficient, rose from about 0.6 in 1820 to about 0.7 in 1910, and then stabilized around 0.7 between 1910 and 2020. It is too early to say whether the decline in the global Gini coefficient observed since 2000 will continue. Income is measured per capita after pension and unemployment insurance transfers and before income and wealth taxes.* **Sources and series:** *wir2022.wid.world/methodology and Chancel and Piketty (2021).*

Another approximation of the long-term fortunes of global inequality by Gini coefficient estimates. Source: "Methodology," World Inequality Report 2022, https://wir2022.wid.world/methodology, citing Lucas Chancel and Thomas Piketty, "Global Income Inequality, 1820–1920: The Persistence and Mutation of Extreme Inequality," World Inequality Lab Working Paper, no. 2021/19, accessed at World Inequality Database, https://wid.world/document/longrunpaper.

what it shows is that global inequality did not begin to abate significantly until very recently, likely reaching its historical high point sometime between 1970 and 1980, or possibly even as late as 2000.

Research on global wealth inequality is less advanced, and also more difficult to calculate. But given that wealth distribution tends to diverge even more sharply than that of income, the trends are likely even more extreme. The bottom line is that throughout the Great Leveling the distance between the global north and the global south continued to grow, expanding the immense chasm between them. Or, to put it another way, the Great Compression was experienced in much of the global south as a Great Squeeze, a continuation of the pressures and forces that had drawn its labor and extracted its resources since the advent of empire, and that did not abate as the soldiers and viceroys withdrew.[76]

Even without such concrete data at their disposal, actors in the Third World had few illusions about the standing of their nations vis-à-vis the First World. In their anger, they could be as straightforward as the abbé Sieyès with respect to the provenance of the welfare of the First and Second Estates. "Europe is literally the creation of the Third World," Frantz Fanon observed in his 1961 classic *Les damnés de la terre* (*The Wretched of the Earth*). "The wealth which smothers her is that which was stolen from the under-developed peoples." Aimé Césaire, for his part, was quick to remark that the "barbarism" of Europe was surpassed only by that of the United States. The points were not subtle; nor were they intended to be. Both men saw clearly that the West's "piles of speeches on the equality of human beings" were predicated on exclusions those speeches failed to acknowledge, but were plain for the Third World to see.[77]

That the rich world, which has spoken continuously since the long eighteenth century of equality, does not like to hear such things, and still less to see them, is a point that Myrdal clearly appreciated. What he described as the "equality doctrine" had been a powerful animating ideal in the Western nations beginning at the time of the Enlightenment. "In a queer way, however, the equality doctrine, in so far as it concerned international relations, was from the beginning almost entirely blotted out from practical attention and much more completely so than it ever was in regard to purely national issues," Myrdal wrote. That was the West's "blind spot," and as Myrdal came to appreciate, it was only exacerbated by decolonization, which had the effect of further sheltering the populations of the former imperial metropoles from the extremes of inequality their nations had helped to create.[78]

The welfare state, tragically, compounded the West's myopia, encouraging its citizens to see their egalitarian commitments and horizons largely in national terms. Just as liberals in the nineteenth century proclaimed liberty at home, while making myriad "exceptions" in their empires, their counterparts in the twentieth century thought of equality at home and abroad on separate tracks.[79]

Symptomatic in this respect was the philosophy of John Rawls. Arguably the greatest liberal theorist of the national welfare state, he had nothing to say on the matter of global inequalities in his main work, *A Theory of Justice* (1971). And although by the late 1960s and 1970s, it was becoming harder and harder to avert one's gaze from the plight of the world, he and others were forced to focus more intently on urgent problems at home that national welfare states had also tended to ignore. Problems of race, gender, and identity, all with imperial entanglements of their own, were forcing themselves on public consciousness in much of the world, and most dramatically in the United States.[80]

11

DREAM

*The Guiding Hand of Equality and
the Moral Arc of the Universe*

On the steps of the Lincoln Memorial in the "symbolic shadow" of the emancipator, Martin Luther King Jr. revealed his famous dream. That "one day this nation will rise up and live out the true meaning of its creed—we hold these truths to be self-evident, that all men are created equal." That one day the country would be truly great. It was the 28th of August, 1963, nearly "five score years" after the Emancipation Proclamation, as King reminded his listeners, the some 250,000 men and women who had marched to Washington, DC, and gathered on the National Mall to hear him. But Black Americans were still very far from free. The redemption of the country, and the realization of its promise, King insisted, were bound up with their ultimate deliverance.[1]

King was a seer of vision, who looked to the past as well as to the future. He was also a master rhetorician. And so in expounding his dream and elaborating his faith he touched on nearly every one of the "figures" of equality examined in this book, serving as their interpreter, receiver, and heir. He summoned an image of *reversal* in his account of the formerly enslaved who had freed themselves once and who would free themselves again to shed "the manacles of segregation and the chains of discrimination." He invoked exile and *loss*, the "long night of captivity" that preceded "the daybreak of hope." He spoke of *fellowship* and *fraternity*, inviting all to sit as equals as God's children at the "table of brotherhood." And he invoked, like the German theologian whose name he shared, the *recovery* of the full freedom and equality that human beings had fatally lost in their sin.[2]

Repeatedly, too, King spoke of *justice* and of the *leveling* and true *balance* that justice would bring. "One day, every valley shall be exalted," he exclaimed, like Amos and Isaiah and the other prophets of old, "and every hill and mountain shall be made low, the rough places will be made plain, and the crooked places shall be made straight, and the glory of the Lord shall be revealed, and all flesh shall see it together."[3]

This was no *illusion*. King refused to countenance equality in the figure favored by Marx and many conservatives. He spoke instead of equality as *dream*. A dream that might one day be realized and made true. A dream that one day men and women would be judged by the content of their character, not the color of their skin. A dream that one day the country's most "vicious racists" would be sidelined along with their words of interposition, when all those who sought the substance of equality in *domination* over others would be cast aside. Then, King dreamed, "little black boys and black girls will be able to join hands with little white boys and white girls as sisters and brothers." The human family would be bound together, hand in hand. King concluded his speech with that same image, conjuring an ecumenical vision of the spread of freedom "when all of God's children—black men and white men, Jews and Gentiles, Protestants and Catholics, will be able to join hands and sing in the words of the old Negro spiritual, 'Free at last, free at last; Thank God almighty, we are free at last.'"[4]

King had invoked that dream before, using many of the same words. As he said in a speech of 1961, it was an "American dream," as "yet unfulfilled":

A dream of equality of opportunity, of privilege and property widely distributed. A dream of a land where men will not take necessities from the many to give luxuries to the few; a dream of a land where men will not argue that the color of a man's skin determines the content of his character; a dream of a nation where all our gifts and resources are held not for ourselves alone but as instruments of service for the rest of humanity; the dream of a country where every man will respect the dignity and worth of human personality—that is the dream.

Both here and on the Mall in Washington, DC, King was reinterpreting, as Lincoln had done, the history of equality, and at the same time reimagining its future.[5]

King's was a vision that took in much of what had come before, synthesizing, sorting, and combining to create a new ideal and a new horizon. It drew from the millenarian strains of the social gospel tradition of liberal Protestantism, and it took in the teachings of the Axial faiths, as well as those of progressive movements for social justice pursued since the eighteenth century, and of

The March on Washington, DC, August 28, 1963. Leonard Freed / Magnum Photos 02-Stock (Estate).

anticolonial activists and people of color in the global south. In so doing, it gave voice to a tough-minded optimism, announcing, in the figure of a dream charged with yearning and hope, yet bolstered by determination, that the "arc of the universe is long but it bends toward justice." All who could summon the strength to join him were called to march in that direction, binding themselves together in their humanity. Free and equal in their irreducible difference, they would be linked as human beings, hand in hand, one as God's children, yet simultaneously distinct.

The Reverend Dr. King was fond of hands. He offered his freely, and took those of others warmly in his own. When he greeted followers from the podium or stage, he did so like the good shepherd he was, with palm facing outward in a gentle wave.

There are well over 1,400 references to hands in scripture—the hands of mortals, the hand of God. Joined hands, King knew, meant "the bond of Christian love." He secured that bond as a man of the cloth, and he reaffirmed it continually, marching in Christian fellowship. But he was also well aware that that power and symbolism of clasping hands, like the image of the hand itself, extended well beyond the frontiers of any strictly Christian meaning.[6]

Hands, in fact, have long served as symbols for what makes human beings human. They turn up in outline in the very first examples we have of human art, registering a collective presence on the walls of prehistoric caves, where individual identities are obscured. But at the same time hands are markers of singularity and difference. In ancient Babylon and China, handprints served as seals, unique markings that, like signatures, were difficult to forge. As the British eugenicist Francis Galton would discover in the late nineteenth century, each of us possesses an absolutely unique set of fingerprints that do not change over the course of our lives. Quite literally, no two person's hands are alike. Everyone is different.

Yet as working people have always known, human beings can be reduced to their hands, severed from their humanity and

Hand paintings in Sumpang Bita cave, Indonesia, dating back 39,000 years. Similar handprints have been found at Altamira, Spain, and other ancient sites. Remi Masson / Nature Picture Library / Science Photo Library.

alienated from the fruits of their labor, treated not as unique individuals but as instruments and factors of production, cogs in a machine. King noted pointedly, in a speech delivered in Nashville, Tennessee, in 1962, that the white gentry in the antebellum South had referred to the enslaved as their "hands." It was, he remarked, a violation of Immanuel Kant's categorical imperative that "all men must be treated as *ends* and never as mere *means*." That all must be respected in their dignity.[7]

Labor leaders and socialists made similar points in their analyses of the exploitation of *manual* workers. The hand in the word is slightly hidden in English (from the Latin root *manus*, "hand"). But in other languages the association is in plain sight. A *Handwerker* in German is an artisan, a craftsman whose work is distinctly made, but whose individual expression, as Karl Marx took pains to note, is effaced by the conditions of mass production under capitalism. It was in part for that reason that workers of the proletariat joined their hands in solidarity as an expression of mutual recognition and as a sign of collective power. Although clasped hands are a gesture with an iconographic tradition dating back at least to the sixteenth and seventeenth centuries—and the shaking of hands served as a ritual gesture of reconciliation at peacemaking ceremonies long before that—from the time of the French Revolution they came to serve as a powerful symbol of "fraternity." Ever after the so-called "fraternal hands" (*Brüderhände*) were adopted as ubiquitous symbols of solidarity among workers.[8]

King was undoubtedly aware of the broader significance of his gestures. How we hold and how we play our hands, he knew, is crucial. When taken in that of another, the hand of individual difference becomes the hand of human solidarity. And when clasped in fellowship and recognition, the hand becomes part of what King described as the "the most durable power," a "weapon of love."[9]

King helped forge that weapon fresh out of divinity school as a young pastor in the streets of Montgomery, Alabama, where he moved in 1954 to become minister of the Dexter Avenue Baptist Church. Soon he was clasping hands with people who had worked for years to challenge segregation in the city, such as JoAnn Robinson, the head of a women's civic organization, who earlier had petitioned the Montgomery City Council to redress the mistreatment of passengers on the city's bus lines; or the seamstress and seasoned NAACP activist Rosa Parks. Parks famously refused to give up her bus seat to a white passenger on December 1, 1955, in a premeditated plan of protest, after others had done the same. And several days later, King assumed the leadership of the Montgomery Improvement Society, charged with helping coordinate the protests and thirteen-month boycott that ensued.[10]

King, like Parks, was but a single, courageous voice in a great "collective struggle," part of an extensive network of grassroots organizers and disciplined cadres made up of men and women who did the busy work of knocking on doors and stuffing envelopes, signing petitions and shuttling passengers across the city in volunteer taxi brigades during the long boycott. The Supreme Court ruling that followed in December 1956, outlawing segregation in public transportation, came on the heels of the court's earlier decision, in *Brown v. Board of Education* (1954), outlawing segregation in the public schools. The victory thrust King into the national—and international—spotlight. But it was, above all, the methods employed in Montgomery, and the ethics that underlay them, that attracted the greatest attention. By joining hands together in peace rather than in violence, tens of thousands of individuals were able to show how much collective power could be channeled by restraint.[11]

"From the beginning a basic philosophy guided the movement," King recalled in his 1958 memoir of the boycott, *Stride Toward Freedom*. That philosophy would be referred to variously as "nonviolent resistance, noncooperation, and passive resistance." But the phrase most often heard in the early days was "Christian love." King had only recently completed his doctorate in theology at Boston University, where he had grappled with Christian reflection on the different expressions of love in scripture (*eros, philia, agape*). Drawing on the Swedish theologian Anders Nygren, whose 1953 study *Agape and Eros* had singled out the disinterested love of Christ (*agape*) as the most creative power in the universe, King moved *agape* to the center of his moral vision. "*Agape* is disinterested love," he wrote. "It is a love in which the individual seeks not his own good, but the good of his neighbor (1 Cor. 10:24). *Agape* does not begin by discriminating between worthy and unworthy people, or any qualities people possess. It begins by loving others *for their sakes*." *Agape* makes no distinction between "friends and enemies." It is directed toward both.[12]

Whereas some considered the distinction between friends and enemies the very basis of politics, King dissolved it entirely. *Agape* would restore wholeness and dignity to people of color, who, as King noted elsewhere, had been treated since their arrival "on the shores of this nation in 1619, one year ahead of the Pilgrim

Fathers," not as persons to be respected but as things to be used. So, too, would it heal the white man, whose "personality is greatly distorted by segregation," and whose "soul is greatly scarred." "The Negro must love the white man, because the white man needs his love to remove his tensions, insecurities, and fears."[13]

That was hard Christian teaching. It recalled the injunction of Jesus to love one's enemies as one's friends. Its goal was the creation and restoration of community: "*Agape* is a willingness to go to any length to restore community." It would require the willingness to forgive on the scale of the Jubilee, "not seven times, but seventy times seven." It would demand the recognition that human beings are social creatures, that "creation is so designed that my personality can only be fulfilled in the context of community." And it would demand the recognition of the ties that bind us: "In the final analysis, *agape* means a recognition of the fact that all life is interrelated. All humanity is involved in a single process, and all men are brothers." That connection, for King, demanded an ethics of nonviolence, for we are all our brothers' keepers.[14]

King was able to ground and justify a philosophy of nonviolent resistance firmly in a Christian theology of love. But he readily acknowledged in the very same work that if "Christ furnished the spirit and motivation" of nonviolent resistance, it was Gandhi who "furnished the method." Gandhi, as it happens, was also fond of hands. He wrote of them often, considering them carefully as a source of strength. "If a fist containing salt be clenched, none dare to open it," Gandhi wrote in reference to those preparing to take part in the Great Salt March of the spring of 1930, a galvanizing act of nonviolent civil disobedience that strongly influenced King. "They may open fire upon you," Gandhi had said. "Men may come with bayonets and sticks and use them on you, but salt should not be taken out of your hands."[15]

Here was an example of the tremendous power of nonviolent resistance, of the strength of the disciplined hand which refused to strike out in anger. It moved King and his supporters powerfully.

The "inspiration of Mahatma Gandhi," King wrote, exerted an influence from the first days of the Montgomery boycott. Soon "people who had never heard the name of the little brown saint were now saying his name with an air of familiarity."[16]

Gandhi by that point was long dead, of course, assassinated in 1948 by a zealot who succeeded only in transforming the "great-souled one" into a martyr. But in death, Gandhi's ideas took on renewed life, and King drew sustenance from them, reading Gandhi's works, corresponding with his disciples, and creatively reinterpreting his thought as he did that of Christian thinkers such as Nygren, Paul Tillich, or Reinhold Niebuhr.

With respect to the notion of "civil disobedience," though, King's American appropriation was also something of a coming home, insofar as Gandhi himself had been greatly inspired on the subject by Henry David Thoreau's celebrated essay of that same name. In King's handling, civil disobedience and the philosophy of nonviolence were forged, as they were in Gandhi's *satyagraha*, as weapons in the fight against injustice, means to effectively resist. Nor were those weapons "passive." On the contrary, their soul-force was a new kind of strength that propelled its possessors into the fray, readying them to endure violence and suffering themselves, whether inflicted by firehoses or fists, bullets, truncheons, or snarling dogs. King was sober about the consequences, citing Gandhi to the effect that "rivers of blood may have to flow before we gain our freedom, but it must be our blood."[17]

Indeed, to an even greater degree than his Indian counterpart, King as a Christian understood suffering as redemptive, an imitation of Christ's passion and admonition to turn the other cheek that had "tremendous educational and transforming possibilities." But he was no less clear about its tactical effects. Again, he cited Gandhi: "Suffering is infinitely more powerful than the law of the jungle for converting the opponent and opening his ears which are otherwise shut to the voice of reason." Persuasion was crucial, for the principle of nonviolence applied not just to the flesh but to the spirit. It aimed always to foster respect for one's opponents, targeting structure and systemic forces, not persons. "We are out to defeat injustice," King emphasized, "and not white persons who may be unjust."[18]

By wedding the Christian doctrine of love to Gandhian philosophy and methods, King and thousands of grassroots protesters were able to do just that, defeating injustice in Montgomery. Many suffered in the process, and many, including King, spent time in jail for their actions. But in doing so they honed their techniques of nonviolent resistance, what King described as "one of the most potent weapons available" to Black Americans in their "struggle for freedom." Directly following the victory in Montgomery, King established the Southern Christian Leadership Conference (SCLC) to serve as an umbrella organization to coordinate nonviolent protest movements across the South, and in the coming years he brought that potent weapon to bear in voter registration drives and mass demonstrations in places such as Birmingham and Selma, and eventually in Washington, DC.[19]

It is fitting that during this period of burgeoning national and international prominence, King also took time to visit India with his wife, Coretta Scott King, at the invitation of Prime Minister Jawaharlal Nehru. "To other countries I may go as a tourist," King declared at a press conference upon his arrival. "But to India I come as a pilgrim." The Kings toured the country for over a month in February and March 1959, and they used their time to deepen their understanding of Gandhian principles. King met with Gandhi's son, grandsons, and disciples, and laid a wreath at Gandhi's entombed ashes at Raj Ghat. Everywhere, he spoke of the profound influence of Gandhi on his thought. And he came away with a much deeper appreciation of the common challenges facing India and the United States with regard to equality.[20]

In one instance, King visited a high school in the state of Kerala in the south whose students were from Dalit families. He was introduced to the group proudly as "a fellow untouchable from the United States." King was shocked by this description and even annoyed. He was, after all, a guest of the prime minister, received at the very highest levels of state. But quickly he came to realize how apt the comparison was, telling himself, "Yes, I am an untouchable, and every Negro in the United States is an untouchable." It was a recognition of the clear, if seldom fully acknowledged, structural similarities between racial segregation in the United States and the caste system that prevailed in India. "We call it race in America," King observed. "They call it caste in India. In both places it means that some are inferior."[21]

King's epiphany was a recognition of the profound ties that bound the oppressed. B. R. Ambedkar had observed something similar years earlier, writing to Du Bois in 1946 to emphasize that "there is so much similarity between the position of the Untouchables in India and the position of the Negroes in America." Du Bois, who had famously described himself as an "outcast" in *The Souls of Black Folk* (1903), was ever mindful of the international resonance of racial and class oppression and a central figure in early efforts to build global and pan-African solidarities. But if the Black radical tradition had always been cognizant of the global dimensions of racial oppression, in the second half of the twentieth century, with decolonization and the increasing awareness of the kindred struggles of people of color, that cognizance only grew. King, among others, was deeply inspired by the 1955 Bandung Conference, which brought together Asian and African heads of state in support of the "equality of all races," and in 1957 he traveled to Ghana, where Du Bois would later become a citizen, to attend the country's independence ceremony at the invitation of Kwame Nkrumah. All of this impressed upon King the degree to which the problem of race relations in the United States was bound up in struggles genuinely global in their sweep. He came away from his trip to India further impressed by the ties of solidarity and the reception he had received. "We were looked upon as brothers," he observed, noting that "the strongest bond of fraternity was the common cause of minority and colonial peoples in America, Africa and Asia struggling to throw off racialism and imperialism."[22]

That widespread realization across segments of the civil rights movement helped afford its American leaders a special place on the world stage as spokespersons for concerns that transcended national frontiers. King's Nobel Prize in 1964 was testimony to that development, which extended to other Black leaders in the United States. "As long as we think . . . that we should get Mississippi straightened out before we worry about the Congo, you'll never get Mississippi straightened out," Malcolm X observed in the same year, amid a steady pace of travel between Africa and the United States. The struggles were conjoined. As King put it, employing the metaphor of the "World House" that he adopted toward the end of his life, "All inhabitants of the globe were now neighbors, common occupants and heirs of a great 'world house' in which we have to live together— black and white, Easterner and Westerner, Gentile and Jew, Catholic and Protestant, Muslim and Hindu." It followed that the civil rights struggle in the United States, though necessarily reflecting American history and circumstances, was bound up with "world development." And it followed, too, that simply to strive for equality on American shores, while ignoring destitution, inequality, and strife in the rest of the world, was insufficient. "Equality with whites [in the United States]," King observed, "will not solve the problems of either whites or Negroes if it means equality in a world society stricken by poverty and in a universe doomed to extinction by war."[23]

Such acknowledgment won for King and other civil rights leaders in the United States an intense appreciation around the world. Yet the struggle for hearts and minds was hardest at home, where King urged repeatedly the need to fight firmly, yet with the utmost understanding. "Our aim must never be to defeat or humiliate the opponent," he insisted, must never be to humiliate the white man, "but to win his friendship and understanding." That goal followed naturally from the principles of Christian love and the soul-force of nonviolence. Yet its full realization eluded him.[24]

Instead, King experienced what one political theorist has described as the "paradox of equality," the fate of numerous moral reformers who seek to induce change by changing hearts and minds, only to find that hearts and minds are fickle and reactive. Especially in democracies, where citizens tend to believe that their own opinions are as good as anyone else's, that very egalitarian belief can lead them to turn on crusaders for reform when they are perceived as straying too far from broadly shared civic values and ideals.[25]

Whether or not that precise dynamic was at play in King's case, it is overwhelmingly clear that in the last years of his life, when he was speaking out against the Vietnam War and leading protests that emphasized how achieving dignity and full equality for Black Americans would require economic sacrifice and structural change, his disapproval ratings soared, reaching nearly 75 percent of the population, according to a 1968 poll. Many northern whites who were ready to decry segregation in the South as inconsistent with American ideals were less ready to contemplate the need for changes closer to home. To watch footage from those years—of the marches for fair housing in Chicago, say—is to be confronted, as with the earlier actions at Montgomery, Birmingham, or Selma, with searing images of hatred and rebuke. The noose, the swastika, and the Confederate flag flit across the screen, along with the sight, as King recalled of the Chicago suburbs in 1966, of "a rain of rocks and bottles" and "the thunder of jeering thousands, many of them waving Nazi flags."[26]

Such images are as shocking in grainy footage as were those transmitted on live television from the nation's capital on January 6, 2021. Yet it is important to register their presence. For they are graphic reminders that this, too, is who Americans are. However much some may wish to obfuscate the fact, America's highest ideals, including liberty and equality themselves, were conceived and established on foundations of racial animus and exclusion, which long cordoned off the country's circle of equals from those who stood outside. The history of American democracy, in fact, is a telling illustration of Carl Schmitt's point that "every actual democracy rests on the principle that not only are equals equal but that unequals will not be treated equally." Schmitt took glee in exposing the hypocrisy of those who denied it, and he enjoyed rubbing the faces of liberals and Democrats in the prospect, as he put it, that "inequality always belongs to equality," that it is equality's natural and "necessary correlate." Americans need not do the same, and still less need they embrace the consequences, concluding, like Schmitt, that a homogeneity of type is the only substance from which equality can be made. Still, it is difficult to deny that as an observer of how equality has functioned historically in liberal and democratic regimes, Schmitt was disconcertingly apt. Both explicitly and in more hidden ways, equality in America has long relied on the substance and exclusion of race. Which meant that King's most rabid opponents were being true, in their way, to an understanding of equality consistent with the country's racist founding and democratic history.[27]

King certainly understood this. In 1967, amid a reflection on the "magnitude of the gap between existing realities and the goal of equality," he observed that "there is not even a common language when the word 'equality' is used. Negro and white have a fundamentally different definition." Whereas Black Americans "proceeded from a premise that equality means what it says," white Americans, "including many persons of goodwill, proceed from a premise that equality is a loose expression for improvement." King recounted how the civil rights movement had proceeded in phases. In the first phase, which began in the 1950s and culminated with Selma and the passage of the Civil Rights Act of 1964, ending legal segregation, and the Voting Rights Act of 1965, white Americans had largely sympathized with the effort to overcome the worst forms of white supremacist barbarism. "For the vast majority of white Americans, the past decade—the first phase—had been a struggle to treat the Negro with a degree of decency, not of equality," King wrote. "White America was ready to demand that the Negro should be spared the lash of brutality and coarse degradation, but it had never been truly committed to helping him out of poverty, exploitation or all forms of discrimination." And so now, "when Negroes looked for the second phase, the realization of equality, they found that many of their white allies had quietly disappeared." White America was not "psychologically organized to close the gap," King avowed, and it would not be ready to do so anytime soon. "As the nation passes from opposing extremist behavior to the deeper and more pervasive elements of equality, white America reaffirms its bonds to the status quo."[28]

Those words are a testament to King's realism—to his recognition that the mainstream understanding of equality in the United States was predicated on the substance of race. To proceed as if that were not the case, he charged, as many white moderates and advocates of "racial liberalism" had long tended to do, was to assume a posture of perpetual deferment, with the dream of equality always on the horizon, but never within reach.[29]

Yet King refused to abandon the idealism and courage of hope, which he seeded into the past as well as the future. It was the hope of Lincoln, and before him Frederick Douglass, for whom America's "true" principles had been distorted and misunderstood from the start. All three men sought to recover those true principles and to write, if not an alternative history of the United States, then at least a different history of its founding promise, a different history of its futures past. It was why all three returned again and again to the Declaration of Independence and its beguiling proposition that all men were created equal, finding there what King described as a "declaration of intent" and a "promissory note" to be redeemed in time.[30]

It is doubtful, as we have seen, that the Declaration intended any such thing, and still less that Jefferson's well-worn proposition was meant to portend the coming equality of all. King likely knew that too. Elsewhere he was quick to lambast the "fantasy of self-deception and comfortable vanity" that led well-meaning white Americans, the majority of whom "consider themselves sincerely committed to justice for the Negro," to contend that "American society is essentially hospitable to fair play and to steady growth towards a middle-class Utopia embodying racial harmony." To assume that the underlying logic of the country would eventually work itself out—that the founding principle of equality would somehow force Americans into line by dint of its inherent justice and right—was to risk "complacency" and "comforting myth." King was anything but complacent. For him to seed hope in the declarations of the past, while looking for their bloom on the horizon, was not to engage in a fantasy of self-deception. It was, rather, a means, as it had been for Lincoln, to cultivate a dream that might save the country from itself.[31]

Still, King readily acknowledged that his hope required faith. He made that abundantly clear from early on, writing in Montgomery that a "basic fact about nonviolent resistance is that it is based on the conviction that the universe is on the side of justice. Consequently, the believer in nonviolence has deep faith in the future." It was a faith that allowed nonviolent resisters to accept suffering without retaliation. It was a faith that girded them to persist in the face of setbacks and reversals. It was a faith that protected them from despair. And while King granted that there were devout believers in nonviolence who found it difficult to accept a personal God, he held that even they believed that there was some "creative force in this universe that works to bring the disconnected aspects of reality into a harmonious whole."[32]

King reiterated that conviction throughout his career, often playing on a line from the nineteenth-century abolitionist minister Theodore Parker to assert that "the arc of a moral universe is long, but it bends towards justice." The assertion rested on a providential understanding of the workings of the world. And yet it recognized fully, as King put it elsewhere, that "the line of progress is never straight." It could, and would, veer off course. In the white response to the gains of the civil rights movement and the general reluctance to pursue Black equality further, King perceived the signs of the "inevitable counterrevolution that succeeds every period of progress." Faith would be required to persevere—"an audacious faith in the future of mankind"—along with great measures of forbearance and patience.[33]

Yet patience was precisely what was wearing thin for many Black Americans, and King well understood it. "The Negro wants absolute and immediate freedom and equality, not in Africa or some imaginary state, but right here in this land today," he insisted in his aptly entitled book *Why We Can't Wait* (1964). Black Americans had waited patiently since the Emancipation Proclamation, but "equality had never arrived." It was already a hundred years late, and people of color in the United States "were no longer tolerant of or interested in compromise." In King's last major work, *Where Do We Go from Here: Chaos or Community?* (1967), he returned to the theme, emphasizing that "the present upsurge of the Negro people of the United States grows out of a deep and passionate determination to make freedom and equality a reality 'here' and 'now.'" Their determination, he added, was "a world development," part of the very arc of justice he so often described and an illustration of his ultimate faith that "oppressed people cannot remain oppressed forever." Time was on justice's side, but its arc was long, and patience was running short. By the time of King's assassination, it was all but exhausted. With chaos or community at stake, many were ready to take matters into their own hands and to use their hands in different ways.[34]

Two women of evident resolve stare directly at the camera, their fists raised in gestures of defiance. One is Black, the other white. One sports an afro and hoop earrings, the other has blonde hair with a center-part still redolent of the 1960s. Both are clad in turtlenecks, though of slightly different shades, and together they radiate solidarity and power. Shot in 1971 by the photographer Dan Wynn for the American men's magazine *Esquire*, the picture is now housed in the National Portrait Gallery in Washington, DC, and with good reason. For, however staged, it captures perfectly the

Gloria Steinem and Dorothy Pitman Hughes, New York, 1971. National Portrait Gallery, Smithsonian Institution. © Dan Wynn Archive and Farmani Group, Co Ltd.

Cartoon published in the Industrial Workers of the World journal *Solidarity*, June 30, 1917.

tenacity of its two principal subjects, the feminist activists Dorothy Pitman Hughes and Gloria Steinem, as well as the ethos of an era. The two women embody the readiness to confront the powers and conventions that be in the service of expanding equality, channeling the resistance of an era in their fists.

The fist is as iconic in that posture as the clasped hands of the freedom marchers, and as a symbol, it is nearly as old. From the nineteenth century it served as an emblem of unity and strength, favored above all by labor movements, whose manual workers made their livings with their hands. Then, in the 1960s and 1970s, a wide range of activists and revolutionaries on both sides of the Atlantic adopted it as a symbol for their own movements. Supporters of Black Power were among those to raise the fist, with the athletes Tommie Smith and John Carlos famously brandishing it on the podium at the 1968 Olympic Games in Mexico City. Students for a Democratic Society put the fist on fliers they distributed at the 1968 Democratic National Convention in Chicago, and striking radicals in Paris did the same on their protest posters and banners. Cesar Chavez and the United Farm Workers in California raised the fist, as did gay activists in the wake of the Stonewall Riots. Carl Wittman's *Gay Manifesto* (1970), with its call to come "out of the closet and into the streets," featured four clenched fists on its cover. And the feminist Robin Morgan incorporated a clenched fist in the button she designed for a women's movement protest of the 1969 Miss America pageant. Painted in "menstrual red," it was set inside the biological female symbol.[35]

In standing together as they did in Wynn's photo, and in speaking together as they did at speeches and rallies across the country, Steinem and Pitman Hughes were signaling to militants for equality, and above all to women Black and white, that they could "come together," as the Beatles sang in 1969, in collective unity and strength. And by adopting the gesture of the fist, they made clear that they were prepared to fight to defend their rights, taking power into their own hands.

Women's liberation movement button, c. 1970. Contraband Collection / Alamy Stock Photo.

A Black Panther poster from the 1960s. Peter Newark American Pictures / Bridgeman Images.

Not that they intended injury to others. With its thumb upright and exposed, Steinem's fist would likely have inflicted more pain on herself, had it been used in violence, than on any other. But that was not the point. Steinem, in fact, had been schooled, like King, in the principles of nonviolent struggle (*satyagraha*), having spent two years in India directly after college on a fellowship from 1957 to 1959. She had traveled from village to village there with a Gandhian group and learned of the need to respect one's opponents and listen to their views with placid firmness and inner calm. Pitman Hughes, for her part, was known above all as a community organizer and an advocate and defender of children. A woman of strength, yes, but hardly of harm. Everything we know about the enduring threat of violence against women in modern societies reinforces a sense that their fists were raised first and foremost in postures of defense.[36]

Still, fists are necessarily menacing signs, and to clench them in defiance was to adopt a different orientation to power. King reflected on the matter in the context of his debates with the civil rights activist Stokely Carmichael, who in an electrifying speech in Mississippi in the spring of 1966 first invoked the term "Black Power." Carmichael, an organizer with the Student Nonviolent Coordinating Committee (SNCC), had traveled to the state on a freedom march to protest the shooting of the renowned activist James Meredith, and was arrested on a trumped-up charge while there. Upon Carmichael's release, he spoke to a gathering of some six hundred in Greenwood, Mississippi: "This is the twenty-seventh time I have been arrested," Carmichael declared. "I ain't going to jail no more. What we gonna start saying now is 'Black Power!'" As Carmichael later acknowledged, the use of the phrase was premeditated, and it had the desired effect. Calling out to the crowd like a preacher in a Black church, he cried, "What do we want?" And six times the crowd answered back in unison, "Black power!" Later they raised their fists in defiance as they marched. King, who met with Carmichael shortly thereafter, acknowledged the resonance of the phrase. It was a cry of disappointment and frustration at the failure of white power to embrace change, he deemed. It was a call for political and economic agency, independence, and means. And it was an effort to throw off the psychological shackles of inherited deference, dependence, and self-denial instilled by hundreds of years of slavery and segregation.[37]

With all those goals King was in sympathy, and indeed, to a greater degree than is often acknowledged, he sympathized with a number of the goals of the man who did the most to prepare the way for the movement of Black Power taken up by Carmichael. That man was Malcolm X, and though he did not use the phrase "Black Power," it described the social movement he led, which aimed above all to recover Black agency, Black pride, and Black appreciation for the beauty, strength, and achievements of Black people. Engaging in a systematic and institutional critique of the mechanisms of white supremacy, Malcolm taught how the structures of white domination colluded to deny education, opportunity, and possibility to Black people, effacing in the process their cultural memory and sense of self. "History has been so 'whitened' by the white man," he observed in the *Autobiography of Malcolm X*, that Black people had forgotten their heritage and the glory of "ancient objects produced by black hands . . . that no human hand today can equal." The necessary response, he taught, was for Black people to reclaim their heritage and to recover their dignity and power. He used his adopted Islamic faith as a means to that end, preaching self-discipline, self-determination, and self-empowerment as a way to actively challenge white oppression.[38]

Although King and Malcolm never developed close personal ties, and their styles and bases of support were undoubtedly different, scholars have emphasized recently how their political visions grew closer throughout their lives, particularly in their later years, when King began to stress the structural and economic dimensions of Black oppression, calling with greater insistence for economic justice and security for the poor. "Equality meant dignity," King recognized, echoing both Kant and the UN Declaration's assertions to that effect, "and dignity demanded a job that was secure and a paycheck that lasted throughout the week." Power—social, political, economic—was necessary to reclaim dignity, and one of the crucial problems that Black Americans confronted was a lack of it. Thus, insofar as "Black Power, in its broad and positive meaning,

[was] a call to black people to amass the political and economic strength to achieve their legitimate goals," King fully concurred.[39]

King worried, however, that the movement for Black Power, in its vigorous and explicit rejection of assimilation, would thwart the goal of racial cooperation. Malcolm X's parents had been supporters of Marcus Garvey, and his time with the Nation of Islam leader Elijah Muhammad only reinforced an intense Black nationalism that stressed not only economic self-sufficiency and community control, but also, ultimately, revolutionary separatism. The "basis of freedom, justice, and equality," Malcolm emphasized, was, in the final reckoning, land. "A revolutionary wants land so he can set up his own nation, an independent nation." The civil rights marchers who locked arms and sang "We shall overcome" were not "asking for any nation," he said. "They're trying to crawl back on the plantation." Black nationalists, by contrast, across the United States and around the world, sought revolution and independence. Black nationalism, Malcolm insisted, was simply a necessary counterpart to white nationalism.[40]

King, who had alluded in his famous "Letter from a Birmingham Jail" (1963) to the "hatred and despair" of Black nationalists, saw in such attitudes a distorted image of the exclusionary stance of white separatists. His entire political career, after all, had been devoted to combating the legal sleight of hand embedded in the 1896 Supreme Court decision *Plessy v. Ferguson*, which had ruled that the conditions of Blacks and whites could be "separate but equal." In practice, of course, they were nothing of the sort, but even if Black institutions and facilities, whether schools or water fountains, waiting rooms or public housing, could be made perfectly equal to those of whites, to live "separate but equal" ran counter to what King regarded as the universal promise of the nation and humanity. "Black Power," then, which King described as "an implicit and often explicit belief in black separatism," was in his view a false route, a recipe for increasing division in the country.[41]

The other fatal error King saw in the Black Power movement was its willingness to countenance violence. It is true that Malcolm

X's explicit overtures to violence have been overstated, and that for all of the militant posturing of later groups, such as the Black Panthers, founded in 1966 to protect citizens of color from police brutality, they were never remotely comparable to that of such white terrorist organizations and crime syndicates as the Ku Klux Klan or the Hells Angels. And yet Malcom X readily acknowledged that the Black Revolution, like all revolutions, would involve violent struggle. "Revolution is bloody," he affirmed. "Revolution is hostile, revolution knows no compromise, revolution overturns and destroys everything that gets in its way." He famously repeated a line from the anticolonial militant and Martinican intellectual Frantz Fanon, whose essay "Why We Use Violence" had insisted on the need to wage war against colonial regimes "by any means necessary." "We want freedom by any means necessary," Malcolm intoned. "We want justice by any means necessary. We want equality by any means necessary." *"By any means necessary,"* he emphasized. "That is our motto."[42]

Stokely Carmichael, too, was ready after the spring of 1966 to leave all options on the table. Despite the fact that he was elected chairman of SNCC, an organization ostensibly committed to nonviolence, he was purposely vague when pressed not long after by a white television reporter as to whether he advocated taking Black Power by "force and violence." "The question of violence and nonviolence just happens to be tactical, as far as we are concerned," Carmichael replied evasively, echoing a claim he had made to King in Greenwood. And though King fully agreed that there was an important tactical dimension to the question, he came to a different conclusion regarding "Black Power." The slogan "carried the wrong connotations," he argued, giving the impression that "we are talking about black domination rather than black equality." King suggested "black consciousness" or "black equality" instead, while cautioning that a turn to violence would be both destructive and futile.[43]

Whatever the tactical considerations in play, King's opposition to violence was always essentially moral, grounded in his deeply held spiritual beliefs and the principles of Gandhi and Christ, who had both asked human beings to turn the other cheek. It was a position that, rhetorically at least, grew harder and harder to uphold. As Malcolm X asked pointedly in one of his speeches, "How are you going to be nonviolent in Mississippi and Alabama, when your churches are being bombed, and your little girls are being murdered . . . ?" Fanon had likewise insisted on the point that "the colonial regime is a regime instituted by violence." How else could one confront and overthrow it than by force? It was violence that had established slavery and enforced segregation, and violence loomed behind white supremacy in all its forms. It had taken the life of Emmett Till and the Birmingham Four. It meted out beatings to protesters at lunch counters, and marchers in the streets. It lynched. It blasted with fire hoses. It confined to ghettos. It sneered in contempt. And it was violence, in the end, that consumed both Malcolm X, in a fratricidal rage, and violence's greatest opponent, Martin Luther King Jr. Jesus may have counseled forbearance. But for many mortals, that was impossible. To raise a fist is as human a gesture as extending an open hand.[44]

And so that gesture was taken up—not only by Black Americans and people of color waging revolution and anticolonial struggles around the world, but also by all those who had had enough of being beaten and cast aside, who had tired of passive resistance and patient response. And while again, to raise the fist was not necessarily to threaten harm, it was a sign that one was ready to defend oneself with force if need be, coming together in militant defense to assert rights and power in solidarity with those who shared a common identity.

Coming together, however, in social movements, as in nations, is never an easy task. Carmichael highlighted one of the difficulties in a legendary speech delivered at the University of California, Berkeley, in 1966, the same year in which the SNCC senior staff moved, by a vote of 19–18, to expel their twenty-four white colleagues. Carmichael reiterated opposition to Black-white collaboration on a

"psychological ground." "The fact is that all black people often question whether or not they are equal to whites," he said, "because every
time they start to do something, white people are around showing
them how to do it. If we are going to eliminate that for the generation
that comes after us, then black people must be seen in positions of
power, doing and articulating for themselves." Carmichael described
his position, invoking an expression of the French philosopher Jean-
Paul Sartre, as that of an "antiracist racist." He was working to restore
Black confidence, independence, and strength. A "reverse racist,"
by contrast, acted purely out of animus, without consideration for
future social health. The distinction, however, was not always clear,
and as King pointed out, it effectively renounced the goal of "racial
understanding," which had to be "created by the fact of contact,"
and would never be discovered "ready-made." If Blacks and whites
renounced the difficult task of working together and seeking to
understand one another, the prospect of an interracial society would
remain as elusive as the present one fell short of the mark.[45]

Stokely Carmichael was willing, at least in the near term, to
forgo racial collaboration in order to cultivate Black Power. But
his movement faced resistance from another powerful constituency—Black women—who were beginning to see that their
own interests and identity could be effaced in the quest to come
together in pursuit of a common end. Carmichael was likely
joking in an off-color way when, in answer to the question of the
"position" of women in the movement, he replied that their only
position was "prone." Yet many Black women came to feel that
they were being mistreated all the same, "consigned to roles," as
the Black activist Toni Cade Bambara recalled, where they were
expected to answer the phones and fix coffee while "the men
wrote the position papers and decided on policy." "What had
begun as a movement to free all black people from racist oppression," the feminist theorist bell hooks adds, "became a movement
with its primary goal the establishment of black male patriarchy."

The appeal to Black Power, the women charged, was in truth an appeal to the power of Black men.[46]

Of course, the assigning of "roles" was hardly unique to the offices of SNCC or the corridors of Black Power, where women such as Angela Davis, in any case, refused to accept them. Unequal gender division was the norm throughout American society in the 1950s and 1960s, as it had been since the country's founding. That extended to the civil rights movement of King and the SCLC, just as it did to the Students for a Democratic Society and progressive groups of the New Left. Women, to be sure, participated centrally in the protests and petitions, the canvassing and sit-ins, while performing crucial work behind the scenes. They were, as the civil rights leader Andrew Young observed, the "spine of our movement." But that didn't change the fact that decision-making and leadership were concentrated overwhelmingly in the hands of men. Farsighted in so many ways, King remained in that respect, like Gandhi, a man of his times.[47]

Still, in his efforts to pursue dialogue with women, King acknowledged that "assumptions of male superiority are as widespread and deep-rooted . . . [and] crippling to the woman as the assumptions of white supremacy are to the Negro." That was in fact a venerable comparison. The early feminist Margaret Fuller had observed, in her *Woman in the Nineteenth Century* (1845), that opposition to slavery was a logical step for members of her sex, a "natural following out of principles." Other feminists drew comparisons between bondage in the home and bondage in the fields, hoping to channel energy in support of abolition into the movement for women's rights. Frederick Douglass certainly understood that connection. A conspicuous and forceful presence at Seneca Falls, he was, like later notable Black intellectuals such as Du Bois, a lifelong advocate of women's suffrage and women's rights. At the same time, a host of Black women, including Mary Church Terrell, Amanda Berry Smith, Anna Julia Cooper, and, most famously, Sojourner Truth, worked actively on behalf of women and the enslaved or disenfranchised together, constituting a "vanguard" in the broader struggle for equality.[48]

The struggle for Black and female liberation could thus seem naturally conjoined. But as Black men and women had both learned to their chagrin in the nineteenth century, even in the most broad-minded circles, race got in the way. Prominent white suffragettes, including Susan B. Anthony and Elizabeth Cady Stanton, opposed the Fifteenth Amendment, which granted the vote to Black men following the Civil War, arguing that white women should take precedence. And with the passage of the Nineteenth Amendment that secured the suffrage for women in 1919, many white women did little to oppose the Jim Crow laws that barred Blacks of either sex from going to the polls. Meanwhile, the extensive Women's Christian Temperance Union (WCTU), which campaigned not only for prohibition, but for suffrage and equality before the law and in the workplace, nominally opened its doors to women of every kind. But as was the case with organizations lobbying on behalf of male workers and farmers, such as the Knights of Labor and the Grange, the WCTU effectively left white supremacy intact, segregating Black women in specific branches of the organization, where they were "separate and unequal." And although Black women founded their own networks and associations in response, struggling on parallel tracks, tensions with white feminists endured.[49]

Those tensions did not abate with the swell of second-wave feminism, which began to form, by common consensus, with the publication of Betty Friedan's *The Feminine Mystique* (1963). Friedan's contention that the fundamental problem for women of her time was "a crisis of identity" built upon an insight of the philosopher Simone de Beauvoir, who had argued famously in *The Second Sex* (1949) that "one is not born, but rather, becomes a woman." Women, that is, assume and inhabit identities—as mothers, daughters, wives, and homemakers—fashioned for them in patriarchal societies that were organized around male needs.

Inauthentically constructed, those identities, not surprisingly, left many women alienated and unfulfilled.[50]

Friedan illustrated the bitter consequences of this fatal "mystique" by reference to her own life, and in the years that followed, many took to heart her broad injunction to fashion new identities for themselves. Rendering the personal political and the political personal, they asked more of equality than simply the right to vote. They demanded sovereignty over their bodies, pressing for sexual liberation through birth control, the right to abortion, and a heightened awareness of male violence against women and the ubiquity of rape. They fought for legislation banning bias in hiring and in the workplace, and for equal offerings and opportunities at schools (Title IX). They lobbied for equal pay for equal work, equal credit, and, through the ill-fated Equal Rights Amendment to the Constitution—twice broached, but unratified to this day by the requisite three-quarters of all states—equal rights. And to pursue those ends collectively they came together, forming local associations for women's liberation and new countrywide organizations, such as Friedan's National Organization for Women (NOW) and the National Women's Political Caucus (NWPC) that followed. When the Women's Strike for Equality packed the streets of New York City in 1970 to mark the fiftieth anniversary of the suffrage, it was the largest women's march to date, and very different issues were on the table from a century, indeed a decade, before.[51]

Those issues—of power and patriarchy, along with the central question, for so long seemingly settled, of just what it meant to be a woman in the first place—were of deep concern to women who were Black. Yet feminists of color could claim, with reason, that their white counterparts too often invoked the category of "woman" as a convenient way of saying women who were white; that appeals to universal "sisterhood" were specious. Friedan's critique of the stultifying constraints of middle-class domesticity, which she likened in an overblown comparison to "a comfortable concentration camp," was certainly foreign to many Black ears.

Others complained that the mainstream feminist movement as a whole was insufficiently sensitive to the specific plight of those who were doubly victimized by sex and race. As Frances Beal, a member of SNCC's Black Women's Liberation Committee, put it in a landmark essay in 1969, to be Black and female was "double jeopardy." Gay women, too, objected (as did gay men) that their own complex identities were too often subsumed into broader categories claiming universality, or were fixed in ways that were distorting. Differences needed to be acknowledged. And there were many more differences, and many more identities, than just male and female, Black and white, gay and straight.[52]

Steinem and Pitman Hughes's much-publicized collaboration was an acknowledgment of—and an attempt to redress—the cleavages along racial lines that persisted in the women's liberation movement. There were other such undertakings—good faith efforts to draw comparisons between "Jim Crow" and "Jane Crow," or between racial and sexual "castes."[53]

Gay men and women at times drew similar comparisons and sought similar alliances. When, not long after midnight on June 28, 1969, police attempted, yet again, to roust the revelers from 53 Christopher Street, the site of the Stonewall Inn in the Greenwich Village neighborhood of New York City, and those same revelers refused to be pushed aside, participants described the resistance as our "Rosa Parks moment." On the West Coast not long thereafter, gay activists in San Francisco and Berkeley modeled the newly formed "Committee for Homosexual Freedom" on Black militant groups. As one of their members observed, "The black man found self-respect and dignity when he said, 'Black is beautiful, and I am proud.' Now homosexuals are starting to say, 'Gay is good, and I too am proud.'" Meeting with the Black Panther leader Huey P. Newton, who encouraged them to fight fiercely for gay rights, they even styled their picketers "Pink Panthers" in a nod of solidarity.[54]

Others, however, were more circumspect. Speaking of the "awakening of gay liberation ideas and energy" in San Francisco,

Carl Wittman's *Gay Manifesto* acknowledged that "black people and their freedom movement" were a source of inspiration. Yet he later pointed out, in a section titled "On Coalition," that ties to the Black liberation movement were "tenuous right now because of the uptightness and supermasculinity of many black men (which is understandable)," a problem that in his view was "basically the same" for "Chicanos," because of what he called the "super up-tightness and machismo among Latin cultures." And though he expressed support for both Latinos and Blacks, along with women's and lesbian liberation, he made clear that his manifesto spoke "from the gay male viewpoint," and that it would be "arrogant" to try to speak for others. "Right now," he emphasized, "the bulk of our work has to be among ourselves—self-educating, fending off attacks, and building free territory. Thus, basically we have to have a gay/straight vision of the world until the oppression of gays is ended." In the short term, at least, gay men would focus on the struggle they knew best.[55]

The women of the Combahee River Collective largely agreed. One of a number of Black feminist groups that sprouted up in the late 1960s and early 1970s, Combahee, operating in the Boston area between 1973 and 1980, was a self-described "Black lesbian, socialist, feminist organization." The group took its name from the famed Civil War action led by Harriet Tubman and a contingent of Black Union soldiers that freed over seven hundred slaves at Combahee Ferry, South Carolina, on June 2, 1863.[56]

The women of the collective modeled themselves in Tubman's image of forceful leadership. And while they recognized affinities and solidarities with other oppressed groups—and indeed pioneered new forms of integrated social analysis that highlighted how systems of hegemony were intersectional and "interlocking"— they emphasized, at the same time, the deep personal origin of their commitment and their unique subject position as Black lesbians. As three of their members, Demita Frazier, Barbara Smith, and Barbara's twin sister, Beverly, declared in the collective's major theoretical statement, "We realize that the only people who care enough about us to work consistently for our liberation are us." The words echoed the sentiment Wittman had expressed with respect to gay men. And although issues of race, class, gender, and sexual orientation cut across complicated lines, meaning that no movement could be treated in isolation, for now the core of the Combahee River Collective's energy and commitment would be generated by "a healthy love for ourselves, our sisters and our community." In a key passage, the authors highlighted and justified their inward turn, observing, "This focusing upon our own oppression is embodied in the concept of identity politics. We believe that the most profound and potentially most radical politics come directly out of our own identity, as opposed to working to end somebody else's oppression."[57]

Those words appear to be the first explicit reference to "identity politics" as such, although the sentiment certainly had deeper roots, especially in the Black nationalist and Black Power movements with their overt calls for self-definition, self-consciousness, and self-love. As Stokely Carmichael and Charles V. Hamilton put it in their 1967 manifesto *Black Power: The Politics of Liberation*, "Our basic need is to reclaim our history and our identity from what must be called cultural terrorism." "Black Pride" and the affirmation "Black Is Beautiful" aimed to exorcise centuries of internalized oppression and to reclaim the full dignity, agency, and respect of those who shared a common experience.[58]

Similar sentiments were echoed in the appeal to gay pride— "Say it loud and proud!"—and the feminist rallying cries "Women unite!" and "Sisterhood is powerful." Variations on those appeals soon emerged among the growing array of groups staking out identity claims in American society. Most of them had long been there, or, like Blacks, Latinos, and the indigenous, had been there from the beginning—but they now called attention to themselves with growing self-consciousness and assertion. And while appeals to identity were necessarily diverse, one word emerged from the clash of many voices to provoke a tension in understandings of equality, and ultimately a reevaluation of its meaning. That word was "difference."

Difference was hardly foreign to discussions of equality, of course. But it had long functioned as a way of justifying exclusions from the circle of equals. As Simone de Beauvoir argued at length, sexual difference was the basis on which women were classified and considered "Other" in relation to the allegedly universal male norm. A powerful current of European philosophy in the twentieth century, which Beauvoir accessed through her sometime lover and longtime friend Jean-Paul Sartre, channeled that same analysis to show how racism and antisemitism functioned in a similar fashion. Whether on the basis of religion, sex, race, caste, class, virtue, sexual orientation, alleged capacity of reason, or some other defining characteristic, difference was most often ascribed to stigmatize those who were deemed unalike in some way, and to establish relations of superiority and inferiority.[59]

It was largely for that reason that excluded groups, particularly since the eighteenth century, had tended to wage struggles for equality on the basis of appeals to their likeness and similarity. Differences between men and women, feminists of the first wave had argued, were negligible and superficial, particularly with regard to the capabilities and aptitudes necessary for political and professional life. It had taken the repeated assertion of that claim to assail the formidable apparatus of law, science, and received prejudice used to justify fundamental distinctions (and formal inequalities) between men and women on the basis of nature.

Much the same was true of efforts to counter invidious distinctions based on ethnicity and race. The Black abolitionist David Walker's famous *Appeal to the Colored Citizens of the World* of 1829 posed a simple question: Are we not men? The same question applied to "the Indians of North and of South America—the Greeks—the Irish . . . the Jews . . . in fine, [to] all the inhabitants of the earth," Walker wrote. Like many Christian abolitionists, he justified the fundamental likeness of human beings on the grounds of monogenism. But it was only in the aftermath of World War II, when scientists were able to discredit the racial taxonomies elaborated since the eighteenth century and undermine the foundations of eugenics and scientific racism, that those universal claims acquired scientific heft. Researchers, in time, would deprive the very category of "race" of scientific grounding and legitimacy, even though simple prejudice proved more stubborn.[60]

Those demonstrations, like parallel efforts to undermine the scientific authority of sexism, were nonetheless important. And they gave added power to the message of that purveyor of the social gospel, Martin Luther King Jr., who preached universal human equality emphatically on Christian grounds. Differences in the family of humanity and among individual persons, each of whom was unique, were irrelevant, he argued. To fixate on them was to acknowledge the slow pace of progress and the imperfect perspective of God's children. But King foresaw a day when "all who work for a living will be one, with no thought of their separateness as Negroes, Jews, Italians, or any other distinctions." That would be the "full realization of the American dream," and he saw it on the horizon. "I am convinced that we shall overcome," he concluded in the same speech in 1961, "because the arc of the universe is long but it bends toward justice."[61]

But if the arc of the universe bends, whether by the force of God's hand or humanity's own, justice, too, appears different according to the laws of relativity, varying with the position of the observer in space and time. And by the 1970s, justice was beginning to appear as the recognition of difference itself. The project of recovery and celebration of identity first advocated by Black nationalists and the movement for Black Power was taken up by women and homosexuals and in turn by many other groups, who likewise celebrated their uniqueness. In effect, it was a rejection of a model of universal assimilation in a world coded male and white, the founding identity of identity politics, though too seldom acknowledged as such.

The (white) anthropologist Margaret Mead came to see this in 1971 in a famous debate with the (Black) novelist James Baldwin. A onetime advocate of color-blind assimilation in the United States, Mead, at Baldwin's insistence, was pressed to acknowledge that the "integration position was a one-sided one":

MEAD: [The] offer that well-intentioned white people made is: "If you will be like us—"

BALDWIN: "You could join our clubs and come to our houses—"

MEAD: "And we'll pretend that you're just like us."

BALDWIN: Yeah.

MEAD: Which means of course that we'll deny you.

BALDWIN: Exactly.

To claim to be color-blind was in fact to be blind. Differences needed to be recognized and acknowledged.[62]

But what would that recognition mean for equality? Some acknowledged that difference and equality were in tension or at odds, while others showed themselves ready to accept that the two might be trade-offs. As one observer put it in 1968, "In black women's liberation we don't want to be equal with men, just as in black liberation we're not fighting to be equal with the white man. We are fighting for the right to be different and not to be punished for it." There were gay and lesbian separatists who likewise scoffed at the pursuit of "equality" with heterosexuals or members of the opposite sex: not for them traditional marriage or the trappings of bourgeois life.[63]

So-called "difference feminists," meanwhile, began to charge that women's aspirations to be "equal" to men were misguided when they meant denying aspects of their gender or sex that made their experience and subjectivity unique. What of childbirth and motherhood? What of female sexuality and female subjectivity? What of female consciousness and even femininity? To seek an androgynous equality as disembodied beings was self-enforced assimilation, they argued, an effort to conform to (male) values and standards that were not women's own. In response, those intent on building a gender-neutral society warned that such speculation was naïve: to admit of essential differences between women and men was to leave the door open to precisely the kind of invidious distinctions that had long served as the basis for oppression. Difference was the lever of patriarchy, meaning that women must continue to erase all differences of gender and sex in order to be treated as the full equals they were and are.[64]

Debates around these issues, pitting "difference" against "equality," raged into the 1980s and 1990s on both sides of the Atlantic, generating in the process a diverse set of reflections on the meanings and relations of the terms. There is probably some truth to the general observation that European feminists, and particularly those from Italy and France, were more comfortable extolling difference, while their Anglo-American counterparts pressed more consistently for equality. But such broad distinctions tended to break down in the fray, where positions on both sides of the Atlantic dissolved any easy or straightforward dichotomy. Historians of feminist movements pointed out that equality and difference have always been bound up together, with activists placing emphasis sometimes on the one and sometimes on the other.[65]

Indeed, as the historian and feminist theorist Joan Scott insisted in an important intervention, it could not have been otherwise. Not only were "equality" and "difference" bound together, she argued, they were mutually constitutive. That was feminism's founding "paradox." "Feminism was a protest against women's political exclusion," she observed. "Its goal was to eliminate 'sexual difference' in politics" and so attain equality. But it did so by making claims on behalf of a distinct group, "women," which it produced discursively through appeals to "sexual difference." "To the extent that it acted for 'women,'" Scott noted, "feminism produced 'the sexual difference' it sought to deny."[66]

Scott's response to that paradox was in effect to embrace it, refusing in the process what she cast as the misleading alternatives of the equality and difference binary, which she worked to deconstruct. "When equality and difference are paired dichotomously," she observed elsewhere, "they structure an impossible choice. If one opts for equality, one is forced to accept the notion that difference is antithetical to it. If one opts for difference, one admits that equality is unattainable." Such blackmail had the consequence of obscuring how difference had always figured in the construction of equality, while simultaneously suggesting that sameness was the only basis on which equality could be established. The only alternative, she concluded, was "to refuse to oppose equality to difference and insist continually on differences—differences as the condition of individual and collective identities, differences as the constant challenge to the fixing of those identities, history as the repeated illustration of the play of differences, difference as the very meaning of equality itself."[67]

To insist on difference *as the very meaning of equality itself* was in the long run of egalitarian reflection a novel claim. But it was by no means exclusive to Scott. Already in the late 1970s, creative voices like the Black lesbian poet Audre Lorde were refusing the opposition of difference and equality. "As women," she noted, "we have been taught to either ignore our differences or to view them as causes for separation and suspicion rather than as forces for change." But that was a mistake. For differences were interdependent strengths that, when "acknowledged and equal," would creatively reshape ways of being and coexisting in the world. "Difference," Lorde affirmed, was that "raw and powerful connection from which our personal power is forged." It would be the motive force of social equality, social justice, and social change.[68]

Although Lorde was an early voice, her position was influential, and increasingly it was adopted more widely, so that by the end of the twentieth century, the feminist philosopher Sonia Kruks could describe the affirmation and embrace of difference as symptomatic of identity politics as a whole:

> What makes identity politics a significant departure from earlier, pre-identarian forms of the politics of recognition is its demand for recognition on the basis of the very grounds on which recognition has previously been denied: it is *qua* women, *qua* blacks, *qua* lesbians that groups demand recognition. The demand is not for inclusion within the fold of "universal humankind" on the basis of shared human attributes; nor is it for respect "in spite of" one's differences. Rather, what is demanded is respect for oneself *as* different.

Kruks uses here the language of recognition and respect. It is one that critics of "identity politics"—a loaded term, it should be stressed, that is often used pejoratively—frequently dismiss as divisive and distracting, an allegedly resentful and insatiable plea for emotional validation that politics are supposedly ill-placed to provide. No matter that all human beings seek recognition: it is, as psychologists and sociologists of status confirm, one of our most basic human drives. And as populist politicians of the Right have arguably understood far better than most in recent years, politics is well placed to provide it.[69]

But more to the point, identity politics is not chiefly about the desire to be recognized; it is about the desire to be recognized as equals. And insofar as difference has come to be regarded, in Scott's words, as "the very meaning of equality itself," identity politics does indeed mark an extraordinary, even utopian, departure from previous understandings of the term. In its way, it is even more demanding than King's universal love. Whereas King taught that Christian *agape* must begin by "loving others *for their sakes*," all differences be damned, it is another step again to love others *for their differences*, not despite them.[70]

Yet both are pleas to heal community. "*Agape* is a willingness to go to any length to restore community," King insisted, and his

Christian sentiments reinforced the need to attend to the plight of the most vulnerable. The women of Combahee made a similar plea for the plight of Black women, and they dreamed that their liberation would spell redemption for all other identities. "If Black women were free, it would mean that everyone else would have to be free since our freedom would necessitate the destruction of all the systems of oppression." Was the moral arc of the universe a vast chromatic spectrum, each band vivid and distinct, bound together in their difference? Or did the colors of the rainbow intersect and merge?[71]

Yet another question lingered in the politics of identity: If the last would be first and all free at last, what would become of those, not farthest down, but long on top? The women of Combahee admitted they did not know, and why should they? Their statement's penultimate line quotes Robin Morgan, who had written, in her 1970 feminist classic *Sisterhood Is Powerful*—an anthology with a fist on its cover in its first edition, set in the female sign in menstrual red—"I haven't the faintest notion what possible revolutionary role white heterosexual men could fulfill, since they are the very embodiment of reactionary-vested-interest-power." The Combahee statement then concludes with a commitment to revolutionary struggle. Even as Morgan herself had floated a provisional answer to the quandary of what white men could do—"possibly not exist"—she begged an important question. What would be the place of those embodied white men in the new moral arc of humanity?[72]

Their place was ambiguous, and it arguably remains so within identity politics today. King's answer to the problem was forgiveness. *Agape* would forgive those who had slapped away an open hand, and those who raised a fist in anger. It would even forgive those whose forefathers had made hands of human beings themselves. But, more recently, others have been inclined to argue that forgiveness without a corresponding acknowledgment of guilt—and reparations for damage done—is pointless. Equality is about power, and power is possible only with proper resources. Until those are balanced more equitably, talk of forgiveness is moot.

And so, it would seem, is talk of shared citizenship. That, at any rate, has been the response of critics who worry that too much talk of difference is divisive. They point out ruefully that the original identity of white men has been reconstituted, with "White Power" as an angry and self-conscious response to "Black Power." White identity now reenters the fray of contemporary politics with a vengeance, empowered by populists and white supremacists who extol their own respective difference. All talk of the common identity of citizens as equals would seem to be lost.[73]

Not that equality is sameness. Those who defend equality as difference and the many identities built upon it are right to insist on the point. This book began, in fact, by stressing precisely that, pointing out that although equality propositions always involve comparisons, they do so from a limited point of view. The host property or thing compared can be virtually anything at all, but it is never everything at once. When equal things are equal in every possible way, they are not equal, but identical. It follows naturally that not only is equality compatible with difference, it demands it. The question is deciding which differences matter and which don't matter at all.[74]

But if that much is undeniable, it is also the case, as this book has emphasized, that a tension between individual difference and the sameness or solidarity of the group runs throughout the history of equality in both practice and thought. Time and again we have seen controversies play out over equality's "substance" and the degree to which it could admit of difference. Did equality imply common religious or national belonging? Was it delimited by sex, title, or race? Or did it free up individuals to make claims on the collective regardless of the fortunes of their birth?

Movement between the poles of homogeneity and heterogeneity is evident in the great Atlantic revolutions in the United States, Haiti, and France, as we have seen. Proximate contemporaries, such as

Tocqueville, called attention to the fact, worrying aloud that equality was a leveling force, making everyone more and more alike, even as citizens took pains to exaggerate a host of "artificial and arbitrary" differences among themselves. A similar tension has animated the long socialist tradition, with its aspirations toward universal human emancipation, on the one hand, and the need to impose uniformity and even leveling on the other. The fascist regimes, for their part, were brutally forthright in their assertion that equality demanded homogeneity. Difference was disqualifying; equals must be, or claim to be, alike. And finally, for all the high-minded talk of "global equality" in recent times, its contours have most often been imagined from within the walls of nation-states, where equality extends only to those who share a passport and more often than not a place of birth. The point being that although equality cannot be reduced to sameness, sameness has been, historically, its close companion.[75]

Which makes the aspiration to treat difference as equality's true meaning a challenging proposition, however laudable the goal. "Equality and particularity are not necessarily reconcilable," one scholar who has thought much about these matters observes. Whether they are or not, solutions will be sought in the rough and tumble of politics or politics by other means.[76]

And that is where we are now, if "we" can be taken to mean all those very different people in the contemporary United States, and in many other places of the world, who are currently trying to reconcile their differences within borders and across them. What the place of equality will be in those efforts—and how it will even be conceived—is very far from clear. And neither is the use we will make of our hands.

CONCLUSION

The Crisis of Equality

Well into the early twenty-first century it was possible to believe, even in some quarters to assume, that the world was plodding steadily along in the direction of greater equality. People were not always reasonable, it is true. But when they were, philosophers assured, they would be forced to confess that equality was the only logical outcome—"axiomatic," as the philosopher and constitutional scholar Ronald Dworkin memorably asserted in 1978. Advanced political reflection, he concluded in a later work, had reached a kind of egalitarian "plateau," an elevated place on which all ethical discussion should henceforth be conducted. The Canadian philosopher Will Kymlicka echoed that thought, observing that "every plausible political theory has the same ultimate value, which is equality." Everyone, it seemed, was an egalitarian nowadays. And though philosophers might dispute the means to get there, or debate the type of equality we should be aiming for, they tended not to call into question the place of arrival. As one scholar put it in his introduction to an important anthology of readings on equality first published in 1997, "It is one of the basic tenets of almost all contemporary moral and political theory that humans are essentially equal, of equal worth, and should have this ideal reflected in the economic, social, and political structures of society."[1]

From the lofty heights of the egalitarian plateau, it was easy enough to conclude that there was an "inner logic" inherent not only in the idea of equality but in the process of modernity itself. Slowly working itself out over time, that idea was always vague, but remarkably malleable. To some extent it was a natural heir to the modernization theories of the 1950s, and in the hands of neoliberals in the 1980s and 1990s it functioned as such. But the idea had older roots, stretching all the way back to the late eighteenth century and the first theories of "cascade" that imagined equality spilling out and down, like water over rocks, to gather in a gradually widening pool that someday would encompass the surface of the earth. Someday.

With the increasingly reliable data at the disposal of economists in the early twenty-first century, it was possible to point to facts that encouraged that belief. Global inequalities of wealth and income were falling, it could be shown, as economic development in China and the "Asian Tigers" pulled tens and eventually hundreds of millions of men and women out of poverty and closer to the global mean. The fall of the Soviet Union hastened that development, as did the demise of Maoist experiments in social leveling. Why should states level nations in poverty when they could raise the floor of wealth and bring their citizens closer to the prosperous? Liberal internationalists cheered. They believed, with the public intellectual Francis Fukuyama, that "the end of history" was on the horizon and that it was the "march of equality" that was taking us there, to a time when political evolution would end in liberal democracy for all.[2]

But it was not simply erstwhile Cold Warriors, and liberals old and new, who shared the belief that equality was advancing by its own inner logic. Many of the marginalized groups who fashioned identities for the politics of identity saw themselves as working to expand equality's promise, long truncated by its myriad exclusions but now tasked with accommodating the many differences it once refused. The promise would only be fully redeemed in the future, but movement toward it could be measured in the past. Scholars chronicled at length the historical struggles of the oppressed in their effort to live as equals, and "struggle" was the operative word. Paired with equality, it has figured in hundreds of titles written since the 1990s that indicate both the goal on the horizon and the difficult steps that must be taken toward it.

Consider only a few. There is *The Struggle for Black Equality*, a book, and Civil Rights and the Struggle for Black Equality in the Twentieth Century, a book series comprising twenty-eight titles. There is *Women's Struggle for Equality: The First Phase, 1828–1876*, and many struggles after that. There is *Gay America: The Struggle for Equality*; and *Dangerous Liaisons: Blacks, Gays and the Struggle for Equality*. There is *The Afro-Cuban Struggle for Equality*, the subtitle of *Our Rightful Share*, which can be read as part of a more general movement that includes *Toward Freedom Land: The Long Struggle for Racial Equality in America*. In the Discrimination Series of the 1990s, there is *Native Americans Struggle for Equality*, with similar volumes discussing Chinese Americans, Japanese Americans, Hispanic Americans, Jewish Americans, and many others.[3]

Written in English, and most often by American authors, these titles reflect particularly American concerns. But their subject matter has not been limited to the United States or confined to the English language. Consider *And Justice for All: Arthur Chaskalson and the Struggle for Equality in South Africa*; *The Struggle for Equality: India's Muslims and Rethinking the UPA Experience*; or *La Florida del Inca: The Struggle for Social Equality in Colonial Latin America*. Not to mention *Canadian Women and the Struggle for Equality*; *The Struggle for Equality: Urban Women Workers in Prestate Israeli Society*; *Black French Women and the Struggle for Equality, 1848–2016*; or *Christians Versus Muslims in Modern Egypt: The Century-Long Struggle for Coptic Equality*. One could easily pursue the struggle for equality around the world.

Which is not to make light of these histories or the important stories they tell, even if it is to poke fun at publishers' lack of creativity in choosing titles. But the titles themselves are revealing, pointing to a shared sense that the world was somehow moving in the direction of what all those documented struggles aimed to effect. The books are "movement" histories in two senses of the word. They trace, on the one hand, protest movements in the past, and the individuals and groups who led them. And they chronicle, on the other, the general movement of history *toward* equality. No matter how well the scholarship is carried out—and very often it has been of the highest caliber—a certain teleology lingered in the accounts, with the past examined for evidence of progress toward a determined end, even when that progress was judged, as it often was, wanting.

The general framing of the struggle toward equality and the logic that appeared to guide it proved remarkably malleable. And not just in scholarship. For the same framing found in historical accounts extended to contemporary politics, where group after group entered the fray of the public sphere demanding recognition as equals. The demand itself was an avowal that reality had yet to conform, but the succession of voices maintained the momentum of expectation, with equality on the horizon as the outcome of persistent struggle. History was on equality's side. All would be equal. Someday.

A dream inherited from the 1960s, the hope for equality was now refashioned to meet the proliferating demands of diversity and difference. President Bill Clinton spoke repeatedly of the need to be on "the right side of history," as did First Lady Hillary Rodham Clinton in her later role as US secretary of state, in the context of the "struggle for equality" and equal rights for all. President Barack Obama, whose own election appeared to many a sign that history was headed in the right direction, echoed those phrases. He made bold to add another, taken directly from Dr. King, invoking "the arc of the moral universe" and its inflection toward justice some thirty-three times in official speeches while in office. As he observed in his Second Inaugural Address in 2013, equality was shaping both the struggle and its trajectory:

We, the people, declare today that the most evident of truths—
that all of us are created equal—is the star that guides us still;
just as it guided our forebears through Seneca Falls, and Selma,
and Stonewall; just as it guided all those men and women,
sung and unsung, who left footprints along this great Mall, to
hear a preacher say that we cannot walk alone; to hear a King
proclaim that our individual freedom is inextricably bound to
the freedom of every soul on Earth.

Equality remained both the polestar of humanity and its promised
land. We were moving there together.[4]

And who could deny that progress had been made? Michelle
Obama called attention to the fact when she observed, with
reverent wonder, that as First Lady she inhabited "a house that
was built by slaves." The Black poverty rate was cut almost in half
between 1960 and 2011, while Black life expectancy and education
rates improved significantly. And there were other signs of progress for those who cared to look. Whereas in 1900, women could
vote in a single country on the planet (New Zealand), by the early
twenty-first century they could vote in every country where men
could, with the sole exception of Vatican City. Women's share of
the global workforce expanded for much of the twentieth century,
as did their presence since the 1960s in important sectors such as
education, media, government, and sport. The gains have been
significant, to such an extent that one recent inequality scholar has
argued of our own time that "working for gender equality means
focusing on boys rather than girls."[5]

Social scientists also mustered global data about the gradual
spread of "liberal values," noting a decline in racial and ethnic
prejudice since 1950, along with the retraction of official policies
of legal discrimination and segregation. The incidence of racist,
misogynist, and homophobic speech in public discourse seemed
to be on the wane in many countries by the close of the century,
while the expression of support for the view that people of different

races, ethnicities, and religions should be accorded equal rights seemed to grow. Meanwhile, the decriminalization of homosexuality underway for much of the twentieth century gathered pace, increasing sharply after 1970. It was a reflection of more tolerant attitudes. In the global north, especially, momentum in favor of gay marriage accelerated dramatically, exerting its own shaping force on the universe's moral arc. Legal scholars confidently proclaimed that equality for lesbian and gay people was "inevitable," as advocates for trans people sometimes do today, touting the corresponding "inevitability" of arguments for same-sex marriage. In a number of countries, those predictions proved to be correct. In short, just as the Great Compression gave credence to views articulated in the 1950s about the prospects for expanding material equality, the reality of more recent gains in civil, social, and political status lent support to the audacity of hope.[6]

Yet a funny thing happened on the way to equality, and it was the end of the Great Compression that provided the setup for the "joke." That decades-long reduction in income and wealth inequalities in the global north began to slow in the 1970s, and by the 1980s a reversal was underway. It gathered force in the following decades, which witnessed the return of inequalities in income and wealth, above all in the United States, which eventually reached levels not experienced since the eve of World War I.

There was no shortage of critics at the time who protested the policies that led to that reversal—the rollbacks in welfare and transfer payments, deregulation and changes in tax and trade policies, the assault on unions and worker protections. And yet its true *historical* dimensions and cumulative consequences only became fully apparent later, as economists and economic historians did the work of sifting through the data that clarified the new trends. The fallout of the 2007–2008 financial crisis and the Occupy Wall Street movement that followed in its wake in 2011 helped to focus the issue.

It was in that year that the Nobel Prize–winning economist Joseph Stiglitz popularized the pejorative term "the one percent."

In a provocatively entitled article in *Vanity Fair*, "Of the 1%, by the 1%, for the 1%," he drew public attention to the massive and growing inequality that was distorting American society "in every conceivable way." The following year, Stiglitz elaborated on these distortions in his best-selling *The Price of Inequality: How Today's Divided Society Endangers Our Future*, which made the case that the country's stark divisions—where the richest 1 percent owned 40 percent of the country's wealth and took in nearly 25 percent of its income—not only imperiled the well-being and opportunities of other Americans, but posed a threat to future economic growth and indeed to democracy itself.[7]

Stiglitz's book made use of the data gathered by a host of economic experts and historians, and one of them, the French economist Thomas Piketty, published his own weighty volume that quickly became an unlikely global best-seller, *Le Capital au XXIᵉ siècle* (*Capital in the Twenty-First Century*). The French edition was released in 2013, the very year that Obama waxed eloquently about the star of equality in his Second Inaugural Address. Piketty saw something different on the horizon. Bringing together years of research, the book detailed long-term trends in the patterns of income and wealth inequality that cast the present in historical relief. When considered in the context of the preceding two centuries, the news was not good. For although Piketty's research highlighted the historical achievement of the Great Compression, with its successful reduction of inequality in the global north, he also detailed the long-term and steady rise of inequality that preceded it, while demonstrating that the pattern had resumed again with a vengeance. The details of his general conclusion—that inequalities would widen inexorably if left to their own devices, because the rate of return on capital (r) outstripped the rate of economic growth (w)—were disputed and controversial. But that did little to blunt the impact of his overall demonstration of just how much inequality had grown since the 1980s. Nor did it soften his general contention, with the weight of history behind it, that, in the absence of active measures to the contrary, it would likely continue to do so.[8]

Quickly translated into English and a host of other languages and discussed around the world, Piketty's work captured the public imagination. Already by the end of 2013, Obama had pivoted to describe inequality as "the defining challenge of our time," and researchers rushed to meet that challenge in a flurry of new studies and investigations. Economists, social scientists, historians, and humanists turned their attention to exploring inequality in the present and the past. NGOs took up the issue in position papers, think tanks crunched the data, and journalists emblazoned inequality in headlines across the world. Even the one percent took notice. As anxious about the future of their investments and the prospects for social stability as anyone else, they broached the issue of inequality at the World Economic Forum at Davos and other elite gatherings.[9]

Soon equality's horizon was receding from public view, to be replaced by what the British sociologist Mike Savage has aptly called the new "inequality paradigm," which focuses attention on inequalities of every kind. From the glaring disparities in wealth and income between rich and poor, north and south, present or past, to the disparate effects of climate change or pandemics, to the ongoing impacts of colonialism and slavery, to vastly different outcomes in education, life chances, and health owing to ethnicity, gender, or place of birth, the subject is as expansive as the inequalities that divide the people of the world.[10]

If the new inequality paradigm was ushered in by the growing awareness of economic disparities, it was heightened and reinforced by developments in politics and culture. The global resurgence of right-wing populism since 2016, the year of Brexit and the election of Donald Trump, cast a harsh new light on the fissures dividing societies around the world.

Groups that had been displaced—or that claimed to have been displaced—by the egalitarian striving of others made up at least part of the constituency of those supporting the resurgence. The so-called Elephant Curve, first conceived by the economists Branko Milanovic and Christoph Lakner in 2013, helps to make sense of that development. Plotting percentiles of global income distribution against the cumulative percentage of real income gain over time, the graph assumed the shape of an elephant's body, with a long thin tail rising up to a high back and an even higher head, and then jutting down like a trunk reaching to the ground before swooping upward at the end. The graph made our global extremes clear: there had been very little growth in the poorest regions of the world and phenomenal growth among the world's top one percent. But the more revelatory data could be found on the back and the peak of the ear together with the plunging part of the trunk. For what this reflected was the rise of countries such as China, India, Indonesia, Thailand, and Vietnam, whose surging economies were pumping citizens out of poverty and into the global middle class (and so reducing

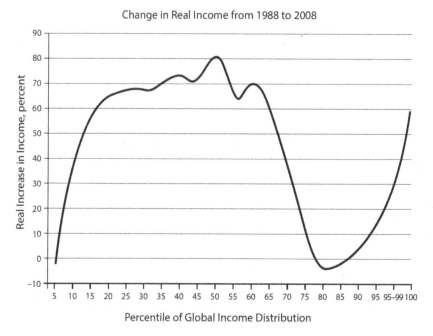

Change in Real Income from 1988 to 2008

The Elephant Curve. By permission of Branko Milanovic.

global inequality), while the comparatively better-off working and lower-middle classes in the global north experienced almost no growth at all.

Here, many argued, was an explanation for populism's support. The tremendous economic growth fueled by deregulation, globalization, and the dismantling of welfare states may have been good for global equality, but it did little for the comparatively prosperous working classes in the global north. The latter saw their wages threatened by competition from workers abroad and immigrants at home, weakening their place in their own societies, where wages stalled or in real terms fell, undermining their respectable status vis-à-vis fellow citizens, as well as their privileged status vis-à-vis much of the rest of the world.[11]

Those workers grumbled at times about wealthy elites in their own societies who skimmed off the gains of global growth. But on the whole, populist-plutocrats and their well-heeled funders have been remarkably adept at displacing such resentment and channeling it toward immigrants and the marginalized groups in their own societies who have so long struggled for a modicum of equality themselves.

A "backlash," it became clear, had been forming for years, targeting feminists and proponents of identity politics who, clustered in the media and at universities, were conveniently cast as a different kind of elite. Too often, they played the part, and their thinly veiled scorn and condescension toward "deplorables," "leavers," and (white) "trash" (such a horrible word) was easily exploited and weaponized against them. The "deplorables" had different names in different places, but they knew who their "enemies" were. And they warmed to those who vowed to treat them as friends with a modicum of respect. Acknowledgment, and a bit of recognition—status—is what most human beings seek. A little goes a long way, and populists have provided a steady drip of both, if only in words.[12]

Their "enemies," of course, had long asked for much the same—dignity and recognition as equals—although the baseline ask was surely considerably less: not to be fondled at work or beaten at home or raped in the streets, not to be suffocated in a chokehold or shot while putting their hands above their heads. The women who came forward in #MeToo and its kindred movements around the world, and the millions of peaceful protesters who affirmed the plaintive truth that Black Lives Matter (BLM), shed as much light as resurgent populists on the inequalities of power and privilege that lay hidden in plain sight. To them it was painfully clear that the struggle was far from over. And though some wondered, in hindsight, if the turn to identity had been a distraction from the economic forces that powered exclusion, others answered that they were always of a piece. Inequalities were "intersectional" in their connections, "visceral" in the way they are experienced in bodies colored and classed, gendered and sexed. And so the struggle against inequality would have to be waged on multiple fronts, where disadvantage and discrimination coincide.[13]

Caught up in the crossfire of these debates are not only competing claims to status, but competing ideas of equality itself, which gesture to older deployments while also signaling something new. On the Left, the very elusiveness of equality as difference has led some to speak of equality in different terms. Although they vehemently deny a genetic basis for life's outcomes, critics regularly assert nonetheless that birth determines life chances in highly unequal ways, owing to inherited privilege and structural discrimination. On this view, heterosexual white men, and to a lesser extent white women, are seen as beneficiaries of the bounty of the past, while women, the indigenous, and peoples of color, those of alternative sexualities, and other disadvantaged groups are held back by its weight. To speak of "equality" in such cases, critics argue, is misplaced. And so equality has gradually given way in recent years in the vocabulary of the Left to "equity." As one diversity officer at an Ivy League college put it frankly in a session on faculty hiring: "We are definitely in an equity and not an equality culture, and that is a good thing." They added that "human beings are rich and varied and not equal." The not-so-veiled message was that candidates should be considered differently.[14]

A widely circulated cartoon narrated by vice presidential candidate Kamala Harris in 2020 made a similar point. The clip showed two figures, one white, one Black, attempting to get up a mountain with a length of rope. "Equality suggests that everyone should get the same amount," Harris comments in the voice-over, in a tone that American politicians tend to adopt when talking to "folks." But the "problem with that [is] not everyone is starting out from the same place." The clip proceeds to explain that if some start out farther back and get the same amount, they'll still lag behind. That is equality. Equity, by contrast, is about "giving everyone the resources and the support they need so that everyone can be on equal footing." The cartoon shows the ground being raised—literally leveled up—so that the Black figure is able to reach the rope and pull himself to the top. The end goal, we learn, is for "everyone [to be] on equal footing so that they can compete on equal footing." "Equitable treatment means we all end up at the same place."[15]

In some respects, the language of equity is just a new iteration of the logic of affirmative action and the older socialist belief that resources should be tailored to differing needs in the service of providing more equal results. But the clip is misleading in that it suggests that competition on equal footing will lead people to an equal place, which it never does. That, as we have seen, was the whole point of the meritocratic claims to equality put forth in the eighteenth century—to provide a mechanism for identifying a new elite of hard work, talent, and intelligence to replace the old ones based on clientage, caste, and aristocratic blood.

The language of equity also quickly passes over an uncomfortable point of contention: that in order to make people equal in the long run, they will need to be treated unequally (equitably) in the near term. The etymologies of the word are revealing. "Equity" (*aequitas*) historically has meant that branch of jurisprudence that deals with exceptions or supplements to the law in the interests of serving justice. It has also long referred to shareholder value, as in the amount of "equity" you have in a company. In its most recent usage, the two meanings are combined. By making exceptions to the law and so treating people unequally for a time, one aims to correct for past injustice and give targeted groups more of a stake.[16]

There is certainly a logic to that view, just as there is a logic for paying reparations for slavery, and for other gross historical injustices. But it shouldn't surprise anyone that those who are not beneficiaries of special consideration, particularly the white working class, often hear talk of equity with deep suspicion. To them it is a thinly veiled code word of identity politics, and as populist leaders skillfully insist, another example of how the system is "rigged." For they, too, complain that meritocracy is a sham, and they rail about the privileges and preferment doled out in universities, corporations, and government agencies to the supposedly underprivileged. Very often that populist response is dismissed as simple prejudice, which it certainly can be. But however much one might dispute the rationales of resentment on grounds of justice, it is difficult to deny the feeling of resentment itself. And the feeling has proved explosive.

Equality is always about feeling, about passions and emotions. It is also about status and power, and very often, about domination and exclusion. That dynamic has shadowed equality from the start, but it was most clearly on view in the first half of the twentieth century among ideologues of the extreme Right. Once again it is on view today among their admirers and heirs among the New Right and Alt-Right, who return to that period self-consciously to mine its intellectual resources. Not surprisingly, they regularly fulminate "against equality" and the dream that it can be expanded to all in no uncertain terms.[17]

The British Alt-Right philosopher Nick Land is typical in that regard, if perhaps more amusing than most. "To call the belief in substantial human equality a superstition is to insult superstition," he writes. "It might be unwarranted to believe in leprechauns, but at least the person who holds to such a belief isn't *watching them not exist*, for every waking hour of the day. Human inequality, in contrast, and in all of its abundant multiplicity, is constantly on display." Land proceeds to list the many ways human beings exhibit variation, and like others on the New Right today, he is more than ready to entertain racial and genetic explanations to account for them. "People are not equal," he concludes. "They do not develop equally, their goals and achievements are not equal, and nothing can make them equal."[18]

Insofar as Land's point is that no two people are alike, who would disagree? Certainly not many of those who insist on the need to respect diversity, identity, and difference. But the latter terms have figured for some time now not just in the vocabulary of the Left. They feature centrally in that of the "Identitarian" New Right as well, which likewise invokes a "right to difference" and inveighs against what it regards as the oppressive universalism of modernity and the persecution of particular peoples and races, refashioning white identities to counter those of color. Nor is the right-wing language of today without its own appeals to the "true" equality of favored peoples, races, nations, and tribes, who are also imagined as the victims of forces who impede them. Like the fascists and national socialists of the first half of the twentieth century, they combat equality in the name of a higher equality, offering status to those to whom, they claim, it has been denied.[19]

Thus, competing languages of identity have emerged that are diametrically opposed and increasingly zero-sum. Like languages marshaling equality in the past, they are about power and status, and whether invoking sameness or difference, they depend upon exclusions—explicitly so in the case of the New Right, and in more veiled ways in the left-wing politics of identity, where white heterosexual men are cast as uncertain allies and privileged exceptions to the rest of humanity. Together these languages combine to sow doubt about the very possibility of pursuing a politics of common purpose.

They also collectively undermine, in the United States as elsewhere, a founding faith in meritocracy through free and fair competition. Free and fair competition, of course, has never been such, though it remains one of America's most cherished myths. Nor has opportunity ever been equal. And yet the millions of immigrants who traveled to the United States in the nineteenth and twentieth centuries saw more of it there than anyplace else, giving the myth a certain credence. There was opportunity in the land of opportunity, and the prospects for some to rise on the basis of talent and hard work were real.

Those prospects today, however, are more daunting, and as a number of critics have recently pointed out, meritocracy itself is part of the problem. For not only does it guarantee unequal outcomes— that was always the point—but it also imbues winners with the self-righteous conviction that their unequal places are earned and deserved. To inequality is added entitlement, and the entitled have shown themselves to be supremely adept at holding on to their places and then passing them on to their children and friends. The effect for social mobility in the United States, as elsewhere, has been cata- strophic, with one critic observing that "meritocracy has become the single greatest obstacle to equal opportunity in America today," further polarizing society and eviscerating its middle class. And while it is not entirely clear what those critics would put in meritocracy's place—More and better meritocracy? Promotion by lottery? Equal outcomes for all?—even the most resolute defenders of the "aristoc- racy of talent" acknowledge that there is force to their critiques.[20]

Meanwhile, lingering suspicions that genetic endowment may grant superior advantage or penalize people from the start further undermine faith in fair competition. For some the social consequences of the genetic lottery is a problem to be faced up to and solved; for others it is a fact of life to be selected for and even celebrated; for still others, it is a dangerous myth, providing cover for racism and misogyny and the historical injustices they have perpetrated. But in all of these cases, the view that human beings are born equal and should be treated as such ends up falling by the wayside.[21]

It is easy, in such circumstances, to despair about the future of equality, which can seem ever more elusive. There is much to be bleak about. If the Great Compression really was, as it appears, a great exception, an anomaly in the long-term economic history of the world, then the resurgence of economic inequalities since the 1980s is simply a return to form. They will remain and even grow unless we take active measures to contain them. And even if we do, it is not clear that active measures alone will suffice. Without the help of the four horsemen of leveling that have attended significant compression in the past—total war, lethal pandemics, state failure, and violent revolution—political will may not be enough. By that reckoning, egalitarians should be careful what they wish for.[22]

Nor does the dark speculation end there. Consider that the silver lining of the surging inequalities of the past three decades in the richest nations of the world has been not just the wealth that has gilded the toilets of the one percent, but the tremendous growth generated beyond them. That growth has been disproportionate, to be sure, and in the very poorest regions of the world, slight. But the tremendous development in China and India, along with that of Indonesia, Vietnam, South Korea, Singapore, Thailand, and Brazil, has helped to pull hundreds of millions of people out of poverty and lowered global inequality as a function of the total number of people in the world since the 1980s. It is among the most rapid, and the most extraordinary, shifts in global income distribution in world history, carried out in just decades.

But those globally equalizing effects won't continue forever, and they may already have ceased. China has now surpassed the global mean of gross domestic product per capita, with the consequence that subsequent growth there will contribute to global divergence among the world's people, not global equality. Meanwhile, inequalities within China's own borders, as within those of other growth nations, such as India and South Korea, are on the rise. One possible specter is that inequalities between nations will be increasingly "internalized"—with yesterday's differences between people in rich and poor nations counting for less than tomorrow's gap between the rich and poor people within each country. A recent study suggests that has already started to happen, with the upshot that the within-country component of global inequality may now count for more than the between-country component.[23]

If that trend continues, the world could come to resemble more what it looked like before the Industrial Revolution, with tremendous inequalities between the rich and poor within nations, but less divergence between them. Much like the aristocrats and haute bourgeoisie of old, who regarded each other across borders as rough equals and peers, but who looked on the commoners in their midst as species of another kind, the global plutocrats of tomorrow may share more in common with one another than they do with their fellow citizens.

In many ways, they already do. In gated compounds and private planes, the super-rich live "cordoned lives," foreign to all but themselves. It is a symptom of what has been described as "asocial inequality," an inequality so siloed and extreme that society's members lose all sense of common belonging. Their lives are no longer even "comparable" in the sense of the word that derives from the Latin *compar* (*com*, "with," and *par*, "equal"), meaning "equal" or "like." Elites and ordinary people instead come to regard each other as alien species, living in worlds apart.[24]

Driven by inequalities of income and wealth, divisions and alienation of this kind are compounded by inequalities of knowledge. Analysts describe the latter as "epistemic inequality," which increasingly divides those in the know from those in the dark. And while it is true that knowledge has always been power, what has changed is the scale. Massive and massively rich companies, such as Meta, Google, TikTok, and Amazon, now control vast amounts of data on all manner of our lives. Authoritarian states do much the same, making use of the very same platforms when they can get away with it. The predictive power and actionable intelligence they have amassed over our preferences, our positions, our health, and our thoughts is without precedent, and the consequences are clear. As one expert underscores, "Unequal knowledge about us produces unequal power over us, turning epistemic inequality into a critical zone of social contest in our time."[25]

The specter of a small number of people amassing vast stores of data in order to dominate wide swaths of humanity may sound like dystopian science fiction or *1984*. The dark strain evident in much current reflection on inequality can at times resemble both, particularly when "rising inequality" is tied to concerns about climate catastrophe and ecological disaster, and the unequal effects those will have on the peoples of the earth.[26]

Still, the grounds for pessimism are real, and advances in robotics and artificial intelligence (AI) are quickly making scientific facts of dystopian science fictions, increasing the prospects of unequal concentration. The historian and public intellectual Yuval Noah Harari warns that as "algorithms push humans out of the job market, wealth and power might become concentrated in the hands of the tiny elite that owns the all-powerful algorithms, creating unprecedented social and political inequality." Harari worries that a new class of upgraded "superhumans" may be able to leverage improvements in health, technology, and AI that would render the mass of humankind superfluous. These would be the god-kings of the next generation, cyborg-pharaohs who would make the god-kings of the archaic states look powerless by comparison, an analogue one percent. Again, that may sound like science fiction. But we should bear in mind that what happened at the dawn of civilization with comparatively primitive tools can happen once more.[27]

Such is our civilization and its present discontents. But while the causes for concern are real, it is important to appreciate that the doom and gloom can be distorting. The inequality paradigm that dominates our time focuses attention on differences and divisions, on cleavages and divides. And while that is surely vital work in a highly unequal age, it has the necessary effect of restricting the realm of possibility. "Changing the terms of debate from 'equality' to 'inequality,'" one observer points out, is a move of retrenchment, which "abandons the prospect of equality and instead repositions thinking around limiting the damage of excessive inequality." It is the work of a disillusioned age, one that has given up on the possibility of progressive social change.[28]

Yet disillusion never springs eternal. Sooner or later, it will yield again to hope and illusions reborn. If nothing else, this entire book should serve as a reminder of what we have lately forgotten—that the human capacity to imagine equality is protean, and that the concept itself is tremendously adaptable and resilient. Periods far more unequal than our own have generated not just illusions, but productive hopes and dreams. And even now, some have begun to dream again.

Piketty, for one, refuses the pessimism of the times, and even, some might say, what the weight of his data suggests. Lately, he has attempted to build a case that "at least since the end of the eighteenth century there has been a historical movement toward equality." If so, that movement has been far from linear or consistent, as my own book has tried to show. Still, Piketty holds fast to the belief that we have it in our power to make the world a more equal place, and he maps out an ambitious, if implausible, strategy toward a "democratic, ecological, and multicultural socialism" on the world scale. "Human progress exists," he insists, adding that "the movement toward equality is a battle that can be won," even if it is "a battle whose outcome is uncertain."[29]

The British sociologist Mike Savage largely agrees. He has done more than any other observer to call out the new "inequality paradigm," and his work forces a full reckoning with the cumulative "weight of history," by which he means the inertial mass of accumulated social, economic, and cultural forces that make the pull of inequality so strong. Yet, like Piketty, he, too, dares to dream, sketching out a "radical manifesto" on the model of Lenin's famous pamphlet "What Is to Be Done?," imagining a politics that would draw on revolutionary energies of the past to build a more equal world for the future.[30]

Finally, to take one other example, the historian Peniel E. Joseph, among America's leading scholars of Black history in the twentieth century and an insightful commentator on contemporary race relations, argues that the country's recent racial strife is an opportunity. "A nightmare," he points out, "is still a dream," and the dream is that the upheavals unleashed in the wake of the Obama presidency—the election of Donald Trump, the resurgence of white supremacy, and the BLM activism following the murder of George Floyd—offer the prospect of a "Third Reconstruction," a program of reconciliation, redemption, and reparation in the service of racial justice. Just as the First Reconstruction following the Civil War made efforts, however fleeting and incomplete, to integrate the formerly enslaved into the nation as citizens; and the Second Reconstruction, spanning the civil rights movement of the 1950s and 1960s, energized that effort again; the Third Reconstruction offers an "opportunity to reimagine [America's] past, present, and future." It is an opportunity to launch "a new struggle for radical equality," to finally make reality of a dream.[31]

There are, then, distinguished voices putting the power of imagination to work right now, aiming to revivify revolutionary energies from centuries past and to carry them forward. Whether such voices can succeed in generating broader political movements—rooting imaginary equality in the social imaginary—is far from clear. Some will find them visionary, others utopian. But we should bear in mind that equality has always had a central place in utopian thinking for good reason: human beings often long to relate to one another more equally than they do, especially when the gaps between them are achingly apparent. Utopian visions express that longing. And even though they rarely succeed in bringing profoundly different worlds into being, they can help us reform the world we inhabit.[32]

Is there any doubt our world needs reforming? Cynics and contrarian optimists sometimes say, as inequalities spiral out of control, that inequality doesn't matter—that what is important is fairness in competition and the minimum floor of wealth and power, not the distances between us. If everyone has enough to get by, they contend, why bother about the gaps? To the many studies that suggest, on the contrary, that inequality matters quite a lot—to health and well-being, to life expectancy and crime, to social mobility, social capital, and all manner of social dysfunction—those same contrarians and optimists commonly reply that correlation is not causation. They are right about that. But when correlations occur over and over again, when profoundly unequal societies also reveal themselves to be profoundly dysfunctional, we ought to begin to see a pattern, and take notice.[33]

Studies of our primate cousins certainly make it clear that hierarchies of domination are not good for the creatures on the bottom. They induce stress, inflammation, weakened immune response, and other changes that adversely affect health. Our human ancestors seem to have figured much of that out for themselves many thousands of years ago, prompting them to resist, and to reverse, the dominance hierarchies that their own nonhuman ancestors long endured.[34]

Resisting hierarchy is part of who we are as a species. But we are also better than any other at building it back up, using the vaunted wisdom of *Homo sapiens* to construct regimes of hierarchy and domination of a scale and intensity unknown in the animal kingdom. We will never make them go away entirely, and we must be mindful of how our views of equality can serve to reinforce them. But we hold it in our power to make them less severe, and more fair, by recalling the vigilance of our ancestors who have fiercely resisted upstarts and fought against the force of things, imagining equality in different figures and forms. Lest the ink on the palimpsest of equality fade altogether, and the old figures be obscured beyond recognition, we would do well to recover them now, and to begin to form them anew.

ACKNOWLEDGMENTS

When I attended public middle school in the late 1970s, students at the Walter Colton Junior High School in Monterey, California, chose their own lockers. The lockers were outside, on four terraced levels carved into the hillside campus, and they ranged from A-level at the bottom to D-level at the top. The students decorated them with shelves and shag carpeting, put mirrors on the inside and stickers on the outside, and sometimes wrote messages on the painted metal in lipstick or Sharpie: Surfers Rule! Disco Sucks! Dead Kennedys! AC/DC! Most students secured their contents— which ranged from books and papers to roach clips and plastic baggies of pot—with a combination or key lock. But the toughest kids brazenly left their locker doors open, daring anyone to mess with them. Few did. Lockers were turf, claimed and defended. They signaled who you were.

They also signaled *where* you were in the crude and sometimes brutal hierarchy of American student life. Place was all-important, and, as a rule, it was better to be on top. The star athletes, the prettiest girls, the cool, the popular, the strong, clustered on D-level along with all those who aspired to be, and they often shared a locker to solidify friendships and alliances. Occasionally, an unsuspecting interloper or a student new to the school would innocently try to claim a space in the territory of the status elite, and he or she would be rousted out, sometimes with violence, books and belongings flung into the surrounding bushes.

On A-level were the "study-buddies" and nerds, kids with overbearing backpacks, thick glasses, and high-water pants, who went about their business, ignoring taunts and occasional cuffs to the head, taking a longer view of the path to success.

On B-level were those who claimed not to care, opting out of the hierarchy to do their own thing, but occupying a place nonetheless: the surfers, the skaters, the punks, who had their own niches. Here also were the self-described "fishermen," young men of predominately Sicilian origin who dressed alike in blue jackets, boots with red laces, and muscle tees, brandishing their Italian-stallion horns on gold chains. The sons of Monterey's commercial fishermen, they went to Alaska on their families' boats each year and returned with lucrative hauls. They cashed in on their profits when they turned sixteen, purchasing hotrods and flashy trucks with side pipes, racing stripes, and mag wheels. They stuck together and looked out for their own.

C-level was something of an outlier: there were the stoners and the disaffected youth, who rebelled against the system and sometimes actively fought it. One even tried to blow up the school by placing a homemade pipe bomb in his locker, as if to lash out at domination at its source. The plot was foiled, and no one was hurt. But it was a frightening premonition of things to come.

Finally, there were our Black classmates, the majority of them bussed in from the less affluent neighboring town as part of the country's failed experiment in the integration of public schools. Predictably, they tended to cluster in their own groups and kept largely to themselves. The sizable community of Asian Americans and the smaller number of Latinos mixed a little more freely, although they too had their groups, as we all did.

In its simplest and crudest form, this was what sociologists call a status hierarchy. The students participated in it, as human beings do everywhere, by playing status games, constantly jockeying for position, seeking attention and respect. Spontaneously organized, the hierarchy was internally policed. Teachers and administrators had nothing to do with it. Perhaps they should have. And perhaps a more farsighted architect would have organized the distribution of lockers in a more communal way. Space matters. There was striving and resentment, movement and friendships across levels. But for the most part, the young men and women found their place and stuck to it, seeking out "equals" on their level, those who were largely the same.

I have thought about junior high school often during the past few years. For, in retrospect, it is clear that it helped spark an early interest in subjects bound up with this book: status, hierarchy, and the elusive nature of equality, as well as the ways in which human beings work at cross-purposes to bring them into being.

I have also thought often about my friend group from that era, which in my part of town, at least, was remarkably varied, and in the less structured and more intimate environment of the neighborhood, less stratified than at school. There was a strong concentration of Asian Americans—Japanese, Chinese, and Filipino—and I fondly recall their names: Hope Yoshida, Ken Ogura, Jeff and Betty Kinoshita, Mary Morita, Nancy Ma. There were some Latinos—above all Morris Reyes-Mendoza, an immigrant from El Salvador, with whom I worked as a dishwasher, then as a busboy, and finally as a waiter, practicing my Spanish in the peninsula's restaurants. My Black friends from that time—Benny Gordon, John Tucker, Troy Cole—were all from the neighborhood, and the countless hours we spent playing pickup games in abandoned lots and on weed-grown courts seem to me an American childhood at its best. None of us were openly gay, or openly trans, though some of us surely, if secretly, were. We all knew that the local bar down the street on Lighthouse Avenue, the After Dark, was queer, and that the two men living together in a house on the corner of my street were, too. But in those halcyon days in 1970s California, no one really seemed to care that much. We tried to get along.

Of course, I romanticize the past, as people of a certain age are wont to do. I know as a historian, as this book recounts, that the very same period was a turbulent time, when society was already wrestling with the problems that are at the root of our present discontents. That serves as a reminder that we are all caught up in historical forces and structures we tend not to see. Still, in my mind's eye, I see in my childhood the tail end of another country, another America, that we don't hear about much anymore. I am grateful to my playmates and friends from that era for giving me a glimpse of the country's extraordinary diversity and its citizens' prosaic, but often beautiful and successful, efforts to coexist. Notwithstanding the bad haircuts and the bell-bottom jeans, there is something to regret of the world we have lost.

All books, in my experience, are difficult to write, but this one has been more difficult than most. I am therefore especially grateful to the many individuals who helped me along the way and who leavened the thousands of hours of silent and often lonely labor that is scholarship with their solidarity and support.

Special thanks go to Siep Stuurman, a pioneer in the study of the intellectual history of equality, and now its doyen. We have carried on a rich exchange over the past several years, and he has generously read and commented on many of my chapters with his characteristic acumen, grace, and good cheer.

Teresa Bejan has done the same, with a passion for conceptual distinction that I admire enormously but cannot match. She read the manuscript in its entirety and has freely and generously shared her deep knowledge of the history of equality, which her own forthcoming book on the subject will fundamentally rewrite.

In the long aftermath of the pandemic, it was a special delight to take part with Siep and Teresa in a colloquium at the University of Utrecht in May 2022 on the history of equality, organized by fellow historian Devin Vartija. Several generations of scholars who study equality were in attendance, and I left the gathering feeling less like a historian working on my own project than as if I were part of a pressing collective endeavor. Warm thanks to Devin and to all those in attendance—especially Lars Behrisch, Annelien de Dijn, Ido de Haan, Lynn Hunt, Shiru Lim, Anne Phillips, David Lay Williams, and (remotely) William Max Nelson. I have learned a great deal from them all.

David Bell, to whom this book is dedicated, and David Armitage, longtime collaborator and dear friend, also read the manuscript in its entirety with their customary intelligence, kindness, and care. I owe them both more than I can say here, but they can rest assured that they will hear it in a toast, glass in hand.

Tiraana Bains, Christian Olaf Christiansen, Aylon Cohen, Jorge Dagnino, Matthew Delmont, Udi Greenberg, Christy Pichichero, Julia Rabig, and Charles Walton all read and commented on individual chapters with collegial generosity, much to the improvement of the book and my great thanks.

I am grateful to Estela Roselló Soberón, Jorge Dagnino, and Hector Maldonado Felix for invitations to speak with stimulating audiences in Mexico City, Santiago, and Lima. In Helsinki, Cesare Cuttica, Jani Marjenen, Stefan Nygård, Johanna Rainio, Kaari Saastamoinen, and the many other good people at the Centre for Intellectual History hosted a wonderful set of discussions, then took me out for a lively evening, during which I lost my computer (but in fine Finnish fashion, I got it back again unscathed the next morning). Sophie Rosenfeld kindly arranged for a spirited event at the University of Pennsylvania, with razor-sharp responses to my paper by François Furstenberg and Natasha Wheatley. Christian Olaf Christiansen was a delightful host in Aarhus and a delightful visitor in Dartmouth and has been a close and admired colleague in the study of equality throughout. Petter Hellström and Sven Widmalm kindly organized a wonderful gathering at the University of Uppsala. Finally, thoughtful audiences at the Davis Center at Princeton and the history department at the University of Warwick assembled by David Bell and Charles Walton gave me much to ponder.

David Gelber at the *Literary Review* kept his eye out for relevant books to send my way and encouraged my thoughts. My colleagues at the Toynbee Prize Foundation, past president Dominic Sachsenmeier and his successor, Glenda Sluga, helped make for a memorable gathering in Seoul. Toynbee, along with Andrew Cohn, Nicole CuUnjieng Aboitz, and Timothy Nunan, also enabled rich discussions about equality and other matters over the years with prizewinners and panelists, including Lauren Benton, Dipesh Chakrabarty, Vanessa Ogle, Jürgen Osterhammel, Jennifer Pitts, and Kenneth Pomeranz.

My colleagues at *Modern Intellectual History*, and above all Tracie Matysik, Duncan Kelly, and Angus Burgin, made my five years there as coeditor fly by, as did the superb Modern Intellectual History postdoctoral fellows at Dartmouth, Jeremy Dell, Danny Steinmetz-Jenkins, and Tiraana Bains. Thank you.

Dartmouth itself has been a model of institutional support, forthcoming with funding, understanding, and time, including a year's sabbatical leave, and another thanks to the generosity of the Guggenheim Foundation. I couldn't ask for a better institutional home, for better colleagues, or for better students, who I boast (in all my acknowledged bias) are among the very best in the world. I would like to thank in particular those who took part in my history of equality seminar in the summer of 2018 and organized an impressive online exhibition on the struggle over female integration at Dartmouth (www.dartmouth.edu/library/rauner/exhibits/coeds_cohogs.html). I am also especially grateful to Yoo Jin Chae, Ashley Dupuy, Joseph Estrada, Zachary Lang, Eliza Mahoney, Christopher Meister, and Kathryn Sachs, who all assisted me in various ways with the research for this book, as did Xingzhi Guo, who in addition translated sources from Chinese.

Fellow Enlightenment scholar Anton Matytsin translated several important Russian sources. He also had me to Oberlin

College many years ago for an enjoyable visit on which I tried out some of my very first ideas on equality.

Thanks are due as well to the many other friends and colleagues who answered queries, offered insights, or provided support or suggestions along the way. They include, in no other order save that of the alphabet, Wes Alcenat, Naomi J. Andrews, Robert Bonner, Pascal Bruckner, D. Graham Burnett, Leslie Butler, Brandon Byrd, Carl Cederström, Henry C. Clark, Nicholas Cronk, Pamela Crosley, Annelien de Dijn, Pascal Dupuy, Dan Edelstein, Steven Ericson, Cecilia Gaposchkin, Dan Gilbert, Adam Grant, Jonathan Haidt, Susannah Heschel, Lynn Hunt, Douglas Irwin, Margaret Jacob, Martin Jay, Mark Juergensmeyer, René Koekkoek, Larry Kritzman, Mark Lilla, Antoine Lilti, Stefan Link, Suzanne Marchand, Anton Matytsin, Jennifer Miller, Bethany Morreton, Samuel Moyn, Paul Musselwhite, Priya Nelson, James Pawelski, Anne Phillips, Naaborko Sackeyfio-Lenoch, Jeffrey Ravel, Glauco Schettini, Martin Seligman, Walter Simons, Miranda Spieler, Roberta Stewart, K. Steven Vincent, Pamela Voekel, Thalia Wheatley, Meik Wiking, Miroslav Wolf, and Rebecca Zorach.

In his empathy and understanding, Howard Burton reaffirmed my conviction that all Canadians are fundamentally good people, however much he has tried to convince me otherwise. Other friends who listened to my laments with compassion and good cheer include Michael Friedman, William Moses, and James Younger. They invariably made them go away. And for the hundreds of hours of pleasant distraction and the needed reminder that there are more important things in life than books, my warm thanks go to Eric and Jen Berniker, Bill and Carrie Shope, Jon and Sara Deren, Jay and Julie and Endich, Amanda Foster and Marinka Hudonogov, Andrew Goldman and Robin Henry, Noah and Weatherly Hammond, Matt and Kate Moneyhon, Greg Naughton and Kelli O'Hara, and Brett and Tara Varsov.

Warm thanks to Alex Kane at WME, to Tina Bennett, as ever, and to my publisher Lara Heimert, an exacting editor, but a dear and accommodating friend. I am also grateful for the painstaking efforts of the copy editor who worked on the manuscript, Kathy Streckfus.

Finally, my family, I fear, has borne the brunt of my scholarly solipsism throughout this project. I ask for their indulgence, and offer my love and gratitude in return.

NOTES

INTRODUCTION: IMAGINARY EQUALITY

1. Timothy A. Kohler and Michael E. Smith, eds., *Ten Thousand Years of Inequality: The Archaeology of Wealth Differences* (Tucson: University of Arizona Press, 2018); Walter Scheidel, *The Great Leveler: Violence and the History of Inequality from the Stone Age to the Twenty-First Century* (Stanford, CA: Stanford University Press, 2017); Atossa Araxia Abrahamian, "The Inequality Industry," *The Nation*, October 8–15, 2018; Ricardo Fuentes-Nieva and Nicholas Galasso, "Working for the Few: Political Capture and Economic Inequality," *Oxfam Briefing Paper*, January 20, 2014, www.oxfam.org/en/research/working-few; Katrina vanden Heuvel, "Voters Must Catch on to the Republicans' Con on Health Care," *Washington Post*, October 23, 2018. Mike Savage addresses the "new equality paradigm" in his trenchant *The Return of Inequality: Social Change and the Weight of the Past* (Cambridge, MA: Harvard University Press, 2021).
2. Thomas Piketty, *Capital in the Twenty-First Century*, trans. Arthur Goldhammer (Cambridge, MA: Harvard University Press, 2014); Branko Milanovic, *Global Inequality: A New Approach for the Age of Globalization* (Cambridge, MA: Harvard University Press, 2018).
3. Aldo Schiavone, *Eguaglianza: Una nuova visione sul filo della storia* (Turin: Einaudi, 2019), vii; Pierre Rosanvallon, *The Society of Equals*, trans. Arthur Goldhammer (Cambridge, MA: Harvard University Press, 2013), 8.
4. The classic statement on the impossibility of writing the history of ideas such as equality is Quentin Skinner, "Meaning and Understanding in the History of Ideas," *History and Theory* 8, no. 1 (1969): 3–53 (esp. 10, 35, 39). I discuss the lack of historical attention to equality at greater length in my article "To Write the History of Equality," *History and Theory* 58, no. 1 (March 2019): 112–125. See also David Armitage, foreword to R. R. Palmer,

The Age of Democratic Revolutions: A Political History of Europe and America, 1760–1800 (Princeton, NJ: Princeton University Press, 2014), xx; Jonathan Israel, *Enlightenment Contested: Philosophy, Modernity, and the Emancipation of Man, 1670–1752* (Oxford: Oxford University Press, 2006), 545.

5. See the conclusion for a discussion of such works.

6. Amartya Sen, "Equality of What?," in *The Tanner Lectures on Human Values*, ed. S. M. McMurrin (Salt Lake City: University of Utah Press, 1980).

7. David Graeber and David Wengrow, *The Dawn of Everything: A New History of Humanity* (New York: Farrar, Straus and Giroux, 2021), 32, 56.

8. A more literal translation of the Latin would be "Nature has birthed all men as equal." For a full discussion of Pope Gregory on equality, see Chapter 5 below.

9. For my thoughts on "imaginary equality" I am indebted to the historian Siep Stuurman. See his pioneering "How to Write a History of Equality," *Leidschrift* 19, no. 3 (2004): 23–38, and, more generally, *The Invention of Humanity: Equality and Cultural Difference in World History* (Cambridge, MA: Harvard University Press, 2017), esp. 1–6. See also Otto Dann, "Gleichheit," in *Geschichtliche Grundbegriffe: Historisches Lexikon zur politisch-sozialen Sprache in Deutschland*, ed. Otto Brunner, Werner Conze, and Reinhart Koselleck, 8 vols. (Stuttgart: Klett-Cotta, 1975), 2:997–998; Ulrike Davy and Antje Flüchter, "Concepts of Equality: Why, Who, and What For?," in *Imagining Unequals, Imagining Equals: Concepts of Equality in History and Law*, ed. Ulrike Davy and Antje Flüchter (Bielefeld: Bielefeld University Press, 2022), 11–31. On the term "host property," coined by the legal theorist John Coons, see Jeremy Waldron, *One Another's Equals: The Basis of Human Equality* (Cambridge, MA: Belknap Press of Harvard University Press, 2017), 85–88.

10. W. E. B. Du Bois, "The Immediate Program of the American Negro," *The Crisis* 9, no. 6 (April 1915): 310–312; Otto Dann, "Gleichheit," 2:997–998.

11. On equality-as-balance, see Teresa M. Bejan's *First Among Equals: A History of Equality in Theory and in Practice* (Cambridge, MA: Harvard University Press, forthcoming), ch. 1.

12. Lars Behrisch, "Notions and Practices of Equality," ch. 3 of *States, Revolutions and the Birth of Democracy in Early Modern Europe*, unpublished manuscript, forthcoming with Cambridge University Press, kindly shared in manuscript form with the author (italics in original).

13. See, for example, *Le dictionnaire de l'Académie Française*, 2 vols. (Paris: Chez la veuve de Jean Baptiste Coignard, 1694), 1:358; Samuel Johnson, *A Dictionary of the English Language*, vol. 1 (London: W. Strahan, 1755), entries for "equality" and "equal" (unpaginated); Noah Webster, *A Compendious Dictionary of the English Language* (New Haven, CT: Sidney's Press, 1806), 105; "Webster's Dictionary 1828," *American Dictionary of the English Language*, n.d., https://webstersdictionary1828.com.

14. Noah Webster, *An American Dictionary of the English Language*, revised and enlarged by Chauncey A. Goodrich (Springfield, MA: George and Charles Merriam, 1861), 405. On the close connections between dignity, rank, and equality, see Jeremy Waldron, *Dignity, Rank, and Rights*, ed. and intro. Meir Dan-Cohen (Oxford: Oxford University Press, 2015), 13–46.

15. Karl Marx, *The Poverty of Philosophy*, trans. Institute of Marxism Leninism (Moscow: Progress Publisher, 1955), ch. 2, sec. 1, accessed at www.marxists.org/archive/marx/works/1847/poverty-philosophy/ch02.htm (italics in original).

16. Carl Schmitt, *The Crisis of Parliamentary Democracy*, trans. Ellen Kennedy (Cambridge, MA: MIT Press, 1988), 9.

17. Cecilia L. Ridgeway, *Status: Why Is It Everywhere? Why Does It Matter?* (New York: Russell Sage Foundation, 2019). The science journalist Will Storr provides a readable summary of the status literature in *The Status Game: On Social Position and How We Use It* (London: William Collins, 2021), as does Alain de Botton in his older *Status Anxiety* (New York: Vintage, 2004).

18. Norberto Bobbio, *Left and Right: The Significance of a Political Distinction*, trans. and intro. Allan Cameron (London: Polity, 1996), 60–71. The description of equality as a "protest ideal" is that of the Enlightenment historian Franco Venturi.

19. See Louis Dumont, *Homo Hierarchicus: The Caste System and Its Implications*, complete revised English edition, trans. Mark Sainsbury, Louis Dumont, and Basia Gulati (Chicago: University of Chicago Press, 1980), 19; Stephen C. Angle, Kwame Anthony Appiah, Julian Baggini, Daniel Bell, Nicolas Berggruen, Mark Bevir, Joseph Chan, et. al., "In Defense of Hierarchy," *Aeon*, March 22, 2017, https://aeon.co/essays/hierarchies-have-a-place-even-in-societies-built-on-equality.

20. On the distinction between hierarchy and domination, I follow the late sociologist Robert Bellah, in *Religion in Human Evolution: From the Paleolithic to the Axial Age* (Cambridge, MA: Belknap Press of Harvard University Press, 2011), 178, 640n7.

21. The classic reference is Erich Auerbach, "Figura," in *Time, History, and Literature: Selected Essays of Erich Auerbach*, trans. Jane O. Newman, ed. James I. Porter (Princeton, NJ: Princeton University Press, 2016), 65–113, which is insightfully discussed by James I. Porter in "Disfigurations: Erich Auerbach's Theory of Figura," *Critical Inquiry* 44 (Autumn 2017): 80–113.

22. Thomas Piketty, *A Brief History of Equality*, trans. Steven Rendall (Cambridge, MA: Belknap Press of Harvard University Press, 2022), 1.

CHAPTER ONE: REVERSAL

1. I first learned of the Cova Remigia paintings from a brief reference in the insightful work of Peter Turchin, *Ultra Society: How 10,000 Years of War Made Humans the Greatest Cooperators on Earth* (Chaplin, CT: Beresta Books, 2016), 106.

2. The exclusion scene is nicely represented in Jean Guillaine and Jean Zammit, *The Origins of War: Violence in Pre-History*, trans. Melanie Hersey (London: Blackwell, 2005), 115, fig. 34.

3. Christopher Boehm, *Hierarchy in the Forest: The Evolution of Egalitarian Behavior* (Cambridge, MA: Harvard University Press, 1999); Richard B. Lee and Richard Daly, eds., *The Cambridge Encyclopedia of Hunters and Gatherers* (Cambridge: Cambridge University Press, 2010 [1999]); Alan Barnard, ed., *Hunter-Gatherers in History, Archaeology, and Anthropology* (Oxford: Berg, 2004).

4. Richard B. Lee, *The !Kung San: Men, Women, and Work in a Foraging Society* (Cambridge, MA: Harvard University Press, 1976), 244–246; James Suzman, *Affluence Without Abundance: The Disappearing World of the Bushmen* (New York: Bloomsbury, 2017), 181–188.

5. Suzman, *Affluence Without Abundance*, 186.

6. Boehm, *Hierarchy in the Forest*, 43–63.

7. Ibid., 85.

8. Frans de Waal, *Our Inner Ape: A Leading Primatologist Explains Why We Are Who We Are* (New York: Riverhead Books, 2005).

9. Donna Haraway, *Primate Visions: Gender, Race, and Nature in the World of Modern Science* (New York: Routledge, 1999); Cordelia Fine, *Testosterone Rex: Myths of Sex, Science, and Society* (New York: W. W. Norton, 2017); Erika Lorraine Milam, *Creatures of Cain: The Hunt for Human Nature in Cold War America* (Princeton, NJ: Princeton University Press, 2019).

10. Jean-Jacques Rousseau, *Discourse on the Origin of Inequality*, in *The Basic Political Writings*, trans. and ed. Donald A. Cress, intro. Peter Gay (Indianapolis: Hackett, 1987), 33.

11. Sandra L. Vehrencamp, "A Model for the Evolution of Despotic Versus Egalitarian Societies," *Animal Behavior* 31 (1983): 667–682.

12. I draw here on the pioneering work of Jane Goodall, particularly *The Chimpanzees of Gombe* (Cambridge, MA: Belknap Press of Harvard University Press, 1986); and Frans de Waal, *Chimpanzee Politics: Power and Sex Among Apes* (Baltimore: Johns Hopkins University Press, 2007 [1982]).

13. De Waal, *Inner Ape*, 32.

14. The group of eminent scholars includes Stephen C. Angle, Kwame Anthony Appiah, Julian Baggini, Daniel Bell, Nicolas Berggruen, Mark Bevir, Joseph Chan, et al., in "In Defense of Hierarchy," *Aeon*, March 22, 2017, https://aeon.co/essays/hierarchies-have-a-place-even-in-societies-built-on-equality.

15. Robert M. Sapolsky, *Behave: The Biology of Humans at Our Best and Our Worst* (New York: Penguin, 2017), 425–444; Jessica E. Koski, Hongling Xie, and Ingrid R. Olson, "Understanding Social Hierarchies: The Neural and Psychological Foundations of Status Perception," *Social Neuroscience* 10, no. 5 (2015): 527–550; Cecilia L. Ridgeway, *Status: Why Is It Everywhere? Why Does It Matter?* (New York: Russell Sage Foundation, 2019).

16. Samuel Bowles and Herbert Gintis, *A Cooperative Species: Human Reciprocity and Its Evolution* (Princeton, NJ: Princeton University Press, 2011).

17. Goodall, *Chimpanzees of Gombe*; de Waal, *Chimpanzee Politics*.

18. TED Blog Video, "Two Monkeys Were Paid Unequally: Excerpt from Frans de Waal's TED Talk," YouTube, www.youtube.com/watch?v=meiU6TxysCg.

19. Donna Hart and Robert Sussman, *Man the Hunted: Primates, Predators, and Human Evolution* (New York: Westview Press, 2005), 191.

20. Edward O. Wilson, *The Social Conquest of the Earth* (New York: W. W. Norton, 2012), 248; de Waal, *Inner Ape*, ch. 6 ("The Bipolar Ape"). On human beings' complicated ways of relating to one another, see also Alan Page Fiske, *Structure of Social Life: Communal Sharing, Authority Ranking, Equality Matching, Market Pricing* (New York: Free Press, 1991).

21. Ian Tattersall, *Masters of the Planet: The Search for Our Human Origins* (New York: St. Martin's Press, 2012), 110.

22. Charles Darwin, *The Descent of Man, and Selection in Relation to Sex*, intro. John Tyler Bonner and Robert M. May (Princeton, NJ: Princeton University Press, 1981), 144.

23. For recent debates and a summary of the literature, see J. Michael Plavcan, "Sexual Size Dimorphism, Canine Dimorphism, and Male-Male Competition in Primates—Where Do Humans Fit In?," *Human Nature* 23 (2012): 45–67; Clark Spencer Larsen, "Equality for the Sexes in Human Evolution? Early Hominid Sexual Dimorphism and Implication for Mating Systems and Social Behavior," *PNAS* 100, no. 16 (August 5, 2003): 9103–9104.

24. Boehm, *Hierarchy in the Forest*, 171–181.

25. On the general importance of throwing, see Tattersall, *Masters of the Planet*, 53–56. The case for *Homo erectus* is made in Neil T. Roach and Brian G. Hammond, "Clavicle Length, Throwing Performance and the Reconstruction of the *Homo erectus* Shoulder," *Journal of Human Evolution* 80 (March 2015): 107–113. On the leveling effects of weapons use, see Boehm, *Hierarchy in the Forest*, 177–181, and Turchin, *Ultra Society*, 95–110. See also Hobbes, *Leviathan*, ch. 13.

26. In what follows I rely heavily on the detailed account in Boehm, *Hierarchy in the Forest*, as does Turchin in *Ultra Society*, 95–111. See also Boehm's more recent *Moral Origins: The Evolution of Virtue, Altruism, and Shame* (New York: Basic Books, 2012).

27. The line was recorded by the anthropologist Harold Schneider in his *Livestock and Equality in East Africa: The Economic Basis for Social Structure* (Bloomington: Indiana University Press, 1979), and cited by Boehm, *Hierarchy in the Forest*, 124.

28. Yuval Harari, *Sapiens: A Brief History of Mankind* (New York: HarperCollins, 2015), 37.

29. David Graeber and David Wengrow, *The Dawn of Everything: A New History of Humanity* (New York: Farrar, Straus and Giroux, 2021), 86–87 and passim.

30. Walter Scheidel, *The Great Leveler: Violence and the History of Inequality from the Stone Age to the Twenty-First Century* (Princeton, NJ: Princeton University Press, 2017), 31; Erik Trinkhaus, Alexandra P. Buzhilova, Maria B. Mednikova, and Maria V. Dobrovolskaya, *The People of Sunghir: Burials, Bodies, and Behavior in the Earlier Upper Paleolithic* (Oxford: Oxford University Press, 2014).

31. David Graeber and David Wengrow, "How to Change the Course of Human History," Eurozine, March 2, 2019, www.eurozine.com/change-course-human-history.

32. Scheidel, *Great Leveler*, 32. On early Gini coefficients, see Kenneth A. Bollen and Pamela Paxton, "Democracy Before Athens," in *Inequality, Democracy, and Economic Development*, ed. Manus I. Midlarsky (New York: Cambridge University Press, 2014), 13–44; and Ian Morris, *Foragers, Farmers, and Fossil Fuels: How Human Values Evolve* (Princeton, NJ: Princeton University Press, 2015), 36.

33. Boehm, *Hierarchy in the Forest*, 4–11; Morris, *Foragers, Farmers, and Fossil Fuels*, 39–41.

34. On plasticity in humans and animals, see Frans de Waal, *Different: Gender Through the Eyes of a Primatologist* (New York: W. W. Norton, 2002); Lucy Cooke, *Bitch: On the Female of the Species* (New York: Basic Books, 2022). On hunter-gatherers, see Karen L. Endicott, "Gender Relations in Hunter-Gatherer Societies," in Lee and Daly, *Cambridge Encyclopedia of Hunters and Gatherers*, 411–418.

35. Raymond Hames and Katherine Starkweather, "A Survey of Non-Classical Polyandry," *Human Nature* 23 (June 2012): 149–172.

36. On Genghis Kahn, see Sapolsky, *Behave*, 367. On the incidence of polygyny, see Nicholas A. Christakis, *Blueprint: The Evolutionary Origins of a Good Society* (New York: Little Brown, 2019), 135, and, more generally, 134–158.

37. Christopher Ryan and Cacilda Jethál, *Sex at Dawn: The Prehistoric Origins of Modern Sexuality* (New York: HarperCollins, 2010).

38. On pair bonding, see Christakis, *Blueprint*, 169–176.

39. Adrienne Zihlman, "The Paleolithic Glass Ceiling: Women in Human Evolution," in *Women in Human Evolution*, ed. L. Hager (London: Routledge, 1997), 91–113; Mark Dyble, Gul Deniz Salali, Nikhil Chaudhary, Abigail E. Page, Daniel Smith, J. Thompson, Lucio Vinicius, Ruth Mace, and Andrea Bamberg Migliano, "Sex Equality Can Explain the Unique Social Structure of Hunter-Gatherer Bands," *Science* 15 (May 2015): 796–798.

40. Hart and Sussman, *Man the Hunted*, 215; Linda Owen, *Distorting the Past: Gender and the Division of Labor in the European Upper Paleolithic* (Tübingen: Kerns Verlag, 2005).

41. Paul Seabright, *The War of the Sexes: How Conflict and Cooperation Have Shaped Men and Women from Prehistory to the Present* (Princeton, NJ: Princeton University Press, 2012), 75.

42. Lawrence H. Keeley, *War Before Civilization: The Myth of the Peaceful Savage* (New York: Oxford University Press, 1996), 36–39.

43. Sapolsky, *Behave*, ch. 11 ("Us Versus Them"); Wilson, *Social Conquest*, ch. 7 ("Tribalism Is a Fundamental Human Trait"); Jonathan Haidt, *The Righteous Mind: Why Good People Are Divided by Politics and Religion* (New York: Vintage, 2012), 161–165.

44. Steven Pinker, *The Better Angels of Our Nature: Why Violence Has Declined* (New York: Penguin, 2011), 522–525; Felicia Pratto, Jim Sidanius, and Shana Levin, "Social Dominance Theory and the Dynamics of Intergroup Relations: Taking Stock and Looking Forward," *European Review of Social Psychology* 17, no. 1 (2006): 271–320.

45. Graeber and Wengrow, "How to Change the Course of Human History."

46. On the *Homo sapiens Blitzkrieg* and its consequences, see Harari, *Sapiens*, 70–72.

47. Hart and Sussman, *Man the Hunted*, 33–135, 150–155.

48. On *Homo sapiens'* gradual and always imperfect "disarticulation" from nature, see Calvin Luther Martin, *In the Spirit of the Earth: Rethinking History and Time* (Baltimore: Johns Hopkins University Press, 1992).

CHAPTER TWO: LOSS

1. Richard Heinberg, *Memories and Visions: Exploring the Universal Myth of a Lost Golden Age*, rev. ed. (Wheaton, IL: Quest Books, 2005); Arthur O. Lovejoy and George Boas, *Primitivism and Related Ideas in Antiquity* (Baltimore: Johns Hopkins University Press, 1935).

2. Unless otherwise stated, all biblical quotations are from the New Revised Standard Version, Anglicised (NRSVA), accessed at Bible Gateway, www.biblegateway.com.

3. See the discussion in James L. Kugel, *How to Read the Bible: A Guide to Scripture, Then and Now* (New York: Free Press, 2007), 54–56.

4. Walter Scheidel, *The Great Leveler: Violence and the History of Inequality from the Stone Age to the Twenty-First Century* (Princeton, NJ: Princeton University Press, 2017), 33–42.

5. My account of the "ascent of man" story draws heavily on James C. Scott, *Against the Grain: A Deep History of the Earliest States* (New Haven, CT: Yale University Press, 2017), 1–16.

6. Ibid., 3–5; Turchin, *Ultra Society: How 10,000 Years of War Made Humans the Greatest Cooperators on Earth* (Chaplin, CT: Beresta Books, 2016), 138–139; Scheidel, *Great Leveler*, 39–45. On alternate social forms and their endurance, see David Graeber and David Wengrow, *The Dawn of Everything: A New History of Humanity* (New York: Farrar, Straus and Giroux, 2021), 276–441; and David Stasavage, *The Decline and Rise of Democracy: A Global History from Antiquity to Today* (Princeton, NJ: Princeton University Press, 2020), 29–99.

7. The account in this paragraph and the two that follow draws on a large body of research that I summarize in my article "From the Paleolithic to the Present: Three Revolutions in the Global History of Happiness," in *Handbook of Well-Being*, ed. Ed Diener, Shigehiro Ishi, and Louis Tay (Salt Lake City: Def Publishers, 2018), esp. 2–4.

8. Scott, *Against the Grain*, 96–115.

9. Marshall Sahlins, "The Original Affluent Society," in *Stone Age Economics* (Chicago: Aldine Atherton, 1972), 1–40.

10. Turchin, *Ultra Society*, 210–211.

11. The term "god-kings" is Turchin's. See his *Ultra Society*, 131–147.

12. Charles Tilly, "War Making and State Making as Organized Crime," in *Bringing the State Back In*, ed. Peter B. Evans, Dietrich Rueschemeyer, and Theda Skocpol (New York: Cambridge University Press, 1985), 169–191; Bruce G. Trigger, *Understanding Early Civilizations: A Comparative Study* (Cambridge: Cambridge University Press, 2003), 264.

13. Trigger, *Early Civilizations*, 88, 475–482; Steven Pinker, *The Better Angels of Our Nature: Why Violence Has Declined* (New York: Penguin, 2011), 135.

14. Trigger, *Early Civilizations*, 157–160; Scott, *Against the Grain*, 155–156; Adam Hochschild, *Bury the Chains: Prophets and Rebels in the Fight to Free an Empire's Slaves* (New York: Houghton Mifflin, 2005), 2; "Modern Slavery Is on the Rise," United Nations, www.un.org/en/observances/slavery-abolition-day.

15. Gerda Lerner, *The Creation of Patriarchy* (New York: Oxford University Press, 1986), 76–100.

16. Ibid., 101–106.

17. Graeber and Wengrow, *Dawn of Everything*, 432–433.

18. Trigger, *Early Civilizations*, 167–194. On Napoleon, see Mary Ann Glendon, *The Transformation of Family Law: State, Law, and Family in the United States and Western Europe* (Chicago: University of Chicago Press, 1997), 89n8.

19. Ernst Gellner, *Plough, Sword, and Book: The Structure of Human History* (Chicago: University of Chicago Press, 1990), 275; Ian Morris, *Foragers, Farmers, and Fossil Fuels: How Human Values Evolve* (Princeton, NJ: Princeton University Press, 2015), 44–92; Graeber and Wengrow, *Dawn of Everything*, 210–275; Scott, *Against the Grain*, 44.

20. Scheidel, *Great Leveler*, 40. See, more generally, Timothy A. Kohler and Michael E. Smith, eds., *Ten Thousand Years of Inequality: The Archaeology of Wealth Differences* (Tucson: University of Arizona Press, 2018).

21. Scott, *Against the Grain*, 128–149.

22. Scheidel, *Great Leveler*, 43–53; Yuval Harari, *Sapiens: A Brief History of Mankind* (New York: HarperCollins, 2015), 101.

23. Scheidel, *Great Leveler*, 33–42; Kent Flannery and Joyce Marcus, *The Creation of Inequality: How Our Prehistoric Ancestors Set the Stage for*

Monarchy, Slavery, and Empire (Cambridge, MA: Harvard University Press, 2012), 207.

24. Jared Diamond, "The Worst Mistake in the History of the Human Race," *Discover*, May 1987, 64–66. See, more broadly, his *Gun, Germs, and Steel: The Fates of Human Societies* (New York: W. W. Norton, 1999), esp. ch. 14 ("From Egalitarianism to Kleptocracy").

25. Jean-Jacques Rousseau, *Discourse on the Origin of Inequality*, in *The Basic Political Writings*, trans. and ed. Donald A. Cress, intro. Peter Gay (Indianapolis: Hackett, 1987), 69. See, especially, Flannery and Marcus, *Creation of Inequality*, whose account I summarize here and in the following paragraph.

26. Ara Norenzayan, *Big Gods: How Religion Transformed Cooperation and Conflict* (Princeton, NJ: Princeton University Press, 2013), 118–121 and passim.

27. Turchin, *Ultra Society*, 149–180; Robert L. Carneiro, *The Muse of History and the Science of Culture* (New York: Kluwer Academic, 2000).

28. Turchin, *Ultra Society*, 140–142; Diamond, *Guns, Germs, and Steel*, 278–292; Allen W. Johnson and Timothy Earle, *The Evolution of Human Societies: From Foraging Group to Agrarian State*, 2nd ed. (Stanford, CA: Stanford University Press, 2000); Morris, *Foragers*, 143.

29. Scott, *Against the Grain*, 8, 137–139, 219–256; James C. Scott, *The Art of Not Being Governed: An Anarchist History of Upland Southeast Asia* (New Haven, CT: Yale University Press, 2009); Benoît Dubreuil, *Human Evolution and the Origin of Hierarchies: The State of Nature* (Cambridge: Cambridge University Press), 188–227; Harari, *Sapiens*, 98.

30. Flannery and Marcus, *Creation of Inequality*, x (and 95 on later "rubbish men"); Turchin, *Ultra Society*, 137–138.

CHAPTER THREE: FELLOWSHIP

1. Ahmad ibn Hanbal, *Al-Musnad*, ed. Shu'ayb al-Arn'aut et al., 50 vols. (Beirut: Mua'ssasa al-Risala, 1993–2001), 38:474 (italics mine). I am grateful to Dr. Rushain Abbasi who kindly called this passage to my attention and translated it for me. For other examples and commentary, see Louise Marlow, *Hierarchy and Egalitarianism in Islamic Thought* (Cambridge: Cambridge University Press, 1997).

2. Karl Jaspers, *The Origin and Goal of History*, trans. Michael Bullock (Abingdon, UK: Routledge, 2010 [1949]); Robert B. Bellah and Hans Joas, eds., *The Axial Age and Its Consequences* (Cambridge, MA: Harvard University Press, 2012).

3. Jaspers, *Origin and Goal*, 6.

4. Confucius, *Analects*, 15.39, cited in Tongdong Bai, *Against Political Equality: The Confucian Case* (Princeton, NJ: Princeton University Press, 2020), 33; Siep Stuurman, *The Invention of Humanity: Equality and Cultural Difference in World History* (Cambridge, MA: Harvard University Press, 2017), 97–111; Confucius, *Analects*, 6.4, in *Analects: With Selections*

from Traditional Commentary, trans. Edward Slingerland (Indianapolis: Hackett, 2003), 53.

5. Zhuangzi, *Basic Writings*, trans. Burton Watson (New York: Columbia University Press, 2003), 31–45; Massimiliano Lacertosa, "The Ethical Stance of the 'Qiwulun (Discourse on Corresponding Things),'" *Dao* 18 (April 2019), 183–196.

6. Eske J. Møllgaard, "Sage-Knowledge and Equality in the *Zhuangzi*," *Journal of Daoist Studies* 7 (2014): 147–162.

7. See SungAe Ha, "Alternative Paths to Equality in Zhuangzi: An Asian Feminist Perspective," *Quest: Studies on Religion and Culture in Asia* 1 (May 2016), accessed at www.theology.cuhk.edu.hk/quest/index.php/quest/article/view/17; John Altmann and Bryan W. Van Norden, "Was the Ancient Taoist [Zhuangzi] the First Philosopher of Disability?," *New York Times*, July 8, 2020.

8. Robert Bellah, *Religion in Human Evolution: From the Paleolithic to the Axial Age* (Cambridge, MA: Harvard University Press, 2011), 573–576. Bellah draws on Jürgen Habermas's well-known concept of "legitimation crisis," as articulated in Habermas's "Towards a Reconstruction of Historical Materialism," in *Communication and the Evolution of Society*, trans. Thomas McCarthy (Boston: Beacon Press, 1976).

9. Bellah, *Religion in Human Evolution*, 573–576.

10. Stuurman, *Invention of Humanity*, 67.

11. Bellah, *Religion in Human Evolution*, 576–585; Brian Calvert, "Slavery in Plato's Republic," *Classical Quarterly* 37, no. 2 (1987): 367–372. On Plato as a critic of economic inequality, see David Lay Williams, *The Greatest of All Plagues: Economic Equality in Western Political Thought* (Princeton, NJ: Princeton University Press, forthcoming), ch. 1.

12. Stuurman, *Invention of Humanity*, 89–96; G. B. Kerferd, "The Concept of Equality in the Thought of the Sophistic Movement," in *Equality and Inequality of Man in Ancient Thought*, ed. Iiro Kajanto (Helsinki: Societa Scientiarum Fennica, 1984), 7–14.

13. Joshua A. Berman, *Created Equal: How the Bible Broke with Ancient Political Thought* (New York: Oxford University Press, 2008), esp. 60–62, 78–80, 81–108.

14. Norman Solomon, "Economics of the Jubilee," in *The Jubilee Challenge: Utopia or Possibility*, ed. Hans Ucko (Geneva: World Council of Churches Publications, 1997), 150–164 (esp. 151); John Bergsma, *The Jubilee from Leviticus to Qumran: A History of Interpretation* (Leiden: Brill, 2007). See also Eric Nelson, *The Hebrew Republic: Jewish Sources and the Transformation of European Political Thought* (Cambridge, MA: Harvard University Press, 2010), 4, 57–88.

15. Howard S. Levy, "Yellow Turban Religion and Rebellion at the End of the Han," *Journal of the American Oriental Society* 76, no. 4 (October–December 1956): 214–227; David Ownby, "Chinese Millenarian Traditions: The

Formative Age," *American Historical Review* 104, no. 5 (December 1999): 1513–1530. On the Taiping Rebellion, see Jonathan D. Spence's classic *God's Chinese Son: The Taiping Heavenly Kingdom of Hong Xiuquan* (New York: W. W. Norton, 1996).

16. Peter Turchin, *Ultra Society: How 10,000 Years of War Made Humans the Greatest Cooperators on Earth* (Chaplin, CT: Boresta Books, 2016), 182–187, and, more generally, 181–209. See also Turchin, "Religion and Empire in the Axial Age," *Religion, Brain and Behavior* 2, no. 3 (2012): 256–260.

17. Ara Norenzayan, *Big Gods: How Religion Transformed Cooperation and Conflict* (Princeton, NJ: Princeton University Press, 2013). Turchin draws out the implications of both Bellah and Norenzayan's arguments in *Ultra Society*, 181–209.

18. Turchin, *Ultra Society*, 211–212. The U-curve, which is invoked by Bellah, was first proposed by B. M. Knauft, "Violence and Sociality in Human Evolution," *Current Anthropology* 32, no. 4 (1991): 391–409.

19. Marcus Aurelius, *Meditations with Selected Correspondence*, trans. Robin Hard, intro. Christopher Gill (New York: Oxford University Press, 2011), 10 (Book 2.1). Cicero's observations are from *De Legibus*, 1.29.

20. Berman, *Created Equal*, 56.

21. On the universalist-dualist dynamic, see Stuurman, *Invention of Humanity*, 34–36.

22. On Mao's comment see Møllgaard, "Sage Knowledge and Equality," 149–150, 158–160. On equality and degrees of humanity, I draw on Anne Phillips, *Unconditional Equals* (Princeton, NJ: Princeton University Press, 2021), 40–62.

23. Mencius, *Mengzi*, 3A4, cited in Møllgaard, "Sage-Knowledge and Equality," 154.

24. Louis Dumont, *Homo Hierarchicus: The Caste System and Its Implications*, complete revised English edition, trans. Mark Sainsbury, Louis Dumont, and Basia Gulati (Chicago: University of Chicago Press, 1980).

25. A classic modern statement of the theme of religion as a force legitimating hierarchy is Peter Berger, *The Sacred Canopy: Elements of a Sociological Theory of Religion* (New York: Doubleday, 1967). On Bakunin, see G. D. H. Cole, *A History of Social Thought*, vol. 2, *Marxism and Anarchism, 1850–1890* (London: Macmillan, 1954), 220–221.

26. Alan Paige Fiske, "The Four Elementary Forms of Sociality: Framework for a Unified Theory of Social Relations," *Psychological Review* 99, no. 4 (1992): 689–723. See also Jonathan Haidt, *The Righteous Mind: Why Good People Are Divided by Politics and Religion* (New York: Vintage, 2012), 167–169.

27. On Gandhi, see Chapter 10.

CHAPTER FOUR: JUSTICE

1. Herodotus, *The Histories*, rev. ed., trans. Aubrey de Sélincourt, ed. and intro. John Marincola (New York: Penguin, 2003), 340 (5.78).

2. Ibid.

3. Paul Cartledge, "Comparatively Equal," in *Dēmokratia: A Conversation on Democracies, Ancient and Modern*, ed. Josiah Ober and Charles Hedrick (Princeton, NJ: Princeton University Press, 1996), 178.

4. Herodotus, *Histories*, 3.80; Gregory Vlastos, "Isonomia," *American Journal of Philology* 74, no. 4 (1953): 337–366; Jürgen Mau and Ernst Günther Schmidt, *Isonomia: Studien zur Gleichheitsvorstellung im griechischen Denken* (Berlin: Akademie Verlag, 1964); Kurt Raaflaub, *Die Entdeckung der Freiheit: Zur historischen Semantik und Gesellschaftgeschicte eines politischen Grundbegriffes der Griechen* (Munich: Verlag C. H. Bech, 1985), 115–118; Mogens Herman Hansen, *Was Athens a Democracy? Popular Rule, Liberty and Equality in Ancient and Modern Political Thought*, Historisk-filosofiske Meddelelser 59 (Copenhagen: Royal Danish Academy of Sciences and Letters, 1989), 25–26.

5. Herodotus, *Histories*, 207 (3.80); David Stasavage, *The Decline and Rise of Democracy: A Global History from Antiquity to Today* (Princeton, NJ: Princeton University Press, 2020), 29–61.

6. Kurt Raaflaub, "Homer to Solon: The Rise of the Polis. Written Sources," in *The Ancient Greek City-State*, ed. M. H. Hansen (Copenhagen: Royal Danish Academy of Sciences and Letters, 1993), 41–105; Kurt Raaflaub,"Equalities and Inequalities in Athenian Democracy," in Ober and Hedrick, *Dēmokratia*, 150; Aristotle, *Politics*, Book 4, 1295b25–26 (following Paul Cartledge's translation). On "semblance of equality," see Paul Cartledge, "Spartan Contributions to Greek Citizenship Theory," in *Defining Citizenship in Archaic Greece*, ed. Alain Duplouy and Roger Brock (Oxford: Oxford University Press, 2018), 184.

7. Gregory Vlastos, "Equality and Justice in Early Greek Cosmologies," *Classical Philology* 42, no. 3 (July 1947): 156–178; Carl Werner Müller, *Gleiches zu Gleichem: Ein Prinzep Frügriechischen Denkens* (Weisbaden: Otto Harrassowitz, 1965), 12–104.

8. Vlastos, "Equality and Justice," 158–164.

9. Ibid., 156–158.

10. Joel Kaye, *A History of Balance, 1230–1375: The Emergence of a New Model of Equilibrium and Its Impact on Thought* (Cambridge: Cambridge University Press, 2014). On early representations of justice, see Judith Resnik and Dennis Curtis, *Representing Justice: Invention, Controversy, and Rights in City-States and Democratic Courtrooms* (New Haven, CT: Yale University Press, 2011), 18–22. On equality-as-balance in ancient thought, and the image of the scale, see the pathbreaking work of Teresa M. Bejan, "On the Historical Emergence of Basic Human Equality" (forthcoming), kindly shared with the author in draft form.

11. Raaflaub, "Equalities and Inequalities," 143–150; Josiah Ober, "The Original Meaning of 'Democracy': Capacity to Do Things, Not Majority Rule," *Constellations* 15, no. 1 (2008): 3–9.

12. On Lincoln's interest in Euclid in relation to his thinking about equality, see Dan van Haften and David Hirsch, *Abraham Lincoln and the Structure of Reason* (New York: Savas, 2015), 24–30, 267; Adam Kucharski, "Euclid as Founding Father," *Nautilus* 41 (October 7, 2016), https://nautil.us/euclid-as-founding-father-236144.

13. On the "strong principle of equality," which he borrows from political theorist Robert Dahl, see Ian Morris, "The Strong Principle of Equality and the Archaic Origins of Greek Democracy," in Ober and Hedrick, *Dēmokratia*, 19–48.

14. Solon, fragment 24.18–20, cited in Raaflaub, "Equalities and Inequalities," 144; Josiah Ober, *Mass and Elite in Democratic Athens: Rhetoric, Ideology, and the Power of the People* (Princeton, NJ: Princeton University Press, 1989), 60–66.

15. T. E. Rihill, "Classical Athens," in *Cambridge World History of Slavery*, ed. Keith Bradley and Paul Cartledge, vol. 1 (Cambridge: Cambridge University Press, 2011), 48–73; Peter Hunt, *Ancient Greek and Roman Slavery* (Malden: Wiley Blackwell, 2018).

16. Josiah Ober, "The Athenian Revolution of 508/7 B.C.: Violence, Authority, and the Origins of Democracy," in *The Cultural Politics of Archaic Greece*, ed. Leslie Kurke and Carol Dougherty (Cambridge: Cambridge University Press, 1993), 215–232.

17. Ober, *Mass and Elite in Democratic Athens*, 68–76; Josine Blok, *Citizenship in Classical Athens* (Cambridge: Cambridge University Press, 2017).

18. Jean-Jacques Rousseau, *The Social Contract* (Book 2, ch. 11), in *The Basic Political Writings*, trans. and ed. Donald A. Cress, intro. Peter Gay (Indianapolis: Hackett, 1987), 171.

19. Raaflaub, "Equality and Inequality," 149; Walter Scheidel, *The Great Leveler: Violence and the History of Inequality from the Stone Age to the Twenty-First Century* (Princeton, NJ: Princeton University Press, 2017), 84–85, 192–199, though compare, despite their sacrifice and valor, the experience of African Americans, as recounted in Mathew Delmont, *Half American: The Epic Story of African Americans Fighting World War II at Home and Abroad* (New York: Viking, 2022).

20. Pericles cited in Thucydides, *The Peloponnesian War*, trans. Martin Hammond, intro. P. J. Rhodes (Oxford: Oxford University Press, 2009), 92 (Book 2, ch. 40).

21. On the "middling men," see Ian Morris, "Strong Principle," in Ober and Hedrick, *Dēmokratia*, 21–22; Josiah Ober, *Rise and Fall of Classical Greece* (Princeton, NJ: Princeton University Press, 2015), 89–90. See also Peter W. Rose, *Class in Archaic Greece* (Cambridge: Cambridge University Press, 2012), 74n50; and the general discussion in Larry Patriquin, *Economic Equality and Direct Democracy in Ancient Athens* (New York: Palgrave, 2015).

22. Paul A. Rahe, *Republics Ancient and Modern*, vol. 1, *The Ancien Régime in Classical Greece* (Chapel Hill: University of North Carolina Press, 1994), 56–57, 195.

23. Scheidel, *The Great Leveler*, 192–198.

24. Aristotle, *The Politics* and *The Constitution of Athens*, trans. Benjamin Jowett, ed. Stephen Everson (Cambridge: Cambridge University Press, 1996), 107–108 (1295b24–40).

25. Plato, *The Laws* (Books 1–6), trans. R. G. Bury, Loeb Classical Library 187 (Cambridge, MA: Harvard University Press, 1926), 413. See, in general, Aristotle, *Nicomachean Ethics*, 1130b–1132b; Aristotle, *Politics*, 1282b–1283a22, 1301a26–1302a15; Plato, *Laws*, 757a–d.

26. Aristotle, *Politics*, trans. Ernest Barker, intro. R. F. Stalley (New York: Oxford University Press, 1995), 180 (1301b26–29). See also *Politics*, 1302a22–29.

27. Plato, *Laws*, 411–415 (757a–d), and the same passages in Plato, *Laws*, trans. Trevor J. Saunders, in *Plato: Complete Works*, ed. John M. Cooper (Indianapolis: Hackett, 1997), 1433.

28. Hans van Wees, "Luxury, Austerity, and Equality in Sparta" and "The Common Messes," both in vol. 1 of *A Companion to Sparta*, ed. Anton Powell (London: John Wiley and Sons, 2018), 202–235, 236–268.

29. Plutarch, "Lycurgus," in *On Sparta*, trans. and intro. Richard J.A. Talbert (London: Penguin, 1988), 3–38; Stephen Hodkinson, *Property and Wealth in Classical Sparta* (London: Duckworth, 2000).

30. Thucydides, *Peloponnesian War*, 1.6.4; J. Peter Euben, "Political Equality and the Greek Polis," in *Liberalism and the Modern Polity: Essays in Contemporary Political Theory*, ed. Michael J. Gargas McGrath (New York: Decker, 1978), 214. See, more generally, Lin Foxhall and John Salmon, eds., *When Men Were Men: Masculinity, Power, and Identity in Classical Antiquity* (London: Routledge, 1998).

31. Blok, *Citizenship in Classical Athens*, esp. 147–187; David M. Pritchard, "The Position of Attic Women in Democratic Athens," *Ancient History* 41–44 (2011–2014): 43–65.

32. Thucydides, *Peloponnesian War*, trans. Hammond, 38, 302, 307 (1.76.10–12; 5.89.8–11, 5.116.11–13); Chester G. Starr, *The Influence of Sea Power on Ancient History* (New York: Oxford University Press, 1989), 38.

33. Aristole, *Politics*, 1332b27–8 (in the translation of Benjamin Jowett).

34. Euben, "Political Equality and the Greek Polis," 216.

35. Hannah Arendt, *On Revolution*, intro. Jonathan Schell (New York: Penguin, 2006 [1963]), 20–21, 267. See also Arendt, *The Human Condition*, 2nd ed., intro. Margaret Canovan (Chicago: University of Chicago Press, 1998 [1958]), 32–33, 40–41.

36. Louis, chevalier de Jaucourt, "Natural Equality," in Denis Diderot, *Denis Diderot's* The Encyclopedia: *Selections*, trans. and ed. Stephen J. Gendzier

(New York: Harper and Row, 1967), accessed at The Encyclopedia of Diderot & d'Alembert: Collaborative Translation Project, Michigan Publishing, University of Michigan Library, http://hdl.handle.net/2027/spo.did2222.0001.312.

37. Josiah Ober, *Mass and Elite in Democratic Athens*, 7 (italics in original).

38. Aristotle, *The Politics and the Constitution of Athens*, 109 (1296b1–3).

CHAPTER FIVE: RECOVERY

1. St. Augustine, *Confessions*, 13.11.12. On the early Christian "theology of equality," I am indebted to the brief but insightful remarks of Aldo Schiavone in *Eguaglianza: Una nuova visione sul filo della storia* (Turin: Einaudi, 2019), 68–75.

2. St. Augustine, *De Trinitate*, 7.6.11, in *On the Trinity*, trans. Rev. Arthur West Haddan, ed. Paul A. Boër Sr. and William G.T. Shedd (Edmond, OK: Veritatis Splendor, 2012), 285. I have consulted the Latin original throughout and made several minor alterations to this translation for reasons of phrasing and style. See also Basil of Caesarea, *Letters*, 236.6, accessed at New Advent, www.newadvent.org/fathers/3202236.htm.

3. St. Augustine, *De Trinitate*, 1.4.7, 6.9.10, 7.6.12, and 9.12.18, in *On the Trinity*, 64, 265, 289, 334.

4. John L. Gresham, "The Social Model of the Trinity and Its Critics," *Journal of Scottish Theology* 46, no. 3 (August 1993): 325–343.

5. St. Augustine, letter 120, 2.7, *The Works of Saint Augustine: A Translation for the 21st Century, II/2, Letters 100–155*, trans. Roland Teske, ed. Boniface Ramsey (Hyde Park, NY: New City, 2003), n. 33. For contemporary reflection on the Trinity as a model of ecclesial and social community, see Miroslav Volf, *After Our Likeness: The Church as the Image of the Trinity* (Grand Rapids, MI: William B. Eerdmans, 1998), 191–220.

6. Otto Zöckler, "Religiöse Sinnbilder aus vorchristlicher und christlicher Zeit," pt. 3, "Trinitäts-Symbole," *Der Beweis des Glaubens*, n.f. 2 (1881): 297; Rebecca Zorach, *The Passionate Triangle* (Chicago: University of Chicago Press, 2011), esp. ch. 3 ("The Triangle and the Trinity").

7. I draw here on the work of David Lay Williams, who kindly shared with me his draft chapter, "'Through the Eye of a Needle': Wealth, Greed, and Inequality in Early Christianity," from his *The Greatest of All Plagues: Economic Inequality in Western Political Thought* (Princeton, NJ: Princeton University Press, forthcoming).

8. In addition to Williams, see N. T. Wright, *Early Christian Letters for Everyone* (Louisville, KY: Westminster John Knox Press, 2001), 34; John Barton and John Muddiman, *The Oxford Bible Commentary* (Oxford: Oxford University Press, 2001), 932; Flavius Josephus, *The Jewish War; or the History of the Destruction of Jerusalem*, in *The Genuine Works of Flavius Josephus*, trans. William Whiston (London: W. Bowyer, 1737), 2.8.3,

accessed at Penelope, University of Chicago, http://penelope.uchicago.
edu/josephus/war-2.html.

9. Peter Brown, *Through the Eye of a Needle: Wealth, the Fall of Rome, and the Making of Christianity in the West, 350–550 AD* (Princeton, NJ: Princeton University Press, 2012), xxiv.

10. B. D. Shaw, "The Divine Economy: Stoicism as Ideology," *Latomus* 64 (1985): 16–64 (esp. 17) (italics in original); Marcia L. Colish, *The Stoic Tradition from Antiquity to the Early Middle Ages*, vol. 2, *Stoicism in Christian Latin Thought Through the Sixth Century* (Leiden: E. J. Brill, 1990); Tuomas Rasimus, Troels Engberg-Pedersen, and Ismo Dunderberg, eds., *Stoicism in Early Christianity* (Grand Rapids, MI: Baker Academic, 2010); Michel Spanneut, *Le stoïcisme des pères de l'église de Rome à Clément d'Alexandrie* (Paris: Seuil, 1957).

11. Cicero, *De finibus bonorum et malorum*, with an English translation by H. Rackham (Cambridge, MA: Harvard University Press, 1994 [1914]), 285 (3.64); Seneca, *Epistles 93–124*, trans. Richard M. Gummere (Cambridge, MA: Harvard University Press, 1920), 90–91, 78–79 (95.33–52).

12. Cicero, *De re publica / De legibus*, with an English translation by Clinton Walker Keyes (Cambridge, MA: Harvard University Press, 1928), 329 (1.10.29–30, 43). I have made minor changes to the English translation.

13. Denise Eileen McCoskey, *Race: Antiquity and Its Legacies* (London: Bloomsbury, 2012). The classic account is Frank Snowden Jr., *Before Color Prejudice: The Ancient View of Blacks* (Cambridge, MA: Harvard University Press, 1983). Contrast Benjamin Isaac, *The Invention of Racism in Classical Antiquity* (Princeton, NJ: Princeton University Press, 2004); Seneca, *De benificis*, 3.20.

14. *Musonius Rufus: The Roman Socrates. Lectures and Fragments*, ed. and intro. Cora E. Lutz, vol. 10, Yale Classical Studies (New Haven, CT: Yale University Press, 1947).

15. Epictetus, *Discourses*, 1.2.7–11, in *The Discourse of Epictetus: The Handbook, Fragments*, trans. Robin Hard, ed. Christopher Gill (London: Everyman, 1995), 8.

16. Mary Beard, *SPQR: A History of Ancient Rome* (New York: Liveright, 2015), 319; Neal Wood, *Cicero's Social and Political Thought* (Berkeley: University of California Press, 1988), 96–97.

17. Cicero, *De re publica*, 1.34.51, in Cicero, *De re publica / De legibus*, 79; Wood, *Cicero's Social and Political Thought*, 4, 93, 95–96.

18. See Julie Zauzmer, "Christians Are Almost Twice as Likely to Blame a Person's Poverty on Lack of Effort," *Washington Post*, August 3, 2017, on polling in the contemporary United States.

19. Schiavone, *Eguaglianza*, 37, 51. The discussion of law that follows draws heavily on Schiavone's authoritative account both here and in his *The Invention of the Law in the West*, trans. Jeremy Carden and Antony Shugaar (Cambridge, MA: Belknap Press of Harvard University Press, 2012); Livy,

Ab urbe condita, 3.43.3, cited in Schiavone, *Invention of the Law*, 97–98; and Jed W. Atkins, *Roman Political Thought* (Cambridge: Cambridge University Press, 2018), 48.

20. Cicero, *De oratore*, 1.42.88.
21. Schiavone, *Eguaglianza*, 52.
22. Teresa M. Bejan, "What Was the Point of Equality?," *American Journal of Political Science* 66, no. 3 (July 2022): 604–616 (esp. 607–608).
23. Schiavone, *Eguaglianza*, 51–52.
24. Max Radin, "Roman Concepts of Equality," *Political Science Quarterly* 38, no. 2 (June 1923): 262–280 (esp. 274).
25. Beard, *SPQR*, 527–530; Atkins, *Roman Political Thought*, 66–67.
26. For the broader historical significance, see Frederick Cooper, *Citizenship, Inequality, and Difference: Historical Perspectives* (Princeton, NJ: Princeton University Press, 2018).
27. David Johnston, "The Jurists," in *The Cambridge History of Greek and Roman Political Thought*, ed. Christopher Rowe and Malcolm Schofield (Cambridge: Cambridge University Press, 2005), 616–634 (esp. 621); Tony Honoré, *Ulpian: Pioneer of Human Rights* (Oxford: Oxford University Press, 2002), 76–94.
28. Ulpian, *Ad Sabinum*, 43, in *Corpus iuris civilis* [henceforth *CIC*], vol. 1, *Institutiones, Digesta*, ed. Paul Krueger, Theodor Mommsen, and Wolfgang Kunkel (Berlin: Weidmannsche Verlagsbuchhandlung, 1954), D. 50.17.32; Ulpian, *Institutiones* I, in *CIC* 1, D. 1.14. See the general discussion in Schiavone, *Invention of the Law*, 452–456, and Robert Warrand Carlyle, *History of Medieval Political Theory in the West*, 6 vols. (Edinburgh: Blackwell and Sons, 1903–1936), 1:33–54.
29. Florentinus, *Disputationes* 7, in *CIC*, D. 12.6.64; Florentinus, *Institutiones* 9, in *CIC*, D. 1.5.4; Ulpian, Liber 43 ad Sabinum, in *CIC*, D. 50.17.32.
30. Schiavone, *Invention of the Law*, 458–459; Schiavone, *Eguaglianza*, 72.
31. Minucius Felix, *Octavius*, 37.10, accessed at Perseus Digital Library, ed. Gregory R. Crane, Tufts University, http://data.perseus.org/citations/urn:cts:latinLit:stoa0203.stoa001.perseus-lat1:37.10.
32. Lactantius, *Divine Institutes*, 5.15. I have used the English translation accessible at New Advent, www.newadvent.org/fathers/07015.htm, altering it slightly in comparison with the Latin, accessible at Documenta Catholica Omnia, www.documentacatholicaomnia.eu/02m/0240-0320,_Lactantius,_Divinarum_Institutionum_Liber_V,_MLT.pdf.
33. St. Jerome, "Tractatus de Psalmo LXXXI," 4.15–16, in *Tractatus sive homiliae in psalmos*, ed. D. Germanus Morin (Maredsous: Apud Editorem, 1895), 71; St. Ambrose, *De Nabuthae*, accessed at Open Greek and Latin Perseus Digital Library, Scaife Viewer, https://scaife.perseus.org/reader/urn:cts:latinLit:stoa0022.stoa038.opp-lat1:2?q=similes%20creat&qk=form; S. Gregorii Magni, *Moralia in Job Libri XI–XXII*, ed. Marci Adriaen

(Turnhout: Brepols Editores Pontificii, 1979), 1082 (21.15.4–5 and 21.15.12–14). On the agreement of the church fathers regarding our original nature, see Carlyle, *History of Medieval Political Theory*, 1:114.

34. Gregorii Magni, *Moralia in Job*, 1082 (21.15.13–14); Adam Serfass, "Slavery and Pope Gregory the Great," *Journal of Early Christian Studies* 14, no. 1 (Spring 2006): 77–103.

35. On Stoic and other accounts of the vanished golden age, see Arthur O. Lovejoy and George Boas, *Primitivism and Related Ideas in Antiquity* (Baltimore: Johns Hopkins University Press, 1935), 260–287.

36. Augustine, *De civitate Dei*, 19.13–15. I have consulted the Latin version available at The Latin Library, www.thelatinlibrary.com/augustine/civ19. shtml, but the English translations, with only minor changes, are from St. Augustine, *Concerning the City of God Against the Pagans*, trans. Henry Bettenson, intro. John O'Meara (London: Penguin, 1984), 870–875. On women's standing in Augustine's account, see Judith Chelius Stark, "Augustine on Women: In God's Image but Less So," in *Feminist Interpretations of Augustine*, ed. Judith Chelius Stark (University Park: Pennsylvania State University Press, 2007), 215–241.

37. St. Augustine, *De doctrina christiana*, trans. and ed. R. P. H. Green (Oxford: Clarendon, 1995), 33 (1.47). On Ambrose and property, see Brown, *Eye of a Needle*, 131–134. On the widespread notion that private property arose from sin, see Janet Coleman, "Property and Poverty," in *Cambridge History of Medieval Political Thought c. 350–450*, ed. J. H. Burns (Cambridge: Cambridge University Press, 2008), 607–648; and Carlyle, *History of Medieval Political Theory*, 1:132–146.

38. Gregory, *Moralia in Job*, 1082 (21.15.2–19).

39. Gregory, *Pastoral Rule* (Book 2, ch. 6), accessed at New Advent, www. newadvent.org/fathers/36012.htm; Gregory, "Gregorius universis episcopis Galliarum, qui sub regno Childeberti sunt" (August 12, 595), *Mense augusto indictione*, 13.5.59, in *Monumenta Germaniae historica. Epistolarum*, vol. 1 (Gregorii registrii L. I–VII) (Berolini Apud Weidmannos, 1891), 371.

40. Pseudo-Dionysius, "The Mystical Hierarchy," in *The Complete Works*, trans. Colm Luibheid, intro. Jaroslav Pelikan (New York: Paulist Press, 1987), 153–154.

41. Gregory, "Gregorius universis episcopis Galliarum," 371–372. Here I have used the English translation of James Barmby, edited by Philip Schaff and Henry Wace, accessed at Documenta Catholica Omnia, www. documentacatholicaomnia.eu/01p/0590-0604,_SS_Gregorius_I_Magnus,_ Registri_Epistolarum_%5BSchaff%5D,_EN.pdf, pp. 771–772.

42. St. Thomas Aquinas, vol. 13 of *Summa theologiae: Latin Text and English Translation*, trans. and ed. Edmund Hill (Cambridge: Blackfriars, 1964), 129–135 (Part I, Question 96, secs. 3–4). I have made slight alterations to the translation.

43. Ibid. Aquinas's reference to Gregory's assertion is from *Moralia in Job*, 21.15. His quote from the Bible ("The things that are from God . . .") is from Romans 13:1, and his quote from Augustine is from *De civitate Dei*, 19.13.

44. The classic account is Arthur O. Lovejoy, *The Great Chain of Being: A Study in the History of an Idea* (Cambridge, MA: Harvard University Press, 1964 [1936]).

45. On the use of the triangle to represent hierarchy, see Zorach, *The Passionate Triangle*, 54–80.

46. On monastic ideals of sharing and equality, see Brown, *Eye of a Needle*, 171–184, 416–418.

47. Gratian as translated and discussed in Philip Knox, "Human Nature and Natural Law in Jean de Meun's *Roman de la Rose*," in *The Roman de la Rose and Thirteenth-Century Thought*, ed. Jonathan Morton, Marco Nievergelt, and John Marenbon (Cambridge: Cambridge University Press, 2002), 137–138. See also Norman Cohn, *The Pursuit of the Millennium*, revised and expanded ed. (New York: Oxford University Press, 1970), 193–195.

48. Herman Pleij, *Dreaming of Cockaigne: Medieval Fantasies of the Perfect Life*, trans. Diane Webb (New York: Columbia University Press, 1997), 12, 309; Paul E. Sigmund, "Hierarchy, Equality, and Consent in Medieval Christian Thought," in *Equality*, ed. J. Roland Pennock and John W. Chapman (New York: Atherton Press, 1967), 134–153.

49. On Meun, see Juhana Toivannen, "The Personal and the Political: Love and Society in the Roman de la Rose," in Morton et al., *The Roman de la Rose*, 111–130; Christine de Pizan, *The Book of the City of Ladies*, trans. and intro. Rosalind Brown-Grant (London: Penguin, 1999), 23 (pt. 1.9).

50. Thomas Walsingham, *Historia Anglicana*, 2 vols., ed. Henry Thomas Riley (London: Longman, 1863), 2:32–33; Norman Cohn, *The Pursuit of the Millennium*, 198–200. Siep Stuurman also discusses this line and its wider European impact in the introduction to his forthcoming *Gelijkheid en Ongelijkheid in Economie en Politik*, which he kindly shared with me in draft form. On the spread of Ball's lines, see Sylvia Resnikov, "The Cultural History of a Democratic Proverb," *Journal of English and Germanic Philology* 36 (1937): 391–405.

51. See, notably, Lars Behrisch, *States, Revolutions and the Birth of Democracy in Early Modern Europe* (Cambridge: Cambridge University Press, forthcoming); and Teresa M. Bejan, *First Among Equals: A History of Equality in Theory and Practice* (Cambridge, MA: Harvard University Press, forthcoming).

52. Luther, *An Open Letter to the Christian Nobility of the German Nation Concerning the Reform of the Christian Estate* (1520), in *The Works of Luther*, trans. C. M. Jacobs (Philadelphia: A. J. Holman Company, 1915) accessed at Christian.net, https://christian.net/pub/resources/text/wittenberg/luther/web/nblty-03.html.

53. Thomas Kaufmann, *Luther's Jews: A Journey into Antisemitism*, trans. Lesley Shapre and Jeremy Noakes (Oxford: Oxford University Press, 2017).

54. Jaroslav Pelikan, *The Christian Tradition: A History of the Development of Doctrine*, vol. 1, *The Emergence of Catholic Tradition (100–600)* (Chicago: University of Chicago Press, 1975), 297–298.

55. Ernst Troeltsch, *The Social Teaching of the Christian Churches*, vol. 1, trans. Olive Wyon, intro. H. Richard Niebhur (Chicago: University of Chicago Press, 1960), 74; John Calvin, *The Institutes of the Christian Religion*, trans. Henry Beveridge (Grand Rapids, MI: William B. Eerdmans, 1989), 206 (Book 3, ch. 21, sec. 5). I have altered the first clause of Beveridge's translation to more literally reflect the Latin.

56. Luther, "The Freedom of a Christian," in *The European Reformation*, rev. ed., ed. Hans Hillerbrand (New York: Harper Perennial, 2009).

57. Rothman cited in Cohn, *The Pursuit of the Millennium*, 266; Anthony Arthur, *The Tailor-King: The Rise and Fall of the Anabaptist Kingdom of Münster* (London: St. Martin's Press, 2001).

58. Martin Luther, *Admonition to Peace: A Reply to the Twelve Articles of the Peasants in Swabia*, trans. Charles M. Jacobs, ed. Theodore G. Tappert, rev. Robert C. Schultz (Philadelphia: Fortress Press, 1967), 3:323.

59. Troeltsch, *The Social Teaching*, 74; Sanford A. Lakoff, "Christianity and Equality," in Pennock and Chapman, *Equality*, 115–133; Calvin, *Institutes* (Book 3, ch. 7, sec. 4), 9.

60. Andrew Bradstock, *Radical Religion in Cromwell's England: A Concise History from the English Civil War to the End of the Commonwealth* (London: I. B. Tauris, 2011), 18.

61. Teresa M. Bejan, "No Respecter of Persons," *Journal of Biblical Literature* 140, no. 4 (2021): 831–836.

62. On "hat honor" and its refusal, see Teresa M. Bejan, "Hobbes and Hats," *American Political Science Review* (2023): 1–14. See also Gerrard Winstanley, *The New Law of Righteousness*, in *Complete Works of Gerrard Winstanley*, vol. 1, ed. Thomas N. Corns and Ann Hughes (Oxford: Oxford University Press, 2009), 513, 521–522.

63. Abiezier Coppe, *A Fiery Flying Roll* (London, 1649), 2–4.

64. Rainsborough cited in Andrew Sharp, "Introduction: The English Levellers, 1645–1649," in *The English Levellers*, ed. Andrew Sharp (Cambridge: Cambridge University Press, 1998), xv; John Lilburne, "The Freeman's Freedom Vindicated, A Postscript, Containing a General Proposition," in Sharp, *The English Levellers*, 31.

65. See, for example, Elizabeth Anderson, *Private Government: How Employers Rule Our Lives (and Why We Don't Talk About It)*, intro. Stephen Macedo (Princeton, NJ: Princeton University Press, 2017), 7–17; Jeremy Waldron, *One Another's Equals: The Basis of Human Equality* (Cambridge, MA: Belknap Press of Harvard University Press, 2017), esp. 94, no. 24; and Waldron's pioneering *God, Locke, and Equality: Christian Foundations in*

Locke's Political Thought (Cambridge: Cambridge University Press, 2002), 1–20. Compare Bejan, "What Was the Point of Equality?," 604–615.

66. Jacques-Bénigne Bossuet, "Unité et égalité parfaite du père et fils," in *Méditations sur l'Évangile*, 2 vols. (Paris: Perisse Frères, 1839), 2:260–267.

67. Lakoff, "Christianity and Equality," 119–123.

68. Cited in Perry Miller, "Equality in the American Setting," in *The Responsibility of Mind in a Civilization of Machines: Essays by Perry Miller*, ed. John Crowell and Stanford J. Searle Jr. (Amherst: University of Massachusetts Press, 1979), 245.

CHAPTER SIX: FRATERNITY

1. Richard Sharpe Patterson, *The Eagle and the Shield: A History of the Great Seal of the United States* (Washington, DC: Office of the Bureau of Public Affairs, 1978), 6–27; Martin Levey, "The First Museum of Natural History," *ISIS* 42, no. 1 (April 1951): 10–12.

2. Adams cited in Patterson, *Eagle and Shield*, 18.

3. James A. Leith, "Symbols in the French Revolution: The Strange Metamorphoses of the Triangle," in *Symbols in Life and Art*, ed. James A. Leith (Montreal: McGill-Queen's University Press, 1987), 105–118.

4. On the novelty of society and nation-making in the eighteenth century, see David A. Bell, *The Cult of the Nation in France: Inventing Nationalism, 1680–1800* (Cambridge, MA: Harvard University Press, 2001), 7–8.

5. St. Augustine, *Confessions*, 4.8.13; Cicero, *De amicitia*, 25.92 (and 21.8); Cicero, *De officiis*, 1.17.56; Aristotle, *Nicomachean Ethics*, ed. Roger Crisp (Cambridge: Cambridge University Press, 2014), 147, 155 (1158a1–2, 1161a27–29).

6. On the complicated history of friendship, see the essays in Barbara Caine, ed., *Friendship: A History* (London: Routledge, 2014).

7. Louis Dumont, *Homo Hierarchicus: The Caste System and Its Implications*, complete revised English edition, trans. Mark Sainsbury, Louis Dumont, and Basia Gulati (Chicago: University of Chicago Press, 1980), 11–12. On the "invention of equality" and the "credo" of revolutionaries, see Pierre Rosanvallon, *The Society of Equals*, trans. Arthur Goldhammer (Cambridge, MA: Harvard University Press, 2013), 12–75, 87; and Siep Stuurman, *François Poulain de la Barre and the Invention of Modern Equality* (Cambridge, MA: Harvard University Press, 2004). For the "test of truth," see Mona Ozouf, "Equality," in *A Critical Dictionary of the French Revolution*, trans. Arthur Goldhammer, ed. François Furet and Mona Ozouf (Cambridge, MA: Belknap Press of Harvard University Press, 1989), 673. On the Enlightenment as a foundational moment of origins, see also Pierre Fala, "Les termes de l'égalité et de l'inégalité: Flux et reflux," in *In/Égalité/s: Usages lexicaux et variations discursives (18ᵉ–20ᵉ siècles)*, ed. Pierre Fala (Paris: L'Harmattan, 1999), 7–20. For accounts that place the origin of modern equality in the seventeenth century among either English

Protestants or the Radical Enlightenment tradition tracing to Spinoza, see Jeremy Waldron, *God, Locke, and Equality: Christian Foundations in Locke's Political Thought* (Cambridge: Cambridge University Press, 2002); and Jonathan Israel, *Enlightenment Contested: Philosophy, Modernity, and the Emancipation of Man, 1670–1752* (Oxford: Oxford University Press, 2006), 545–571.

8. The *locus classicus* for the extensive literature on sociability, the public sphere, and equality is Jürgen Habermas, *The Structural Transformation of the Public Sphere: An Inquiry into a Category of Bourgeois Society*, trans. Thomas Burger (Cambridge, MA: MIT Press, 1989). For a careful consideration of the legacies of both Marx and Tocqueville, and a creative interpretation of the role of the "empire of fashion" in creating civic equality, see William H. Sewell Jr., *Capitalism and the Emergence of Civic Equality in Eighteenth-Century France* (Chicago: University of Chicago Press, 2021), 3–8, 103–147, 227–242.

9. Siep Stuurman, *The Invention of Humanity: Equality and Cultural Difference in World History* (Cambridge, MA: Harvard University Press, 2017), 258–346; Devin J. Vartija, *The Color of Equality: Race and Common Humanity in Enlightenment Thought* (Philadelphia: University of Pennsylvania Press, 2021). On Radical Enlightenment, see Israel, *Enlightenment Contested*, 545–571. On novels and human rights, see Lynn Hunt, *Inventing Human Rights: A History* (New York: W. W. Norton, 2007), esp. 35–70 (citation on 58).

10. David A. Graeber and David Wengrow, *The Dawn of Everything: A New History of Humanity* (New York: Farrar, Straus and Giroux, 2021). But compare the trenchant critique of David A. Bell, "A Flawed History of Humanity," *Persuasion*, November 19, 2021, www.persuasion.community/p/a-flawed-history-of-humanity.

11. Lincoln, "Speech in Independence Hall, Philadelphia, Pennsylvania, February 21, 1861," in *Collected Works of Abraham Lincoln*, vol. 4, ed. Roy P. Basler (New Brunswick, NJ: Rutgers University Press, 1953), accessed at University of Michigan Library, Library Digital Collections, https://quod.lib.umich.edu/l/lincoln/lincoln4/1:376?rgn=div1;view=fulltext.

12. For the Declaration as inspiration, see Danielle Allen's stirring *Our Declaration: A Reading of the Declaration of Independence in Defense of Equality* (New York: W. W. Norton, 2014); Ruth Bogin, "'Liberty Further Extended': A 1776 Antislavery Manuscript by Lemuel Haynes," *William and Mary Quarterly* 40, no. 1 (January 1983): 85–105; Mia Bay, "'See Your Declaration Americans!!!': Abolitionism, Americanism, and the Revolutionary Tradition in Free Black Politics," in *Americanism: New Perspectives on the History of an Ideal*, ed. Michael Kazin and J. A. McCartin (Chapel Hill: University of North Carolina Press, 2006), 25–52; David Armitage, *The Declaration of Independence: A Global History* (Cambridge, MA: Harvard University Press, 2008); Pauline Maier, "The Strange History of 'All Men

Are Created Equal,'" *Washington and Lee Law Review* 56, no. 3 (1999): 873–888. Compare James L. Huston, *The American and British Debate over Equality, 1776–1920* (Baton Rouge: Louisiana State University Press, 2017), 21.

13. On the "axiomatic" nature of natural equality and natural liberty in Scholastic thought, see Harro Höpfl, *Jesuit Political Thought: The Society of Jesus on the State, c. 1540–1630* (Cambridge: Cambridge University Press, 2004), 204–208. And Robert Filmer, *Patriarcha*, in *Patriarcha, and Other Political Writings*, ed. Johann P. Sommerville, Cambridge Texts in the History of Political Thought (Cambridge: Cambridge University Press, 1991), 3. On Hobbes, see Kinch Hoekstra, "Hobbesian Equality," in *Hobbes Today: Insights for the 21st Century*, ed. S. A. Lloyd (Cambridge: Cambridge University Press, 2012), 76–112.

14. Algernon Sidney, *Discourses Concerning Government*, ed. Thomas G. West (Indianapolis: Liberty Fund, 1996), 45; John Locke, *Two Treatises on Government*, ed. Peter Laslett (Cambridge: Cambridge University Press, 1988), 269–270; Thomas Hobbes, *Leviathan*, revised student edition, ed. Richard Tuck (Cambridge: Cambridge University Press, 1996), 107.

15. Thomas Jefferson to Henry Lee, May 8, 1825, accessed at Founders Online, https://founders.archives.gov/documents/Jefferson/98-01-02-5212.

16. On the meaning of the phrase, see Richard D. Brown, *Self-Evident Truths: Contesting Equal Rights from the Revolution to the Civil War* (New Haven, CT: Yale University Press, 2017), esp. ch. 1; Jack P. Greene, "All Men Are Created Equal: Some Reflections on the Character of American Revolution," Inaugural Lecture Delivered Before the University of Oxford, 1976; Huston, *American and British Debate*, 10–37; J. R. Pole, *The Pursuit of Equality in American History* (Berkeley: University of California Press, 1978), esp. ch. 2; and Gordon Wood, *Radicalism of the American Revolution* (New York: Vintage, 1991), 229–243.

17. Teresa M. Bejan, "What Was the Point of Equality?," *American Journal of Political Science* 66, no. 3 (July 2022): 604–616; Christopher Brooke, "Non-Intrinsic Egalitarianism from Hobbes to Rousseau," *Journal of Politics* 82, no. 4 (October 2020): 1406–1417.

18. Carl Schmitt, *Constitutional Theory*, trans. Jeffrey Seitzer (Durham, NC: Duke University Press, 2008), 258. The extensive literature on what she labels "constitutive exclusion" is summarized and developed by Sina Kramer in *Excluded Within: The Unintelligibility of Radical Political Actors* (New York: Oxford University Press, 2017), 1–25.

19. Edmund S. Morgan, "Slavery and Freedom—The American Paradox," *Journal of American History* 59, no. 1 (1972): 5–29; Jack P. Greene, "The Symbiotic Relationship Between Liberty and Inequality in the Cultural Construction of Colonial British America and the United States: An Overview," *American Political Thought: A Journal of Ideas, Institutions, and Culture* 5 (Fall 2016): 549–566; Annelien de Dijn, *Freedom: An Unruly History* (Cambridge, MA:

Harvard University Press, 2020), 6–7, 17, 20, 25–34; Tyler Stovall, *White Freedom: The History of an Idea* (Princeton, NJ: Princeton University Press, 2021), esp. 1–134.

20. Stuurman, *Invention of Humanity*, 259.

21. On the Christian and theological dimensions to Locke's thinking, and to modern equality more generally, see Waldron, *God, Locke, and Equality*. On Sidney, see Michael P. Winship, "Algernon Sidney's Calvinist Republicanism," *Journal of British Studies* 49, no. 4 (2010): 753–773.

22. For a modern scholarly dismissal, see, for example, Rosanvallon, *Society of Equals*, 16–18. See also Thomas Paine, *The Rights of Man, Part I*, in *Political Writings*, ed. Bruce Kuklick (Cambridge: Cambridge University Press, 2000), 85; [Rochefoucauld], *Lettre d'un banquier de Londre a M.—, à Anvers* (September 2, 1776), cited in Armitage, *Declaration of Independence*, 77; and Peter Paulus, *Verhandeling over de vrage: In welken zin kunnen de menschen gezegd worden gelyk te zyn? En welke zyn de regten en pligten die daaruit voordvloeien?* (Haarlem: C. Plaat, 1793).

23. Alexis de Tocqueville, *Democracy in America*, trans. Arthur Goldhammer (New York: Library of America, 2004), 4–6, 12; Friedrich Nietzsche, *The Will to Power*, trans. Walter Kaufmann and R. J. Hollingdale, ed. Walter Kaufmann (New York: Vintage, 1967), 401 (fragment 765).

24. In addition to Waldron's *God, Locke, and Equality*, see his *One Another's Equals: The Basis of Human Equality* (Cambridge, MA: Belknap Press of Harvard University Press, 2017), 1, 16–17, 175–215; Wood, *Radicalism of the American Revolution*, 235; and James Kloppenberg, *Toward Democracy: The Struggle for Self-Rule in European and American Thought* (Oxford: Oxford University Press, 2016), 311.

25. Bejan, "What Was the Point of Equality?," 607–609.

26. Jean-Jacques Rousseau, *Discourse on Inequality* and *Social Contract*, in *The Basic Political Writings*, trans. and ed. Donald A. Cress, intro. Peter Gay (Indianapolis: Hackett, 1987), 39, 153, 81.

27. [François Xavier Talbert], *Discours qui a remporté le prix de l'Académie des sciences de Dijon en l'année 1754* (Dijon, 1754), 5–8, 15.

28. Ibid., 19.

29. Rousseau, *Discourse on Inequality*, 77–78, 106. On Rousseau's "secular theodicy" and his analysis of the psychology of inequality, see Frederick Neuhouser, *Rousseau's Theodicy of Self-Love: Evil, Rationality, and the Drive for Recognition* (Oxford: Oxford University Press, 2008), and Michael Locke McLendon, *The Psychology of Inequality: Rousseau's Amour-Propre* (Philadelphia: University of Pennsylvania Press, 2019). On the place of pride more generally in Enlightenment thought and the persistent Augustinian streak, see Christopher Brooke, *Stoicism and Political Thought from Lipsius to Rousseau* (Princeton, NJ: Princeton University Press, 2012); John Robertson, *The Case for the Enlightenment: Scotland and Naples, 1680–1760* (Cambridge: Cambridge University Press, 2005); and David Wooton,

Power, Pleasure, and Profit: Insatiable Appetites from Machiavelli to Madison
(Cambridge, MA: Belknap Press of Harvard University Press, 2019).

30. Rousseau, *Discourse on Inequality*, 80. On Rousseau's theodicy, see
Neuhouser, *Rousseau's Theodicy*, 2–9, 187–190, 265–267.

31. Hans-Jörg Sigwart, "Rousseau in Amerika: Liberale Tradition und
demokratischer Dissens im US-Amerikanischen Selbstverständigungs-
diskurs," *Jahrbuch für Recht und Ethik* 20 (2012): 195–220; Paul M.
Spurlin, *Rousseau in America, 1760–1809* (Tuscaloosa: University
of Alabama Press, 1969). I am indebted to my former student Daniel
Bring for expanding my knowledge of Rousseau's fate in America in his
undergraduate honors thesis, "The American Reception of Rousseau,
1760–1850" (Dartmouth College, 2021). On the persistence of sin, see
Perry Miller, "Equality in the American Setting," in *The Responsibility
of Mind in a Civilization of Machines: Essays by Perry Miller*, ed. John
Crowell and Stanford J. Searle Jr. (Amherst: University of Massachusetts
Press, 1979), 240–254.

32. Daniel R. Mandell, *The Lost Tradition of Economic Equality in America,
1600–1870* (Baltimore: Johns Hopkins University Press, 2020), 38, and,
more generally, 32–58.

33. Adams cited in Brown, *Self-Evident Truths*, 17–18. For a model account
of American attitudes toward the indigenous, see Colin Colloway, *The
Indian World of George Washington: The First President, the First Peoples,
and the Birth of the Nation* (Oxford: Oxford University Press, 2018). See
also Nicolas Guyatt, *Bind Us Apart: How Enlightened Americans Invented
Racial Segregation* (New York: Basic Books, 2016), 39–60.

34. Thomas Jefferson to the Marquis de Chastellux, June 5, 1785, accessed
at Founders Online, https://founders.archives.gov/documents/Jefferson/
01-08-02-0145. For Jefferson on race, see the judicious comments of
Annette Gordon-Reed in *The Hemingses of Monticello: An American Family*
(New York: W. W. Norton, 2008), esp. 141, 267–268, 271–272.

35. Buffon cited and analyzed in Stuurman, *Invention of Humanity*, 301–312.
On the reception of Buffon's "extraordinarily influential" work in America
and its influence on Jefferson, see Guyatt, *Bind Us Apart*, 22–28. On
Buffon in the context of eighteenth-century science and thought, see
Emma Planinc, "Regenerating Humanism," *History of European Ideas* 46,
no. 3 (2020): 242–256.

36. In addition to Stuurman on these points, see Andrew S. Curran's excellent
The Anatomy of Blackness: Science and Slavery in an Age of Enlightenment
(Baltimore: Johns Hopkins University Press, 2011), esp. 74–117, and
Henry Louis Gates Jr. and Andrew S. Curran, *Who's Black and Why? A
Hidden Chapter in the Eighteenth-Century Invention of Race* (Cambridge,
MA: Belknap Press of Harvard University Press, 2022), 3–46.

37. John Millar, *The Origin of the Distinction of Ranks*, ed. and intro. Aaron
Garrett (Indianapolis: Liberty Fund, 2006), 85.

38. Adam Ferguson, *An Essay on the History of Civil Society*, ed. Fania Oz-Salzberger (Cambridge: Cambridge University Press, 1995), 74–106 (pt. 2, "Of the History of Rude Nations"). On stadial theory, see Ronald L. Meeks, *Social Science and the Ignoble Savage* (Cambridge: Cambridge University Press, 1976), and, as applied specifically to thinking about the New World, J. G. A. Pocock, *Barbarians, Savages and Empires* (Cambridge: Cambridge University Press, 2005), 157–229. Silvia Sebastiani treats the racial and gender aspects of stadial theory in her excellent *The Scottish Enlightenment: Race, Gender, and the Limits of Progress* (New York: Palgrave, 2013), esp. ch. 3; and see the critical account in Graeber and Wengrow, *Dawn of Everything*, 27–62.

39. Stuurman, *Invention of Humanity*, 289–290.

40. Adam Smith, *An Inquiry into the Nature and Causes of the Wealth of Nations*, ed. R. H. Campbell and A. S. Skinner, 2 vols. (Indianapolis: Liberty Fund, 1982), 2:712 (V.i.b.7); Dennis Rasmussen, "Adam Smith on What Is Wrong with Economic Inequality," *American Political Science Review* 110, no. 2 (2016): 342–352; Dennis Rasmussen, *The Problems and Promise of Commercial Society: Adam Smith's Response to Rousseau* (University Park: Penn State University Press, 2009), 51–91.

41. Helvétius cited in Meeks, *Social Science*, 93. On Helvétius's extensive thoughts on equality, see David Wooton, "From Radical Enlightenment to Revolution," *Political Theory* 28, no. 3 (2000): 307–366. See also Louis, chevalier de Jaucourt, "Natural Equality," in Denis Diderot, *Denis Diderot's* The Encyclopedia: *Selections*, trans. and ed. Stephen J. Gendzier (New York: Harper and Row, 1967), accessed at The Encyclopedia of Diderot & d'Alembert: Collaborative Translation Project, Michigan Publishing, University of Michigan Library, http://hdl.handle.net/2027/spo.did2222.0001.312.

42. Montesquieu, *The Spirit of the Laws* (Book 2, ch. 3), in *Selected Political Writings*, trans. and ed. Melvin Richter (Indianapolis: Hackett, 1990), 163.

43. Eric Nelson, *The Greek Tradition in Republican Thought* (Cambridge: Cambridge University Press, 2004), 1–18.

44. Talbert, *Discours*, 31; Mably cited in Nelson, *Greek Tradition*, 178. On Mably's thinking about equality, see Johnson Kent Wright, *A Classical Republican in Eighteenth-Century France* (Stanford, CA: Stanford University Press, 1997), 94–109.

45. Aristotle, *The Politics* and *The Constitution of Athens*, trans. Benjamin Jowett, ed. Stephen Everson (Cambridge: Cambridge University Press, 1996), 107–108 (1295b24–40); Ganesh Sitaraman, *The Crisis of the Middle-Class Constitution: Why Economic Inequality Threatens Our Republic* (New York: Knopf, 2017), 23–34.

46. See Wooton, "Equality in Machiavelli," in *Power, Pleasure, and Profit*, Appendix C, 259–265; James Harrington, *The Commonwealth of Oceana*

and a System of Politics, ed. J. G. A. Pocock (Cambridge: Cambridge University Press, 1992), 20. On Harrington's influence in America, see Edmund S. Morgan, *Inventing the People: The Rise of Popular Sovereignty in England and America* (New York: W. W. Norton, 1988), esp. 85–87, 291; Sitaraman, *Middle-Class Constitution*, 53–58. On the Jewish connection in Harrington, see Eric Nelson, *The Hebrew Republic: Jewish Sources and the Transformation of European Political Thought* (Cambridge, MA: Harvard University Press, 2010), 78–86.

47. Harrington, *Commonwealth*, 33.

48. Jean-Pierre Gross, *Fair Shares for All: Jacobin Egalitarianism in Practice* (Cambridge: Cambridge University Press, 1997), 93.

49. Adams cited in Sitaraman, *Middle-Class Constitution*, 68. On property requirements and other restrictions on citizenship, see Alexander Keyssar, *The Right to Vote: The Contested History of Democracy in the United States* (New York: Basic Books, 2000), 1–42; Rogers M. Smith, *Civic Ideals: Conflicting Visions of Citizenship in U.S. History* (New Haven, CT: Yale University Press, 1997), 1–136.

50. On European visitors, see Kloppenberg, *Toward Democracy*, 460, and, continuing into the nineteenth century, Huston, *American and British Debate*, 59–68; Jefferson discussed and cited in Nelson, *Greek Tradition*, 194, and de Dijn, *Freedom*, 194–195.

51. Peter H. Lindert and Jeffrey G. Williamson, *Unequal Gains: American Growth and Inequality Since 1700* (Princeton, NJ: Princeton University Press, 2016), 37; Mandell, *Lost Tradition*, 46.

52. Mandell, *Lost Tradition*, 7–31; Nelson, *Greek Tradition*, 230–231; Nelson, *Hebrew Republic*, 66–83; Montesquieu, *Spirit of the Laws* (Book 5, chs. 5–6), 142–143.

53. In addition to Mandell, *Lost Tradition*, see Sean Wilentz, *The Politicians and the Egalitarians* (New York: W. W. Norton, 2016), 31–66, 69–124; [Thomas Gordon], *Cato's Letters*, no. 45 (September 16, 1721), "Of the Equality and Inequality of Men," in *Cato's Letters, or Essays on Liberty, Civil and Religious, and Other Important Subjects*, ed. Ronald Hamowy, 2 vols. (Indianapolis: Liberty Fund, 1995), 1:306–310.

54. Sophia Rosenfeld, *Common Sense: A Political History* (Cambridge, MA: Harvard University Press, 2011); Thomas Paine, *Common Sense*, 11; Adams cited in William Doyle, *Aristocracy and Its Enemies in the Age of Revolution* (Oxford: Oxford University Press, 2009), 94; Thomas Jefferson to John Adams, October 28, 1813, accessed at Founders Online, https://founders.archives.gov/documents/Jefferson/03-06-02-0446.

55. George Washington to Thomas Jefferson, March 15, 1795, accessed at Founders Online, https://founders.archives.gov/documents/Washington/05-17-02-0441. On the Society of Cincinnati affair, see Doyle, *Aristocracy*, 99–137. See also Cassius and Samuel Adams cited in Doyle, *Aristocracy*, 103, 105.

56. Harrington, *Commonwealth*, 23; Paine, *Rights of Man, Part I*, 120; Adams to Benjamin Rush, January 25, 1806, accessed at Founders Online, https://founders.archives.gov/documents/Adams/99-02-02-5119; Hamilton, *The Federalist*, no. 36 (January 8, 1788), accessed at The Avalon Project, Yale Law School, https://avalon.law.yale.edu/18th_century/fed36.asp.

57. Hamilton cited and analyzed in Nelson, *Greek Tradition*, 224; David Ramsay, *An Oration on the Advantages of American Independence* (Charleston, SC, 1778), 2–3; Wood, *Radicalism*, 233–234. On natural aristocracy and the politics of merit, see John Carson, *The Measure of Merit: Talents, Intelligence, and Inequality in the French and American Republics, 1750–1940* (Princeton, NJ: Princeton University Press, 2007), 11–38; Joseph F. Kett, *Merit: The History of a Founding Ideal from the American Revolution to the 21st Century* (Ithaca, NY: Cornell University Press, 2013), 15–38; and Adrian Wooldridge, *The Aristocracy of Talent: How Meritocracy Made the Modern World* (London: Allen Lane, 2021), 175–205.

58. On eighteenth-century debates over whether talent was acquired or innate, see Darrin M. McMahon, *Divine Fury: A History of Genius* (New York: Basic Books, 2013), 78–92; David Hume, "On the Original Contract," in *Essays, Moral, Political, and Literary*, ed. Eugene F. Miller (Indianapolis: Liberty Fund, 1987), 467–468; Smith, *Wealth of Nations*, 1:28–29.

59. Adams cited and discussed in Wood, *Radicalism*, 238; and Greene, "All Men Are Created Equal," 7–8.

60. Wilson cited in Greene, "All Men Are Created Equal," 6.

61. Rousseau, *Discourse on Inequality*, 37–38; Ozouf, "Equality," 673.

62. Luke Mayville, *John Adams and the Fear of American Oligarchy* (Princeton, NJ: Princeton University Press, 2016); Alfred F. Young, Gary B. Nash, and Ray Raphael, eds., *Revolutionary Founders: Rebels, Radicals, and Reformers in the Making of the Nation* (New York: Vintage, 2012).

63. Montesquieu, *Spirit of the Laws* (Book 8, ch. 3), 163.

64. The "brief window of opportunity" is the phrase of Rosemarie Zagarri, *Revolutionary Backlash: Women and Politics in the Early American Revolution* (Philadelphia: University of Pennsylvania Press, 2007), 181–182. On Godwin, Wollstonecraft, and "negotiating equality" in London, see Mark Philp, *Radical Conduct: Politics, Sociability and Equality in London, 1789–1815* (Cambridge: Cambridge University Press, 2020).

65. On the New Jersey exception, see Zagarri, *Revolutionary Backlash*, esp. 30–37.

66. Christine Levecq, *Slavery and Sentiment: The Politics of Feeling in Black Atlantic Antislavery Writing, 1770–1850* (Hanover, NH: University Press of New England, 2008), 153–154; David Ramsay to Thomas Jefferson, May 3, 1786, accessed at Founders Online, https://founders.archives.gov/documents/Jefferson/01-09-02-0370; Thomas Jefferson, *Notes on the State of Virginia*, ed. and intro. Frank C. Shuffleton (New York: Penguin, 1999), 150–151.

67. Guyatt, *Bind Us Apart*, 22–28.

68. On the Masons' central role in fostering equality, see Margaret Jacob, *The Origins of Freemasonry: Facts and Fictions* (Philadelphia: University of Pennsylvania Press, 2006), 5, 115–117; and Margaret Jacob, *Living the Enlightenment: Freemasonry and Politics in Eighteenth-Century Europe* (Oxford: Oxford University Press, 1991). On the same in the United States, see Steven C. Bullock, *Revolutionary Brotherhood: Freemasonry and the Transformation of the American Social Order, 1730–1840* (Chapel Hill: University of North Carolina Press, 1996), esp. 5.

69. Jacob, *Origins of Freemasonry*, 75; James Anderson, *Constitutions of the Freemasons* (London, 1723), 55.

70. Early constitution (1741) cited in Jacob, *Origins of Freemasonry*, 72.

71. On Freemasons' love of drink, see John Dickie, *The Craft: How the Freemasons Made the Modern World* (London: Hodder and Stoughton, 2020), 69.

72. Carey Wilson McWilliams, *The Idea of Fraternity in America* (Berkeley: University of California Press, 1973); Dana D. Nelson, *National Manhood: Capitalist Citizenship and the Imagined Fraternity of White Men* (Durham, NC: Duke University Press, 1998); Levecq, *Slavery and Sentiment*, 139–164.

73. Kenneth Loiselle, *Brotherly Love: Freemasonry and Male Friendship in Enlightenment France* (Ithaca, NY: Cornell University Press, 2014), 167–168, 229–231. On sociability more generally and on what he calls the "unequal equality" of the Parisian salons, see Antoine Lilti, *The World of the Salons: Sociability and Worldliness in Eighteenth-Century Paris*, trans. Lydia G. Cochrane (Oxford: Oxford University Press, 2020), 77–81. American Mason cited in Bullock, *Revolutionary Brotherhood*, 149.

74. White clergyman cited in Dickie, *The Craft*, 194; Hall cited and discussed in Richard S. Newman, "Prince Hall, Richard Allen, and Daniel Coker: Revolutionary Black Founders, Revolutionary Black Communities," in Young et al., *Revolutionary Founders*, 309 (italics in original).

75. Guyatt, *Bind Us Apart*, 197–245; Huston, *American and British Debate*, 33–36. Huston comments pointedly on the "unspoken understanding" in the eighteenth century "that the idea of equality applied to people in a homogeneous ethnic community, of one type of people in each nation-state" (35).

CHAPTER SEVEN: LEVELING

1. Hector Fleischman, *La guillotine en 1792 d'après des documents inédits des Archives nationales* (Paris: Publications Modernes, 1908), 223; Guillaume Debat, "La Guillotine révolutionnaire: De l'incarnation de l'humanisme pénal à une machine effroyable (1789–1794)," *Annales historiques de la révolution française* 402, no. 4 (October 2020): 33–57; Albert Soboul, *Les sans-culottes parisiens dans l'an II: Mouvement populaire et gouvernement révolutionnaire* (Paris: Librerie Clavreuil, 1958), 578–579.

2. Cited in Fleischman, *La guillotine en 1792*, 223.

3. *Sans-culottes* ditty in Michel Vovelle, *La mentalité révolutionnaire: Société et mentalités sous la Révolution française* (Paris: Éditions Sociales, 1985), 128; Charles-Frédéric Reinhard, *Le néologiste français, ou vocabulaire portatif des mots les plus nouveaux de la langue française* (Nurnberg, 1796); Max Frey, *Les transformations du vocacbulaire français a la époque de la révolution (1789–1800)* (Paris: Presses Universitaires de France, 1923).

4. James A. Leith, "Symbols in the French Revolution: The Strange Metamorphoses of the Triangle," in *Symbols in Life and Art*, ed. James A. Leith (Montreal: McGill-Queen's University Press, 1987), 105–118; Claudia Hattendorff, "Gleicheit," in *Lexikon der Revolutions-Ikonographie in der europäischen Druckgraphick (1789–1889)*, ed. Rolf Reichardt (Münster: Rhema, 2017), 1001–1016; Jeffrey Revel, "Plus de rois, de dames, de valets: Playing Cards During the French Revolution," unpublished manuscript kindly shared with the author.

5. Edmund Burke, *Reflections on the Revolution in France*, ed. Frank M. Turner (New Haven, CT: Yale University Press, 2003), 42. On equality in Burke, see Richard Bourke, *Empire and Revolution: The Political Life of Edmund Burke* (Princeton, NJ: Princeton University Press, 2015), 700–708.

6. Declaration as translated in Lynn Hunt, *The French Revolution and Human Rights: A Brief Documentary History* (Boston: Bedford / St. Martin's Press, 1996), 77–79.

7. Keith Michael Baker, "The Idea of a Declaration of Rights," in *The French Idea of Freedom: The Old Regime and the Declaration of Rights of 1789*, ed. Dale Van Kley (Stanford, CA: Stanford University Press, 1994), 154–199; Price cited in J. C. D. Clark, "How Did the American Revolution Relate to the French? Richard Price, the Age of Revolutions, and the Enlightenment," *Modern Intellectual History* 19, no. 1 (March 2022): 105–127.

8. *Archives parlementaires, Prémière serie (1789–1799)*, vol. 9, *Du 16 septembre au 11 novembre 1789*, ed. M. J. Mavidal (Paris: Librairie Administrative de Paul Dupont, 1877), 393 (October 9, 1789). On dignity and "leveling up," see Jeremy Waldron, *Dignity, Rank, and Rights*, ed. and intro. Meier Dan-Cohen (Oxford: Oxford University Press, 2012), 30–36.

9. Lynn Hunt, *The Family Romance of the French Revolution* (Berkeley: University of California Press, 1992), 41; Suzanne Desan, *The Family on Trial in Revolutionary France* (Berkeley: University of California Press, 2006), esp. 141–178; Lameth cited in Richard Popkin, *A New World Begins: The History of the French Revolution* (New York: Basic Books, 2019), 213.

10. *Révolutions de Paris*, no. 1 (July 12, 1789): 1.

11. Emmanuel Joseph Sieyès, *What Is the Third Estate?*, in *Political Writings*, trans., ed., and intro. Michael Sonenscher (Indianapolis: Hackett, 2003), 162, 124; Sieyès, *Essay on the Privileges* in *Political Writings*, 76.

12. Sieyès, *What Is the Third Estate?*, 107. On Sieyès's bizarre proposal to breed a new race of men, see William H. Sewell Jr., *A Rhetoric of Bourgeois Revolution:*

The Abbé Sieyès and What Is the Third Estate? (Durham, NC: Duke University Press, 1994), 153–158; Laurent Dubois, *A Colony of Citizens: Revolution and Slave Emancipation in the French Caribbean, 1787–1804* (Chapel Hill: University of North Carolina Press, 2004), 173–176; and most fully, William Nelson, *Enlightenment Biopolitics* (Chicago: University of Chicago Press, forthcoming), esp. ch. 5 ("New Citizens, New Slaves"), which I cite at the paragraph's end.

13. Sieyès, *What Is the Third Estate?*, 107; Popkin, *New World Begins*, 187.

14. Nelson, *Enlightenment Biopolitics*, ch. 5.

15. Sieyès, *What Is the Third Estate?*, 128; Mona Ozouf, "Equality," in *A Critical Dictionary of the French Revolution*, trans. Arthur Goldhammer, ed. François Furet and Mona Ozouf (Cambridge, MA: Belknap Press of Harvard University Press, 1989), 671.

16. Michel-Rolf Trouillot, *Silencing the Past: Power and the Production of History* (Boston: Beacon Press, 1995), 76, and, more generally, Anne Phillips, *Unconditional Equals: Why Equality Cannot Be Conditional on a Shared Human "Nature" but Has to Be for All* (Princeton, NJ: Princeton University Press, 2021).

17. Karen Offen, *European Feminisms, 1700–1950* (Stanford, CA: Stanford University Press, 2000), 31–35; Siep Stuurman, *François Poulain de la Barre and the Invention of Modern Equality* (Cambridge, MA: Harvard University Press, 2004).

18. Londa Schiebinger, "Skeletons in the Closet: The First Illustrations of the Female Skeletons in Eighteenth-Century Anatomy," *Representations* 14 (1986): 42; Londa Schiebinger, *The Mind Has No Sex? Women in the Origins of Modern Science* (Cambridge, MA: Harvard University Press, 1989); Thomas Laqueur, *Making Sex: Body and Gender from the Greeks to Freud* (Cambridge, MA: Harvard University Press, 1992); Siep Stuurman, *The Invention of Humanity: Equality and Cultural Difference in World History* (Cambridge, MA: Harvard University Press, 2017), esp. ch. 6; Geneviève Fraisse, *Reasons's Muse: Sexual Difference and the Birth of Democracy*, trans. Jane Marie Todd (Chicago: University of Chicago Press, 1994); Anne C. Vila, *Enlightenment and Pathology: Sensibility in the Literature and Medicine of Eighteenth-Century France* (Baltimore: Johns Hopkins University Press, 1998); Nelson, *Enlightenment Biopolitics*, ch. 4.

19. Stuurman, *François Poulain de la Barre*, 286–289; Helena Rosenblatt, "On the 'Misogyny' of Jean-Jacques Rousseau: The Letter to D'Alembert in Historical Context," *French Historical Studies* 25, no. 1 (Winter 2002): 91–114; Joan B. Landes, *Women and the Public Sphere in the Age of the French Revolution* (Ithaca, NY: Cornell University Press, 1988); Joan Wallach Scott, *Only Paradoxes to Offer: French Feminists and the Rights of Man* (Cambridge, MA: Harvard University Press, 1996); Hunt, *Family Romance*, 53–89.

20. Nelson, *Enlightenment Biopolitics*, ch. 4.

21. Condorcet, "Sur l'admission des femmes au droit de cité," *Journal de la Société de 1789* 5 (July 3, 1790): 1–12 (esp. 3).

22. See, for example, Shanti Marie Singham, "Betwixt Cattle and Men: Jews, Blacks, and Women, and the Declaration of Rights," in Kley, *The French Idea of Freedom*, esp. 138–150; Darline Gay Levy and Harriet B. Applewhite, "A Political Revolution for Women? The Case of Paris," in *Becoming Visible: Women in European History*, 3rd ed., ed. Renate Bridenthal, Susan Mosher Stuard, and Mary E. Wiesner (Boston: Houghton Mifflin, 1998), 265–295; and Carla Hesse, *The Other Enlightenment: How French Women Became Modern* (Princeton, NJ: Princeton University Press, 1993).

23. Jodin cited in Stuurman, *Invention of Humanity*, 363; Singham, "Betwixt Cattle and Men," 146; Olympe de Gouges, "Declaration of the Rights of Women," in Hunt, *The French Revolution and Human Rights*, 124–129. On de Gouges, see Scott, "The Uses of Imagination: Olympe de Gouges in the French Revolution," in *Only Paradoxes*, 19–57.

24. Lynn Hunt, *Inventing Human Rights: A History* (New York: W. W. Norton, 2007), 169. On the backlash in France and then throughout Europe, see Offen, *European Feminisms*, 66–76; Carole Pateman, *The Sexual Contract*, 30th anniv. ed. (Stanford, CA: Stanford University Press, 1988).

25. Sue Peabody, *"There Are No Slaves in France": The Political Culture of Race and Slavery in the Ancien Régime* (New York: Oxford University Press, 1996), 4; Pierre H. Boulle, *Race et esclavage dans la France de l'Ancien Régime* (Paris: Perrin, 2007), 109; Érick Noël, *Être noir en France au XVIIIᵉ siècle* (Paris: Tallandier, 2006).

26. Nelson, *Enlightenment Biopolitics*, ch. 3; Trouillot, *Silencing the Past*, 76; Devin J. Vartija, *The Color of Equality: Race and Common Humanity in Enlightenment Thought* (Philadelphia: University of Pennsylvania Press, 2021), 198–199; Andrew S. Curran, *The Anatomy of Blackness: Science and Slavery in an Age of Enlightenment* (Baltimore: Johns Hopkins University Press, 2011), esp. chs. 2–3; Henry Louis Gates Jr. and Andrew S. Curran, *Who's Black and Why? A Hidden Chapter in the Eighteenth-Century Invention of Race* (Cambridge, MA: Belknap Press of Harvard University Press, 2022), 3–46; Stuurman, *Invention of Humanity*, 301–345.

27. Condorcet, *Reflections on Negro Slavery* (1781), in Hunt, *French Revolution and Human Rights*, 55–57, though compare the discussion of Condorcet's "blind spots" in Dubois, *Colony of Citizens*, 177–183. On the contestation of racial and imperial claims, see Vartija, *Color of Equality*, 206–213; Antoine Lilti, *L'heritage des lumières: Ambivalences de la modernité* (Paris: Seuil, 2019), esp. pt. 1; and Sankar Muthu, *Enlightenment Against Empire* (Princeton, NJ: Princeton University Press, 2003).

28. Trouillot, *Silencing the Past*, ch. 3 ("An Unthinkable History: The Haitian Revolution as a Non-Event").

29. C. L. R. James, *The Black Jacobins: Toussaint L'Ouverture and the San Domingo Revolution* (New York: Vintage, 1989 [1963]); Louverture cited in Madison Smart Bell, *Toussaint Louverture: A Biography* (New York: Vintage, 2007), 18.

30. Jeremy D. Popkin, *A Concise History of the Haitian Revolution* (Hoboken, NJ: Wiley-Blackwell, 2012), 66–67. On Dumas's extraordinary story, see Tom Reiss, *The Black Count: Glory, Revolution, Betrayal, and the Real Count of Monte Cristo* (New York: Crown, 2012).

31. Louverture cited in Laurent Dubois, *Avengers of the New World: The Story of the Haitian Revolution* (Cambridge, MA: Belknap Press of Harvard University Press, 2004), 190.

32. Susan Buck-Morss, "Hegel and Haiti," *Critical Inquiry* 26, no. 4 (Summer 2000): 821–865; Dubois, *Avengers of the New World*, 3–7; Dubois, *Colony of Citizens*, 3–8; Robin Blackburn, *American Crucible: Slavery, Emancipation, and Human Rights* (New York: Verso, 2011), 203; Nick Nesbit, *Universal Emancipation and the Radical Enlightenment* (Charlottesville: University of Virginia, 2008). On "inner logic," see Hunt, *Inventing Human Rights*, 150.

33. Samuel Moyn, "On the Nonglobalization of Ideas," in *Global Intellectual History*, ed. Samuel Moyn and Andrew Sartori (New York: Columbia University Press, 2013), 187–204; Adom Getachew, "Universalism After the Post-Colonial Turn," *Political Theory* 44, no. 6 (2016): 821–845.

34. Louis Boisrond Tonnerre, "The Declaration of Independence, 1 January, 1804," in *The Haitian Revolution: A Documentary History*, trans., ed., and intro. David Geggus (Indianapolis: Hackett, 2014), 179–180.

35. Blackburn, *American Crucible*, 198–200.

36. Philippe Girard, "Rebelles with a Cause: Women in the Haitian War of Independence, 1802–1804," *Gender and History* 21, no. 1 (2009): 60–85; David Geggus, "The Caribbean in the Age of Revolution," in *The Age of Revolutions in Global Context, c. 1760–1840*, ed. David Armitage and Sanjay Subrahmanyam (New York: Palgrave-Macmillan, 2010), 97. See also David Armitage and Julia Gaffield, "Introduction: The Haitian Declaration of Independence in an Atlantic Context," in *The Haitian Declaration of Independence*, ed. Julia Gaffield (Charlottesville: University of Virginia Press, 2016), 9.

37. On the strange fortunes of Victor Hugues, see Miranda Spieler, *Empire and Underworld: Captivity in French Guiana* (Cambridge, MA: Harvard University Press, 2012), 76–80.

38. Trouillot, *Silencing the Past*, 95–107; Brandon Byrd, *The Black Republic: African Americans and the Fate of Haiti* (Philadelphia: University of Pennsylvania Press, 2021).

39. Condorcet, *Esquisse d'un tableau historique des progrès de l'esprit humain*, intro. Alain Pons (Paris: Flammarion, 1988), 265–266, 272 (tenth époque); Alexis de Tocqueville, *Democracy in America*, trans. Arthur Goldhammer (New York: Library Classics, 2004), 6; Darrin M. McMahon, "Equality and the Horizon of Human Expectations," *Global Intellectual History* (April 2022): 1–23.

40. On "fecundity," Ozouf, "Equality," 674; on "cascade," Hunt, *Inventing Human Rights*, 147; on "in-built potential," Moyn, "On the Nonglobalization of Ideas," 190.

41. Thomas Piketty, *A Brief History of Equality*, trans. Steven Rendall (Cambridge, MA: Harvard University Press, 2022), 1–2, 10, 18.

42. Montesquieu, *The Spirit of the Laws* (Book 4, chs. 2–3), in *Selected Political Writings*, trans. and ed. Melvin Richter (Indianapolis: Hackett, 1990), 140 (italics mine).

43. On the sentimental revolution, see William R. Reddy, *The Navigation of Feeling: A Framework for the History of Emotions* (Cambridge: Cambridge University Press, 2001). On its connections to equality in the eighteenth century, see Hunt, *Inventing Human Rights*, 35–70; and Vartija, *Color of Equality*, 6, 150, 196–197.

44. Lynn Hunt, "The World We Have Gained: The Future of the French Revolution," *American Historical Review* 108, no. 1 (February 2003): 1–19.

45. Ibid.

46. On the problem of persuasion in Rousseau, see Bryan Garsten, "Persuading Without Convincing: Rousseau," in *Saving Persuasion* (Cambridge, MA: Harvard University Press, 2009), 55–83; Emma Planinc, "The Figurative Foundations of Rousseau's Politics," *Modern Intellectual History* 20, no. 1 (March 2023): 1–26; Jean-Jacques Rousseau, *Social Contract*, in *The Basic Political Writings*, trans. and ed. Donald A. Cress, intro. Peter Gay (Indianapolis: Hackett, 1987), 226 (Book 4, ch. 8).

47. Peter McPhee, *Liberty or Death: The French Revolution* (New Haven, CT: Yale University Press, 2016), 239.

48. Mona Ozouf, *Festivals in the French Revolution*, trans. Alan Sheridan (Cambridge, MA: Harvard University Press, 1988), 262–278.

49. Pierre Louis Roederer, *The Spirit of the Revolution of 1789*, trans. and ed. Murray Forsyth (Aldershot: Scolar Press, 1989), 5; Jacques Necker, *Réflexions philosophiques sur l'égalité*, intro. Jean-Fabien Spitz (Paris: Les Belles Lettres, 2005), 32; François Furet, *Interpreting the French Revolution*, trans. Elborg Foster (Cambridge: Cambridge University Press, 1981), 53.

50. Rabaut cited in Pierre Rosanvallon, *The Society of Equals*, trans. Arthur Goldhammer (Cambridge, MA: Harvard University Press, 2013), 55.

51. Steven C. Bullock, *Revolutionary Brotherhood: Freemasonry and the Transformation of the American Social Order, 1730–1840* (Chapel Hill: University of North Carolina Press, 1996), 5.

52. Rosanvallon, *Society of Equals*, 49–52; Ozouf, "Equality," 673; Charles Walton, "Who Pays? Social Rights and the French Revolution," in *Social Rights and the Politics of Obligation in History*, ed. Steven J.B. Jensen and Charles Walton (Cambridge: Cambridge University Press, 2022), 63–82. On Jacobin social reforms and their limits, see Jean-Pierre Gross, *Fair Shares for All: Jacobin Egalitarianism in Practice* (Cambridge: Cambridge University Press, 1997). On the decline in wealth inequality, see Thomas Piketty, *Capital in the Twenty-First Century*, trans. Arthur Goldhammer

(Cambridge, MA: Belknap Press of Harvard University Press, 2014), 341–342.

53. Samuel Moyn, *Not Enough: Human Rights in an Unequal World* (Cambridge, MA: Harvard University Press, 2018), 12–41; Lisa Dicaprio, *The Origins of the Welfare State: Women, Work, and the French Revolution* (Champaign: University of Illinois Press, 2022). Compare Samuel Fleischacker, *A Short History of Distributive Justice* (Cambridge, MA: Harvard University Press, 2004), 53–79.

54. On "disgraceful opulence," see Eric Hazan, *A People's History of the French Revolution*, trans. David Fernbach (London: Verso, 2014), 366–367. On the law of March 18, 1793, see Gross, *Fair Shares for All*, 93–94. See also Rousseau, *Social Contract*, 170 (Book 2, ch. 11), and Robespierre cited in Gross, *Fair Shares for All*, 39. On property rights more generally, see Rafe Blaufarb, *The Great Demarcation: The French Revolution and the Invention of Modern Property* (New York: Oxford University Press, 2016).

55. Gilbert Romme, "Report on the Republican Era" (September 20, 1793), in *The Old Regime and the French Revolution*, trans. and ed. Keith Michael Baker (Chicago: University of Chicago Press, 1987), 362–365.

56. Joseph-Marie Lequinio, *Des fêtes nationales* (Paris: Imprimerie nationale, n.d. [an 2]), 10, 28–29; Hunt, *Family Romance*, 69–71.

57. Lequinio, *Des fêtes nationales*, 10–11; Ozouf, *Festivals in the French Revolution*, x–xi, 135 (zealous patriot and city government). See also Ozouf, "Equality," 680.

58. Ozouf, *Festivals in the French Revolution*, 60.

59. Richard Cobb, "The Revolutionary Mentality in France," in *The French and Their Revolution: Selected Writings*, ed. and intro. David Gilmour (New York: New Press, 1998), 12.

60. Lynn Hunt, "Freedom of Dress in Revolutionary France," in *From the Royal to the Republican Body: Incorporating the Political in Seventeenth- and Eighteenth-Century France*, ed. Sara E. Melzer and Kathryn Norberg (Berkeley: University of California Press, 1998), 224–25; Richard Wrigley, *The Politics of Appearances: Representations of Dress in Revolutionary France* (Oxford: Berg, 2002). "Eternal principles" cited in Robert Darnton, "What Was Revolutionary About the French Revolution?," *New York Review of Books*, January 19, 1989. Petition cited in McPhee, *Liberty or Death*, 238.

61. Roger de Figuères, *Les noms révolutionnaires des communes de France: Listes par départements et liste générale alphabétique* (Paris, 1901).

62. Jean Mettas, *Répertoire des expeditions négrières françaises au dix-huitième siècle*, ed. Serge Daget, 2 vols. (Paris: Société française d'histoire d'outre-mer, 1978), 1:792–793. I am grateful to Miranda Spieler for pointing me to this reference.

63. Pierre-Henri-Billy, "Des prénoms révolutionnaires en France," *Annales historiques de la Révolution française*, no. 322 (October/December 2000): 39–60.

64. Festival station cited in Dan Edelstein, *The Terror of Natural Right: Republicanism, the Cult of Nature, and the French Revolution* (Chicago: University of Chicago Press, 2009), 181.

65. Furet, *Interpreting the French Revolution*, 55.

66. Randy Larsen and David M. Buss, *Personality Psychology: Domains of Knowledge About Human Nature*, 6th ed. (New York: McGraw Hill, 2017), 199.

67. Montesquieu, *Spirit of the Laws* (Book 5, ch. 5, and Book 8, ch. 3), 142, 163. On the "Atlantic Thermidor," see René Koekkoek, *The Citizenship Experiment: Contesting the Limits of Civic Equality and Participation in the Age of Revolutions* (Leiden: Brill, 2011), esp. 14–24. See also François Antoine de Boissy, *Projet de constitution pour la République français, et discours préliminaire* (Paris: Imprimerie de la Republique, Messidor, an 3 [1795]), 27; Tocqueville, *Democracy in America*, 818 (vol. 2, pt. 4, chs. 6–7); and Rousseau, *Social Contract*, 170 (Book 2, ch. 11).

68. Boissy, *Projet de constitution*, 27.

69. Denis Diderot, *Political Writings*, trans. and ed. J. H. Mason and R. Wokler (Cambridge: Cambridge University Press, 1992), 197–198; Voltaire, "Fertilisation" in the *Questions sur l'Encyclopédie* (1772), *Oeuvres completes de Voltaire* (Lyon: Chez Delamollière, 1792), 58:23. In the better-known article "Égalité" in the *Dictionnaire philosophique* (1764), Voltaire describes equality as "at once the most natural and the most chimerical of things." See also Rousseau, *Social Contract*, 170–171 (Book 2, ch. 11). I have amended Cress's English translation here from "speculative fiction" to "speculative chimera" to better reflect Rousseau's original (*chimère de speculation*).

CHAPTER EIGHT: ILLUSION

1. Philippe Buonarroti, *Conspiration pour l'égalité dite de Babeuf: Suivie du procès auquel elle donna lieu, et des pièces justificatives, etc.*, 2 vols. (Brussels: Librairie romantique, 1828), 1:9; Elizabeth L. Eisenstein, *The First Professional Revolutionist: Filippo Michele Buonarroti, 1761–1837* (Cambridge, MA: Harvard University Press, 1959); Libero Federici, *L'Egualitarismo di Filippo Buonarroti* (Saonara: Il prato, 2006).

2. All citations from the *Manifesto of the Equals* are taken from the translation of Mitchel Abidor, available at Marxists Internet Archive, www.marxists.org/history/france/revolution/conspiracy-equals/1796/manifesto.htm (italics in original). On the conspiracy itself, and the long public trial held in its wake, see Laura Mason, *The Last Revolutionaries: The Conspiracy Trial of Gracchus Babeuf and the Equals* (New Haven, CT: Yale University Press, 2022).

3. Karl Marx and Friedrich Engels, *The Holy Family: Critique of Critical Critique* (Moscow: Foreign Languages Publishing House, 1956), 161.

4. Pierre Leroux, *De l'égalité, nouvelle édition* (Boussac: Imprimerie Pierre Leroux, 1848 [1838]), 1.

5. Martin Malia, *The Soviet Tragedy: A History of Socialism in Russia, 1917–1991* (New York: Free Press, 1994), 34.

6. Tony Wright, *Socialisms Old and New* (London: Routledge, 1996), 31 (italics in original); Gareth Stedman Jones, "European Socialism from the 1790s to the 1890s," in *The Cambridge History of Modern Thought*, vol. 1, *The Nineteenth Century*, ed. Warren Breckman and Peter E. Gordon (Cambridge: Cambridge University Press, 2019), 199; Frank E. Manuel, "From Equality to Organicism," *Journal of the History of Ideas* 17, no. 1 (January 1956): 54–69; Gregory Claeys, "Early Socialism as Intellectual History," *History of European Ideas* 40, no. 7 (2014): 898.

7. Saint-Simon, *Lettres d'un habitant de Génève à ses contemporains* (1803), 68–69, accessed at Gallica, https://gallica.bnf.fr/ark:/12148/bpt6k833303/f104.item.

8. Ibid., 32.

9. Claire G. Moses, "Saint-Simonian Men / Saint-Simonian Women: The Transformation of Feminist Thought in 1830s France," *Journal of Modern History* 54, no. 2 (June 1982): 240–267. See, more generally, Naomi J. Andrews, "The Women Question: Liberal and Socialist Critiques of the Status of Women," in Breckman and Gordon, *Cambridge History of Modern Thought*, 1:255–278.

10. *Doctrine de Saint-Simon: Exposition. Première Année, 1828–1829*, 2nd ed. (Paris: Bureau de l'Organisateur et du Globe, 1830), 38, 41 (published anonymously, but attributed to Émile Barrault in Bibliothèque nationale de France catalog; actually P. Enfantin Bazard, H. Carnot, Olinde Rodrigues, Henri Fournel, and Charles Duveyrier, per Stanford Libraries Catalog, https://searchworks.stanford.edu/view/4536410). The fascinating history of this phrase and its aftermath is traced in Luc Bovens and Adrien Lutz, "'From Each According to Ability; To Each According to Needs': The Origin, Meaning, and Development of Socialist Slogans," *GATE WP 1839–December 2018* (January 8, 2019), available at http://dx.doi.org/10.2139/ssrn.3312190.

11. *Doctrine de Saint-Simon*, 237, 55; Marie-France Piguet, "*Egalité* dans le discours post-révolutionnaire: Montloisier et Saint-Simon," *Mots: Les langages du politique* 69 (2002), available at: http://journals.openedition.org/mots/10653; Auguste Comte, *Cours de philosophie positive (1830–1842)* (Book 6, ch. 1), in *Auguste Comte and Positivism: The Essential Writings*, ed. and intro. Gertrude Lenzer (Chicago: University of Chicago Press, 1975), 206.

12. Fourier on illusions, cited in Jonathan Beecher, *Charles Fourier: The Visionary and His World* (Berkeley: University of California Press, 1986), 32; Charles Fourier, *The Theory of Four Movements*, ed. Gareth Stedman Jones and Ian Patterson (Cambridge: Cambridge University Press, 1996), 6, 277.

13. Fourier, "political poison," cited in Beecher, *Charles Fourier*, 247. "Social poison" cited in Stedman Jones, "Introduction," *Theory of Four Movements*, xx. See also Fourier, *Le Nouveau monde industriel et sociétaire, ou invention du procédé d'industrie attrayante et naturellement distribués en séries passionnées* (Paris: Bossange Père, 1829), 71. On LSD, see Albert S. Lindemann, *A History of European Socialism* (New Haven, CT: Yale University Press, 1983), 38.

14. Fourier, "Harmonie universelle," *Bulletin de Lyon*, 11 frimaire an XII (December 3, 1803), cited in Beecher, *Fourier*, 104–105; Fourier, *Theory of Four Movements*, 87.

15. Karl Marx, *The German Ideology: Part I*, in *The Marx-Engels-Reader*, 2nd ed., ed. Robert C. Tucker (New York: W. W. Norton, 1978), 160.

16. Robert Owen, "Address Delivered by Robert Owen, of New Lanark, on 27 April 1825," in *Selected Works of Robert Owen*, ed. Gregory Claeys, 4 vols. (London: William Pickering, 1993), 2:40–41, 46.

17. Robert Owen, *Book of the New Moral World: First Part* (1842), in *Selected Works*, 3:39–40; Owen, "To the Men and Women of France" (1846), in *Selected Works*, 2:426. On the inequality of age and experience, see "A Development of the Principles and Plans on Which to Establish Self-Supporting Home Colonies" (1841), in *Selected Works*, 2:347, as well as the "General Recapitulation" of the *Book of the New Moral World*.

18. Owen, "The Social System (1826)," in *Selected Works*, 2:85; Owen, "A Development of the Principles and Plans on Which to Establish Self-Supporting Home Colonies" (1841), *Selected Works*, 2:377.

19. Owen, "The New Religion" (1830), in *Selected Works*, 2:182; Owen, "Recapitulation" and "General Recapitulation," at the end of the seventh part of the *Book of the New Moral World* (1844), in *Selected Works* 3:405–409.

20. Nancy L. Green, "Socialist Anti-Semitism, Defense of a Bourgeois Jew and Discovery of the Jewish Proletariat: Changing Attitudes of French Socialists Before 1914," *International Review of Social History* 30, no. 3 (1985): 374–399.

21. Here I follow Gareth Stedman Jones, "Religion and the Origins of Socialism," in *Religion and the Political Imagination*, ed. Ira Katznelson and Gareth Stedman Jones (Cambridge: Cambridge University Press, 2010), 171–189.

22. Ibid., 175; Henri de Saint-Simon, *Nouveau Christianisme, dialogue entre un conservateur et un novateur* (Paris: Bossange Père, 1825); Fourier cited in Stedman Jones, "Religion and the Origins of Socialism," 176; Considérant cited in Edward Berenson, *Populist Religion and Left-Wing Politics in France, 1830–1852* (Princeton, NJ: Princeton University Press, 1984), 40.

23. "A Chartist Funeral Service in Derby" (1841), in *Chartism and Society: An Anthology of Sources*, ed. F. C. Mather (New York: Holmes and Meier, 1980), 301; Wilhelm Weitling, *Das Evangelium eines armen Sünders*

(Bern: Verlag von Jenni, Sohn, 1845); Buchez cited in Berenson, *Populist Religion*, 43.

24. Pierre Leroux, *Du Christianisme et de son origine démocratique* (Paris: Imprimerie de Pierre Leroux, 1848). The work was a reprint of articles Leroux had written in 1837. See Jack Bakunin, "Pierre Leroux: A Democratic Religion for a New World," *Church History* 44, no. 1 (March 1975): 59n15; Leroux, *De l'égalité*, 122.

25. Buchez cited in Berenson, *Populist Religion*, 43. On Blanc's religious views, see Berenson, *Populist Religion*, 43–45. On the theme of competition, see Pierre Rosanvallon, *The Society of Equals*, trans. Arthur Goldhammer (Cambridge, MA: Harvard University Press, 2013), 113–114.

26. Étienne Cabet, *Le vrai Christianisme suivant Jésus-Christ* (Paris: Bureau de Populaire, 1846), 47, 51, 165–167, 619–624. See, esp., ch. 3, sec. 30 ("Égalité"); ch. 3, sec. 31 ("Égalité des salaires"); and ch. 18 ("Le communisme c'est le Christianisme").

27. Étienne Cabet, *Voyage en Icarie* (Paris: Bureau de Populaire, 1848), 215.

28. Ibid., i–iii; Louis Blanc, *Le catéchisme des socialistes* (Paris: Bureau de Nouveau Monde, 1849).

29. Bovens and Lutz, "From Each According to Ability," 5–6. See also Boven's reflections in " 'From Each According to Ability; To Each According to Need'—Tracing the Biblical Roots of Socialism's Enduring Slogan," *The Conversation*, September 4, 2020, https://theconversation.com/from-each-according-to-ability-to-each-according-to-need-tracing-the-biblical-roots-of-socialisms-enduring-slogan-138365; Louis Blanc, *L'Organisation du travail: Neuvième édition refondue et augmentée de Chapitres Nouveaux* (Paris: Bureau du Nouveau Monde, 1850), 72 (capital letters in the original).

30. Louis Blanc, *Organization of Work*, trans. and ed. Marie Paula Dickoré (Cincinnati: University of Cincinnati Press, 1911 [1839]), 59.

31. See the discussion in Rosanvallon, *Society of Equals*, 114–115.

32. Cabet, *Vrai Christianisme*, 170–175.

33. Friedrich Engels, "Progress of Social Reform on the Continent," *New Moral World* 19, 3rd series, November 4, 1843. English original.

34. Pierre-Joseph Proudhon, *What Is Property?*, ed. Donald R. Kelley and Bonnie G. Smith (Cambridge: Cambridge University Press, 1993), 197.

35. Cabet, *Voyage en Icarie*, i–ii, 420 (italics in original). The historical *coup d'oeuil*, the "Tableau historique des progress de la démocatie et de l'égalité," is provided in Part 2, chs. 9–10, 407–464.

36. Leroux, *De l'égalité*, 11.

37. Cabet, *Voyage en Icarie*, 463; Alexis de Tocqueville, *Democracy in America*, trans. Arthur Goldhammer (New York: Library Classics, 2004), 6. On European, chiefly British, reactions to American equality, see James L. Huston, *The American and British Debate over Equality, 1776–1920* (Baton Rouge: Louisiana State University Press, 2017).

38. Harriet Martineau, *Society in America*, 2 vols. (New York: Saunders and Otley, 1837), 1:154; Harriet Taylor, "The Enfranchisement of Women," *Westminster Review* (1851), in *The Complete Works of Harriet Taylor Mill*, ed. Jo Ellen Jacobs and Paula Harms Payne (Bloomington: Indiana University Press, 1998), 51.

39. Holly Case, *The Age of Questions: Or, a First Attempt at an Aggregate History of the Eastern, Social, Woman, American, Jewish, Polish, Bullion, Tuberculosis, and Many Other Questions over the Nineteenth Century, and Beyond* (Princeton, NJ: Princeton University Press, 2018); Leslie Butler, *Consistent Democracy: Self-Government and the "Woman Question" in Nineteenth-Century America* (New York: Oxford University Press, 2023); Stephen W. Sawyer, *Demos Assembled: Democracy and the International Origins of the Modern State, 1840–1880* (Chicago: University of Chicago Press, 2018).

40. Friedrich Engels and Karl Marx, *Manifesto of the Communist Party*, in *The Marx-Engels Reader*, 497–499.

41. Lindemann, *History of European Socialism*, 99–109.

42. Gareth Stedman Jones, "European Socialism," 186–187. The religious dimensions of Marxism and the Soviet experiment are developed at length in Yuri Slezkine, *The House of Government: A Saga of the Russian Revolution* (Princeton, NJ: Princeton University Press, 2017). See also Igal Halfin, *Terror in My Soul* (Cambridge, MA: Harvard University Press, 2003), esp. chs. 1–2; Andrei Znamenski, *Socialism as a Secular Creed: A Modern Global History* (Lanham, MD: Lexington Books, 2021).

43. Lenin, "Karl Marx: A Brief Biological Sketch with an Exposition of Marxism," at Marxists Internet Archive, www.marxists.org/archive/lenin/works/1914/granat/ch02.htm; Engels and Marx, *Communist Manifesto*, 497. Schapper's views as paraphrased by Gareth Stedman Jones, *Karl Marx: Greatness and Illusion* (Cambridge, MA: Belknap Press of Harvard University Press, 2016), 220. See also Marx, *German Ideology: Part I*, 197.

44. Allen W. Wood, "Marx on Equality," in *The Free Development of Each: Studies on Freedom, Right, and Ethics in Classical German Philosophy* (Oxford: Oxford University Press, 2014), 259–260. On Marx as an opponent of equality, see also Jacques Texier, "Marx, Penseur Egalitaire?," in *EGALITE/INEGALITE*, ed. Alberto Burgio, Domenico Losurdo, and Jacques Texier (Urbino: Quattro-Venti, 1989), 201–229; Michelle Barrett, "Marxist-Feminism and the Work of Karl Marx," in *Feminism and Equality*, ed. Anne Phillips (New York: New York University Press, 1987), 44–62; and Richard W. Miller, *Analyzing Marx: Morality, Power, and History* (Princeton, NJ: Princeton University Press, 1984), 19–45.

45. Tocqueville, *Democracy in America*, 649–652 (pt. 2, ch. 20, "How Industry Could Give Rise to an Aristocracy"). On Marx's concern with freedom as nondomination, see William Clare Roberts, *Marx's Inferno: The Political Theory of 'Capital'* (Princeton, NJ: Princeton University Press, 2017).

46. Peter H. Lindert and Jeffrey G. Williamson, *Unequal Gains: American Growth and Inequality Since 1700* (Princeton, NJ: Princeton University Press, 2016), 117. See, for example, Thomas Piketty, *Capital and Ideology*, trans. Arthur Goldhammer (Cambridge, MA: Belknap Press of Harvard University Press, 2020), esp. chs. 5–6.

47. Marx, "On the Jewish Question," in *The Marx-Engels Reader*, 42–43; Anatole France, *The Red Lily*, trans. Winifred Stephens (New York: Dodd-Mead, 1930), 91.

48. Marx, *Economic and Philosophic Manuscripts of 1844*, in *The Marx-Engels Reader*, 99.

49. Marx, *Capital: A Critique of Political Economy*, vol. 1, trans. Ben Fowkes, intro. Ernest Mandel (London: Penguin, 1990), 151–152. For Aristotle's discussion, see *Nicomachean Ethics*, 5.14. I draw here on the reading of Cornelius Castoriadis, "Valeur, égalité, justice, politique de Marx à Aristote et de Aristote à nous," in *Les carrefours de labyrinthe* (Paris: Seuil, 1978), 325–413.

50. On money as the "great leveler," see the discussion in Rosanvallon, *Society of Equals*, 67; Marx, *Capital*, 520, 151–152.

51. Karl Marx and Friedrich Engels, *Die deutsche Ideologie*, in *Werke*, vol. 3 (Berlin: Dietz Verlag), 39, 47, 158, 162; Marx, *Ökonomisch—Philosophische Manuskripten aus dem Jahre 1844*, "Drittes Manuskript," in *Ergänzungsband: Schriften, Manuskripte, Briefe Bis 1844* (Berlin: Dietz Verlag, 1968), 553.

52. Engels, *Anti-Dühring*, ch. 10 ("Morality and Law. Equality"), accessed at Marxists Internet Archive, www.marxists.org/archive/marx/works/1877/anti-duhring/ch08.htm.

53. Engels to August Bebel, March 18–28, 1875, accessed at Marxists Internet Archive, www.marxists.org/archive/marx/works/1875/letters/75_03_18.htm (italics in original).

54. "Das Gothaer Programm," point II, accessed at Marxists Internet Archive, www.marxists.org/deutsch/geschichte/deutsch/spd/1875/gotha.htm; Marx to Engels, July 30, 1862, available at Marxists Internet Archive, https://marxists.architexturez.net/archive/marx/works/1862/letters/62_07_30a.htm. Marx employed the phrases *Juden Itzig* and *jüdische Nigger* on numerous occasions. See Wulf D. Hund, "Der 'jüdische Nigger' Lassalle: Marginalie zu einem Brief von Karl Marx," *Sozial.Geschichte Online* 24 (2018): 103–130.

55. Marx, *Critique of the Gotha Program*, in *Marx-Engels Reader*, 530–531 (italics in original).

56. Ibid., 531.

57. Marx, *The Poverty of Philosophy* (ch. 2, sec. 1), trans. Institute of Marxism Leninism (Moscow: Progress Publisher, 1955), accessed at Marxists Internet Archive, www.marxists.org/archive/marx/works/1847/poverty-philosophy/ch02.htm (italics in original); Wood, "Marx on Equality," 262–265; Samuel Moyn, *Not Enough: Human Rights in an Unequal World* (Cambridge, MA: Belknap Press of Harvard University Press, 2018), 28.

58. On Soviet bloc compression, see Branko Milanovic, *The Haves and the Have Nots: A Brief and Idiosyncratic History of Global Inequality* (New York: Basic Books, 2011), 54–60; and see the insightful comments of Martin King Whyte, *Myth of the Social Volcano: Perceptions of Inequality and Distributive Injustice in Contemporary China* (Stanford, CA: Stanford University Press, 2010), 118–125.

59. Vladimir Ilich Lenin, *State and Revolution* (ch. 5, sec. 3), revised translation (New York: International Publishers, 1935 [1917]), 77; Lenin, "Deception of the People with Slogans of Freedom and Equality," speech delivered on May 19, 1919, in vol. 29 of *Collected Works*, 4th ed. (Moscow: Progress Publishers, 1972), 333–376, accessed at Marxists Internet Archive, www.marxists.org/archive/lenin/works/1919/may/06.htm (italics in original).

60. Remarks on "wage scales" from Stalin's speech "New Conditions—New Task in Economic Construction," delivered on June 23, 1931, cited and translated in S. Dobrin, "Lenin on Equality and the Webbs on Lenin," *Soviet Studies* 8, no. 4 (April 1957): 337–357 (esp. 342). See also Constitution of the USSR (1936), Article 1, ch. 12. For the context of the phrase, see Bovens and Lutz, "From Each According to Ability," 3–4; and Dobrin, "Lenin on Equality," 355–356.

61. Richard Stites, *Utopian Visions and Experimental Life in the Russian Revolution* (New York: Oxford University Press, 1989), 124.

62. Marx as "the denouncer of equality as illusion" is the characterization of Jacques Texier with reference to the work of François Furet (Texier, "Marx, Penseur Egalitaire?," 201). Furet makes the argument himself in his preface to Alexis de Tocqueville, *De la démocratie en Amérique* vol. 1 (Paris: Flammarion, 1981), 40–41. On equality as "psychological mainspring," see François Furet, *The Passing of an Illusion: The Idea of Communism in the Twentieth Century*, trans. Deborah Furet (Chicago: University of Chicago Press, 1999), 26. On equality as socialism's "core moral idea," see Malia, *Soviet Tragedy*, 516. See also Slezkine, *House of Government*, esp. ch. 2 ("The Faith").

63. I. Kryvelev, "Равенство," in *Bolsháya sovétskaya entsiklopédiya*, ed. Otto Yulyevich Schmidt, 1st ed., 67 vols. (Moscow: Sovetskaya Entsiklopediya, 1926–1947), 47:890–896. I am grateful to Professor Anton Matysik for translating this article for me from the Russian original, along with the substantially different unsigned article on equality from the second edition of 1949–1958.

CHAPTER NINE: DOMINATION

1. Salvatore Lupo, "Fasci italiani di combattimento," and Luca Scuccimarra, "Fascio littorio," in Victoria de Grazia and Sergio Luzzatto, *Dizionario del fascismo*, 2 vols. (Turin: Einaudi, 2002), 1:513–518; Simonetta Falasca-Zamponi, *Fascist Spectacle: The Aesthetics of Power in Mussolini's Italy* (Berkeley: University of California Press, 2000), 95–99.

2. See the prescient observations of A. James Gregor, "Introduction," in Giovanni Gentile, *Origins and Doctrine of Fascism*, trans. and ed. A. James Gregor (New Brunswick, NJ: Transaction, 2002), xii.

3. Benito Mussolini, *The Political and Social Doctrine of Fascism*, trans. Jane Soames (London: Hogarth Press, 1933), 14, 16; Adolf Hitler, *Mein Kampf*, trans. Alvin Saunders Johnson, ed. John Chamberlain (New York: Reynal and Hitchcock, 1940), 435.

4. See Darrin M. McMahon, *Enemies of the Enlightenment: The French Counter-Enlightenment and the Making of Modernity* (New York: Oxford, 2001), 41; Edmund Burke, *Reflections on the Revolution in France*, ed. Frank M. Turner (New Haven, CT: Yale University Press, 2003), 166; Sebastiano Ayala, *De la liberté et de l'égalité des hommes et des citoyens avec des considérations sur quelques nouveaux dogmes politiques* (Vienna: Alberti, 1792), ix; Christoph Meiners, *Ueber wahre, unzeitige, und falsche Aufklärung und deren Wirkungen* (Hanover: Helwingischen Hofbuchhandlung, 1794), 86.

5. Arthur de Gobineau, *The Inequality of Human Races*, intro. George L. Mosse (New York: Howard Fertig, 1999), 117, 154, 205. Compare Joseph Anténor Firmin, *De l'égalité des races humaines* (Paris: Cotillon, 1885). On the invention of the "Caucasian," see Bruce Baum, *The Rise and Fall of the Caucasian Race: A Political History of Racial Identity* (New York: New York University Press, 2006), esp. 58–117.

6. Jennifer Pitts, "Ideas of Empire: Civilization, Race, and Global Hierarchy," in *Cambridge History of Modern Thought*, vol. 1, ed. Warren Breckman and Peter E. Gordon (Cambridge: Cambridge University Press, 2019), 447–469. For the liberal context, see Jennifer Pitts, *A Turn to Empire: The Rise of Imperial Liberalism in Britain and France* (Princeton, NJ: Princeton University Press, 2005). See also Thomas Henry Huxley, "On the Natural Inequality of Men" (1890), in *Collected Essays*, vol. 1 (Cambridge: Cambridge University Press, 2011), 290–335.

7. Friedrich Nietzsche, *The Anti-Christ*, trans. H. L. Mencken (New York: Alfred A. Knopf, 1931), 122–123 (sec. 43); Friedrich Nietzsche, *The Gay Science*, aphorism 120, in *Complete Works of Friedrich Nietzsche*, vol. 1, trans. Thomas Common (London: T. N. Foulis, 1910), 163. See, more broadly, James Wilson, "Nietzsche and Equality," in *Nietzsche and Ethics*, ed. Gudrun von Tevenar (Oxford: Peter Lange, 2007), 221–240.

8. Gaetano Mosca, *The Ruling Class (Elementi di scienza politica)*, ed. Arthur Livingston, trans. Hannah D. Kahn (New York: McGraw Hill, 1939), 53; Robert Michels, *Political Parties: A Sociological Study of the Oligarchical Tendencies of Modern Democracy*, trans. Eden Paul and Cedar Paul, intro. Seymour Martin Lipset (New York: Free Press, 1962), esp. 342–357 ("Democracy and the Iron Law of Oligarchy").

9. Langbehn cited in George L. Mosse, *Masses and Man: Nationalist and Fascist Perceptions of Reality* (Detroit: Wayne State University Press, 1987), 206.

10. Udi Greenberg, "Revolution from the Right: Against Equality," in Breckman and Gordon, *Cambridge History of Modern Thought*, 233–258; Federico Finkelstein, "On Fascist Ideology," *Constellations* 15, no. 3 (2008/2009): 320.

11. Maurice Barrès, *Contre les étrangers: Etude pour la protection des ouvriers français* (Paris: Grande Imprimerie Francais, 1893), 13–14.

12. Pierre Rosanvallon, *Society of Equals*, trans. Arthur Goldhammer (Cambridge, MA: Harvard University Press, 2013), 143–149.

13. Carl Schmitt, *The Crisis of Parliamentary Democracy*, trans. Ellen Kennedy (Cambridge, MA: MIT Press, 1988), 8–9.

14. Ibid., 9–10.

15. Ibid.

16. Ibid., 9, 12–13; Chantal Mouffe, "Carl Schmitt and the Paradox of Liberal Democracy," in *The Challenge of Carl Schmitt*, ed. Chantal Mouffe (London: Verso, 1990), 38–53.

17. Schmitt, *Crisis of Parliamentary Democracy*, 7. On Prévost-Paradol and the question of equality, see Stephen W. Sawyer, *Demos Assembled: Democracy and the International Origins of the Modern State, 1840–1880* (Chicago: University of Chicago Press, 2018), 52–79. On America as a German "inspiration," see James Q. Whitman, *Hitler's American Model: The United States and Nazi Race Law* (Princeton, NJ: Princeton University Press, 2018).

18. Schmitt, *Crisis of Parliamentary Democracy*, 10.

19. Carl Schmitt, *Verfassungslehre* (Munich: Duncker and Humblot, 1928), 228–232, 234.

20. Carl Schmitt, *Staat, Bewegung, Volk* (Hamburg: Hanseatische Verlagsanstalt, 1933), 32, 42 (see, in general, pt. 4, "Führertum und Artgleichheit als Grundbegriffe des Nationalsozialistichen Rechts"); Werner Hill, *Gleichheit und Artgleichheit* (Berlin: Duncker and Humblot, 1966), 205–215; Diemut Majer, *"Non-Germans" Under the Third Reich: The Nazi Judicial and Administrative System in Germany and Occupied Eastern Europe, with Special Regard to Occupied Poland, 1939–1945* (Lubbock: Texas Tech University Press, 2014), esp. 35–49.

21. Schmitt, *Staat, Bewegung, Volk*, 42; Hill, *Gleichheit und Artgleichheit*, 264–272; Ville Suuronen, "Carl Schmitt as a Theorist of the 1933 Revolution: 'The Difficult Task of Rethinking and Recultivating Traditional Concepts,'" *Contemporary Political Theory* 20, no. 2 (2020): 341–363; Duncan Kelly, "Carl Schmitt's Theory of Representation," *Journal of the History of Ideas* 65, no. 1 (January 2014): 113–134.

22. Schmitt, *Staat, Bewegung, Volk*, 43; Hill, *Gleichheit und Artgleichheit*, 273–292.

23. Wilhelm Stuckart and Hans Globke, "Kommentare zur deutschen Rassengesetzgebung" (1936), excerpted and translated in *Nazi Culture: Intellectual, Cultural, and Social Life in the Third Reich*, ed. George L. Mosse (Madison:

University of Wisconsin Press, 2003), 328, 332. See also Gustav Adolf Walz, *Artgleichheit gegen Gleichartigkeit: Die beiden Grundprobleme des Rechts* (Hamburg: Hanseatische Verlagsanstalt, 1938).

24. On this variety of terms in the legal discourse, see Majer, *"Non-Germans" Under the Third Reich*, esp. 35–49.
25. Ibid., 36–49.
26. Ulrich Scheuner, "Der Gleichheitsgedanke in der Völkischen Verfassungsordnung," *Zeitschrift für die gesamte Staatswissenschaft* 99, no. 2 (1939): 272–276.
27. Ibid., 245–246.
28. Carl Schmitt, "Faschistische und nationalsozialistische Rechtswissenschaft," *Deutsche Juristen-Zeitung* 41 (May 1936): 619–620. See also the discussion in A. James Gregor, *Mussolini's Intellectuals: Fascist Social and Political Thought* (Princeton, NJ: Princeton University Press, 2005), 179–190. On race in Fascist Italy, see Olindo De Napoli, "The Origin of the Racist Laws Under Fascism: A Problem of Historiography," *Journal of Modern Italian Studies* 17, no. 1 (2012): 106–122.
29. Marinetti cited in Barbara Spackman, *Fascist Virilities: Rhetoric, Ideology, and Social Fantasy in Italy* (Minneapolis: University of Minnesota Press, 1996), 173n11.
30. Giuseppe Bottai, "Corporativismo e principi dell'ottantanove," in *Scritti* (Bologna: Cappelli Editore, 1965), 174–175.
31. Giovanni Gentile, *Che cosa è il fascismo: Discorsi e polemiche* (Firenze: Vallechi Editore, 1924), 133. Gentile quoted Spaventa's *La politica della Destra* (Bari: Laterza, 1910), edited by Benedetto Croce, Spaventa's foster child. See also Mussolini, *The Political and Social Doctrine of Fascism*, 19. On the complexities of the reckoning with the French Revolution in Fascist Italy, see Antonino de Francesco, *Mito e storiografia della "grande rivoluzione"* (Napoli: Alfredo Guida Editore, 2006). See also Bottai, "Corporativismo e principe dell'ottantanove," 175–176; Bottai, "La Rivoluzione francese e la Rivoluzione fascista," *Critica Fascista* 23, no. 8 (December 1, 1930): 441–445.
32. *Der illustrieter Beobachter*, May 1, 1935; George Mosse, "Fascism and the French Revolution," *Journal of Contemporary History* 24, no. 1 (January 1989): 5–26; Carlo Talarico, *Le due rivoluzioni: Dall'eguaglianza dinanzi alla legge all'eguglianza dinanzi al lavoro* (Milan: La Prora, 1939), 69–70.
33. Ibid., 70–72.
34. Ibid., v.
35. Merlino is cited, and his broad influence discussed, in David D. Roberts, *The Syndicalist Tradition and Italian Fascism* (Manchester: Manchester University Press, 1979), 60–63, 162–163. On Sorel, see Zeev Sternhell, *Neither Right nor Left: Fascist Ideology in France*, trans. David Maisel (Princeton, NJ: Princeton University Press, 1986), 66–77.
36. *Rerum novarum* (On Capital and Labor), encyclical of Pope Leo XIII, May 15, 1891, available at The Holy See, www.vatican.va/content/leo-xiii/en/

encyclicals/documents/hf_l-xiii_enc_15051891_rerum-novarum.html;
James Chappel, *Catholic Modern: The Challenge of Totalitarianism and
the Remaking of the Church* (Cambridge, MA: Harvard University Press,
2018), 59–108 (quotation on 79).

37. Talarico, *Le due rivoluzioni*, 235–239. On "true equality" (*vera eguaglianza*), see, for example, Giuseppe Chiarelli, *Lo stato corporativo* (Padua:
Cedam, 1936), 243.

38. Guido Bortolotto, *La dottrina del fascismo* (Milan: Editore Enrico Hoepli,
1939), 203, 313–314.

39. Roberts, *Syndicalist Tradition*, 132; Marcel Déat, *Pensée allemande et pensée
française* (Paris: Aux armes de France, 1944), 110–111.

40. Scheuner, "Der Gleichheitsgedanke," 246–247.

41. Richard J. Evans, *The Third Reich in Power* (New York: Penguin, 2005),
498–499.

42. Stanley G. Payne, *A History of Fascism, 1914–1945* (Madison: University
of Wisconsin Press, 1995), 13; Spackman, *Fascist Virilities*; Victoria de
Grazia, *How Fascism Ruled Women: Italy, 1922–1945* (Berkeley: University
of California Press, 1993); Jill Stevenson, *Women in Nazi Germany* (New
York: Longman, 2001); Kevin Passmore, ed., *Women, Gender, and Fascism
in Europe, 1919–1945* (Manchester: Manchester University Press, 2003).

43. Joseph Goebbels, "Deutsches Frauentum," March 18, 1933, and Adolf
Hitler, "Speech to the National Socialist Women's Organization,"
September 9, 1934, reproduced and translated in *The Third Reich Source-
book*, ed. Anson Rabinbach and Sander L. Gilman (Berkeley: University of
California Press, 2013), 316–319, 311–314.

44. A[ntonino] Pagliaro, "Eguaglianza," in *Dizionario di politica a cura del
Partito nazionale fascista*, 4 vols. (Rome: Istituto della Enciclopedia Ital-
iana, 1940), 2:42–44.

45. Wolfgang Schivelbusch, *Three New Deals: Reflections on Roosevelt's America,
Mussolini's Italy, and Hitler's Germany, 1933–1939* (New York: Picador,
2006). On the international resonance of the New Deal, see Kiran Klaus
Patel, *The New Deal: A Global History* (Princeton, NJ: Princeton University
Press, 2016).

46. Mussolini cited in Maria Sophia Quine, *Italy's Social Revolution: Charity
and Welfare from Liberalism to Fascism* (London: Palgrave, 2002), 100;
Jean-Guy Prévost, *A Total Science: Statistics in Liberal and Fascist Italy*
(Montreal: McGill-Queen's University Press, 2009), 208–220; Francesco
Cassata, *Il fascismo razionale: Corrado Gini fra scienza e politica* (Rome:
Carocci, 2006); Giacomo Gabbuti, "Between Pareto and Gini: The Origins
of Personal Inequality Measurement in Italy, 1894–1939," *History of Polit-
ical Economy* 52, no. 2 (2020): 535–554.

47. Hitler cited in Götz Aly, *Hitler's Beneficiaries: Plunder, Racial War, and
the Nazi Welfare State*, trans. Jefferson Chase (New York: Metropolitan, 2005), 30; David Schoenbaum, *Hitler's Social Revolution: Class and
Status in Nazi Germany, 1933–1939* (New York: W. W. Norton, 1980),

55. Compare the more modest assessment in Evans, *Third Reich in Power*, 477–503, and the criticism of Adam Tooze, "What Held Nazi Germany Together? The Aly-Tooze Debate Revisited," in *Adam Tooze* (blog), January 25, 2017, https://adamtooze.com/2017/01/25/ what-held-nazi-germany-together-the-aly-tooze-debate-revisited.

48. Evans, *Third Reich in Power*, 492; Samuel Moyn, *Not Enough: Human Rights in an Unequal World* (Cambridge, MA: Belknap Press of Harvard University Press, 2018), 37; Quine, *Italy's Social Revolution*, 108.

49. Quine, *Italy's Social Revolution*, 111, 296–302; Evans, *Third Reich in Power*, 499–500; María Gómez León and Giacomo Gabbuti, "The Other Halves of Fascist Italy: Income Inequality from Dynamic Social Tables, 1900–1950," Working Paper DT 2104, July 19, 2021, available at Public University of Navarre (UPNA), www2.unavarra.es/gesadj/depEconomia/ repec/DocumentosTrab/DT2104.PDF.

50. I have used the French edition, Henri de Man, *Au-delà du marxisme*, 2nd ed., intro. Michel Brelaz and Ivo Rens (Paris: Editions du Seuil, 1974 [1926]), accessed at Université du Québec à Chicoutimi, http:// classiques.uqac.ca/clas siques/de_man_henri/au_dela_du_marxisme/au_ dela_du_marxisme.pdf.

51. Ibid., 77–78. De Man's work is discussed at length in Sternhell, *Neither Right nor Left*, 119–141.

52. De Man, *Au-delà du marxisme*, 77–79.

53. Ibid., 79–84; Alexis de Tocqueville, *Democracy in America*, trans. Arthur Goldhammer (New York: Library Classics, 2004), 226, 584. On resentment in Nietzsche and Scheler, see Robert Schneider, *The Return of Resentment: The Rise and Decline and Rise Again of a Political Emotion* (Chicago: University of Chicago Press, 2023), 74–90.

54. Schoenbaum, *Hitler's Social Revolution*, 273–274, 55–64; Evans, *Third Reich in Power*, 499–500; *Der Angriff*, October 2, 1937, cited in Schoenbaum, *Hitler's Social Revolution*, 64. For further insight into how the Nazis operated as a "status generating machine," see Will Storr, *The Status Game: On Social Position and How We Use It* (London: William Collins, 2021), 200–215.

55. Hitler, speech of March 1, 1935, at Saarbrücken, in *Hitler: Reden and Proklamationen, 1932–1945*, ed. Max Domarus (Leonberg: Pamminger and Partner, 1973), 486; Hitler, *Mein Kampf*, 647–648.

56. Menno ter Braak, "National Socialism as a Doctrine of Rancour" (1937), trans. Robert van Krieken, *Theory, Culture, and Society* 36, no. 3 (2019): 105–106.

57. Ibid., 107–108, 115 (italics in original).

58. Ibid., 109–112 (italics in original).

CHAPTER TEN: BALANCE

1. United Nations Charter, www.un.org/en/about-us/un-charter/full-text; Hans Kelsen, "The Principle of Sovereign Equality of States as a Basis for

International Organization," *Yale Law Journal* 53, no. 2 (March 1944): 207–220; Mudaliar cited in Siep Stuurman, *The Invention of Humanity: Equality and Cultural Difference in World History* (Cambridge, MA: Harvard University Press, 2017), 495.

2. Du Bois cited in Marilyn Lake and Henry Reynolds, *Drawing the Global Color Line: White Men's Countries and the International Challenge of Racial Equality* (Cambridge: Cambridge University Press, 2008), 346. On the wider context of Black Americans' reactions to the drafting of the charter, see Carol Anderson, *Eyes off the Prize: The United Nations and the African American Struggle for Human Rights, 1944–1955* (Cambridge: Cambridge University Press, 2003), 8–58. See also Amitav Acharya, "'Idea-Shift': How Ideas from the Rest Are Reshaping World Order," *Third World Quarterly* 37, no. 7 (2016): 1157.

3. The two leading scholars are Sunil Amrith and Glenda Sluga, in "New Histories of the United Nations," *Journal of World History* 19, no. 3 (September 2008): 258. See also Lucas Chancel and Thomas Piketty, "Global Income Inequality, 1820–1920: The Persistence and Mutation of Extreme Inequality," World Inequality Lab Working Paper, no. 2021/19, accessed at World Inequality Database, https://wid.world/document/longrunpaper.

4. Samuel Moyn, *Not Enough: Human Rights in an Unequal World* (Cambridge, MA: Belknap Press of Harvard University Press, 2018), 91; Christian Olaf Christiansen, "The Making of *Global Inequality*: A Conceptual History, 1945–1980," *Contributions to the History of Concepts* 16, no. 2 (Winter 2021): 83–107; Vincent Bonnecase, "Inequality, the Emergence of a Political Idea in the 20th Century," in *Reducing Inequalities: A Sustainable Development Challenge*, trans. Jim and Katell Johnson, ed. Rémi Genevey, Rajendra K. Pachauri, and Laurence Tubiana (New Delhi: The Energy and Resources Institute, with Agence française de développement and Institut du développement durable et des relations internationales, 2013), 61–73.

5. Thucydides, *The Peloponnesian War*, trans. Martin Hammond, intro. P. J. Rhodes (New York: Oxford University Press, 2009), 38, and see Chapter 4 above.

6. Emer de Vattel, *The Law of Nations*, ed. and intro. Béla Kapossy and Richard Whatmore (Indianapolis: Liberty Fund, 2008), 75 (Preliminaries, sec. 18).

7. Ibid., 281–288 (Book 2, ch. 3). From the extensive literature on sovereign equality, I have found the following works to be useful: Edwin Witt de Dickinson, *The Equality of States in International Law* (Cambridge, MA: Harvard University Press, 1920); Robert A. Klein, *Sovereign Equality Among States: The History of an Idea* (Toronto: University of Toronto Press, 1974); Lora Anne Viola, Duncan Snidal, and Michael Zürn, "Sovereign (In)Equality in the Evolution of the International System," in *Oxford Handbook of Transformations of the State*, ed. Stephan Leibfried, Evelyne

Huber, Matthew Lange, Jonah D. Levy, Frank Nullmeier, and John D. Stephens (Oxford: Oxford University Press, 2015); and Ulrich K. Preuß, "Equal States—Its Meaning in a Constitutionalized Global Order," *Chicago Journal of International Law* 9, no. 1 (2008): 17–49.

8. On the proliferation of nation-states and their appeal to separate and equal station, see David Armitage, *The Declaration of Independence: A Global History* (Cambridge, MA: Harvard University Press, 2008); and David Armitage, *Foundations of Modern International Thought* (Cambridge: Cambridge University Press, 2013), 191–233. Marshall and the "standard account" of Lassa Oppenheim are cited in Gerry Simpson, *Great Powers and Outlaw States: Unequal Sovereigns in the International Legal Order* (Cambridge: Cambridge University Press, 2004), 27.

9. Simpson, *Great Powers*, 25–62.

10. On the demolition of the myth of Westphalia, see David Armitage, "The Fifty Years' Rift: Intellectual History and International Relations," *Modern Intellectual History* 1, no. 1 (2004): 97–109. On Vattel, I have relied heavily on Jennifer Pitts, *Boundaries of the International: Law and Empire* (Cambridge, MA: Harvard University Press, 2018), 68–91; and Jennifer Pitts, "Intervention and Sovereign Equality: Legacies of Vattel," in *Just and Unjust Military Intervention: European Thinkers from Vitoria to Mill*, ed. Stefano Recchia and Jennifer M. Welsh (Cambridge: Cambridge University Press, 2013), 132–153.

11. Vattel, *Law of Nations*, 496 (Book 3, ch. 3, sec. 47); Michael Sheehan, *The Balance of Power: History and Theory* (London: Routledge, 1996).

12. Edward Keene, *Beyond the Anarchical Society: Grotius, Colonialism, and Order in World Politics* (Cambridge: Cambridge University Press, 2009).

13. Barbosa cited in Dickinson, *Equality of States*, 183–184. See the general accounts in Klein, *Sovereign Equality*, 54–62; and Simpson, *Great Powers*, 133–154.

14. See Aristotle, *Politics*, 1301b26; Vattel, *Law of Nations*, 497 (Book 3, ch. 3, sec. 48).

15. Erez Manela, *The Wilsonian Moment: Self-Determination and the International Origins of Anticolonial Nationalism* (New York: Oxford University Press, 2007); Adom Getachew, *Worldmaking After Empire: The Rise and Fall of Self-Determination* (Princeton, NJ: Princeton University Press, 2019), 37–70.

16. On the Japanese proposal, see Naoko Shimazu, *Japan, Race, and Equality: The Racial Equality Proposal of 1919* (London: Routledge, 1998); and Lake and Reynolds, *Drawing the Global Colour Line*, 284–309. For Du Bois, see Pankaj Mishra, *From the Ruins of Empire: The Revolt Against the West and the Remaking of Asia* (New York: Picador, 2012), 2. For other responses to the Japanese victory in 1905, see Cemil Aydin, *The Politics of Anti-Westernism in Asia: Visions of World Order in Pan-Islamic and Pan-Asian Thought* (New York: Columbia University Press, 2019), 71–91.

17. Tessa Morris-Suzuki, "Debating Racial Science in Wartime Japan," *Osiris* 13 (1998): 354–375.

18. Siep Stuurman, *The Invention of Humanity*, 419–485 (ch. 8, "The Globalization of Equality"); Aishwary Kumar, *Radical Equality: Ambedkar, Gandhi and the Rise of Democracy* (New Delhi: Navayana, 2019), 1–56 (ch. 1, "Of Faith in Equality: Toward a Global Measure"), and 146–148, 347n1.

19. See Leila J. Rupp, *Worlds of Women: The Making of an International Women's Movement* (Princeton, NJ: Princeton University Press, 1997), 51–81, and 250n96 (on the historiography of "feminist orientalism" and "imperial feminism"); and Glenda Sluga, "Women, Feminisms, and Twentieth-Century Internationalisms," in *Internationalisms: A Twentieth-Century History*, ed. Glenda Sluga and Patricia Clavin (Cambridge: Cambridge University Press, 2017), 61–84.

20. Du Bois cited in Stuurman, *Invention of Humanity*, 442. On the subsequent influence and contradictions of Boas and Boasian anthropology, see Mark Anderson, *From Boas to Black Power: Racism, Liberalism, and American Anthropology* (Stanford, CA: Stanford University Press, 2019).

21. Pan-African manifesto in *W. E. B. Du Bois, International Thought*, ed. Adom Getachew and Jennifer Pitts (Cambridge: Cambridge University Press, 2022), 56. For a full account, see Hakim Adi, *Pan-Africanism: A History* (London: Bloomsbury, 2018), esp. 43–59.

22. On Gandhi's evolving views of Africans, see Ramachandra Guha, *Gandhi Before India* (New York: Vintage, 2015), 292–293, 309, 379, 395–396.

23. Mohandas K. Gandhi, "Speech at Tanjore" (September 16, 1927), in *Penguin Gandhi Reader*, ed. Rudrangshu Mukherjee (New York: Penguin, 1996), 207 (italics in original).

24. Gandhi cited in Samir Banerjee, *Tracing Gandhi: Satyarthi to Satyagrahi* (London: Routledge, 2019), 80.

25. Indian constitution, https://cdnbbsr.s3waas.gov.in/s380537a945c7aaa788 ccfcdf1b99b5d8f/uploads/2023/05/2023050195.pdf; Debjani Ghosal, "B. R. Ambedkar: The Messiah and Emancipator of Indian Women," *Contemporary Voice of Dalit*, February 3, 2022, https://doi.org/10.1177/ 2455328X211067113; Soumyabrata Choudhury, *Ambedkar and Other Immortals: An Untouchable Research Programme* (New Delhi: Navayana Publishing, 2018), 31–33; Anupama Rao, *The Caste Question: Dalits and the Politics of Modern India* (Berkeley: University of California Press, 2009).

26. Kumar, *Radical Equality*, 2–3; Ananya Vajpeyi, *Righteous Republic: The Political Foundations of Modern India* (Cambridge, MA: Harvard University Press, 2009), 10.

27. Gandhi on "doctrine of equality" from an article in the *Times of India*, August 19, 1899, cited in Stuurman, *Invention of Humanity*, 467. See also Sharon Kay Dobbins, "The Principles of Equity and the Sermon on the Mount as Influence in Gandhi's Truth Force," *Journal of Law and Religion* 6, no. 1 (1988): 131–144. Gandhi on "rock bottom" from

a speech of September 29, 1927, cited in Ankur Barua, "Revisiting the Gandhi-Ambedkar Debates over 'Caste': The Multiple Resonances of *Varna*," *Journal of Human Values* 25, no. 1 (2019): 33. See also B. R. Ambedkar, "My Philosophy of Life," in *Dr. Babasaheb Ambedkar: Writings and Speeches*, vol. 17, pt. 3 (Mumbai: Dr. Babasaheb Ambedkar Source Material Publication Committee, 2003), 503.

28. Daniel Kent-Carrasco, "A Battle over Meanings: Jayaprakash Narayan, Rammanohar Lohia and the Trajectories of Indian Socialism in Early Independent India," *Global Intellectual History* 2, no. 3 (2017): 370–388; Cemil Aydin, *The Idea of the Muslim World* (Cambridge, MA: Harvard University Press, 2017); Faisal Devji, "Pan-Islamic Politics," *Modern Intellectual History* (forthcoming).

29. My discussion of Chinese reflection on equality draws on the doctoral dissertation of Weiyu Qui (/邱伟云), 中国近代平等观念的形成 (The formation of the idea of equality in contemporary China), National Chengchi University of Taiwan, 2013, as summarized and interpreted by my outstanding student Xingzhi Guo; Tan Sitong, *Ren Xue (A Study of Benevolence)*, ed. Runguo Jia (Shenyang, Liaoning: Liaoning Renmin Chubanshe, 1994), 65.

30. K'ang Yu-wei, *Ta T'ung Shu: The One World Philosophy of K'ang Yu-wei*, trans. and intro. Lawrence G. Thompson (London: George Allen, 1958).

31. He-Yin Zhen, "On the Revenge of Women," in *The Birth of Chinese Feminism: Essential Texts in Transnational Theory*, ed. Lydia H. Liu, Rebecca E. Karl, and Dorothy Ko (New York: Columbia University Press, 2013), 122–146.

32. He-Yin Zhen, "On the Revenge of Women," 122–146. See also He-Yin's "Feminist Manifesto" (1907) and Liang Qichao, "On Women's Education," in the same volume, 191–192, 200–201.

33. Sun Yat-sen, *The Three Principles of the People*, trans. Frank W. Price, ed. L. T. Chen (Vancouver: Soul Care, 2011 [1927]), 1. I have altered Chen's translation here in consultation with scholars to emphasize Sun's reiteration, in the original, of the character 平等 (píngděng) for equal.

34. Ibid., 141–145.

35. Ibid., 155–156, 287–288.

36. Martin King Whyte, *Myth of the Social Volcano: Perceptions of Inequality and Distributive Injustice in Contemporary China* (Stanford, CA: Stanford University Press, 2010), 20–25, 118–125.

37. Tim Harper, *Underground Asia: Global Revolutionaries and the Assault on Empire* (Cambridge, MA: Belknap Press of Harvard University Press, 2021).

38. Timothy Brook, Michael van Walt van Praag, and Miek Boltjes, eds., *Sacred Mandates: Asian International Relations Since Chinggis Khan* (Chicago: University of Chicago Press, 2018), 1–24; Lydia H. Liu, *The Clash of Empires: The Invention of China in Modern World Making* (Cambridge,

MA: Harvard University Press, 2004), 31–70; Yue Du, "From Dynastic State to Imperial Nation: International Law, Diplomacy, and the Conceptual Decentralization of China, 1860s–1900s," *Late Imperial China* 42, no. 1 (June 2021): 177–220; James L. Hevia, "Making China 'Perfectly Equal,'" *Journal of Historical Sociology* 3, no. 4 (December 1999): 379–400.

39. See Naoki Sakai, "From Relational Identity to Specific Identity: On Equality in Nationality," in *Values, Identity, and Equality in Eighteenth- and Nineteenth-Century Japan*, ed. James E. Ketelaar, Yasunori Kojima, and Peter Nosco (Leiden: Brill, 2015), 290–320.

40. The complaint is the first point of the "Declaration of the Rights of Negro Peoples of the World," proclaimed in Harlem on August 13, 1920, at a mass gathering of Garvey's Universal Negro Improvement Association, available at History Matters, George Mason University, http://historymatters.gmu.edu/d/5122. "Close ranks" is taken from Garvey's *Message to the People: The Course of African Philosophy*, ed. Tony Martin, foreword Charles L. James (Dover, MA: Majority Press, 1986), 25. On Garvey's complicated sympathy for fascism, see Mark Christian Thompson, *Black Fascism: African American Literature and Culture Between the Wars* (Charlottesville: University of Virginia Press, 2007), 45–47. On his reception among women, see Keisha N. Blain, *Set the World on Fire: Black Nationalist Women and the Global Struggle for Freedom* (Philadelphia: University of Pennsylvania Press, 2018). On his mixed legacy, see Wilson Jeremiah Moses, *The Golden Age of Black Nationalisms, 1850–1925* (New York: Oxford University Press, 1978), 197–270.

41. Lake and Reynolds, *Drawing the Global Colour Line*, 343.

42. Ibid., 339–343; Stuurman, *Invention of Humanity*, 489–497; Anderson, *Eyes off the Prize*, 25–47.

43. Rupp, *Worlds of Women*, 222; Steven L.B. Jensen, *The Making of International Human Rights: The 1960s, Decolonization, and the Reconstruction of Global Values* (Cambridge: Cambridge University Press, 2016), 21–37; Michael Rosen, *Dignity: Its History and Meaning* (Cambridge, MA: Harvard University Press, 2012).

44. The leading scholar is Getachew, *Worldmaking*, 71, 74 ("inevitable outgrowth"). Logan cited in Anderson, *Eyes off the Prize*, 55; Du Bois cited in Getachew, *Worldmaking*, 79; Armitage, *Declaration*, 106.

45. Walter Scheidel, *The Great Leveler: Violence and the History of Inequality from the Stone Age to the Twenty-First Century* (Princeton, NJ: Princeton University Press, 2017), 5–9.

46. Ibid., 130–173; Peter H. Lindert and Jeffrey G. Williamson, *Unequal Gains: American Growth and Inequality Since 1700* (Princeton, NJ: Princeton University Press, 2016), 194–219. On the "Great Redistribution," see Thomas Piketty, *A Brief History of Equality*, trans. Steven Rendall (Cambridge, MA: Belknap Press of Harvard University Press, 2022), 121–150. On "benign" and "malign" forces, see Branko

Milanovic, especially his *Global Inequality: A New Approach for the Age of Globalization* (Cambridge, MA: Belknap Press of Harvard University Press, 2016), 4–5, 55–57.

47. Tony Judt, *Postwar: A History of Europe Since 1945* (New York: Penguin, 2005), 360–389; Frank Nullmeier and Franz-Xavier Kaufman, "Post-War Welfare State Development," in *The Oxford Handbook of the Welfare State*, ed. Francis G. Castles, Stephan Leibfried, Jane Lewis, Herbert Obinger, and Christopher Pierson (New York: Oxford University Press, 2010), 81–82; Darrin M. McMahon, "Equality and the Horizon of Human Expectations," *Global Intellectual History* (April 2022): 1–23.

48. T. H. Marshall and Tom Bottomore, *Citizenship and Social Class* (London: Pluto Press, 1992 [1950]), 4–8; R. H. Tawney, *Equality*, intro. Richard M. Titmuss (London: George Allen and Irwin, 1964 [1931]), 10. On the broad context for these remarks, see Ben Jackson, *Equality and the British Left: A Study in Progressive Political Thought, 1900–1964* (Manchester: Manchester University Press, 2011), esp. 29–30, 58–90, 203–218.

49. Raymond Aron, *Eighteen Lectures on Industrial Society* (London: Weidenfield and Nicolson, 1968 [1961]), 34–36, 42–43, 241. Compare, though, Aron's darker portrayal of the "dialectic of equality" in his later *Progress and Illusion: The Dialectics of Modern Society* (New York: New American Library, 1968), 21–69.

50. On Keynes and postwar optimism about equality, see David Singh Grewal and Jedidiah Purdy, "Inequality Rediscovered," *Theoretical Inquiries in Law* 18, no. 61 (2017): 61–82.

51. Simon Kuznets, "Economic Growth and Economic Equality," *American Economic Review* 45, no. 1 (1955): 1–28; Milanovic, *Global Inequality*, 46–117; Piketty, *Capital*, 11–15.

52. Shils cited and Rostow paraphrased in Nils Gilman's indispensable *Mandarins of the Future: Modernization Theory in Cold War America* (Baltimore: Johns Hopkins University Press, 2003), 1, 202. "Foreign-policy counterpart" is Gilman's expression (17).

53. Colin Clark, *Growthmanship: A Study in the Methodology of Investment* (London: Barrie and Rockcliff, 1961); Erhard cited in Philipp Lepenies, "Products Before People: How Inequality Was Sidelined by Gross National Product," in *Histories of Global Inequality: New Perspectives*, ed. Christian Olaf Christiansen and Steven L.B. Jensen (Cham: Palgrave Macmillan, 2019), 104; John Kenneth Galbraith, *The Affluent Society*, 40th anniv. ed. (Boston: Houghton Mifflin, 1998 [1958]), 69, 80.

54. Galbraith, *Affluent Society*, 69–71. On the marginalization of inequality in economics and the slow gathering of data and statistics, see, in addition to the articles by Christiansen, Lepenies, and Bonnecase cited above, Eli Cook, "Historicizing Piketty: The Fall and Rise of Inequality Economics," and Pedro Ramos Pinto, "Inequality by Numbers: The Making of a Global Political Issue?," in Christiansen and Jensen, *Histories of Global Inequality*,

35–57, 107–128; and Branko Milanovic, "The History of Global Inequality Studies," November 8, 2020, accessed at *Global Inequality* (blog), http://glineq.blogspot.com/2020/11/the-history-of-global-inequality-studies.html.

55. On the political use of justifications of short-term inequality in developing economies, see Seung Jin Baek, "Is Rising Income Inequality Far from Inevitable During Structural Transformation? A Proposal for an Augmented Inequality Dynamics," *Journal of Economics and Political Economy* 4, no. 3 (2017): 224–237. The two experts are Christian Olaf Christiansen and Steven L.B. Jensen, in "Histories of Global Inequality: Introduction," in *Histories of Global Inequality*, 18.

56. Albert O. Hirschman and Michael Rothschild, "The Changing Tolerance for Income Inequality in the Course of Economic Development," *Quarterly Journal of Economics* 87, no. 4 (November 1973): 544–566.

57. On the "temporality of not yet," see Dipesh Chakrabarty, *Provincializing Europe: Post-Colonial Thought and the Historical Difference* (Princeton, NJ: Princeton University Press, 2000), 8–9.

58. The analysis of the "gap" and the change in mood regarding convergence in the 1960s is discussed at length by Christian Olaf Christiansen in a draft chapter, "Wide, Wider, Widening: Human Rights in an Age of Rising Inequality (1960–1973)," from his forthcoming book, *A Miscalculated Bet*. I am grateful to him for allowing me to consult this rich work in progress.

59. Andrés Rivarola Puntigliano and Örjan Appelqvist, "Prebisch and Myrdal: Development Economics in the Core and on the Periphery," *Journal of Global History* 6, no. 1 (2011): 29–52; Edgar J. Dosman, *The Life and Times of Raul Prebisch, 1901–1986* (Montreal: McGill-Queen's University Press, 1988); Margarita Fajardo, *The World That Latin America Created: The United Nations Economic Commission for Latin America in the Development Era* (Cambridge, MA: Harvard University Press, 2022).

60. Gunnar Myrdal, *Development and Under-Development: A Note on the Mechanism of National and International Economic Inequality* (Cairo: National Bank of Egypt, 1956), 47; Myrdal, *An International Economy: Problems and Prospects* (New York: Harper and Brothers, 1956), 323 (italics in original); Myrdal, *Beyond the Welfare State: Economic Planning and Its International Implications* (New Haven, CT: Yale University Press, 1960), 148. On Myrdal's concept of a welfare world, see Moyn, *Not Enough*, 104–109; Marianne Johnson, "Swedish Intellectual Thought on Inequality and a 'Welfare World,'" *Global Intellectual History* (April 2022), https://doi.org/10.1080/23801883.2022.2062415; Isaac Nakhimovsky, "An International Dilemma: The Postwar Utopianism of Gunnar Myrdal's *Beyond the Welfare State*," *Humanity: An International Journal of Human Rights, Humanitarianism, and Development* 8, no. 1 (Spring 2017): 185–194.

61. *Mater et Magistra* (On Christianity and Social Progress), encyclical of Pope John XXIII, May 15, 1961, sec. 157, available at The Holy See, www.vatican.va/content/john-xxiii/en/encyclicals/documents/hf_j-xxiii_

enc_15051961_mater.html, cited and analyzed in Christiansen, "Wide, Wider, Widening"; Barbara Ward, *The Rich Nations and the Poor Nations* (New York: Norton, 1962), 14–15.

62. Ward, *Rich Nations and Poor Nations*, 14; Kwame Nkrumah, *NeoColonialism: The Last Stage of Capitalism* (London: Panaf Books, 1987 [1965]), xix. On colonial humanism and welfare, see Moyn, *Not Enough*, 98–99, 240n16, as well as Gary Wilder, *The French Imperial Nation-State: Negritude and Colonial Humanism Between the Two World Wars* (Chicago: University of Chicago Press, 2005), 43–75.

63. On the genesis of the "Third World" and the "rich traditions of egalitarianism" of the "Third World Project," see Vijay Prashad, *The Darker Nations: A People's History of the Third World* (New York: New Press, 2007), 6–11; and Vijay Prashad, *The Poorer Nations: A Possible History of the Global South*, intro. Boutros Boutros-Ghali (New York: Verso, 2014), 25. See also Aimé Césaire, *Discourse on Colonialism*, trans. Joan Pinkham, intro. Robin D.G. Kelley (New York: Monthly Review Press, 2000 [1955]), 52.

64. On the understudied subject of welfare provisions in the postcolonial states, see the seminal work of Moyn, *Not Enough*, ch. 4 ("Globalizing Welfare After Empire"); and Getachew, *Worldmaking*, 107–175. On social rights, see Steven L.B. Jensen and Charles Walton, eds., *Social Rights and the Politics of Obligation in History* (Cambridge: Cambridge University Press, 2022).

65. Göran Therborn, *The Killing Fields of Inequality* (Cambridge, UK: Polity, 2013), 48–54, 79–89; Angus Deaton, *The Great Escape: Health, Wealth, and the Origins of Inequality* (Princeton, NJ: Princeton University Press, 2013), 152–156; Leandro Prados de la Escosura, *Human Development and the Path to Freedom: 1870 to the Present* (Cambridge: Cambridge University Press, 2022), 37–95.

66. Chancel and Piketty, "Global Income Inequality," esp. tables 5–8. On compression in the Soviet sphere, see Branko Milanovic, *The Haves and the Have Nots: A Brief and Idiosyncratic History of Global Inequality* (New York: Basic Books, 2011), 54–60.

67. Dia cited in Moyn, *Not Enough*, 104; Nkrumah, *Neo-Colonialism*, ix.

68. Bandung principles at Bandung Spirit, https://bandungspirit.org/spip.php?article99. On the Black Atlantic federations, see Getachew, *Worldmaking*, 107–141.

69. Fajardo, *World That Latin America Created*, 37–38, 178–182.

70. UN General Assembly, "Declaration on the Establishment of a New International Economic Order," 1974, United Nations Digital Library, https://digitallibrary.un.org/record/218450. In addition to the accounts of the NIEO in Moyn and Getachew, I have benefited from Vanessa Ogle, "States Rights Against Private Capital: The New International Economic Order and the Struggle over Aid, Trade, and Foreign Investment, 1962–1981," *Humanity: An International Journal of Human Rights, Humanitarianism,*

and Development 5, no. 2 (Summer 2014): 211–234; and Nils Gilman, "The New International Economic Order: A Reintroduction," *Humanity: An International Journal of Human Rights, Humanitarianism, and Development* 6, no. 1 (Spring 2015): 1–16.

71. Myrdal, "The Equality Issue in World Development," Lecture to the Memory of Alfred Nobel, March 17, 1975, Nobel Prize, www.nobelprize. org/prizes/economic-sciences/1974/myrdal/lecture/ (italics in original).

72. Mark Mazower, *Governing the World: The History of an Idea* (New York: Penguin, 2012), 304; Getachew, *Worldmaking*, 171–175; Moyn, *Not Enough*, 117–118.

73. Quinn Slobodian, *Globalists: The End of Empire and the Birth of Neoliberalism* (Cambridge, MA: Harvard University Press, 2018), 218–262.

74. Indian trade delegate cited in ibid., 219; Julius Nyerere, "The Plea of the Poor: New Economic Order Needed for the World Community," *New Directions* 4, no. 4, article 8 (1977), https://dh.howard.edu/newdirections/vol4/iss4/8.

75. Ngaire Woods, "Order, Globalization, and Inequality in World Politics," in *Inequality, Globalization, and World Politics*, ed. Andrew Hurrell and Ngaire Woods (Oxford: Oxford University Press, 2002), 14–16.

76. Kenneth Pomeranz, "The Data We Have vs. the Data We Need: A Comment on the State of the 'Divergence' Debate (Part I)," *The NEP-HIS Blog*, March 19, 2017, https://nephist.wordpress.com/2017/06/06/the-data-we-have-vs-the-data-we-need-a-comment-on-the-state-of-the-divergence-debate-part-i; Prasannan Parthasarathi, *Why Europe Grew Rich and Asia Did Not: Global Economic Divergence* (Cambridge: Cambridge University Press, 2011); Milanovic, *Global Inequality*, 118–154; François Bourguignon, *The Globalization of Inequality*, trans. Thomas Scott-Railton (Princeton, NJ: Princeton University Press, 2015), 9–40; Angus Maddison, *Contours of the World Economy 1–2030 AD: Essays in Macro-Economic History*, illustrated ed. (Oxford: Oxford University Press, 2007), 294–321; Piketty, *Brief History of Equality*, 48–66; Chancel and Piketty, "Global Income Inequality," 7–10, and Figures 1–3. On the complexities of the data and the influence of factors beyond the purely economic, see Robert J. Holton, *Global Inequalities* (London: Palgrave, 2014), 49–150; and Mike Savage, *The Return of Inequality: Social Change and the Weight of the Past* (Cambridge, MA: Harvard University Press, 2021), esp. 101–168.

77. Frantz Fanon, *The Wretched of the Earth*, trans. Constance Farrington (New York: Grove Press, 1963 [1961]), 102, 89. In the book's preface, Fanon calls North America a "super-European monster" (26). See also Césaire, *Discourse on Colonialism*, 47. Nkrumah argues similarly that Western "colonial earnings" were diverted to "finance the 'Welfare State'" (*Neo-Colonialism*, xiii).

78. Myrdal, *Rich Lands and Poor: The Road to World Prosperity* (New York: Harper and Brothers, 1957), 148; Jamie Martin, "Gunnar Myrdal and

the Failed Promises of the Postwar International Economic Settlement," *Humanity: An International Journal of Human Rights, Humanitarianism, and Development* 8, no. 1 (Spring 2017): 167–173. On "sheltering," see Frederick Cooper, "Afterword: Social Rights and Human Rights in the Time of 'Decolonization,'" *Humanity: An International Journal of Human Rights, Humanitarianism, and Development* (Winter 2012): 473–492 (esp. 487).

79. On liberal exceptions, see Uday Singh Mehta, *Liberalism and Empire: A Study in Nineteenth-Century British Liberal Thought* (Chicago: Chicago University Press, 1999); Karuna Mantena, *Alibis of Empire: Henry Maine and the End of Liberal Imperialism* (Princeton, NJ: Princeton University Press, 2010); and Pitts, *Turn to Empire.*

80. On Rawls, see Milanovic, *Haves and Have-Nots,* 203–208; Moyn, *Not Enough,* 147–148. The inequities of national welfare states with regard to gender and race have drawn much scholarship in recent decades. See Susan G. Pederson, *Family, Dependence, and Origins of the Welfare State: Britain and France, 1914–1945* (Cambridge: Cambridge University Press, 1995); Alice Kessler-Harris, *In Pursuit of Equity: Women, Men, and the Quest for Economic Citizenship in 20th-Century America* (Oxford: Oxford University Press, 2001); Ira Katznelson, *When Affirmative Action Was White: An Untold Story of Racial Inequality in Twentieth-Century America* (New York: W. W. Norton, 2006); Laura Levine Frader, *Breadwinners and Citizens: Gender and the Making of the French Social Model* (Durham, NC: Duke University Press, 2008).

CHAPTER ELEVEN: DREAM

1. Martin Luther King Jr., "I Have a Dream," in *A Testament of Hope: The Essential Writings and Speeches,* ed. James M. Washington (New York: HarperOne, 1986), 217–220.
2. Ibid.
3. Ibid., 219. See the allusion to leveling in Isaiah 40:4 and Amos 7:7–10.
4. Ibid., 219–220. On the context and broader significance of the speech, see Eric J. Sundquist, *King's Dream: The Legacy of Martin Luther King's "I Have a Dream" Speech* (New Haven, CT: Yale University Press, 2009).
5. King, Speech Before the Fourth Constitutional Convention of the AFL-CIO, December 11, 1961, in *Testament of Hope,* 206–207.
6. King, *Stride Toward Freedom: The Montgomery Circle* (New York: Harper and Row, 1958), 86.
7. King cited from "The Ethical Demands for Integration," first published in *Religion and Labor* 6 (1963), and reprinted in *Testament of Hope,* 119 (italics in original). On dignity in Kant and its broader history, see Michael Rosen, *Dignity: Its Meaning and History* (Cambridge, MA: Harvard University Press, 2012), esp. 19–31.

8. On the iconography of hands, see Gottfried Korff and Larry Peterson, "From Brotherly Handshake to Militant Clenched Fist: On Political Metaphors for the Worker's Hand," *International Labor and Working Class History* 42 (Fall 1992): 70–81. On handshakes in peacemaking, see Hanna Vollrath, "The Kiss of Peace," in *Peace Treaties and International Law in European History: From the Late Middle Ages to World War One*, ed. Randall Lesaffer (Cambridge: Cambridge University Press, 2004), 162–183.

9. King, "The Most Durable Power," *Christian Century* 74 (June 5, 1957): 708.

10. Jeanne Theoharis, *The Rebellious Life of Mrs. Rosa Parks* (Boston: Beacon Press, 2013).

11. Jeanne Theoharis, *A More Beautiful and Terrible History: The Uses and Misuses of Civil Rights History* (Boston: Beacon Press, 2018), 17, 62–82.

12. King, *Stride Toward Freedom*, 84, 104–105 (italics in original).

13. King, "Nonviolence and Racial Justice," *Christian Century* 74 (February 6, 1957): 165–167; King, *Stride Toward Freedom*, 105.

14. King, *Stride Toward Freedom*, 105–106.

15. Ibid., 85; Gandhi cited in Aishwary Kumar, *Radical Equality: Ambedkar, Gandhi and the Risk of Democracy* (New Delhi: Navayana, 2019), 99, and see pp. 98–105 for Kumar's apt reflections on what he calls Gandhi's "discourse of the hand."

16. King, *Stride Toward Freedom*, 85.

17. Ibid., 103.

18. Ibid.

19. Ibid., 101.

20. "Account by Lawrence Dunbar Reddick of Press Conference in New Delhi on 10 February 1959," available at Stanford University, Martin Luther King, Jr., Research and Education Institute, https://kinginstitute.stanford.edu/king-papers/documents/account-lawrence-dunbar-reddick-press-conference-new-delhi-10-february-1959.

21. King as "untouchable" cited in Isabel Wilkerson, *Caste: The Origins of Our Discontents* (New York: Random House, 2022), 22; King, "My Trip to the Land of Gandhi" (1959), in *Testament of Hope*, 27.

22. Ambedkar cited in Wilkerson, *Caste*, 26; King, "My Trip to the Land of Gandhi," 24.

23. Malcolm X, "At the Audubon," in *Malcom X Speaks: Selected Speeches and Statements*, ed. George Breitman (New York: Grove Press, 1994), 90; King, *Where Do We Go from Here: Chaos or Community?*, foreword Coretta Scott King, intro. Vincent Harding (Boston: Beacon Press, 2010 [1967]), 177–179.

24. King, "The Power of Nonviolence," speech at the University of California, Berkeley, June 4, 1957, in *Testament of Hope*, 12.

25. Andrew Sable, "The Paradox of Equality and the Trials of Martin Luther King," *Society* 36 (May 1999) 32–42.

26. James C. Cobb, "Why Martin Luther King Had a 75% Disapproval Rating in the Year of His Death," *Zócalo*, April 4, 2018, www.zocalopublicsquare.org/2018/04/04/martin-luther-king-75-percent-disapproval-rating-year-death/ideas/essay/; King, *Chaos or Community?*, 2.

27. Carl Schmitt, *The Crisis of Parliamentary Democracy*, trans. Ellen Kennedy (Cambridge, MA: MIT Press, 1987), 9, 12–13.

28. King, *Chaos or Community?*, 3–5, 8.

29. Charles W. Mills, *Black Rights / White Wrongs: The Critique of Racial Liberalism* (New York: Oxford University Press, 2017).

30. King, "A Testament of Hope" (1968), published posthumously in 1969, in *Testament of Hope*, 315; King, "I Have a Dream," 217.

31. King, *Chaos or Community?*, 4–5; King, "A Testament of Hope," in *Testament of Hope*, 315.

32. King, *Stride Toward Freedom*, 106; King, "An Experiment in Love," in *Testament of Hope*, 20.

33. King, sermon delivered on March 31, 1968, at the National Cathedral in Washington, DC, in *Testament of Hope*, 277; King, *Chaos or Community?*, 12–13; King, "Nobel Prize Acceptance Speech," in *Testament of Hope*, 225. Theodore Parker's original reflection on the long arc of the "moral universe" may be found in *Ten Sermons of Religion*, 2nd ed. (Boston: Little, Brown, 1855), 84–85. On the uneven course of Black progress, see Philip A. Klinker and Rogers M. Smith, *The Unsteady March: The Rise and Decline of Racial Equality in America* (Chicago: University of Chicago Press, 1999).

34. King, *Why We Can't Wait*, intro. Dorothy Cotton (Boston: Beacon Press, 2011 [1963/1964]), 3, 155; King, *Chaos or Community?*, 179.

35. For numerous examples, see the exhibition and zine by Mary Coble, *Gestures of Defiance* (2015), available at Gothenburg University Publications Electronic Archive, https://gupea.ub.gu.se/bitstream/handle/2077/42215/gupea_2077_42215_13.pdf.

36. Laura L. Lovett, *With Her Fist Raised: Dorothy Pitman Hughes and the Transformative Power of Black Community Activism* (Boston: Beacon Press, 2021); Gloria Steinem, Meenakshi Mukherjee, and Ira Pande, "A Conversation with Gloria Steinem," *India International Centre Quarterly* 34, no. 2 (Autumn 2007): 90–205.

37. King, *Chaos or Community?*, 20–33; Peniel E. Joseph, *Stokely: A Life* (New York: Basic Books, 2014), 105–115.

38. On King and Malcolm X, see Peniel E. Joseph, *The Sword and the Shield: The Revolutionary Lives of Malcolm X and Martin Luther King Jr.* (New York: Basic Books, 2020); Alex Haley and Malcolm X, *The Autobiography of Malcolm X* (New York: Ballantine Books, 1992), 184.

39. Joseph, *Sword and Shield*, 1–24; King, *Why We Can't Wait*, 17; King, *Chaos or Community?*, 37.

40. Malcolm X, "Message to the Grass Roots," 1963, accessed at Black Past, www.blackpast.org/african-american-history/speeches-african-american-history/1963-malcolm-x-message-grassroots.

41. King, "Letter from a Birmingham Jail," in *Testament of Hope*, 296; King, *Chaos or Community?*, 49.

42. Malcolm X, "Message to the Grass Roots"; Malcolm X, "The Founding Rally of the OAAU," in *By Any Means Necessary (Malcolm X Speeches and Writings)*, ed. John Breitman (New York: Pathfinder Press, 1970), 37 (italics mine); Frantz Fanon, "Why We Use Violence" (1960), in *The Political Writings from Alienation and Freedom*, trans. Steven Corcoran, ed. Jean Khalfa and Robert J. C. Young (London: Bloomsbury, 2021), 117–124; *Face the Nation* interview with Stokely Carmichael, June 19, 1966, transcript accessed at Civil Rights Movement Archive, www.crmvet.org/nars/660619_sncc_stokely_ftn.pdf; King, *Chaos or Community?*, 30–32.

43. Stokely Carmichael, *Face the Nation* interview; King, *Chaos or Community?*, 30–32.

44. Malcolm X, "Message to the Grass Roots"; Fanon, "Why We Use Violence," 118.

45. Stokely Carmichael, "Black Power," October 29, 1966, accessed at Voices of Democracy: The U.S. Oratory Project, https://voicesofdemocracy.umd.edu/carmichael-black-power-speech-text, paragraphs 25–26; King, *Community or Chaos?*, 8.

46. Joseph, *Stokely*, 305–306; Toni Cade Bambara, "On the Issue of Roles," in *The Black Woman: An Anthology*, ed. Toni Cade Bambara (New York: New American Library, 1970), 107; bell hooks, *Ain't I a Woman: Black Women and Feminism* (London: Pluto Press, 1982), 5.

47. Linda Gordon, "The Women's Liberation Movement," in Dorothy Sue Cobble, Linda Gordon, and Astrid Henry, *Feminism Unfinished: A Short, Surprising History of American Women's Movements* (New York: Liveright Publishing, 2014), 104; Young cited in Elisabeth Griffith, *Formidable: American Women and the Fight for Equality, 1920–2020* (New York: Pegasus, 2022), 149; Anne Standley, "The Role of Black Women in the Civil Rights Movement," in *Women in the Civil Rights Movement: Trailblazers and Torchbearers, 1941–1965*, ed. Vicki Crawford, Jacqueline Anne Rousse, and Barbara Woods (Brooklyn, NY: Carlson, 1990), 184.

48. King cited in Griffith, *Formidable*, 160; Margaret Fuller, *Woman in the Nineteenth Century* (New York: Greeley and McElrath, 1845), 18; Martha S. Jones, *Vanguard: How Black Women Broke Barriers, Won the Vote, and Insisted on Equality for All* (New York: Basic Books, 2020).

49. Charles Postel, *Equality: An American Dilemma, 1866–1896* (New York: Farrar, Straus and Giroux, 2019), esp. 113–135, 201–244, 296–312.

50. Betty Friedan, *The Feminine Mystique*, intro. Anna Quindlen (New York: Norton, 2001 [1963]), 131 and ch. 3 ("The Crisis in Woman's Identity"); Simone de Beauvoir, *The Second Sex*, trans. H. M. Parshley, intro. Deirdre Bair (New York: Vintage, 1989), 267.

51. Griffith, *Formidable*, 171.

52. Friedan, *Feminine Mystique*, 426–427; Frances M. Beal, "Double Jeopardy: To Be Black and Female (1969)," in *Meridians, Feminism, Race, Transnationalism* 89, no. 2 (March 2008): 166–176. See also Winifred Breines, *The Trouble Between Us: An Uneasy History of White and Black Women in the Feminist Movement* (New York: Oxford University Press, 2006).

53. Casey Hayden and Mary King, "Sex and Caste: A Kind of Memo," November 18, 1965, available at Civil Rights Movement Archive, www.crmvet.org/docs/sexcaste.pdf; Mary Eastwood and Pauli Miller, "Jane Crow and the Law: Discrimination and Title VII," *George Washington University Law Review* 34, no. 2 (December 1965). See also Kristen Hogan, *The Feminist Bookstore Movement: Lesbian Antiracism and Feminist Accountability* (Durham, NC: Duke University Press, 2016).

54. Stonewall commentator cited in the documentary film *Stonewall Uprising* (2010), directed by Kate Davis and David Heilbroner; Committee for Homosexual Freedom activist cited in Lillian Faderman, *The Gay Revolution: The Story of Struggle* (New York: Simon and Schuster, 2015), 179.

55. Carl Wittman, *Gay Manifesto*, 1–5.

56. On the Combahee River Collective, see Kimberly Springer, *Living for the Revolution: Black Feminist Organizations, 1968–1980* (Durham, NC: Duke University Press, 2005), 56–61, 146; Breines, *Trouble Between Us*, 117–149.

57. Combahee River Collective, *The Combahee River Collective Statement* (April 1977), accessed at Black Past, www.blackpast.org/african-american-history/combahee-river-collective-statement-1977.

58. Gerald Izenberg, *Identity: The Necessity of a Modern Idea* (Philadelphia: University of Pennsylvania Press, 2016), 174–179; Stokely Carmichael and Charles V. Hamilton, *Black Power: The Politics of Liberation in America* (New York: Random House, 1967), 34–35.

59. Manuela Consonni and Vivian Liska, eds., *Sartre, Jews, and the "Other": Rethinking Antisemitism, Race, and Gender* (Berlin: De Gruyter Oldenbourg, 2020).

60. David Walker, *David Walker's Appeal to the Colored Citizens of the World, but Very Expressly, to Those of the United States of America*, rev. ed., intro. Sean Wilentz (New York: Hill and Wang, 1995), 7; Siep Stuurman, *The Invention of Humanity: Equality and Cultural Difference in World History* (Cambridge, MA: Harvard University Press, 2017), 512–520, 561.

61. King, Speech Before the Fourth Constitutional Convention of the AFL-CIO, December 11, 1961, in *Testament of Hope*, 206–207.

62. James Baldwin and Margaret Mead, *A Rap on Race* (New York: J. B. Lippincott, 1971), 11–12. The encounter is analyzed astutely in Mark Anderson, *From Boas to Black Power: Racism, Liberalism, and American Anthropology* (Stanford, CA: Stanford University Press, 2019), 1–7.

63. Margaret Wright, "I Want the Right to Be Black and Me," in *Black Women in White America: A Documentary History*, ed. Gerda Lerner (New York: Vintage, 1992 [1972]), 608.

64. Gisela Bock and Susan James, "Introduction: Contextualizing Equality and Difference," in *Beyond Equality and Difference: Citizenship, Feminist Politics, Female Subjectivity*, ed. Gisela Bock and Susan James (London: Routledge, 1992), 1–13; Anne Phillips, "Introduction," in *Feminism and Equality*, ed. Anne Phillips (New York: New York University Press, 1987), 19–22.

65. Bock and James, "Introduction," 2–5.

66. Joan Wallach Scott, *Only Paradoxes to Offer: French Feminists and the Rights of Man* (Cambridge, MA: Harvard University Press, 1997), 3.

67. Joan W. Scott, "Deconstructing Equality-Versus-Difference: Or, the Uses of Poststructuralist Theory for Feminism," *Feminist Studies* 14, no. 1 (Spring 1988): 43, 46.

68. Audre Lorde, "The Master's Tools Will Never Dismantle the Master's House," in *The Essential Feminist Reader*, ed. and intro. Estelle M. Freedman (New York: Modern Library, 2007), 333.

69. Sonia Kruks, *Retrieving Experience: Subjectivity and Recognition in Feminist Politics* (Ithaca, NY: Cornell University Press, 2001), 85 (italics in original). Notable and contrasting critiques are Nancy Fraser, *Fortunes of Feminism: From State-Managed Capitalism to Neoliberal Crisis* (London: Verso, 2020 [2013]); and Francis Fukuyama, *Identity: The Demand for Dignity and the Politics of Resentment* (New York: Farrar, Straus and Giroux, 2018). On the sociology of status, see Cecilia L. Ridgeway, *Status: Why Is It Everywhere? Why Does It Matter?* (New York: Russell Sage Foundation, 2019).

70. King, *Stride Toward Freedom*, 105 (italics in original). On recognition of equals, see Anne Phillips, *Unconditional Equals* (Princeton, NJ: Princeton University Press, 2021), 65–70, 97–103.

71. King, *Stride Toward Freedom*, 105; *Combahee River Collective Statement*.

72. *Combahee River Collective Statement*; Robin Morgan, "Introduction: The Women's Revolution," in *Sisterhood Is Powerful: An Anthology of Writings from the Women's Liberation Movement*, ed. Robin Morgan (New York: Vintage, 1970), xxxv.

73. See, notably, Mark Lilla, *The Once and Future Liberal: After Identity Politics* (New York: Harper, 2017).

74. Scott, "Deconstructing Equality-Versus-Difference," 44–45; Phillips, *Unconditional Equals*, 93–107; Kwame Anthony Appiah, *The Ethics of Identity* (Princeton, NJ: Princeton University Press, 2007), 193.

75. Alexis de Tocqueville, *Democracy in America*, trans. Arthur Goldhammer (New York: Library of America, 2004), 710.

76. Frederick Cooper, "Afterword: Social Rights and Human Rights in the Time of 'Decolonization,'" *Humanity* (Winter 2012): 473–492 (esp. 485). See, more generally, his *Citizenship, Inequality, and Difference: Historical Perspectives* (Princeton, NJ: Princeton University Press, 2018).

CONCLUSION: THE CRISIS OF EQUALITY

1. Ronald Dworkin, *Taking Rights Seriously* (London: Bloomsbury, 1978), 7; Ronald Dworkin, "Comments on Narveson: In Defense of Equality," *Social Philosophy and Policy* 1, no. 1 (1983): 24–40 (esp. 25, 31); Will Kymlicka, *Contemporary Political Philosophy* (Oxford: Oxford University Press, 1999), 4; Louis P. Pojman, "Introduction: The Nature and Value of Equality," in *Equality: Selected Readings*, ed. Louis P. Pojman and Robert Westmoreland (Oxford: Oxford University Press, 1997), 1. See also the observations of Jeremy Waldron, *God, Locke, and Equality: Christian Foundations in Locke's Political Thought* (Cambridge: Cambridge University Press, 2002), 1–2.

2. Francis Fukuyama, "The March of Equality," *Journal of Democracy* 11, no. 1 (2000): 11–17. On the "inner logic" of equality, see Anne Phillips, "Gender and Modernity," *Political Theory* 46, no. 6 (2018): 837–860. On the hundreds of millions pulled out of poverty, see François Bourguignon, *The Globalization of Inequality*, trans. Thomas Scott-Railton (Princeton, NJ: Princeton University Press, 2015), who puts the figure at 500 million since 1990 (29).

3. All book titles referencing the "struggle" for equality in this paragraph were freely available on Amazon.com at the time of writing.

4. David A. Graham, "The Wrong Side of 'the Right Side of History,'" *Atlantic*, December 21, 2015, www.theatlantic.com/politics/archive/2015/12/obama-right-side-of-history/420462; Hillary Rodham Clinton, Human Rights Day Speech—Free and Equal in Dignity and Rights, Geneva, Switzerland, December 6, 2011, U.S. Mission to International Organizations in Geneva, https://geneva.usmission.gov/2011/12/06/free-and-equal. On Obama's use of the phrase "moral arc of the universe," see Michael J. Sandel, *The Tyranny of Merit: What's Become of the Common Good?* (New York: Farrar, Straus and Giroux, 2020), 54–57; Barack Obama, Inaugural Address, January 21, 2013, White House, President Barack Obama, https://obamawhitehouse.archives.gov/the-press-office/2013/01/21/inaugural-address-president-barack-obama.

5. Michelle Obama, "Remarks by the First Lady at the Democratic National Convention," July 25, 2016, White House, President Barack Obama, https://obamawhitehouse.archives.gov/the-pressoffice/2016/07/25/remarks-first-lady-democratic-national-convention. The upbeat data is summarized and presented in Steven Pinker, *Enlightenment Now: The Case for Reason, Science, and Progress* (New York: Viking, 2018), 214–232, esp. 219–224. On improvements in the position of women in this time, see also Mike Savage, *The Return of Inequality: Social Change and the Weight of the Past* (Cambridge, MA: Harvard University Press, 2021), 211–215; and Elisabeth Griffith, *Formidable: American Women and the Fight for Equality, 1920–2020* (New York: Pegasus, 2022), 59–95. "One recent scholar" is Richard V. Reeves, cited in Idrees Kahloon, "What's the Matter with Men?," *New Yorker*,

January 30, 2023. See also Richard V. Reeves, *Of Boys and Men: Why the Modern Male Is Struggling, Why It Matters, and What to Do About It* (Washington, DC: Brookings Institution Press, 2022).

6. Pinker, *Enlightenment Now*, 216–223; Laurence H. Tribe, "The Constitutional Inevitability of Same-Sex Marriage," *Maryland Law Review* 71, no. 2 (2012): 471–489; Kent Blore, "Sexuality Law Reform and the Language of Progress: What Lies Behind Statements that Equality for Lesbian and Gay People Is Inevitable?," *Deakin Law Review* 18, no. 2 (2013): 391–423. On gay marriage more broadly, see William N. Eskridge Jr. and Christopher R. Riano, *Marriage Equality: From Outlaws to In-Laws* (New Haven, CT: Yale University Press, 2020).

7. Joseph Stiglitz, "Of the 1%, by the 1%, for the 1%," *Vanity Fair*, May 2011, www.vanityfair.com/news/2011/05/top-one-percent-201105.

8. Thomas Piketty, *Capital in the Twenty-First Century*, trans. Arthur Goldhammer (Cambridge, MA: Harvard University Press, 2014).

9. Barack Obama, "Remarks by the President on Economic Mobility," December 4, 2013, White House, President Barack Obama, https://obamawhitehouse.archives.gov/the-press-office/2013/12/04/remarks-president-economic-mobility.

10. Savage, *Return of Inequality*, 1–27.

11. Branko Milanovic, *Global Inequality: A New Approach for the Age of Globalization* (Cambridge, MA: Harvard University Press, 2018), 10–24.

12. Susan Faludi was exposing the "backlash" against women as early as 1991 in her *Backlash: The Undeclared War Against American Women* (New York: Broadway Books, 2020 [1991]). On the long history of stigmatizing poor whites, see Nancy Isenberg, *White Trash: The 400-Year Untold History of Class in America* (New York: Viking, 2016).

13. Nancy Fraser, *Fortunes of Feminism: From State-Managed Capitalism to Neoliberal Crisis* (London: Verso, 2020 [2013]); Kimberlé Crenshaw, *On Intersectionality: Essential Writings* (New York: New Press, 2022). On "visceral inequality" and the long-term connections between race, gender, and class, see Savage, *Return of Inequality*, 168–228.

14. Meeting attended by the author on September 23, 2022.

15. Kamala Harris (@KamalaHarris), "Equality Versus Equity," Twitter, posted November 1, 2020, https://twitter.com/kamalaharris/status/1322963321994289154.

16. The foundational discussion of "equity" (*epieikeia*) is found in Aristotle, *Nicomachean Ethics*, 1137b–1138a. On how this concept plays out in Western law, see Mark Fortier, *The Culture of Equity in Early Modern England* (London: Routledge, 2005); and Lorenzo Maniscalco, *Equity in Early Modern Legal Scholarship* (Leiden: Brill, 2020).

17. Tomislav Sunic, *Against Democracy and Equality: The European New Right* (Newport Beach, CA: Noontide Press, 2004).

18. Nick Land, *The Dark Enlightenment*, part 4B, accessed at www.thedark enlightenment.com/the-dark-enlightenment-by-nick-land (italics in original).

19. On the language of identity and difference on the Right, see Michael O'Meara, *New Culture, New Right: Anti-Liberalism in Postmodern Europe* (London: Arktos, 2013), 40–45, 258–263; Matthew Rose, *A World After Liberalism: Philosophers of the Radical Right* (New Haven, CT: Yale University Press, 2021), 10–12, 89, 105–106; and throughout Mark Sedgewick, ed., *Key Thinkers of the Radical Right: Behind the New Threat to Liberal Democracy* (New York: Oxford University Press, 2010).

20. Daniel Markovits, *The Meritocracy Trap: How America's Foundational Myth Feeds Inequality, Dismantles the Middle Class, and Devours the Elite* (New York: Penguin, 2019), 27; Sandel, *Tyranny of Merit*; Adrian Wooldridge, *The Aristocracy of Talent: How Meritocracy Made the Modern World* (London: Allen Lane, 2021), 7–8.

21. See, for example, the work and response to Kathryn Paige Harden, *The Genetic Lottery: Why DNA Matters for Social Equality* (Princeton, NJ: Princeton University Press, 2021); Richard J. Herrnstein and Charles Murray, *The Bell Curve: Intelligence and Class Structure in American Life* (New York: Free Press, 1996).

22. Walter Scheidel, *The Great Leveler: Violence and the History of Inequality from the Stone Age to the Twenty-First Century* (Princeton, NJ: Princeton University Press, 2017), 424–444.

23. Lucas Chancel and Thomas Piketty, "Global Income Inequality, 1820–1920: The Persistence and Mutation of Extreme Inequality," World Inequality Lab Working Paper, no. 2021/19, 17, accessed at World Inequality Database, https://wid.world/document/longrunpaper.

24. Bourguignon, *Globalization of Inequality*, 38; Milanovic, *Global Inequality*, 5. The term "asocial inequality" is used by the anthropologist James Ferguson in his *Give a Man a Fish: Reflections on the New Politics of Distribution* (Durham, NC: Duke University Press, 2015), 155. On the latter point, and what she calls "cordoned lives," see also the perceptive comments of Anne Phillips, *Unconditional Equals* (Princeton, NJ: Princeton University Press, 2021), 12–13.

25. Shoshanna Zuboff, "Caveat Usor: Surveillance Capitalism as Epistemic Inequality," in *After the Digital Tornado: Networks, Algorithms, Humanity*, ed. Kevin Werbach (Cambridge: Cambridge University Press, 2020), 174–214 (esp. 180). And see, more broadly, Shoshanna Zuboff, *The Age of Surveillance Capitalism: The Fight for a Human Future at the New Frontier of Power* (New York: Public Affairs, 2020).

26. See, for example, "Rising Inequality Risks Regional Collapse and Climate Catastrophe," Earth4All, www.earth4all.life/news/book-launch.

27. Yuval Noah Harari, *Homo Deus: A Brief History of Tomorrow* (New York: Harper, 2017), 355.

28. Savage, *Return of Inequality*, 16.

29. Thomas Piketty, *A Brief History of Equality*, trans. Steven Rendall (Cambridge, MA: Belknap Press of Harvard University Press, 2022), 1–18; Darrin M. McMahon, "Tomorrow Belongs to Us," *Literary Review* 506 (April 2022): 28–29.
30. Savage, *Return of Inequality*, 309–329.
31. Peniel E. Joseph, *The Third Reconstruction: America's Struggle for Racial Justice in the Twenty-First Century* (New York: Basic Books, 2022), 1–35, 228. The characterization of the book as "a new struggle for radical equality" is that of the writer and sociologist Michael Eric Dyson, provided in the first page of the printed blurbs.
32. On the central place of equality in utopian visions, see Gregory Claeys, *Utopianism and a Dying Planet: Life After Consumerism* (Cambridge: Cambridge University Press, 2022), which came to me right as I was finishing this book.
33. A cogent statement of the contrarian view is Harry G. Frankfurt, *On Inequality* (Princeton, NJ: Princeton University Press, 2015). Richard Wilkinson and Kate Pickett make the case for inequality's adverse effects in *The Spirit Level: Why Greater Equality Makes Societies Stronger* (New York: Bloomsbury, 2010). On the critique of the latter work for conflating correlation and causation, see Pinker, *Enlightenment Now*, 100–101.
34. By way of introduction to a substantial literature by one of its pioneers, see Robert Sapolsky, "The Influence of Social Hierarchy on Primate Love," *Science* 308 (April 29, 2005): 648–652; and Sapolsky, *Behave: The Biology of Humans at Our Best and Our Worst* (New York: Penguin, 2017), 291–296, 434–442.

INDEX

DARRIN M. MCMAHON is the David W. Little Class of 1944 Professor of History at Dartmouth College. He is the author of *Happiness: A History* and *Divine Fury: A History of Genius* and he writes regularly for the national and international press. He lives in Connecticut.